O9-AIE-871

THE AMERICAN EXPRESS POCKET GUIDE TO

PARIS

Christopher McIntosh

Major contributions by

Susan Heller Anderson

Peter Graham

SIMON AND SCHUSTER

NEW YORK

The Author

Christopher McIntosh is an author and journalist. Formerly assistant editor of *Country Life* and deputy editor of *The Illustrated London News*, he has written travel articles for *Travel & Leisure* and other magazines.

Contributors

Susan Heller Anderson (Nightlife, Shopping)
Robert Barton-Clegg (Wine in Paris)
Peter Graham (Hotels, Eating in Paris, Restaurants, Cafés)
William Green (Nightlife)

Acknowledgments

The author and publishers would like to thank the following for their invaluable help and advice: Dr & Mme Robert Amadou, Christine Baker, Annabel Campbell, Pamela Fiori, Pauline Hallam and Martine Williams of The French Government Tourist Office, M. & Mme Robert Jaulin, Hugh Johnson, Margaret Keith, Gisela Kirberg, Jeremy Lawrence, Barbara McIntosh.

Quotations

The author and publishers are grateful to those listed below for their kind permission to reprint the following extracts: Jonathan Cape Ltd. (UK) and Charles Scribner's Sons (USA) for the quotation from *A Moveable Feast* by Ernest Hemingway (p120); Andre Deutsch Ltd. (UK) and Harper and Row Publishers Inc. (USA) for quotations from *Quartet* by Jean Rhys (p86 and p96).

Few travel books are without errors, and no guidebook can ever be completely up-to-date, for telephone numbers and opening hours change without warning, and hotels and restaurants come under new management, which can affect standards. While every effort has been made to ensure that all information is accurate at the time of going to press, the publishers will be glad to receive any corrections and suggestions for improvements, which can be incorporated in the next edition. Price information in this book is accurate at the time of going to press, but prices and currency exchange rates do fluctuate. Dollar amounts appearing are at exchange rates in effect in mid-1982.

Editor Fiona Duncan
Executive Editor Hal Robinson
Chief Sub-Editor Susan Chapman
Researcher Catherine Jackson
Editorial assistants Lynne Lynch, Sue McKinstry, Paddy Poynder

Art Editor Eric Drewery
Designer Sarah Jackson
Illustrators Jeremy Ford (David Lewis Artists), Illustra Design Ltd., Illustrated Arts, Rodney Paull

Editor-in-Chief Susannah Read
Executive Art Editor Douglas Wilson
Production Julian Deeming, Sarah Goodden
Consultant editors Ila Stanger, Maria Shaw (*Travel & Leisure*)

Edited and designed by
Mitchell Beazley International Limited
87–89 Shaftesbury Avenue
London W1V 7AD

Published by Simon and Schuster
A Division of Gulf & Western Corporation
Simon & Schuster Building
Rockefeller Center
1230 Avenue of the Americas
New York, New York 10020

Library of Congress Cataloging in Publication Data.
McIntosh, Christopher.
The American Express pocket travel guide to Paris.
(The Simon and Schuster/ American Express pocket travel guides)
Includes index.
1. Paris (France) — Description — 1975 — Guide-books. I. Title. II. Series.
DC708.M46 914.4'3604838 82–3184
ISBN 0–671–45371–8 AACR2

Maps in 4-color by Clyde Surveys Ltd., Maidenhead, England, based on copyrighted material of IGN-Paris 1982; authorization no. 99-0595; extracts from maps of the Institut Géographique National – France
Metro and autobus plans, property of the RATP, 53 ter, Quai des Grands-Augustins, Paris 6ᵉ
Typeset by Vantage Photosetting Co. Ltd., Southampton, England
Printed and bound in Hong Kong by Mandarin Offset International Ltd.

Contents

How to use this book

The American Express Pocket Guide to Paris is an encyclopedia of travel information, organized in the sections listed on the previous page. There is also a comprehensive **index** (pages 212–219), which is accompanied by a **gazetteer** (pages 220–224) of the most important streets that are shown in the full-color **maps** at the end of the book.

For easy reference, all major sections (**Sights and places of interest, Hotels, Restaurants**) and other sections as far as possible are arranged alphabetically.

Abbreviations

As far as possible only standard abbreviations have been used. These include days of the week and months, points of the compass (N, S, E and W), street names (Av., Bd., Pl., Sq.), Saint and Sainte (St and Ste), C for century, and measurements.

Bold type

Bold type is used in running text primarily for emphasis, to draw attention to something of special interest or importance. It is also used in this way to pick out places – shops or minor museums, for instance – that do not have full entries of their own. In such cases it is usually followed in brackets by the address, telephone number, and details of opening times, printed in italics. Similarly, in *Hotels* and *Restaurants*, it is used to identify places mentioned in one entry which have an entry of their own elsewhere in these sections.

Cross-references

A special type has been used for cross-references. Whenever a place or section title is printed in sans serif italics (for example *Arc de Triomphe* or *Basic information*) in the text, this indicates that you can turn to the appropriate heading in the book for further information.

Cross-references always refer either to sections of the book – *Basic information, Planning, Hotels, Shopping* – or to individual entries in **Sights and places of interest**, such as *Arc*

How entries are organized

Invalides, Les 🏛 ☆

7e. Map 13I5. Metro Invalides, Latour-Maubourg, École-Militaire, Varenne.

When Louis XIV's architects designed this building in the 1670s as a home for his invalided soldiers, they poured into it all the architectural rhetoric of the Sun King's era. The 196m (645ft) long **facade** overlooks a wide **esplanade** stretching down to the *Seine*; the great portico is guarded by statues of *Mars* and *Minerva*; the dormer windows in the roof are framed by huge stone suits of armor; the **courtyard** with its double colonnade is worth seeing; and the **Dôme church** opposite dominates the whole edifice. Most of the building is the work of Libéral Bruand, but the Dôme church was designed by Jules Hardouin-Mansart and the esplanade by Robert de Cotte.

Once this building housed nearly 6,000 old soldiers. Now the number has dwindled to around 100 and Les Invalides has taken on a new role as the home of four museums and as the resting place of Napoleon Bonaparte.

de Triomphe or *Vincennes*. Ordinary italics are used to identify sub-sections. For instance: see *Architecture* in *Culture, history and background*.

Floors

To conform with local usage, "first floor" is used throughout the book to refer to the floor above the ground floor, "second floor" to the floor above that, and so on.

Map references

Each page of the color maps at the end of the book has a page number (2–24), and each map is divided into a grid of squares, which are identified vertically by letters (A, B, C, D, etc.) and horizontally by numbers (1, 2, 3, 4, etc.). A map reference identifies the page and square in which the street or place can be found – thus the **Arc de Triomphe** is located in the square identified as Map 6F3.

Price categories

Price categories are denoted by the symbols and which signify cheap, inexpensive, moderately priced, expensive and very expensive, respectively. In the cases of hotels and restaurants these correspond approximately with the following actual prices, which give a guideline at the time of printing. Although actual prices will inevitably increase, in most cases the relative price category – for example, expensive or cheap – will be likely to remain more or less the same.

Price categories	Corresponding to approximate prices for **hotels** *double room with bath; single not much cheaper*	for **restaurants** *meal for one with service, taxes and house wine*
cheap	under $20	under $10
inexpensive	$20–40	$10–15
moderate	$40–50	$15–25
expensive	$50–70	$25–40
very expensive	over $70	over $40

Bold blue type for entry headings.

Blue italics for address, practical information and symbols, encapsulating standard information and special recommendations. For list of symbols see p6.

Black text for description. Bold type used for emphasis.

Sans serif italics used for cross-references to other entries.

Entries for hotels, restaurants, shops, etc. follow the same organization, and are usually printed across a narrow measure.

In hotels, symbols indicating special facilities appear at the end of the entry.

Étoile

3 Rue de l'Étoile, 75017 Paris

380–36–94 642028. Map 6E3 25 25

Metro Ternes.

***Location:** Close to the Arc de Triomphe.* A small, intimate hotel where you can live like a prince, almost for a song, with color TV, minibar, direct-dial telephone, thick wall-to-wall carpets and functional modern furniture in your room, plus a bar and a mini-library in the lobby.

Key to symbols

- Telephone
- Telex
- Not to be missed
- Worth a visit
- Good value (in its class)
- Tourist information
- Car parking
- Hotel
- Simple (hotel)
- Luxury (hotel)
- Cheap
- Inexpensive
- Moderately priced
- Expensive
- Very expensive
- Number of rooms
- Rooms with private bathroom
- Air conditioning
- Residential terms available
- American Express
- Carte Blanche
- Diners Club
- MasterCard
- Visa
- Secure garage
- Own restaurant
- Meal obligatory
- Quiet hotel
- Elevator
- Facilities for the disabled
- TV in each room
- Telephone in each room
- Dogs not allowed
- Garden on premises
- Outstanding views
- Swimming pool
- Tennis court(s)
- Golf course
- Conference facilities
- Restaurant
- Simple (restaurant)
- Luxury (restaurant)
- À la carte available
- Set (fixed price) menu available
- Good for wines
- Open-air dining available
- Building of architectural interest
- Church or Cathedral
- Entrance free
- Entrance fee payable
- Entrance expensive
- Photography not permitted
- Guided tour available
- Guided tour compulsory
- Cafeteria
- Special interest for children
- Bar
- Disco
- Nightclub
- Casino/gambling
- Live music
- Dancing
- Revue
- Members only

Before you go

Documents required

For citizens of the USA, EEC and British Commonwealth, a passport is the only document required for visits not exceeding three months. For most other nationals a visa must be obtained. Vaccination certificates are not normally required unless traveling from some Far East, South American or African countries. For stays of longer than three months you will need to apply for a *carte de séjour* from the police at: *Préfecture de Police*, Service des Étrangers, 163 Rue Charenton, 12e ☎341–81–49.

If arriving by car, you need a valid driver's license (not provisional) and must be 18 or over. An international driver's license is not required. You also need the vehicle registration certificate (logbook), a national identity plate or sticker displayed at the rear of the vehicle, and a certificate of insurance or international green card proving that you have third party insurance.

Travel and medical insurance

It is advisable to travel with an insurance policy which covers loss of deposits paid to airlines, hotels, tour operators, etc., the cost of dealing with emergency requirements, such as special tickets home and extra nights in a hotel, as well as a medical insurance policy.

The IAMAT (International Association for Medical Assistance to Travelers) has a list of English-speaking doctors who will call for a fee, as well as having member hospitals and clinics in France. Membership of IAMAT is free.

For information and a directory of doctors and hospitals that are members, write to: IAMAT, Suite 5620, 350 Fifth Ave., New York 10001.

There is an American hospital in Paris at 63 Bd. Victor-Hugo, Neuilly-sur-Seine ☎747–53–00, which accepts Blue Cross and Blue Shield medical insurance. It has a 24hr emergency department, which operates seven days a week. There is also a British Hospital at 48 Rue de Villiers, Levallois-Perret ☎757–24–10.

Money

The unit of currency is the franc (f), which consists of 100 centimes (c). There are coins for 5c, 10c, 20c and ½f, 1f, 2f, 5f and 10f, and notes for the following amounts: 10f, 20f, 50f, 100f and 500f.

There is no limit to the amount of currency you can bring into France, but you can take out no more than 5,000f when you leave, unless large sums are declared on entry. Travelers cheques are a good safeguard against theft, and are widely accepted. Make a separate note of the serial numbers, which you will need if you have to report a loss. Cash them at banks rather than at hotels as they can usually offer more competitive rates.

Major international credit cards such as American Express, Diners Club, Eurocard and Visa (known as Carte Bleue), are widely accepted for most goods and services. Do not assume that your card will always be accepted; either check first or carry alternative means of payment. American citizens who also bank in Europe can make use of the Eurocheque scheme whereby they can cash checks with a Eurocheque card.

Customs

If you are visiting France for less than six months, you are entitled to bring, free of duty and tax, all personal effects, except tobacco goods, alcoholic drinks and perfume, which you intend to take with you when you leave. Make sure that you are carrying dated receipts for the most valuable items such as cameras and watches, or you may be charged duty.

In the following list of duty-free allowances, the figures in brackets show the increased allowances for goods obtained duty and tax paid in the EEC. All limits apply to travelers over 17.

Tobacco If you are coming from an EEC country, you are allowed 300 cigarettes *or* 150 cigarillos *or* 75 cigars *or* 400g tobacco. If you are coming from outside Europe, you are allowed 400 cigarettes *or* 200 cigarillos *or* 100 cigars or 500g tobacco; however, if you are coming from a non-EEC European country you are allowed half this amount.

Alcoholic drinks 1(1.5) liters spirits (over 22% alcohol by volume) *or* 2(3) liters of alcoholic drinks of 22% alcohol or less; *plus* 2(4) liters still wines.

Perfume 50g/60cc/2 fl oz(75g/90cc/3 fl oz).

Other goods Commodities and articles to the value of 230f (1,030f); 115f (290f) for travelers under 15.

Certain prohibited and restricted goods cannot be imported, such as narcotics, gold and weapons. A more detailed list can be obtained from the French Government Tourist Office. Visitors are exempt from the Value Added Tax system above a certain limit, although it should be remembered that the business of filling in the necessary forms can be complicated and time-consuming.

Getting there

By air: There are daily flights to Paris from many parts of the world, including many cities in the USA, and an almost hourly shuttle service from London (Heathrow) run by British Airways and Air France.

Paris has three airports: Orly, south of the city; the ultra-modern Roissy/Charles de Gaulle, north of the city; and Le Bourget, which mainly handles internal flights.

Cities in the USA that are connected by direct non-stop flights to France's capital include New York, Washington, Boston, Chicago, Miami and Houston. In Canada there are flights from Montreal and Toronto. Flying time from the East Coast is approximately 6½ hr by subsonic jet, 3½ hr by Concorde. Airlines that fly direct include the following:

From New York: Air France and TWA fly daily; El Al and Pakistan International fly several times weekly. Air France fly Concorde daily to Roissy/Charles de Gaulle.

From Washington: TWA have a daily service and Air France fly Concorde to Roissy/Charles de Gaulle twice a week.

From Boston: TWA fly daily to Charles de Gaulle.

From Chicago: Air France and TWA fly daily.

From Miami: Aeromexico and National fly several times weekly.

From Montreal and Toronto: Air France and Air Canada fly daily.

Getting there from Britain

For those who are traveling to the Continent from Britain there are several options available. Regular flights leave from London's Heathrow and Gatwick airports as well as from

Manchester, Dublin and some other British cities. It is also possible to travel by train from London's Victoria station to Paris (Gare du Nord), and the journey takes about 7hr. There are several different routes across the Channel using ferry or hovercraft for both car and foot passengers. The cheapest means of getting to Paris from England is by bus. Enquire at a travel agent for all further travel details.

Climate
In Aug many Parisians evacuate the city as Paris can be unpleasantly hot – temperatures average 23°C(75°F). Autumn is often warm; spring brings clear blue skies, but can be chilly; and in winter it can be uncomfortably cold.

Clothes
The famous Parisian *chic* is evident wherever you go; both men and women are beautifully turned out, rarely casually or scruffily dressed. The French are, however, tolerant of informality: you don't need to wear a tie to a smart restaurant, and women can wear trousers on virtually any occasion.

General delivery (poste restante)
The central post office in Paris, at 52 Rue du Louvre, 75001 Paris ☎233–71–60, will keep all mail marked *poste restante* unless specifically addressed to another Parisian post office. The addressee's name should be written clearly on the envelope. You will need identification when you collect your mail and may be charged a small fee. If the letter is addressed to two people, e.g. Mr and Mrs, addressees must collect the letter together. Travel companies such as American Express will also hold mail.

Getting around

From the airports to the city
Trains run every 15min between 5:30am–11:30pm to the Gare du Nord from Roissy/Charles de Gaulle (☎862–22–80); the journey takes 35min. Buses take 1hr and leave every 15min, between 6am–11pm, for the Porte Maillot terminal (☎758–20–18). The public buses (nos. 350 and 351) are slow and relatively expensive.

From Orly Airport (☎884–32–10), south of Paris, trains take approximately 40min and leave every 15min for the Gare d'Austerlitz, Gare St-Michel or Gare d'Orsay. The bus goes to Les Invalides air terminal (☎550–32–30) every 15min between 5:45am–11pm; the journey takes 40min. The public buses (nos. 215, 285 and 183a) are slow.

If arriving at Le Bourget Airport (☎862–12–12), there is no train service but buses will take you to the Air France terminal at Porte Maillot or Les Invalides terminal. A public bus, no. 152, will take you to Porte de la Villette.

There are taxis at each airport, but a taxi ride to your destination will certainly be expensive and will not necessarily be any quicker.

Public transport
Paris has one of the best public transport systems in the world, run by the RATP (*Réseau Autonome du Transport Parisien*). Bus

and metro tickets are interchangeable, and it is best to buy a book (*carnet*) of ten, obtainable from bus or metro stations, *tabacs* and, increasingly, from slot machines in the street. *Billets de tourisme* (tourist tickets) are obtainable from major metro and railway stations, RATP offices and certain banks; they are valid for two, four and seven days. For longer stays it is worth buying a *carte orange*, which entitles you to unlimited travel on buses, metro and RER for one month.

Metro
Unlike some subway systems, the Paris metro is very clean, efficient and quite easy to understand. The lines are designated by the names of the end-stations, so, for example, if you want to go from Concorde to Palais-Royal, you must take the line marked 'Direction Château-de-Vincennes.' There are two classes but no smoking compartments. Inside Paris one ticket is valid no matter how far you go or how many changes you make and you must retain your ticket until you reach your destination; there are frequent ticket inspections. The metro runs between 5:30am–1:15am. Metro stations are a popular haunt of musicians; there are also beggars and pickpockets.

RER (Réseau Express Régional)
This is a fast suburban service. Within Paris there is a flat fare which is only slightly more expensive than the metro. If you want to change from RER to metro, or vice versa, you must buy a *billet combiné* (combined ticket).

Buses
On the buses, one ticket is valid for up to two *sections* (fare stages) and two tickets for three stages or more within the city boundary. When you enter the bus you have to *composter* (punch) your ticket by inserting it into the machine behind the driver. On most routes the buses run from 6:30am–9pm.

Taxis
At the last count there were 14,300 taxis in the city. They can be ordered by telephone (☎200–67–89 – you can pay with an American Express card), or hailed in the street. Cabs have two lights on the roof: both lit means free, one lit means occupied, both off means the driver is on his way home. All registered cabs are equipped with meters. There is a surcharge on Sun and between 10pm–6:30am. You will also pay more if you are carrying a lot of heavy or bulky objects or if you are picked up at a station – you can avoid the latter charge (and the lines) by walking 50m(50yd) away from the station.

Taxis will theoretically hold up to four passengers, but most drivers nowadays will only take three unless you offer them financial inducement in advance. This can be awkward for families or groups of four. Under normal circumstances the driver expects a tip of 12–15%.

Beware of pirate drivers who offer to take you for a 'first-class' fare which will be about five times the normal one.

Getting around by car
If you value your bumpers it is wise to avoid driving in Paris – the Parisian drives as if he were in a bumper car at a fairground, and parks as though he were shoving a book into a tight shelf. The parking problem is severe, and meters are ubiquitous – they run from 9am–7pm and are watched over by purple-uniformed ladies popularly known as *aubergines*. There are also a number of underground, multi-story parking lots. In *zones*

bleues, identified by a circular blue sign posted on the curbside, a *disque de contrôle* (parking disc) must be displayed; it is obtainable from hotels, garages and tourist offices.

Speed limits are 60kph(37mph) in the city and in built-up areas, 80kph(50mph) on the Périphérique, 90kph (56mph) on country roads, 130kph(80mph) on toll autoroutes and 110kmp(68mph) on free autoroutes and four-lane highways. It is good to be aware of the following laws: cars coming from the right have the right of way unless otherwise indicated; seat-belts are compulsory; and children under ten must not travel in the front seat.

For further information contact the *Automobile Club de France*, 6 Pl. de la Concorde, 8e ☎265–34–70, or the *Touring Club de France*, 8 Rue Firmin-Gillot, 15e ☎352–22–15. Automobile clubs such as the AAA, AA and RAC are affiliated with these clubs.

Renting a car

Most international car rental companies have offices in Paris and there are also many reliable and often cheaper Paris firms. Payment by credit card avoids the need for a large cash deposit. A current driver's license is required, and the minimum age is usually 21, although some companies have raised it to 25. Make sure the car is fully insured, even if it means making separate arrangements for insurance against damage to other vehicles and injury to your passengers.

Many companies are represented at the airports, and you can make fly-drive arrangements before you leave your home country.

Getting around on foot

Paris is a city built on a human scale and is therefore easy and pleasant to walk in. If you are not in a hurry, this is the most enjoyable way of getting about. Crossing busy roads, however, can be hazardous, even at *passages cloutés* (pedestrian crossings), where drivers are supposed to give way but often don't. It is safer still to walk in one of the traffic-free zones. There is one around Les Halles and another to the E of the Pl. St-Michel.

Railway services

France's railway services are run by the SNCF (*Société Nationale de Chemins de Fer*). When traveling by train, you must validate any ticket purchased in France by stamping it at the machine at the entrance to the platform. If you fail to do this you will be treated as if you are traveling without a ticket and will have to pay a surcharge. The stations listed below are terminals for specific areas of France.

Gare d'Austerlitz (*southwest*) ☎584–16–16
Gare de L'Est (*east*) ☎208–49–90
Gare de Lyon (*southeast*) ☎345–92–22
Gare Montparnasse (*west*) ☎538–52–29
Gare du Nord (*north*) ☎280–03–03
Gare St-Lazare (*northwest*) ☎538–52–29

For general information ☎261–50–50.

Domestic airlines

Air Inter is France's major internal airline. The central office is at 12 Rue Castiglione, 1er ☎260–36–46; reservations ☎539–25–25.

Other transport

If you are prepared to brave the traffic, bicycling in Paris can be an excellent way of exploring the city. Bicycles can be rented from the following:

La Maison du Vélo 8 Rue de Belzunce, 10ᵉ ☎281–24–72
Paris-Vélo 4 Rue du Fer-à-Moulin, 5ᵉ ☎337–59–22
Vélocation 1 Rue de Savoie, 6ᵉ ☎354–67–21

Mopeds (*vélomoteurs*) can be rented from:

Autothèque 80 Rue Montmartre, 2ᵉ ☎236–50–93
Market Moto 19 Pl. du Marché-St-Honoré, 1ᵉʳ ☎261–09–62

For an aerial view of Paris, a series of tours over the city and as far afield as the Loire Valley is offered by *Paris-Hélicoptère*, Héliport de Paris, 15ᵉ ☎554–12–55.

On-the-spot information

Public holidays

New Year's Day, Jan 1; Easter Monday; Labor Day, May 1; VE Day, May 8; Ascension Day (sixth Thurs after Easter); Whit Monday (second Mon after Ascension); Bastille Day, July 14; Assumption, Aug 15; All Saints' Day, Nov 1; Remembrance Day, Nov 11; Dec 25. Most museums close but many shops and restaurants remain open.

Time zones

Like most Western European countries, France is 1hr ahead of GMT in the winter and 2hr ahead in summer, i.e. 6hr ahead of the eastern USA most of the year.

Banks and currency exchange

In general, banks are open Mon–Fri 9am–4:30pm, but there are no standardized banking hours. They all close in the afternoon before a public holiday. *Bureaux de change* at airports and in most stations stay open late and are often open at weekends. The *American Express Office*, 11 Rue Scribe, 9ᵉ ☎266–09–99, is open Mon–Fri 9am–5pm, Sat 9am–noon.

Money can also be exchanged in larger hotels, but the rate will not be as good as in banks. It is advisable to ask about exchange rates and commission as they vary from place to place. Remember that you need your passport when changing money. Checks backed by a Eurocheque card can be cashed at all banks displaying the sign.

Shopping hours

Department stores remain open from 9:30am–6:30pm without interruption from Mon–Sat, and some are open until 8pm on Wed. Smaller boutiques generally open from 10am–6pm Mon–Sat, although they may close for an hour at lunch. While neighbourhood shops often observe the traditional Mon closing, stores in the centre stay open. And, while Aug was once the universal holiday month, most of the larger shops stay open all summer.

Rush hours

Between 7:30–9am and 5–7pm, the metro is packed with workers going to and from their offices. On Fri evenings the weekend traffic out of Paris is very heavy. It is also wise to avoid leaving Paris on the first and last days of Aug when schools and factories have their holidays.

Postal and telephone services

Post offices are marked by a sign with a blue arrow on a white disc or by the letters *PTT*, and are open Mon–Fri 8am–7pm, Sat 8am–noon. The main post office is at 52 Rue du Louvre, 1er (see *Addresses and telephone numbers p15* for other post offices). Stamps can be bought in *tabacs*, hotels and newsstands, and in coin-operated vending machines, painted yellow. Mailboxes are also yellow and marked *boîte aux lettres*. Allow 7–10 days for mail to reach France and for your letters to reach home. Addresses in Paris must all include the post code, which combines 750-- with the numbers of the arrondissements. Thus the post code in the 1er is 75001, and so on, to the 20e where the post code is 75020. Conversely, the post code shows at once the arrondissement in which any address is to be found.

Telegrams can be sent from any post office or over the telephone. For telegrams in English ☎233–21–11; in French ☎444–11–11. For a small extra charge, letters sent by the *pneumatique* (fast-letter service) will be delivered within 3hr. This applies only within the Paris area.

Public telephones are found in post offices and cafés as well as in the street. Most telephones take 50c, 1f and 5f coins. The French telephone system has been modernized in recent years and Paris numbers are changing, so ask the operator if you cannot get the number you want. Paris telephone numbers are made up of seven figures, written in three groups of three, two and two. All other numbers are made up of six figures, written in three groups of two, with a two-figure prefix for the district – not used in local calls. When calling a number outside Paris, you must dial 16 and then the number with its two-figure prefix; if calling Paris from outside the city the code is 1. In pay phones, the coin is normally inserted before dialing, but if the call is not answered your coin is refunded when you hang up. The ringing signal is a shrill intermittent tone, while the busy signal is less shrill and more rapid.

For international calls, look in the telephone code book to see if the place can be dialed direct. Otherwise dial 19, wait for the second tone, then dial 33 for the international operator.

Public rest rooms

Those who knew Paris before modernization started in earnest will remember the abundance of quaint, perforated-iron kiosks known as *vespasiennes*. Now there are only about 100 of these urinals left. However, modern public conveniences are scattered around the city and, on the whole, are clean and well looked after. You will find them in many metro stations and public parks and you can use the facilities of nearly every café. Often you will find a lady presiding who will charge a nominal sum; otherwise in cafés leave a small tip in the saucer at the bar as you go out.

Electric current

The electric current is 220V (50 cycles AC). Plugs are two-pin round, standard European. Adapters (*transformateurs*) can be bought at any good electrical shop or at large department stores in Paris, or before you leave home.

Laws and regulations

There are no particularly surprising laws in France; laws against drug abuse are as strongly enforced as elsewhere, with greater penalties for the buying and selling of drugs. Hitchhiking is forbidden on *autoroutes*, although it is tolerated on other roads. Smoking in public places such as post offices and banks is forbidden and incurs a fine.

Customs and etiquette

The French are among the most manner-conscious of all nations, and observe a rather rigid code of behavior in personal relationships which is, however, just beginning to be broken down by the younger generation. This consciousness is exemplified by the *vous* and *tu* forms of address; the former applying to everyone except relations and close friends. Hand-shaking is common when greeting or saying goodbye among friends, as well as between acquaintances and strangers, and close friends kiss each other energetically on alternate cheeks at least twice and often three times. It is customary when addressing someone to say 'Madame' or 'Monsieur' without using a surname.

Tipping

Tipping is still widely practiced in France, although most bars, restaurants and hotels include 15% service and taxes in their prices (*service compris*). If a meal or the service has been particularly good, you can show your appreciation by leaving a small tip for the waiter. For *service non compris*, a tip of 12–18% is advisable.

Small tips of up to a few francs should be given to cloakroom attendants, tour guides, doormen, hairdressers and cinema usherettes. Airport and railway porters have a fixed charge per item, while taxi drivers expect about 10–15%.

Disabled travelers

Special facilities for the disabled are becoming more and more usual in France and the French Government Tourist Office has some useful leaflets describing them. The leaflets also indicate which hotels cater to wheelchairs. The *Comité National Français de Liaison pour la Réadaptation des Handicapés* (38 Bd. Raspail, 75007 Paris ☎548–90–13) publishes a booklet called *Voyager Quand Même* (*Travel Any Way*) which describes the accessible hotels and sights in most French towns. For further information, US visitors should write to the International Travel Staff, US Customs Service – Room 6316, Washington, D.C. 20229, or send off for the International Directory of Access Guides, Travel Survey-Rehabilitation International, USA, TL Department, 20 W 40th Street, New York, NY 10018. If you are traveling by train, it is worth finding out the facilities available before you leave, as over 300 stations have wheelchairs and mobile steps.

Local publications

Useful publications giving full details of current events, movies, theaters, shows, sports, etc., are the weekly *Pariscope* and *Officiel des Spectacles* (the latter has a useful day-by-day section listing lectures and guided tours of the city) and the monthly *Ville de Paris* and *Paris City* ('the magazine for foreigners in Paris'). These publications can be bought at most kiosks and newspaper stands.

Major English-language bookshops include:

Attica 23 Rue Jean-de-Beauvais, 5e
Brentano's 8 Rue Danielle-Casanova, 2e
Le Nouveau Quartier Latin 78 Bd. St-Michel, 6e
Shakespeare and Co. 37 Rue de la Bûcherie, 5e
W.H. Smith and Son 248 Rue de Rivoli, 1er
Trilby's 18 Rue Franklin, 16e.

Useful addresses

Tourist information

The *Office du Tourisme* (tourist office) has several branches throughout Paris. Major branches, often at large stations and at Les Invalides terminal, can give hotel information and make reservations for you. The central office is at: 127 Av. des Champs-Élysées, 8e ☎723–61–72. Open 9am–10pm in season, 9am–6pm off season, Sun and hols.

Telephone services

Tourist events in English ☎720–88–98
Speaking clock ☎463–84–00
Alarm call ☎463–71–11
Traffic report ☎858–33–33
Weather ☎555–95–90

Post offices

Central post offices (open 24hr):
52 Rue du Louvre, 1er ☎233–71–60
71 Av. des Champs-Élysées, 8e ☎359–55–18

Tour operators

The following companies run bus tours around Paris:
American Express 11 Rue Scribe, 9e ☎266–09–99
Cityrama 4 Pl. des Pyramides, 1er ☎260–30–14
Paris-Vision (*France-Tourisme*) 214 Rue de Rivoli, 1er ☎260–31–25
SNCF Bureau de Tourisme SNCF, 16 Bd. des Capucines, 2e ☎742–00–26, or Syndicat d'Initiative, 127 Av. des Champs-Élysées, 8e ☎723–61–72

River trips

Bateaux Mouches Port de la Conférence, 8e ☎225–22–55
Vedettes de Paris Quai Montebello, 5e ☎326–92–55
Vedettes de Paris Ile-de-France Port de Suffren, 7e ☎705–71–29
Vedettes Parisiens Tour Eiffel Port de la Bourdonnais, 7e ☎705–50–00
Vedettes du Pont Neuf 1er ☎633–98–38

Airways

Air France 119 Av. des Champs-Élysées, 8e ☎720–70–50
Air Inter 12 Rue de Castiglione, 1er ☎260–36–46
British Airways 91 Av. des Champs-Élysées, 8e ☎778–14–14
Pan Am 1 Rue Scribe, 9e ☎266–45–45

Places of worship

For information on all religious events within Paris, contact the *Centre Religieux International*, Palais de Congrés, Porte Maillot, 17e ☎758–21–47.
American Cathedral 25 Av. George-V, 8e ☎720–17–92
American Church 65 Quai d'Orsay, 7e ☎551–38–90
St George's (*Anglican*) 7 Rue Auguste-Vacquerie, 16e ☎720–22–51
St Joseph's English-speaking Catholic Church 50 Av. Hoche, 8e ☎563–20–61
St Michael's English Church (*Anglican*) 5 Rue d'Aguesseau, 8e ☎742–70–88
Synagogue 43 Rue de la Victoire, 9e ☎526–91–89
Union Liberale Israelite Synagogue (*English Rabbi*) 24 Rue Copernic, 16e ☎727–25–76

Major libraries

American Library 10 Rue du Général-Camou, 7e ☎551–46–82

Bibliothèque du Centre National d'Art et de Culture Georges-Pompidou Pl. Georges-Pompidou et Rue Beaubourg, 4e ☎277–12–33

Bibliothèque Nationale 52 Rue de Richelieu, 2e ☎261–82–83

British Council Library 9 Rue Constantine, 7e ☎705–66–20

Embassies and consulates

Australia 4 Rue Jean-Rey, 15e ☎575–62–00
Austria 6 Rue Fabert, 7e ☎555–95–66
Belgium 9 Rue de Tilsitt, 17e ☎380–61–00
Canada 35 Av. Montaigne, 8e ☎723–01–01
Denmark 77 Av. Marceau, 16e ☎720–32–66
Finland 39 Quai d'Orsay, 7e ☎705–35–45
Germany, West 13/15 Av. F.D. Roosevelt, 8e ☎359–33–51
Greece 17 Rue Auguste-Vacquerie, 16e ☎723–72–28
Ireland 12 Av. Foch, 16e ☎500–20–87
Italy 47 Rue de Varenne, 7e ☎544–38–90
Japan Av. Hoche, 8e ☎766–02–22
Netherlands 7 Rue Eblé, 7e ☎306–61–88
New Zealand 9 Rue Léonard-de-Vinci, 16e ☎500–24–11
Norway 28 Rue Bayard, 8e ☎723–99–22
South Africa 59 Quai d'Orsay, 7e ☎555–92–37
Spain 13 Av. George-V, 8e ☎723–61–83
Sweden 17 Rue Barbet-de-Jouy, 7e ☎555–92–15
Switzerland 142 Rue Grenelle, 7e ☎550–34–46
United Kingdom 35 Rue de Faubourg St-Honoré, 8e ☎266–91–42
United States 2 Av. Gabriel, 8e ☎296–12–02

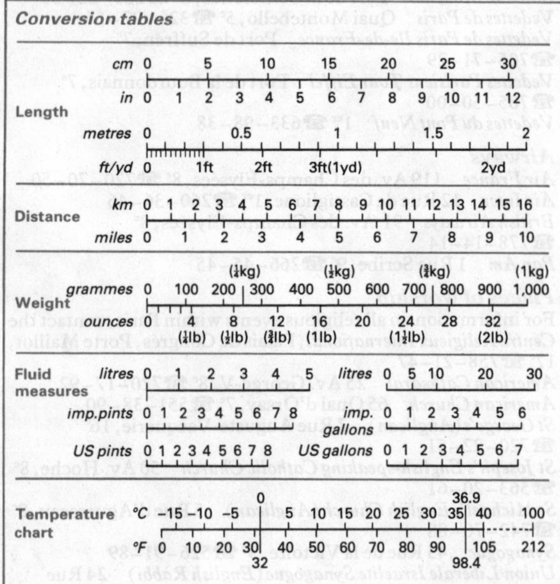

Emergency information

Emergency services

Police ☎17
Ambulance ☎18 or ☎887–27–50
Fire (*Sapeurs pompiers*) ☎18

There is no unified ambulance service – the operator will offer you the numbers of several companies.

Hospitals

For information on hospitals ☎274–50–50

Medical emergencies

For Paris' general practitioners' 24hr service ☎542–37–00; ☎707–77–77 for *SOS Médecin*, or at night ☎337–77–77 for a doctor.

All-night pharmacy

Pharmacie Dhéry Galerie des Champs, 84 Av. des Champs-Élysées, 8e ☎256–02–41 (all night)

Help lines

English Samaritan services 3pm–11pm ☎723–80–80

Automobile accidents

— Do not admit liability or incriminate yourself.
— Ask any witness(es) to stay and give a statement.
— Contact the police.
— Exchange names, addresses, car details and insurance company details with any other drivers involved.
— In serious accidents, ask the police to contact the sheriff's clerk (*huissier*) to make out a legally acceptable account of the incident. You will have to pay for his services, but in any dispute his report will be accepted as authoritative.

Car breakdowns

— Put on flashing hazard warning lights, and place a portable warning triangle 50m(55yd) behind the car.
— Telephone police or call the *Touring Club de France* if you are a member of a motoring club affiliated with this association. If in a rented car, call the number you have been given.

Lost passport

Contact the local police immediately, and your nearest consulate.

Lost travelers cheques

Contact the police and report the loss to your issuing bank.

Lost property

If you have lost something on public transport, go to the *Bureau des Objets Trouvés*, 36 Rue des Morillons, 15e ☎828–97–30; if you have lost something on the street ☎531–14–80. Report all losses to the police as insurance companies may not accept claims without a police report.

Emergency phrases

Help! *Au secours!*
There has been an accident. *Il y a eu un accident*
Where is the nearest telephone/hospital? *Où se trouve le téléphone/l'hôpital le plus proche?*
Call a doctor/ambulance! *Appelez un médecin/une ambulance!*
Call the police! *Appelez la police!*

Introduction

To go to Paris is not just to experience a beautiful city (some would say the most beautiful of all); it is to feel the pulse of a civilization that has held the admiration of the world for centuries – the civilization of France. The Parisian regards Paris not only as the capital of a great nation but as the capital of all true culture. He can be forgiven if he feels he has no need to travel. Why should he go to the Himalayas when he can look at the Ile de la Cité reflected in the waters of the Seine? Why should he learn other languages when his own is so perfect?

All Parisians, even the most humble, are conscious of their heritage. They may seem arrogant, but they have much to be arrogant about. Think of the countless songs that have been written about Paris, the books that have been inspired by it, the millions of pilgrims who have beaten a path to the city over the centuries.

"Paris", wrote Henry James, "is the greatest temple ever built to material joys and the lust of the eyes." His words are as apt today as when they were written in the 1870s. Paris is indeed a temple, the doors of which are always open to anyone who is receptive to beauty, civilized values and delight of the senses. As a result, the visitor is almost inevitably transformed in some way by the experience. But it is not enough just to walk in and passively wait for the magic to work. You must become a little bit Parisian in the way you look at things and the way you react, understand something of the spirit of Paris and the history and traditions that have shaped it. Also you must avoid rigid preconceptions and expectations. Allow for the unexpected and elusive moments of pleasure that Paris so often gives.

People come here from all over the world and for a variety of reasons: to see the Paris of the travel brochures (the Eiffel Tower, Notre-Dame and Montmartre); to explore the great museums such as the Louvre; to enjoy the famous quality of Parisian food and wine; or to test Paris' reputation as the city of Eros. If you come for the last reason you may not find exactly what you had expected. Paris is not a particularly wicked city compared with many others in Europe despite its red-light districts and its scarlet reputation that was established half a century ago, but what it does have is a subtle sensuality that bubbles over into the whole environment, giving zest to the very air of the city. You can see it in the easy flow of intimacy between young lovers strolling by the Seine or idling on the café terraces. It is impossible not to be affected by it, however imperceptibly.

As for the inhabitants of Paris themselves, they can seem somewhat abrupt, even abrasive to the outsider, but this is usually a surface impression. Underneath you will find a good-humored courtesy and friendliness that does them credit considering the massive influx of visitors with whom they have to deal each year.

Remember that Paris is not just a vast museum for tourists. It is also a busy, thriving metropolis, and one that has coped superbly well with the problems that face all modern cities. While other capitals crumble under the strain, Paris remains one of the smoothest-running urban machines in the world.

What might be called 'Greater Paris,' that is the whole metropolitan area, covers 479sq.km (185sq. miles) and has a population of about 8½ million. But the part that we are focusing on here is the city proper, which is surrounded by the ring road known as the Périphérique. This area, cut in half by the Seine, covers only 106sq.km (41sq. miles) and has just over 2¼ million inhabitants; although these are very tightly crammed into a small area, somehow, by a miraculous sleight of hand, Paris gives an impression of spaciousness. The metro carries 4 million passengers a day – and does the job with the minimum of fuss and with subsidized fares at a very low cost. For the entertainment of its citizens and visitors, the city has 1,260 hotels, 10,000 restaurants, cafés and nightclubs, 80 municipal libraries, 2 city orchestras, 66 theaters, 27 café-theaters, 220 galleries, 465 movie theaters, and 48 concert halls.

Paris is a veritable ocean. Throw in the plumb line and you will never know the depth of it . . .

Balzac, *Père Goriot*

In order to keep the city running smoothly, it is administered by a city council of 109 members who are elected for a 6yr term and meet in the palatial Hôtel de Ville. The council is headed by a mayor who also sits for a 6yr term. For over a century the city had no mayor and was controlled by the national government through a Prefect of Paris. This arrangement proved unsatisfactory because, as a result, the people of Paris had no direct influence over the running of their city. It was partly this state of affairs that enabled some disastrous mistakes in planning to be made during President Pompidou's era, such as the building of the Tour Montparnasse and the construction of a highway along part of the riverside footpath. In 1977 Paris was once again given a mayor in the person of the energetic Jacques Chirac, a former prime minister, who has done much to improve the quality of life and the environment in Paris.

Those who knew Paris 30yr ago, in the days before President de Gaulle came to power, will remember a city that seemed to be a symphony in shades of gray, the prevailing atmosphere one of picture-postcard scruffiness and exquisitely faded charm. The water was hazardous, plumbing was often antediluvian and the franc was a precarious currency. Today all this has changed. Paris, along with the whole of France, has become buoyant, prosperous and confident. A massive cleaning program has transformed the city center, so that the boulevards and squares now gleam with pristine tones of cream and gold. Most houses now have modern plumbing, and old buildings are being restored district by district with grants from the city. The decline in population, one of the great problems of recent years, is being stemmed by housing subsidies and by an attempt to attract light industries back into the city instead of pushing them out in accordance with the mistaken policy exercised before 1977. The recent prosperity of Paris, and of France, and its desire to keep pace with modernization, is well illustrated by the construction of La Défense, the huge, gleaming Manhattan-sur-Seine complex of skyscrapers just outside the city limits.

Inevitably there has been a price to pay for progress. Many charming old districts, such as Montparnasse and the Belleville/Ménilmontant area, have been destroyed, and fine buildings, such as the former Halles market, have been pulled down and brash new ones, such as the Tour Montparnasse, have been erected, marring the fine-grained visual quality of the city. But the scars are few compared to many other great cities, and at the end of the day, Paris remains essentially the same glorious temple that it was in Henry James' time.

Time chart

The Gallic origins

3rdC BC The Parisii, a Gallic tribe, made the Ile de la Cité their fortified capital. They prospered from fishing and the river trade, supplemented by hunting and gathering.

The Roman era

52 BC–c.AD 486 In 52 BC Julius Caesar's Roman legions conquered the island, which they called Lutetia, and in due course it became an important Roman center, with the governor's palace erected on the island, and the forum and arena on the Left Bank.

As early as the 2nd or 3rd decade AD, a society of mercantile watermen had established itself in Paris, and these boatmen were to play an important role in the history of the city. The symbol of Paris is a ship, and her motto is *fluctuat nec murgitur* (she is tossed but does not sink).

In AD 250 St Denis came to Paris with two companions, introducing Christianity and becoming the city's first bishop. But Rome was still officially pagan, and St Denis was decapitated by an angry mob.

Several Roman emperors stayed at Lutetia, notably Constantius Chlorus, who made it his headquarters in AD 292. His son, Constantine the Great (c.274–337), who made Christianity the official religion of the empire, also stayed there for a time, as did Julian the Apostate, who was proclaimed Emperor of Rome at the city in 360. In that year Lutetia was named Paris.

Early Middle Ages

5thC AD In the vacuum left by the departure of the Romans, Paris stood in danger of being engulfed by barbarians, but the morale of the city was restored by a religious young woman from Nanterre, named Geneviève, who, in 451, correctly assured the Parisians that Attila the Hun and his hordes would not attack the city. Ten years later, when the city was besieged by the Franks, she helped relieve the famine. She later became Paris' patron saint.

The Merovingians

508–752 In 508 the Christianized King Clovis of the Frankish Merovingian line, made Paris his capital, and it remained in Merovingian hands until 752, when the last of the dynasty, Childeric, was finally ousted by Pepin the Short, father of Charlemagne.

The Carolingians

752–987 An uneasy period for Paris, with frequent raids by Norman pirates, culminating in a great siege in 885–6 which ended in defeat of the Normans by Count Eudes, who was elected King of France in 887.

The Capetians

987–996 Hugues Capet elected King of France at Senlis; his territories were not extensive, however. His descendants reigned from father to son until 1328, establishing the principle of monarchy in France.

996–1108 The reigns of Robert the Pious, Henri I and Philippe I. The building of Notre-Dame cathedral was begun in Philippe's reign.

1108–1137 Louis VI the Fat. During his reign the mercantile waterman's guild was established.

1137–1180 Louis VII the Young, husband of Eleanor of Aquitaine. Having been divorced by Louis, Eleanor married, in 1152, Henri Plantagenet, subsequently Henry II of England, who ruled both NW France and Aquitaine, far more land than the French king.

1180–1223 Philippe Auguste erected the fortress of the Louvre and constructed a great defensive wall around the city, the Philippe-Auguste girdle. His reign also laid the foundation of the University of Paris, one of the greatest medieval centers of learning.

1223–1285 The reigns of Louis VIII, Louis IX, who was canonized, and Philippe III. In the reign of Louis IX the Sorbonne was established. Pierre de Montreuil built Sainte Chapelle to house relics of the true cross which Louis IX had bought for a vast sum, and he worked on the St-Denis basilica, prototype of the Gothic style. In 1260 the guild of mercantile watermen officially took over the city administration, with their provost acting as mayor.

1285–1314 Philippe IV the Fair. Fair only in looks, Philippe was a cruel and vicious king who crushed the Templars, persecuted the Jews and caused misery and poverty among the Parisians through high taxation, forced labor and debasement of the currency. It was he who built the Conciergerie.

1314–1328 The reigns of Louis X the Quarrelsome, Jean I (a few months only), Philippe V the Tall, and Charles IV the Fair, the last of the Capetians.

The Valois

1328–1350 Philippe VI, first of the Valois kings, whose reign marked the start of a chaotic period for France; the country weakened by war with England.

1350–1364 Jean II. During his reign, Étienne Marcel, provost of the merchants and mayor of the city, led a popular uprising (1358).

1364–1380 Charles V the Wise, who restored order to France, built the Bastille and erected a wall on the Right Bank beyond the Philippe-Auguste wall.

1380–1422 Charles VI the Well-Beloved. A weak king, under whose reign the English invaders, and with them chaos, returned. In 1420 Paris was captured by Henry V of England.

1422–1461 Charles VII the Victorious. In 1429 Joan of Arc relieved Orléans, but tried in vain to recapture Paris, which remained in English hands until 1436, when Charles VII recaptured it. In 1431 Henry VI of England had himself crowned at Notre-Dame. In 1453 the English withdrew from all of France apart from Calais.

1461–1483 Louis XI. A cunning, authoritarian, but enlightened king. Under his reign Paris prospered. The city's first school of medicine was opened and its first printing press was set up, at the Sorbonne, by the German Ulrich Gering.

1483–1515 The reigns of Charles VIII and Louis XII, each of whom married Anne of Brittany; her lands were ceded to France after her death in 1514.

1515–1547 François I, great patron of the arts, who was with Leonardo da Vinci when he died near Amboise. Françoise helped to introduce the Italian Renaissance to France and acquired the first masterpieces for the Louvre. He began the reconstruction of the Louvre, and under his rule many magnificent buildings grew up in Paris.

1547–1559 Henry II was killed in a jousting accident. His wife, Catherine de Medici, began building the Tuileries palace.

1559–1589 The reigns of Henry II and Catherine de Medici's three sons, François II, Charles IX and Henry III. During this period Paris was the scene of bloody conflicts between Catholics and Protestants, culminating in the St Bartholomew's Day massacre in 1572, when 3,000 Huguenots were murdered in Paris. Henry III was forced to flee Paris when the Catholic league turned against him in 1588. He was murdered at St-Cloud while laying siege to Paris in 1589. During his reign the construction of the Pont-Neuf was begun.

The Bourbons

1589–1610 Henry IV *Le Vert Galant* allayed for a time the religious uprisings by converting from Protestantism to Catholicism, and issuing the Edict of Nantes, allowing Protestants some freedom of worship. In Paris, he extended the Louvre and the Tuileries, created the Place des Vosges and completed the Pont-Neuf. He was assassinated by a fanatic named Ravaillac.

1610–1643 Louis XIII. The 17thC was known as 'Le Grand Siècle.' Paris was now growing more magnificent as each year passed. The Ile St-Louis was developed, Marie de Medici built the Luxembourg palace and Cardinal Richelieu, first minister and far more powerful than the young king, built the Palais-Royal and founded the Académie Française. The arts flourished, but brutality was also much in evidence, and gruesome public executions were frequent. In 1622 Paris became a bishopric.

1643–1715 Louis XIV the Sun King, under whom France reached its zenith of power and prestige. Versailles was built and became the royal court, and the capital acquired many splendid new buildings and institutions: Les Invalides, the Salpêtrière, Gobelins, the Louvre colonnade, and the Comédie Française.

In 1648, when Louis XIV was still too young to rule, Paris had been convulsed by the Fronde uprising, a bloody protest against the centralized power of the monarchy. When Louis XIV took the reigns of power in 1661, he tightened the grip, abolishing the municipal institutions and the office of mayor so that Paris was ruled by the state. This was to remain the case until the Revolution. In 1685 the king ordered the Revocation of the Edict of Nantes, causing thousands of Protestants to flee.

1715–1774 Louis XV's reign saw financial crisis, disastrous wars with England over Quebec and West Indian colonies and the growing unpopularity of the crown. But Paris was further enriched architecturally by the Panthéon, the Palais-Bourbon and the Pl. de la Concorde. Another encircling wall, known as the Farmers General Wall, was erected as a customs barrier, and further added to popular discontent.

1774–1792 Louis XVI. The government was now financially, politically and morally bankrupt. Discontent among all classes was rife. Louis XVI, an ineffectual king, was unable to stem the tide of revolution.

The Revolution

1789–1799 One of the great turning points in the history of France, and of the world. The Revolution began symbolically with the storming of the Bastille on July 14, 1789. In Oct of that year a mob invaded Versailles, and the king returned to Paris. At first he remained on the throne while various reforms were carried out, but by 1792 he was deposed and imprisoned, and the following year he and his queen Marie-Antoinette were executed. Extremists, including Danton, Marat and Robespierre, instituted the Reign of Terror, in which 2,800 people in Paris alone were executed, and another 14,000 in the rest of the country.

The Reign of Terror finally ended with the fall and execution of Robespierre in 1794. The Revolution itself could be said to have ended when, in 1799, Napoleon appointed himself First Consul – in effect, dictator of France.

The Consulate and First Empire

1799–1815 After a period of stagnation Paris began, under Napoleon, to enjoy a new period of expansion and prosperity. The Farmers General Wall was done away with, the office of Prefect of the Seine was created, and many of the exiled nobles returned. The foundations of large-scale industry were laid, and the arts flourished once more. On the negative side, the city was terrorized by Napoleon's police under the ruthless first Prefect of Police, Joseph Fouché.

In 1804 Napoleon had himself crowned Emperor in Notre-Dame. Under Napoleon, France was master of Europe until 1814 when Paris fell to the invading allied armies. Napoleon abdicated at Fontainebleau and was exiled to Elba. In 1815 he escaped and returned to France for his final campaign, which ended at Waterloo. He was sent again into exile, this time to St Helena, in the custody of the British government, where he died in 1821.

The Restoration

1815–1848 After Napoleon's defeat, the Bourbon monarchy was restored and Louis XVIII crowned king. He was succeeded in 1824 by Charles X who himself was ousted during the short-lived July Revolution in Paris in favor of Louis-Philippe of the Orléans line.

These were years of modernization for Paris. Between 1812–5 the Ourcq, St-Denis and St-Martin canals were built, and 1837 saw the opening of the first French railway line, from Paris to St-Germain-en-Laye. Pleasure steamers plied the Seine; gas lighting was installed; and a new wall, the Thiers fortifications, was erected around the city in 1841–5. Although this has vanished, it marks the line of the present Périphérique boundary. In 1832, 19,000 Parisians perished in a cholera epidemic.

The Second Republic and Second Empire

1848–1870 Louis-Philippe was ousted in the 'Year of Revolutions' which swept through Europe in 1848; a Second

Republic was declared, only to give way to a Second Empire under Napoleon III (Emperor 1852–70). This was a key period in the development of Paris. Baron Haussmann, Prefect of the Seine, drove his great boulevards through the city, which was divided into the present 20 *arrondissements*. Haussmann's idea behind the building of the boulevards was partly to create streets too wide for barricading in case of further street fighting and revolution. Among other new buildings, the Opéra and Les Halles sprang up, as well as the main stations, the sewers (*égouts*) and the Bois de Boulogne and Vincennes. In 1855 and 1867 spectacular international exhibitions were held in the capital. This gay period was ended by the Franco-Prussian War.

Third Republic

1870–1945 The Third Republic was declared in 1870. Napoleon III surrendered at Sedan. Paris was besieged by the Prussians and fell to them in early 1871. St-Cloud château was burned down, and Napoleon III fled to England. Paris was taken over by the revolutionary government, the Commune, between Mar–May 1871, but it was finally suppressed; the city suffered terrible damage.

After Paris had recovered, a new period of expansion and prosperity set in, symbolized by the World Exhibition of 1889 and the building of the Eiffel Tower. The year 1900 saw the opening of the first metro line in Paris, and the city then played host to another World Exhibition.

During the First World War Paris sustained little physical damage, and comparatively little during the Second, but the population suffered much under Nazi occupation. The city was liberated in 1944. General de Gaulle led the new provisional government, which held power for just over a year.

Since the Second World War

1946 The inauguration of the Fourth Republic. A new constitution. Government by coalition of Socialists, Communists, Radicals and Catholic Democrats.

1958 French army takes power in Algeria. Fourth Republic falls and de Gaulle forms Fifth Republic.

1959 EEC (Common Market) founded, with France included among the six members.

1962 Algeria granted independence.

1968 Student riots and demonstrations in the streets of Paris, reaching a peak in May.

1969 Electoral defeat of de Gaulle. Election of Pompidou as President. Les Halles market transferred to Rungis, in the suburbs.

1970 De Gaulle's death.

1973 Montparnasse Tower and the ring road were completed.

1974 Pompidou's death. Election of Giscard d'Estaing as President.

1977 Election of Jacques Chirac as the first mayor of Paris since 1871.

1981 Electoral defeat of Giscard d'Estaing. A socialist government elected under the leadership of François Mitterand.

Architecture

Perhaps the most striking element of Paris' architecture as a whole is its visual harmony. Although there are samples of many different periods and styles, each blends with the other in such a way as to create an environment that is both diverse and unified. Only in the past two decades have any really disruptive elements been introduced, and even these have not destroyed the overall sense of unity. Most of the great architectural styles are represented in Paris, from Roman to ultramodern.

Roman *(1st–4thC AD)*
The only examples of the Roman era still visible are the Thermal Baths in the Cluny museum and the restored Arènes de Lutèce. Both are evidence of the heavy, grandiose and colossal elements typical of Roman concrete and brick architecture, with massive walls, barrel vaults and big rounded arches. France has comparatively few Gallo-Roman remains, though some traces are evident in the foundations of Paris' St-Denis basilica.

Romanesque *(11th and 12thC)*
Skilful use was made of vaulting and pillars to create a striking sense of space. The style is characterized by rounded arches and monumental simplicity, the columns smooth except perhaps for a flourish of carving at the top. There are few examples of the Romanesque in Paris, but those that there are include the bell tower and small chancel columns of St-Germain-des-Prés, the capitals in St-Pierre, Montmartre, the belfry which abuts the apse in St-Germain l'Auxerrois and the St-Denis basilica crypt.

Early Gothic *(12th and 13thC)*
In place of the rounded arches and plainness of the Romanesque style, the Gothic builders used pointed arches and made great play with stained glass, sculptural decoration and vertical emphasis. It was pre-eminently an ecclesiastical style, with the ideal of liberating as much space as possible, creating a sense of void over solid and, by using verticals rather than horizontals, of producing a soaring, aspiring quality. The precursor of Gothic architecture in Europe was the St-Denis basilica, on the outskirts of Paris, but the outstanding example in Paris is the cathedral of Notre-Dame. In the early Gothic churches, windows were small and decoration comparatively restrained.

Mid-Gothic *(13th and 14thC)*
As the Gothic builders became more skilful at distributing weight through the use of buttresses, they were able to liberate larger areas of wall for stained-glass windows. The Sainte Chapelle in Paris is one of the finest examples of this period to be found anywhere. The cathedral of Notre-Dame at Chartres is one of the most renowned examples of the High Gothic architectural style, and served as the experiment which opened the way for the later and even more spectacular architectural developments.

Late or Flamboyant Gothic *(15thC)*
In the late phase of the Gothic period, builders abandoned themselves to exuberant decoration characterized by Flamboyant (literally 'flame-like') window tracery and columns rising into fan-vaulting, as in the ambulatory of St-Séverin. Other buildings which illustrate this style in Paris are the Hôtel de Sens, Hôtel de Cluny, the Tour St-Jacques and the Billettes Cloister. The church of St-Maclou at Rouen is also an outstanding example of this exotic phase.

Renaissance *(16thC)*
Military campaigns in Italy led the French to a gradual understanding of the Renaissance. In architecture it was marked by a return to Greek and Roman forms and motifs: allegorical sculptures, Classical columns, balustrades, pediments and rounded arches. François I, a patron of the arts, did much to introduce Renaissance architecture to France, where one of its leading exponents was Pierre Lescot who designed part of the Cour Carré in the Louvre. Other examples are: the courtyard of the Hôtel Carnavalet, the Porte Dorée at Fontainebleau, the Fontaine des Innocents at Les Halles and, in interior decoration, the rood-screen at St-Étienne-du-Mont.
French Baroque and Classicism *(17thC)*
In essence, the Baroque style is a more ornate version of Renaissance Classicism. Versailles is a striking instance; another is the E wing of the Louvre. In ecclesiastical architecture, Baroque includes the so-called 'Jesuit' style (based on the church of Gésu in Rome). Paris has many churches of this kind: the Sorbonne church, Val-de-Grâce, St-Paul-St-Louis, all featuring the Baroque predilection for

The Thermal Baths, reminder of Paris' Roman heritage, show the typical use of brickwork and rounded arches.

St Denis' Romanesque crypt; the rest of the basilica is early Gothic.

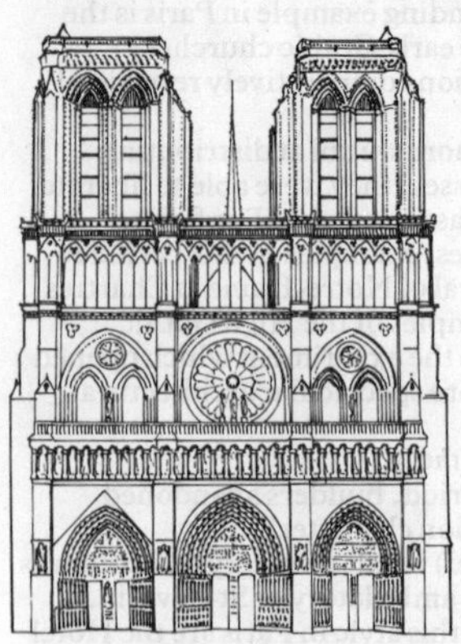
Notre-Dame cathedral. France is rich in superb Gothic cathedrals and this is one of the most exquisite examples.

Sainte Chapelle shows perfectly the Gothic architect's desire to free space for light and stained glass.

domes. One of the outstanding architects of this period was François Mansart, who also gave his name to the high-pitched 'Mansard roof' as on the Val-de-Grâce cloister. His relative, Jules Hardouin-Mansart, married Baroque with the simple lines of Classicism in many superb secular buildings: notably Pl. Vendôme, and the Dôme church at Les Invalides.

***Rococo** (18thC)*

After the death of Louis XIV, and with a child king on the throne, a new, lighter style made its appearance. This was Rococo, called *Rocaille* in French and more restrained than elsewhere and mainly a feature of interior decoration – for example, in Paris, the Oval Salon of the Hôtel de Soubise. The Hôtel Biron, now the Rodin museum, is an example of the refined elegance of the Rococo age. The 18thC Classical, monumental architecture reached its peak in Paris with such buildings as the Louvre Colonnade, the École Militaire, and the Pl. de la Concorde.

***Neo-Classicism** (late 18th–early 19thC)*

Between the 1780s and 1830s, interest in Classical antiquity was revived in contrast to the ornate Rococo style. Once again,

The Flamboyant Gothic style of the late 15thC **Hôtel de Sens** is seen to good effect in the highly decorated turrets and battlements.

The courtyard of the **Hôtel Carnavalet**, below left, is a clear example of the influence of the Italian Renaissance.

The Dôme church, below right, is Jules Hardouin-Mansart's classically proportioned Baroque masterpiece.

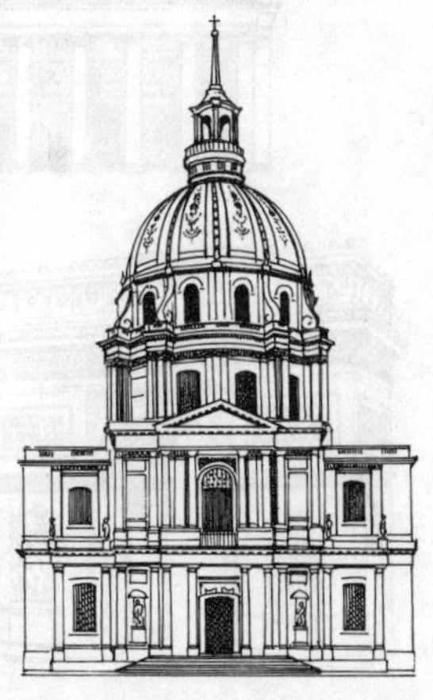

order, balance and clarity became the keynotes. The Madeleine illustrates the style, and Paris has the supreme example of Neo-Classicism in the Panthéon.

Consulate, Empire and Restoration *(early 19thC)*
Buildings of this period are unimaginative, a heavier version of the Classical style, as in the Arc de Triomphe and Madeleine.

Second Empire and early Third Republic *(mid-19th to early 20thC)*
Uniformity went by the board and was replaced by a great mixture of styles, drawing on many periods. Advanced engineering, exemplified by the Eiffel Tower, was often combined with great extravagance of decoration, at least partly because the structural problems solved by the use of iron allowed great decorative freedom. A typical Second-Empire building is Charles Garnier's Opéra. The feeling of extravagant rhetoric was carried into the Third Republic period with such edifices as the Sacré-Coeur, the Grand Palais and Petit Palais, and Pont Alexandre III. The Grand Palais interior illustrates particularly well the combination of practicality and decorativeness, and its use of stylized natural forms can be seen

The Hôtel Biron shows the refined gracefulness of the *Rocaille* period.

The Panthéon is a supreme example of Neo-Classicism.

The Eiffel Tower illustrates the late 19thC's interest in engineering and the diversity of its architectural styles.

The Arc de Triomphe's monumental grandeur elaborates on pure Classicism.

as a precursor of the architectural experiments that characterize Art Nouveau.

Art Nouveau *(late 19th to early 20thC)*
Here the mood changes markedly. Art Nouveau decorations on buildings are fluid in appearance, characterized by many elongated loops and an almost Baroque elaborateness of form. It is most obvious in the original cast-iron entrances to some metro stations, for example at the Louvre.

Inter-war *(1918-39)*
Modernity and functionalism are the keynotes, but echoes of tradition were still retained. The combination can be seen in the Palais de Chaillot and the Palais de Tokyo, where full use is made of reinforced stone and concrete.

Postwar *(1945 to present day)*
Le Corbusier was the most famous exponent of modern architecture in France, but Paris has little of his work. Bleak expanses of glass, steel and concrete can be seen particularly in the Tour Montparnasse, La Défense and the Palais des Congrès. But Paris also has some fine modern buildings such as the Pompidou Center and the Forum des Halles.

The Opéra, Charles Garnier's Second Empire extravaganza.

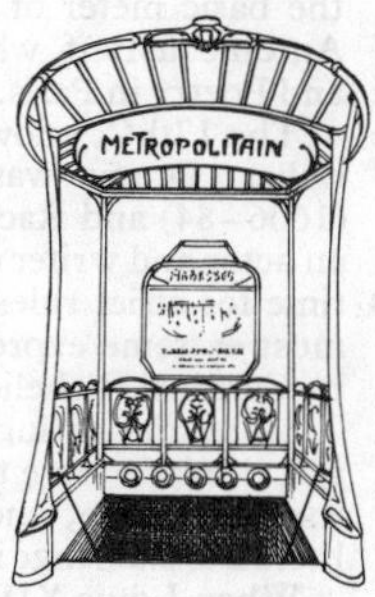

One of the many remaining early 20thC Art Nouveau **metro station** entrances.

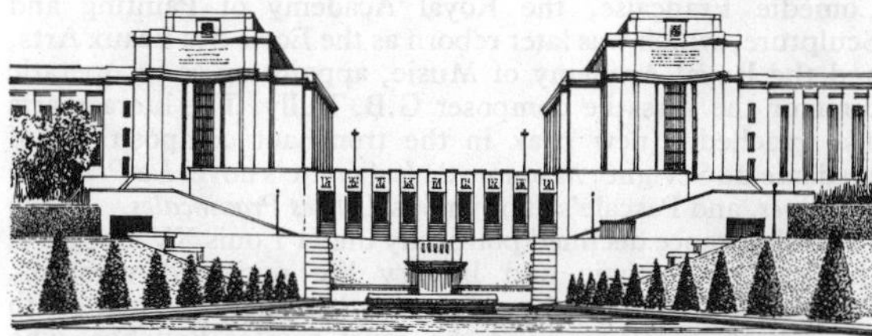

The Palais de Chaillot marries functionalism with more traditional elements of style.

Exposed tubes on its exterior characterize Rogers and Piano's exciting **Pompidou Center**.

The arts in Paris

It is hard to pinpoint the beginning of Paris' greatness as a center of art and culture. Its cultural roots can be traced back as far as the Gallo-Roman period, but in more recent times a point of origin can be seen in François Villon, widely considered to be France's (and Paris') first great poet, who combined the writing of brilliant verse with living as a thief and brigand among the maze of tiny streets and taverns of the Latin Quarter.

Villon was a forerunner of the great cultural outburst that came when Italian Renaissance art and architecture reached France under the influence of François I. François also stimulated a new interest in music, particularly songs accompanied by the lute, which were often heard in his court, and brought important Italian masterpieces – among them the *Mona Lisa* – to Paris. Literature also flourished, and it was at this time that François Rabelais (c.1494–c.1553) wrote his roistering and satirical stories of *Gargantua and Pantagruel*. The same period saw the emergence of the *Pléiade*, a group of seven poets who broke with medieval traditions, introduced Italian Renaissance forms and established the alexandrine (line of 12 syllables) as the basic meter of French verse. One of the group was Jean Antoine de Baïf, who in 1571 established an Academy of Music and Poetry in Paris.

The 17thC, known as 'La Grand Siècle,' was culturally even richer. Drama was dominated by the tragedians Corneille (1606–84) and Racine (1639–99), and by Molière (1622–73), an actor and writer of sparkling comedies. The fondness at this time for strict rules of form in literature and drama found its most extreme expression in the Académie Française, founded by Cardinal Richelieu in 1635.

More stimulating and less conservative as a milieu for writers and thinkers were the *salons*, which began to flourish at about the same time, and provided a forum for philosophers and literati to exchange ideas and sharpen their wits on one another.

When Louis XIV began to rule in 1661, he proved to be the greatest patron of the arts since François I. He founded the Comédie Française, the Royal Academy of Painting and Sculpture, which was later reborn as the École des Beaux Arts, and the Royal Academy of Music, appointing as its operatic director the versatile composer G.B. Lully. The literary arts also reached a new peak in the trenchant compositions of Madame de Sévigné, Madame de Lafayette's novel *La Princesse de Clèves*, and Pascale's anonymous *Lettres Provinçales*.

While France declined politically under Louis XV and XVI, the nation's artistic and literary life remained vigorous. Painting was dominated by Watteau, then later Fragonard with his delicate eroticism, and the court painter Boucher, who became famous for his portraits of Louis XV's mistress, Madame de Pompadour. In music, operas were composed by Rameau and the German, Gluck, who had his greatest successes in Paris. And the world of letters resounded to the philosophy and wit of Voltaire, Rousseau, Montesquieu, Diderot and d'Alembert. In such company, the *salons* enjoyed their heyday under the patronage of some of the most fashionable hostesses, among them Madame de Lambert, Madame de Deffand, Madame Geoffrin and Madame de Pompadour herself. Despite revolution and war, the early half of the 19thC saw the flowering of great artists in all fields: Delacroix in painting, Berlioz in music, Balzac and Victor Hugo in literature.

Under the Second Empire, Parisian life once again became a glorious party, dancing to the tunes of Offenbach and captured in the caricatures of Daumier. But it was in the late 19thC, after Paris had recovered from the Franco-Prussian war, that the period of greatest cultural efflorescence began.

The artistic world felt itself alienated from bourgeois society and had carved out its own territory, 'Bohemia,' the world so vividly portrayed by Henri Murger in his novel *Scènes de la Vie de Bohème*. In the Second Empire, one of the favorite hostelries had been the Brasserie des Martyrs in the Rue des Martyrs, where Murger rubbed shoulders with the poet Baudelaire and the painter Gustave Courbet. Later the scene shifted to other cafés such as the Guerbois and the Nouvelle Athènes, where could be found a remarkable mixture of artistic rebels, drop-outs, and failures and a handful who became famous, among them writers like Zola and painters labeled 'Impressionists': Monet, Pissarro, Renoir and Degas.

The late 19th–early 20thC, and particularly the Belle Époque (1900–14), brought forth many schools in the various branches of the arts. On the stage, Sarah Bernhardt was the toast of Paris. There were the 'Symbolist' poets and painters with their interest in the strange, the surreal, the mythological: Gustave Moreau in painting, Villiers de l'Isle Adam in literature, and there was Marcel Proust with his odyssey *À la Recherche du Temps Perdu*, which shows that even in the early decades of the 20thC the tradition of the *salon* was still alive. At the same time, the foundations of modern art were being laid. Picasso, for example, was already at work in Paris in 1901. He lived and worked in a remarkable artists' and writers' lodging house in Montmartre called the Bateau-Lavoir in the company of other avant-garde painters like Van Dongen, Braque and Juan Gris, and writers such as Max Jacob and Apollinaire.

Montmartre continued to be an artistic center until well into this century – Utrillo, for example, lived there, and its streets appear in many of his paintings. But between the First and Second World Wars most of the artists and writers preferred Montparnasse, and it was here that James Joyce, Henry Miller, Ernest Hemingway, Scott Fitzgerald and Gertrude Stein sought inspiration. Miller's *Tropic of Cancer* and Hemingway's *A Moveable Feast* both vividly describe the Paris they knew.

In the interwar period, Paris gave birth to one of the most influential artistic and literary movements of modern times: Surrealism. Its founder was a poet, André Breton, but its best-known exponents were painters: René Magritte, André Masson, Salvador Dali, and Max Ernst. Literature also flourished in Paris in the interwar and postwar years under the hands of such renowned writers as Gide, Colette, Cocteau, Simenon, Queneau, Camus, Sartre and Simone de Beauvoir.

After the Second World War the focus of intellectual life moved once again, this time to the St-Germain-des-Prés quarter, where the cafés were frequented by Sartre and his circle. The postwar years are also profoundly associated with Edith Piaf, whose compelling voice and passionate lifestyle made her into a legend both in her lifetime and beyond her untimely death in 1963.

Today the cultural life of Paris is as lively as ever, from the theater of Jean-Louis Barrault, the films of Alain Resnais and the music of the Paris Symphony Orchestra to the street poets and musicians who perform with such verve and imagination in front of the Pompidou Center.

Orientation map

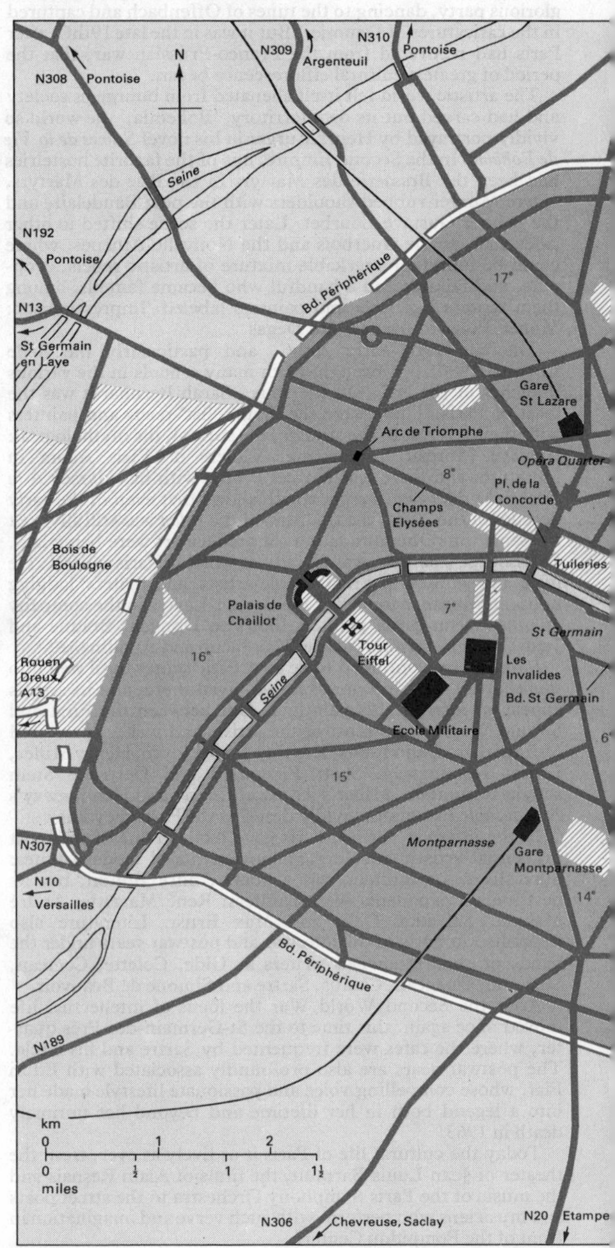

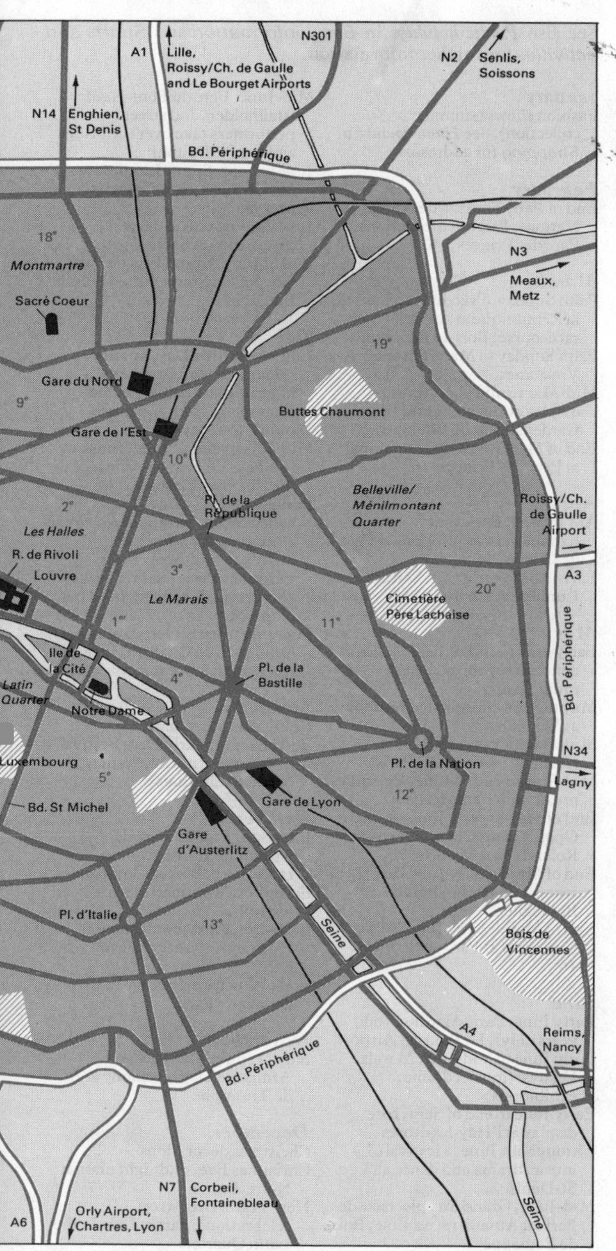

N301
A1
Lille,
Roissy/Ch. de Gaulle
and Le Bourget Airports
N2
Senlis,
Soissons
N14
Enghien,
St Denis
Bd. Périphérique
18°
Montmartre
N3
Meaux,
Metz
Sacré Coeur
19°
Gare du Nord
9°
Buttes Chaumont
Gare de l'Est
10°
Belleville/
Ménilmontant
Quarter
2°
Pl. de la
République
Roissy/Ch.
de Gaulle
Airport
Les Halles
R. de Rivoli
Louvre
3°
A3
Le Marais
20°
Cimetière
Père Lachaise
1er
11°
Bd. Périphérique
Ile de
la Cité
Pl. de la
Bastille
Latin
Quarter
4°
Notre Dame
N34
Pl. de la Nation
Luxembourg
5°
Lagny
12°
Bd. St Michel
Gare de Lyon
Gare
d'Austerlitz
Pl. d'Italie
13°
Seine
Bois de
Vincennes
A4
Reims,
Nancy
Bd. Périphérique
N7
Corbeil,
Fontainebleau
Orly Airport,
Chartres, Lyon
A6
Seine

Calendar of events

See also *Public holidays* in *Basic information* and *Sports and activities* for further information.

January

Fashion shows (summer collection). See *Haute couture* in *Shopping* for addresses

February

End of Feb, Tournoi des Cinqs Nations: Rugby International at Parc des Princes, 16[e]

March

Palm Sunday, Prix du Président de la République at Auteuil racecourse, Bois de Boulogne

Palm Sunday to May, Throne Fair, Vincennes

Mid-Mar to mid-Apr, flower display at Bagatelle and Floral Gardens, Bois de Boulogne

End of Mar, Rugby International at Parc des Princes, 16[e]

April

Apr to May, Paris Fair (commercial exhibition) at Parc des Expositions

Early Apr to early Oct, Son et Lumière at Les Invalides

May

Early May to end of June, series of concerts organized by the municipality

May to Sept, illuminated fountains at Versailles

Mid-May, Paris marathon (running race around Paris)

Mid-May to end of June, Versailles music and drama festival

End of May to early June, French Open Tennis Championships, Roland Garros courts, 16[e]

End of May to early July, display of roses at Bagatelle, Bois de Boulogne

End of May or early June, soccer Cup Final at Parc des Princes, 16[e]

June

Early June, Paris Air Show (odd years only), Le Bourget Airport

Early June to mid-July, Marais Festival (music, drama, exhibitions)

Early June to end of Sept, rose display at l'Hay-les-Roses

Throughout June, a festival of music, drama and dance at St-Denis

Mid-June, Grand Steeplechase de Paris at Auteuil racecourse, Bois de Boulogne

Mid-June, Fête du Pont-Neuf (stallholders and street performers take over the bridge and the Pl. Dauphine)

June to Sept, Son et Lumière at Moret-Sur-Loing (Seine-et-Marne)

June 24, Feux de St-Jean (fireworks) at Sacré-Coeur

End of June, Grand Prix de Paris, Longchamp racecourse, Bois de Boulogne

July

July 14, Bastille Day, holiday celebrated with fireworks, a huge military display in the Champs-Élysées and much public festivity

Mid-July or end of June, finish of the Tour de France cycle race in the Champs-Élysées

Fashion shows (winter collections). See *Haute couture* in *Shopping* for addresses

Mid-July to mid-Sept, Festival Estival de Paris (classical music concerts and recitals), in all parts of the city

Mid-July to early Oct, concerts at Orangerie du Château, Sceaux (metro/RER Sceaux)

September

Festival de Montmartre

End of Sept to early Dec, Festival d'Automne (music, drama, ballet, exhibitions)

October

First Sun, Prix de l'Arc de Triomphe at Longchamp racecourse, Bois de Boulogne

Early Oct, Montmartre wine festival

Early Oct, Paris motor show at Parc des Expositions (even years only)

End of Oct to early Nov, Festival de Jazz de Paris

November

Nov 11, public holiday and Armistice Day ceremony at Arc de Triomphe

December

Christmas decorations

Christmas Eve, midnight mass at Notre-Dame

New Year's Eve, street celebrations, particularly in the Latin Quarter.

When and where to go

The city is at its most hectic and crowded in Apr and May and again in Sept and Oct. Aug is still the quietest month of the year, but no longer dead as it used to be when most Parisians went on their annual holidays and half the city closed down. Nowadays Aug is a relaxing and pleasant time to visit Paris, and only a few of the museums are closed.

Paris is a compact city bounded by a beltway, the Périphérique, and divided into 20 *arrondissements* (districts) which spiral outwards from the center. Each *arrondissement* has its own character – say the word '*seizième*' to a Parisian, and he will conjure up an image of a certain urban ambience and lifestyle, he will even hear a special accent. Within the *arrondissements*, and often overlapping them, are *quartiers* (quarters), such as *Montparnasse*, *Montmartre* and the *Latin Quarter*.

The *Seine* divides the city into Rive Droite (Right Bank) and Rive Gauche (Left Bank) with the two islands, *Ile de la Cité and Ile St-Louis*, in the middle. The Right Bank is conspicuous by its affluence and smartness and its high concentration of imposing buildings, large shops, museums and theaters. The districts of bright lights (and red ones) are also mostly concentrated on the Right Bank. The Left Bank has its share of fine buildings and some dazzle, but on the whole its charm is more subtle, romantic and Bohemian.

From a visitor's point of view the districts of greatest interest are the 1st to the 9th, with a few pockets in outlying places. The areas outside the Périphérique do not belong to Paris proper, except for the *Bois de Boulogne* and *Vincennes*, but there are places of interest on the outskirts, such as *La Défense*, the *Flea Market* and *St-Denis* cathedral.

Area planners and visits

The following list gives a brief account of the most significant areas in the city, with their corresponding *arrondissements* (shown in French by the superior letter 'e' following the number, short for *ième*). The areas are listed in an order that starts at the center of the city and works out in a spiral.

Opéra Quarter (*part of 1er, 2e and 9e; Map 8&9*). An area of grand architecture, smart shops and highbrow culture. Glossy and expensive but somewhat fraying at the edges.

Les Halles (*part of 1er; Map 10H9*). A chaotic but exhilarating mixture of old and ultra-modern, still in a state of flux.

Marais (*3e and part of 4e; Map 10&11*). An old, quiet, gracious district, with many museums, narrow rambling streets, and a strong flavor of the past.

Ile de la Cité and Ile St-Louis (*part of 1er and 4e; Map 10&11*). The former is the historic heart of Paris containing the *Conciergerie*, *Palais de Justice*, *Sainte Chapelle* and *Notre-Dame*. Busy and administrative. The Ile St-Louis, by contrast, is charming, quiet and residential.

Latin Quarter (*5e; Map 15*). Youthful, cosmopolitan, colorful, Bohemian, with a large student population.

St-Germain (*6e and part of 7e; Map 8&9 and 14&15*). A quarter with a wide boulevard, tiny side streets, old buildings, and a thriving café life. Intellectual, artistic, elegant and fastidious.

Eiffel Tower and *Les Invalides* and environs (*remainder of 7e; Map 12&13*). Quiet, mainly residential area dominated by the axes of the *Champ-de-Mars* and *Les Invalides* complex.

Champs-Élysées and *Faubourg St-Honoré* (*8e; Map 6&7*). Busy, expensive, grandiose.

Parc de Monceau and environs (*straddling 8e and 17e; Map 2*). Stolid and residential. The world that Marcel Proust described.

Montparnasse (*straddling 14e and 15e; Map 12*). Cosmopolitan, former Bohemian colony, torn apart by redevelopment, but retaining some of its old character.

Palais de Chaillot and environs (*16e; Map 12*). Cluster of museums set in an opulently residential *arrondissement*.

Montmartre (*18e; Map 4*). Rambling, picture-postcard quaintness, side by side with neon-lit but shabby razzle-dazzle.

Belleville/Ménilmontant (*straddling 19e and 20e; Map 11&12*). Dilapidated charm eroded by developers' bulldozers. Strong North African flavour.

On a short visit to Paris, the way to avoid frustration and cultural indigestion is to be selective. Remember that Paris has the advantage of being small and well-organized for the pedestrian, as well as having a superb metro system, and it is a good idea to plan your sightseeing with this in mind. You may already have decided what you want to see, but if not, here are some suggested programs for a two-day and a four-day visit.

Two-day visit

Day 1 In the morning go to the *Carnavalet* museum to get a bird's-eye view of the history of Paris. Then walk through the lovely old *Marais* district to the *Pompidou Center* for a glimpse of the ultra-modern face of Paris. Go across the *Seine* through the *Ile de la Cité* and have lunch in the *Latin Quarter*. In the afternoon take a boat trip on the Seine from the *Pont-Neuf*.

Day 2 Go up the *Eiffel Tower* and perhaps have lunch in one of its restaurants. Then take the metro from Bir-Hakeim to Charles-de-Gaulle-Étoile metro station and walk from the *Arc de Triomphe* down the *Champs-Élysées* to the *Place de la Concorde*.

Four-day visit

Day 1 Do *Walk 1/Getting to know Paris* (opposite).

Day 2 Return to the *Ile de la Cité* for a closer look at *Notre-Dame* and the *Sainte Chapelle* and perhaps the *Conciergerie* and *Crypte Archéologique*. Have lunch on the *Ile St-Louis*. In the afternoon cross to the Left Bank and explore the *Latin Quarter*.

Day 3 Take the metro to Trocadéro and admire the magnificent view from the *Palais de Chaillot*. Cross the river and climb the *Eiffel Tower*. In the afternoon take a river trip from the Pont d'Iéna.

Day 4 In the morning visit the *Sacré-Coeur* and wander round *Montmartre*. In the afternoon walk through the *Tuileries* gardens to the *Place de la Concorde* and visit the *Jeu de Paume* museum there.

Walks in Paris

Paris is a wonderful city for walking, and the fine texture of its urban landscape is best appreciated on foot.

Walk 1/Getting to know Paris

***Walks 1* and *2* can be traced on the map below.**
Allow 3hr plus, according to how many stops you make.
*Maps **8&9**. Metro Opéra (**1**), Louvre (**13**).*

This walk is designed to introduce the visitor to Paris, taking a spiral route round its heart. It encompasses many well-known landmarks and contrasts the great boulevards and the rambling side streets, the Right Bank and the Left.

Begin at the Pl. de l'Opéra (1), dominated by the ornate *Opéra* itself and forming one of the main intersections of the city. This is the heart of the Paris of Haussmann, creator of grand townscapes, and the area is full of smart shops. Walk SW down the Bd. des Capucines and the Bd. de la Madeleine which ends at the church of the *Madeleine* itself (2), looking, as it is meant to, like a stray building from ancient Rome.

From here, go down the Rue Royale to the *Place de la Concorde* (3) passing between two splendid matching buildings of the Louis XV period, the one on the right housing the famous Hôtel Crillon (see *Hotels*). Cross the river by the Pont de la Concorde (4) opposite the *Assemblée Nationale* and walk down the great artery of the Left Bank, the *Bd. St-Germain* (5), perhaps pausing for coffee at one of its famous cafés (see *Cafés*). At the church of *St-Germain-des-Prés* (6) turn left to browse in the charming maze of old streets between the boulevard and the Seine, with their many little book and antique shops, art galleries and food stalls. Then take the Rue St-André-des-Arts and follow it E to the Pl. St-Michel (7), focal point of the *Latin Quarter*. This would be an ideal place to stop for lunch as the area is full of good restaurants.

From here, cross by the Pont au Double to the *Ile de la Cité* and *Notre-Dame* cathedral (8) and return to the Right Bank by the Pont d'Arcole (9), walking N with the *Hôtel de Ville* on the right and the Gothic eminence of the *Tour St-Jacques* to the

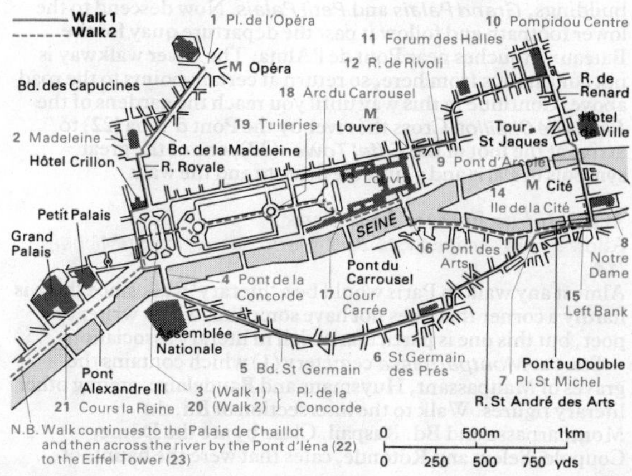

left. Rues de Renard and Beaubourg lead to the E side of the *Pompidou Center* (**10**), Paris' most famous modern building. To reach the main entrance, walk round the lively piazza in front of the building. Having seen the Center, turn W, passing another striking modern development, the *Forum des Halles* (**11**), a shopping complex which has taken the place of the old food market. Now turn left down to the elegant *Rue de Rivoli* (**12**) with its colonnade and luxurious shops and turn right to the *Louvre* (**13**). Whether or not you visit the museum, set off for home from the Louvre metro which, with its low reliefs and statues, is Paris' most attractive metro station.

Walk 2/A riverside walk

Allow 2–3hr. *Maps **9,8,7**&**6**. Metro Cité (**14**), Trocadéro (**23**).*

Most of the great capitals of Europe have their equivalents of the Seine, but few have as intimate a relationship with their rivers as Paris does. History and romance flow thickly in its waters, and Parisians love it tenderly. This walk, beginning and ending at Paris' two greatest landmarks, does not stay on the river banks all the time since the main roads run along much of them, but the Seine will never be far away.

The beginning is where Paris itself began: on the *Ile de la Cité* (**14**). And what could be a more appropriate starting point than the brass compass marker set into the ground by the W door of *Notre-Dame*, from which all distances from the capital are measured? Walk across the Pont au Double, then turn W along the Left Bank (**15**), passing some of the *bouquinistes*, the booksellers with their rows of enticing little hutches full of books. Continue along the Left Bank, from where there are magnificent views across the river, until level with the *Louvre*. Then take what Nancy Mitford in *The Blessing* called "the most beautiful walk in the world". Cross the Pont des Arts (**16**) (during temporary reconstruction cross the next bridge, Pont du Carrousel), enter Louvre by the Passage des Arts near the E end, and walk through the Cour Carrée (**17**), under the *Arc de Triomphe du Carrousel* (**18**), through the *Tuileries* gardens (**19**), and across the *Place de la Concorde* (**20**).

Now return to the river by walking along the Cours la Reine (**21**), staying on the upper level long enough to see the sumptuous *Pont Alexandre III* and the two exhibition buildings, *Grand Palais* and *Petit Palais*. Now descend to the lower footpath and follow it past the departure quay for the Bateaux Mouches near Pont de l'Alma. The lower walkway is not continuous from here, so return at certain points to the road above. Continue in this way until you reach the gardens of the *Palais de Chaillot*. Cross the river by the Pont d'Iéna (**22**) to arrive at the foot of the *Eiffel Tower* (**23**), one of the great symbols of Paris and a suitable place to end the walk.

Walk 3/The literary Left Bank

Allow 2–3hr. *Maps **14**,**15**,**8**&**9**. Metro Raspail (**1**), St-Michel (**14**).*

Almost any walk in Paris would be a 'literary' walk since there is hardly a corner that does not have some link with a writer or poet, but this one is particularly rich in literary associations.

Start at *Montparnasse* cemetery (**1**) which contains the graves of Maupassant, Huysmans and Baudelaire, among other literary figures. Walk to the intersection of Bd. du Montparnasse and Bd. Raspail. Close by are the Dôme, Coupole, Select and Rotonde, cafés that were the haunts of

Hemingway, Fitzgerald, Miller and other expatriate writers of the inter-war years. By the Rotonde on Bd. Raspail stands a cast of Rodin's famous *Balzac*. Turn right along the Bd. du Montparnasse. At the corner of the Bd. and Av. de l'Observatoire is another old haunt of the American literary set, the Closerie des Lilas.

Walk down the Av. de l'Observatoire (2) into the *Luxembourg* gardens where you will find memorials to many writers including (on the E side) to Murger, author of *La Bohème*, Flaubert, Stendhal, George Sand and Lecomte de L'Isle. On the W side is a particularly striking memorial to the poet Paul Verlaine. Leave the gardens on the W side by the Rue Fleurus (3), passing no. 27, where Gertrude Stein lived.

Turn right into the Rue d'Assas. Now follow for a while the walk taken one night by d'Artagnan, in Dumas' *Three Musketeers*, while dreaming of his beloved, as he was "passing along a lane on the spot where the Rue d'Assas is now situated." Turning into what must have been the Rue de Vaugirard, d'Artagnan made for the house of his fellow musketeer Aramis, "situated between the Rue Cassette and the Rue Servandoni" (still in existence). "The hero passed the Rue Cassette and caught sight of the door of his friend's house, shaded by a mass of sycamore and clematis, which formed a vast arch above it." This must have been somewhere near where the Rue Bonaparte begins. Walk down this street (**4**), full of antiquarian bookshops, to the Pl. St-Sulpice (5), described by Henry Miller in *Tropic of Cancer*: "St-Sulpice! The fat belfries, the garish posters over the door, the candles flaming inside. The Square so beloved of Anatole France with that drone and buzz from the altar, the splash of the fountain, the pigeons cooing. . . ."

Continue down the Rue Bonaparte to Pl. *St-Germain-des-Prés* (**6**). Here is the heart of *St-Germain*, once known as the 'Capitale des Lettres' thanks to the presence of poets such as Apollinaire (who lived at 202 Bd. St-Germain) and later of Jean-Paul Sartre, Simone de Beauvoir, Raymond Queneau and Albert Camus. It was in the cafés here that the Existentialist philosophy was nurtured. Continue N on the Rue Bonaparte, then turn right into the Rue des Beaux-Arts (7). "I am dying beyond my means," declared Oscar Wilde, who died at no. 13 in 1900. Even so he would not recognize the luxury of l'Hôtel, as this building is now simply known (see *Hotels*).

Turn right into the Rue de Seine (**8**), where at no. 21 there is

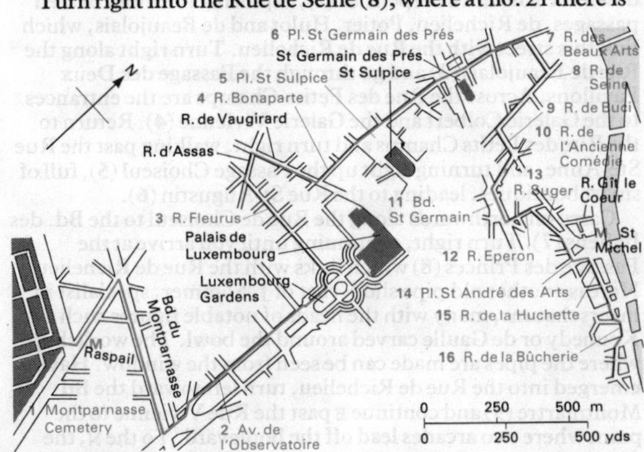

the house once inhabited by George Sand. It is now the Akademia, an art gallery and craft center founded by Isadora Duncan's brother Raymond and now run by his daughter, Ligoa. Turn left into the Rue de Buci (**9**) and right into the Rue de l'Ancienne-Comédie (**10**) and walk S to the Café Procope, no. 13, a literary haunt since it was founded in 1686 (see *Cafés*). Molière and Racine came here when the *Comédie Française* was at no. 14 in the same street. Later it was patronized by Balzac, Hugo, Verlaine and many others.

Back on the Bd. St-Germain (**11**), continue E past the Carrefour de l'Odéon and turn left down the Rue Éperon (**12**) and right into the Rue Suger (**13**) where J.K. Huysmans was born at no. 11 in 1848. This road leads to the Pl. St-André-des-Arts (**14**) where there is a café called Gentilhomme, described by Jack Kerouac in his *Satori in Paris*. Round the corner in Rue Gît-le-Coeur is the Hôtel Vieux Paris where he, Allen Ginsburg and others of the 'Beat Generation' used to stay. From here turn left into the Bd. St-Michel and before the Seine turn right along the Rue de la Huchette (**15**) and on into the Rue de la Bûcherie (**16**), to find the famous bookshop, Shakespeare and Co., at no. 37. The shop is as full of atmosphere as it is of books, and continues the splendid literary tradition of this part of Paris in the lively poetry readings attended by young literati.

Walk 4/The arcades of Paris

Allow 3–4hr. *Maps* ***9*****&*****10****. Metro Palais-Royal (****1****&****21****).*

Long before pedestrian zones came into vogue, Paris had many arcades, covered walkways and colonnades where the elegant *flaneur* could stroll or window-shop unhampered by traffic and sheltered from the rain. At the beginning of the 19thC there were about 140 arcades in Paris. The depredations of Haussmann and later developers have reduced the number to about 30, and many are rather down-at-heel, but they are gradually taking a new lease on life with the increasing pedestrianization of Paris. The first and second *arrondissements* are particularly rich in arcades and passages and by linking them up one can create a charming, off-beat walk.

Begin at the *Palais-Royal* (**1**) by entering at the SE end of the garden and going counter-clockwise round the colonnade, with its stamp and medal dealers, booksellers, and the pipe shop, A l'Oriental. Pipe shops are a feature of the arcades. Double back down the Rue de Montpensier (**2**), exploring the four covered passages, de Richelieu, Potier, Hulot and de Beaujolais, which link this street with the Rue de Richelieu. Turn right along the Rue de Beaujolais (**3**) and go through the Passage des Deux Pavillons. Across the Rue des Petits-Champs are the entrances to the Galerie Colbert and the Galerie Vivienne (**4**). Return to the Rue des Petits Champs and turn right, walking past the Rue Ste-Anne, and turning right up the Passage Choiseul (**5**), full of smart boutiques, leading to the Rue St-Augustin (**6**).

Carry on northwards along the Rue de Choiseul to the Bd. des Italiens (**7**). Turn right, continuing until you arrive at the Passage des Princes (**8**) which links with the Rue de Richelieu. Here is another old pipe shop, that of J. Sommer, specialist in meerschaums, many with the heads of notable figures such as Kennedy or de Gaulle carved around the bowl. The workshop where the pipes are made can be seen from the window. Having emerged into the Rue de Richelieu, turn left toward the Bd. Montmartre (**9**) and continue E past the Rue Vivienne to the point where two arcades lead off the boulevard. To the N, the

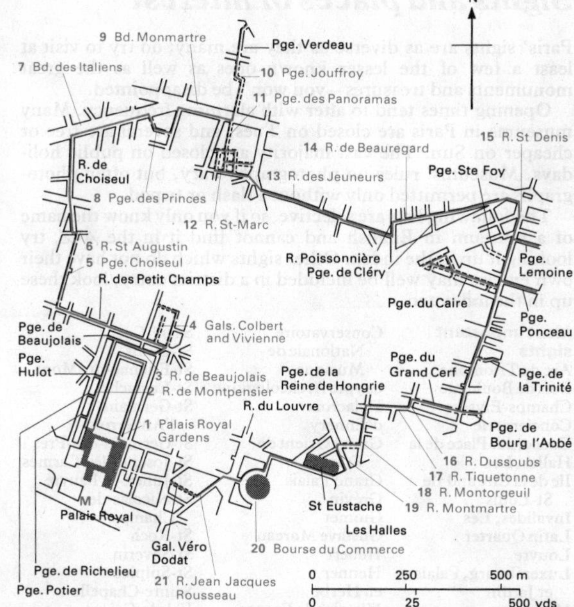

Passage Jouffroy (**10**) extends into the Passage Verdeau. To the S, the Passage des Panoramas (**11**) links up with a small rabbit warren of arcades with a mixture of shops and restaurants.

Exit at the S side of the galleries into the Rue St-Marc (**12**), then head E, walking via the Rue des Jeuneurs (**13**), the Rue Poissonnière and the Rue de Beauregard (**14**) (off which runs the short Passage de Cléry) to the corner of the Bd. de Bonne Nouvelle and the Rue St-Denis (**15**). From here walk S down the Rue St-Denis, exploring in turn each of the seven covered passages that lead off it, to right and left: Passages Lemoine, Ste-Foy, Ponceau, du Caire, de la Trinité, de Bourg-l'Abbé and du Grand Cerf. These once fashionable walkways have come down in the world, but still possess a faded charm. The Passage du Caire has a cornice decorated with Egyptian reliefs and supported by sphinx-like heads. The Passage du Grand Cerf leads out into the Rue Dussoubs (**16**).

Turn right into Rue Tiquetonne (**17**) and left again into Rue Montorgeuil (**18**) to visit the Passage de la Reine de Hongrie, one of the few with no shops. The alley got its name when a woman who ran a stall there gave a petition to Marie-Antoinette. The queen told her that she looked very like the Queen of Hungary, and the name stuck, both to the woman and the place where she worked. Emerge into the Rue Montmartre (**19**) and skirt round the redevelopment area of *Les Halles* by the lovely *St-Eustache* church. Walk through the colonnade surrounding the *Bourse du Commerce* (**20**), then cross the Rue du Louvre and turn left down Rue Jean-Jacques Rousseau (**21**) to the lovely Galérie Véro-Dodat. This arcade, with its gracefully proportioned shop fronts and carved mahogany paneling, brings you back to near the Palais-Royal.

Sights and places of interest

Paris' sights are as diverse as they are many; do try to visit at least a few of the lesser known ones as well as the great monuments and treasures – you won't be disappointed.

Opening times tend to alter with alarming frequency. Many museums in Paris are closed on Tues, and several are free or cheaper on Sun. The vast majority are closed on public holidays. Museums' rules on photography vary, but often photographs are permitted only without a flash or tripod.

The following lists are selective, so if you only know the name of a museum in English and cannot find it in the *A–Z*, try looking it up in the index. Other sights which do not have their own entries may well be included in a district entry; look these up in the index too.

Most important sights

Arc de Triomphe
Bois de Boulogne
Champs-Élysées
Conciergerie
Concorde, Place de la
Halles, Les
Ile de la Cité and Ile St-Louis
Invalides, Les
Latin Quarter
Louvre
Luxembourg, Palais et Jardin
Madeleine
Montmartre
Notre-Dame
Opéra
Panthéon
Place Vendôme
Place des Vosges
Pompidou Centre
Sacré-Coeur
Sainte Chapelle
Tour Eiffel
Tuileries

Museums

Armée, see Les Invalides
Arménian
Art Moderne, National
Art Moderne de la Ville de Paris
Arts Africains et Océaniens
Arts Décoratifs
Arts et Métiers
Arts et Traditions Populaires
Balzac
Bourdelle
Bricard
Carnavalet
Cernuschi
Chasse
Cinéma
Clemenceau
Cluny
Cognacq-Jay
Conservatoire Nationale de Musique
Crypte Archéologique
Delacroix
d'Ennery
Grand Orient de France
Grand Palais
Grévin
Guimet
Gustave Moreau
Hébert
Henner
en Herbe
Histoire de France, see Archives Nationales
Histoire Naturelle, see Jardin des Plantes
Homme
Hôtel des Monnaies
Hugo, Victor
Institut Catholique
Invalides, Les
Jacquemart-André
Jeu de Paume
Le Corbusier
Légion d'Honneur
Louvre
Marine
Marmottan
Mode
Monuments Français
Nissim de Camondo
Observatoire
Palais de la Découverte
Pasteur
Petit Palais
Picasso
Police
Postal
Rodin
Sculpture en Plein Air
Transports Urbains

Churches

Dôme, see Les Invalides
Madeleine
Notre-Dame
Sacré-Coeur
St-Denis
St-Étienne-du-Mont
St-Eustache
St-Germain l'Auxerrois
St-Germain-des-Prés
St-Joseph-des-Carmes
St-Julien-le-Pauvre
St-Nicolas-des-Champs
St-Roch
St-Séverin
St-Sulpice
Sainte-Chapelle
Val-de-Grâce

Districts

Belleville/Ménilmontant Quarter
Latin Quarter
Marais
Montmartre
Montparnasse
Opéra Quarter
St-Germain Quarter

Modern buildings

Cité Universitaire
La Défense
Forum des Halles
Le Corbusier Foundation
Mosque
Palais de Chaillot
Palais de Congrés
Palais de Tokyo
Pompidou Centre
Radio France, Maison de
Tour Montparnasse
UNESCO Building

Parks and gardens

Bois de Boulogne
Buttes Chaumont
Champ-de-Mars
Jardin des Plantes
Luxembourg
Monceau, Parc de
Montsouris, Parc de
Tuileries

Arc de Triomphe 🏛★

Pl. Charles-de-Gaulle, 8e ☎380-31-31. Map **6**F3

Open 10am–5:30 (ticket office closes 4:30). Metro Étoile.

As much of a symbol of Paris as the *Eiffel Tower* or *Notre-Dame*, the Arc de Triomphe is the largest structure of its kind in the world – 50m(164ft) high and 45m(148ft) wide – and its massive bulk dominates the *Place Charles-de-Gaulle*, formerly the Pl. de l'Étoile. It is surely one of the biggest 'white elephants' ever created. The term is curiously appropriate, because an earlier plan for the site was to erect a vast stone elephant containing an amphitheater, banqueting hall and other apartments.

The present arch was begun in 1806 on the orders of Napoleon as a monument to French military victories, but it was still unfinished at the time of his downfall. Under the restored monarchy, work on the arch continued spasmodically, and it was finally completed in 1836. Many artists worked on the decoration of the exterior, which includes four huge relief sculptures at the bases of the pillars: *The Triumph of 1810* by Cortot; *Resistance* and *Peace* by Etex; and *The Departure of the Volunteers* (commonly called 'The Marseillaise') by Rude, generally considered the best of the four.

Higher up are reliefs of battles and a crowded frieze, and engraved around the top are the names of major victories won during the Revolutionary and Napoleonic periods. On the inside walls appear the names of lesser victories and of 558 generals.

Set into the ground under the arch is the **Tomb of the Unknown Soldier**, commemorating the dead of the First and Second World Wars, whose memory is kept alight by an eternal flame – a few years ago, an irreverent person cooked an omelet over it. The arch seems to invite such disrespectful gestures: in 1919 the aviator Godefroy flew under it in an airplane, defying a police ban.

Inside the cross-piece of the building is a **museum of the arch's history** which runs a continuous audiovisual program in French and English recounting the monument's great moments.

Like many other disproportionately large and grandiose monuments in Paris, the arch has merged comfortably into the townscape, settling down to an almost homely, comfortable existence, like a retired general, but no trip to Paris would be complete without a visit, and from the top there is an excellent view over the city of Paris.

Arc de Triomphe du Carrousel

Pl. du Carrousel, 1er. Map **8**H8. *Metro Palais-Royal, Louvre.*

This graceful arch, with its rose-colored marble columns, is linked with the greater *Arc de Triomphe* by the splendid axis formed by the *Champs-Élysées* and the *Tuileries*. Completed in 1809, it commemorates Napoleon's victories in 1805 (including Austerlitz and Ulm) which are depicted on six marble low reliefs. It was formerly surmounted by the four gilded bronze horses from St Mark's in Venice. When these were returned to Italy in 1815 they were replaced by a bronze group, representing the Restoration, riding in a chariot drawn by four horses. The arch once formed the gateway to the Tuileries Palace, burned down in 1871, and now floats in the gardens between the great jaws of the *Louvre* like a dainty morsel about to be swallowed by a whale.

Archives Nationales: Musée de l'Histoire de France *(National Archives: Historical Museum of France)*

🏛 ☆

Hôtel de Soubise, 60 Rue des Francs-Bourgeois, 3e
*☎277–11–30. Map **11**H11 Open 2–5pm. Closed Tues. Metro Rambuteau, Hôtel-de-Ville.*

How many tumultuous events have started with an innocent-looking document? The Revocation of the Edict of Nantes by Louis XIV removed freedom of worship and drove thousands of Protestants out of France. The Revocation and the original Edict are both in the Historical Museum of France, and form part of a collection of documents belonging to the National Archives and housed in one of the great mansions of the *Marais* district, the **Hôtel de Soubise** ☆ Here also are the wills of Louis XIV and Napoleon, the Concordat of 1802 between Napoleon and the Holy See, the Declaration of the Rights of Man, letters of Joan of Arc and Voltaire – snippets of history skillfully displayed and carefully illustrated with the use of maps, photographs and captions to create an intriguing scrapbook of the French nation. The National Archives themselves, which take up 280km(175 miles) of shelving, have been housed in the Hôtel de Soubise since 1808 and in the adjacent **Hôtel de Rohan** ☆ since 1927.

There is more to see than just the documents. The Hôtel de Soubise itself, with its elegant, colonnaded **courtyard**, is worth visiting on its own account. From 1553–1688 it was a residence of the powerful Guise family. It then became the home of the Prince and Princesse de Soubise who had it sumptuously decorated by some of the greatest artists and craftsmen of the era, including Boucher, van Loo and Lemoyne. Leaving the main room of the museum on the first floor, formerly the guard room, one passes through a series of **private apartments** ☆ Notice particularly the Princess' Oval Salon with its eight paintings of the loves of Psyche by Charles Natoire, and also her small bedroom, which now houses a permanent exhibition on the French Revolution. There are also temporary exhibitions in the apartments.

The Hôtel de Rohan (*87 Rue Vieille-du-Temple*), officially called the Hôtel de Strasbourg, as well as being part of the National Archives, is now frequently used for temporary exhibitions. It was lived in by four successive cardinals of Strasbourg who decorated their **apartments** with rich extravagance. One of the rooms, the **Monkey Cabinet**, retains its original panels decorated with animals by Christophe Huet in 1745. The remainder of the interior is the result of skillful restoration. The courtyard has a fine relief by Robert le Lorrain, *The Horses of Apollo*.

Arènes de Lutèce

Entrances in Rue de Navarre and Rue des Arènes, 5e
*Map **16**K10. Metro Monge, Jussieu, Cardinal-Lemoine.*

Turning off the street into what seems like an ordinary Parisian park, you find yourself walking down a stone corridor and suddenly emerging into a Gallo-Roman amphitheater with terraces for spectators. It was unearthed in 1869 by accident when the Rue Monge was being constructed, and it was later restored. Now it is enjoying a second and quieter lease on life surrounded by greenery, and it makes an ideal place for playing *boules* or for simply sitting and imagining life in *Lutetia* – as Paris was known in the Roman era.

Armée, Musée de l' A collection illustrating the history of the French Army. See *Les Invalides*.

Arménian, Musée *(Armenian Museum)*
59 Av. Foch, 16e ▣ *Open Sun only Sept–Mar 1–4pm, Apr–July 1–5pm. Closed Aug. Metro Argentine, Victor Hugo.*
Armenians have suffered conquest, genocide and dispersion, yet, not unlike the Jews, they have still managed to keep their identity. This small museum of works of art, documents and domestic objects provides an intriguing view of their history and culture. It is in the same building as the *d'Ennery* museum, housing the private collection of 19thC dramatist Adolphe d'Ennery and his wife.

Art Moderne, Musée National d' *(National Museum of Modern Art)* ★
Centre Georges Pompidou, Plateau Beaubourg, 4e
☎ *277–12–33. Map* ***10****H10* *Open Mon, Wed, Thurs, Fri noon–10pm, Sat, Sun 10am–10pm. Closed Tues. Metro Hôtel-de-Ville, Rambuteau, Châtelet.*
Housed on the third and fourth floors of the *Pompidou Center*, this is the largest museum of its kind in the world, and one of the most stimulating. The exhibits are arranged on a two-tier system of grouping. Large spaces, designated by letters, are devoted to the great artistic movements of the 20thC, starting with Fauvism (from the French word *fauve*, meaning wild beast) and progressing through Cubism, Abstract Expressionism, Dadaism, Surrealism and other movements to present day. Smaller rooms, opening off these spaces and designated by numbers, emphasize particular aspects of a movement or artist. Thus, for example, under Cubism you will find a number of painters who, in their different ways, shared the same tendencies: an interest in elementary forms, such as the cube and the cylinder, and a renunciation of color in favor of light and shape. The works represented include Georges Braque's *Young Girl with a Guitar*, Picasso's *Seated Woman*, and Fernand Léger's *La Noce*, which also anticipates Futurism in its suggestion of movement through repetition of shapes in a sequence. In a similar way, Surrealism is represented by artists as diverse as Salvador Dali, Max Ernst and Joan Miró, all of whom subsequently developed in very different directions.

Progressing through the galleries you will find that certain artists reappear as they pass through different phases. Picasso crops up at intervals as his style and subject matter change. We see him through a period of interest in classical antiquity, exemplified by his *Minotaur*, then his work becomes increasingly abstract. Other painters – Kandinsky, Matisse, Braque, Léger – also reappear as their styles change. In this manner one perceives the dynamic way in which 20thC art has developed – schools merging, overlapping and breaking away.

The works include many sculptures as well as paintings, for example Constantin Brancusi's deliciously simple *Seal* in gray and white marble, and Raoul Haussmann's Dadaist work *The Spirit of our Times* showing a dummy-like head with a tape-measure, purse, watch and other oddments stuck to the skull.

Part of the fourth floor is taken up by changing exhibitions of works by artists of today, and here you are sure to find creations that challenge the very definition of art.

For a proper understanding of this museum and the way the

paintings are presented, it is worth joining a guided tour with one of the center's lively *animateurs* who know how to make art appreciation fun. Alternatively there is an excellent audio guide to the collection.

Art Moderne de la Ville de Paris, Musée d' *(Museum of Modern Art of the City of Paris)* 🏛 ☆
*Palais de Tokyo, 11 Av. du Président-Wilson, Paris 16e ☎ 723-61-27. Map **12**G3 ▣ ▣ ✱ Open 10am–5pm (Wed until 8:30). Closed Mon. Metro Iéna, Alma-Marceau.*
This lively museum is housed in the **Palais de Tokyo**, which was built for the World Exhibition of 1937. The Palais de Tokyo is a typical example of 1930s style which, at the time, seemed so aggressively modern and now looks quaintly dated – 'modernity' as an earlier generation saw it. Something of the same feeling is also present on entering the building, helping one to see the paintings in the context of their periods. For example, Raoul Dufy's huge canvas *La Fée Electricité* (*The Good Fairy Electricity*) epitomizes the idealistic pride in technological achievement that was still so fresh when the picture was painted in 1937. Other items in this very fine collection include Cubist paintings by Picasso and Braque, canvasses of the Fauve school (Matisse, Derain) and works by the so-called Paris school (Modigliani, Soutine, Pascin). There are also temporary exhibitions.

In addition to the main galleries, the museum has two other sections. On the top floor is ARC (Animation, Recherche, Confrontation) devoted to off-beat contemporary exhibitions and also to concerts, lectures and other cultural events. Down on the lowest level is the **Musée des Enfants** (*entrance at 14 Av. de New York*), where children are able to participate in various creative activities from painting to dancing, under the guidance of teachers.

Arts Africains et Océaniens, Musée des *(Museum of African and Oceanic Arts)*
*293 Av. Daumesnil, 12e ☎ 343-14-54. Map **19**D5. ▣ ✗ by prior arrangement ✱ Open 9:45–noon, 1:30–5:15pm. Metro Porte-Dorée.*
The most remarkable feature of this building, erected in 1931 near the Bois de *Vincennes* and originally called the Colonial Museum, is the immense and striking low relief that covers the entire main facade. It represents "the contribution of the overseas territories to the mother country and to civilization", and serves as a reminder of the days when colonialism flourished. The museum contains a superb collection of ethnic art: Benin bronzes, masks from New Guinea, Aborigine bark paintings and a particularly fine display of North African Islamic art. Down in the basement is one of the best tropical aquariums in Europe, complete with crocodiles.

Arts Décoratifs, Musée des *(Museum of Decorative Arts)* 🏛
*Pavilion de Marsan, 107 Rue de Rivoli, 1er ☎ 260-32-14. Map **8**H7 ▣ ✗ Open 2–5pm. Closed Tues. Metro Palais-Royal, Tuileries.*
Founded in the 1870s as part of an attempt to combat mediocrity in the applied arts, this museum presents a panorama of decorative art from the Middle Ages to the 20thC. Housed in the **Marsan pavilion** of the *Louvre*, exhibits are set

out in a series of rooms furnished and decorated in the style of different eras. Here you can see medieval carvings, chests and tapestry work, Renaissance stained glass, elaborate marquetry furniture of the 17thC, Vincennes porcelain of the 18thC, and Art Nouveau woodwork of the 20thC. One of the most striking rooms is a complete **Italianate salon** of the Second Empire with richly painted and gilt wood paneling.

Frequent temporary exhibitions on design and decoration are held on the ground floor.

Arts et Métiers, Conservatoire des

*292 Rue St-Martin, Paris 3ᵉ ☎ 271–24–14. Map **10**G10 on Wed. Open Mon–Sat noon–5:45pm. Sun 10am–5:30pm. Metro Réaumur-Sébastopol, Arts-et-Métiers.*

The conservatory, a college of technology and a large technical museum, is housed in the former priory of **St-Martin-des-Champs** in the NW corner of the *Marais*. The two most distinguished elements that remain from the medieval priory are the beautifully proportioned and vaulted **refectory**, now a library (visits by prior arrangement only), and the church of **St-Martin-des-Champs** which is now part of the museum. If archeologists of the future ever discover this chapel and its contents they might think that they have come upon a bizarre temple dedicated to the worship of machinery. In the Gothic ambulatory, where the shrines of saints should be, there are engine components, car and airplane motors and similar objects, some of them placed in glass cases like holy relics, suggesting perhaps the cult of 'Our Ford' in Huxley's *Brave New World*.

For the technically minded, the museum is fascinating. Here you can see models and displays demonstrating the technical progress of water power, the automobile, photography, television, musical instruments and more – all examples of man's inventiveness and skill.

Arts et Traditions Populaires, Musée des *(Museum of Popular Arts and Traditions)*

6 Route de Mahatma Gandhi, 16ᵉ ☎ 747–69–80 ✗ by prior arrangement ❋ Open 10am–5:15pm. Closed Tues. Metro Sablons.

A cock from a church steeple, models of fishing boats, Breton peasant costumes, a blacksmith's forge, a clairvoyant's consulting room complete with crystal ball and tarot cards – these and many more curiosities are to be found in this colorful museum dealing with folk art and culture in France from the beginning of the Iron Age to the 20thC. A visit to the museum adds another element to a pleasant morning or afternoon spent in the *Bois de Boulogne* where it is situated.

For location, see map in *Bois de Boulogne*.

Assemblée Nationale: Chambre des Députés The lower house of parliament. See *Palais-Bourbon*.

Balzac, Maison de ☆

*47 Rue Raynouard, 16ᵉ ☎ 548–67–27. Map **12**I1 ✗ Open 10am–5:45pm. Closed Mon. Library open 10am–5:45pm. Closed Sun. Metro Passy, Muette.*

This house is the only survivor of the several Paris homes lived in by the author of the great series of novels, *La Comédie Humaine*. It would no doubt appeal to Balzac's sense of irony to find it being used as a museum to his memory, for he considered it somewhat degrading. He fled there from his creditors in 1840, renting it in the name of his housekeeper to avoid their attentions, and remained in it for 7yr. It was here that he wrote some of his last novels, such as *La Rabouilleuse, Une Ténébreuse Affaire* and *La Cousine Bette*.

Whatever reservations Balzac may have had about it, to the modern visitor his house appears an idyllic place which still possesses the flavor of his era and the stamp of his personality. It is approached from a terrace lying below the level of the Rue Raynouard. Passing through a gate that seems to lead nowhere one suddenly descends some steps into a hidden garden belonging to a charming rustic-looking building with pale turquoise shutters, which appears to be a single-story cottage but is, in fact, the top floor of a large house which has another entrance on a lower street.

The house is full of fascinating mementoes of Balzac, including a series of bills from tradesmen. One of them is from a glovemaker, and the caption reveals that Balzac once bought 60 pairs of gloves in a month. Personal effects on display include his coffee pot – he often drank 30 cups a day to sustain his prodigious output. There is also a library of books by and about Balzac.

The garden, with its two stone sphinxes and its shaded corners, has retained much of the charm that it must have had in Balzac's day.

Bastille, Place de la

*4ᵉ. Map **17**J12. Metro Bastille.*

Built between 1370–82, the Bastille served for four centuries as a fortress and prison – mainly for powerful people who had fallen foul of the king. On July 14, 1789 it was stormed by a Revolutionary mob and afterwards demolished, an event still celebrated annually and with gusto in France. Now all that remains of the Bastille is a line of cobblestones at the W side of the square, marking out the ground plan of the once formidable building with its projecting towers.

How dear the sky has been above this place!
Small treasures of this sky that we see here
Seen weak through prison-bars from year to year.

Dante Gabriel Rossetti, *Poetical Works*

Today the Pl. de la Bastille is a huge, bustling, chaotic crossroads, bounded on the S side by the *St-Martin Canal* and surrounded by rather garish cinemas, cafés and shops. It is dominated by the **July column**, a massive bronze edifice surmounted by an allegorical figure of *Liberty*, which commemorates the Parisians killed in the street-fighting of 1830 (the fall of Charles X) and 1848 (the fall of Louis-Philippe).

Beaubourg Familiar name for Paris' vibrant cultural center. See *Pompidou Center*.

Beaux-Arts, École des *(School of Fine Arts)* 🏛

*17 Quai Malaquais, 6ᵉ ☎ 260-34-57. Map **8**I8. Open Mon–Fri 9am–noon, 2pm–5pm (courtyards). Times of temporary exhibitions vary. Metro Pont-Neuf, Rue-du-Bac.*

In his *Paris Sketch Book*, 150yr ago, William Thackeray wrote of this building: "With its light and elegant fabric, its pretty fountain, its archway of the Renaissance, and fragments of sculpture, you can hardly see, on a fine day, a place more *riant* and pleasing." His words apply equally well today.

Temporary exhibitions from the school's collection are held here about three times a year, but it is a pleasure simply to wander through the courtyards and mingle with the students.

Beaux-Arts de la Ville de Paris, Musée des Objects and paintings from antiquity to 20thC and excellent temporary exhibitions. See *Petit Palais*.

Belleville/Ménilmontant Quarter
*19e and 20e. Map **11**F12. Metro Belleville, Ménilmontant.*
Located at the E end of the Rue du Faubourg du Temple, this is the area to go to if you want to catch a glimpse of the down-at-heel charm that used to characterize so much of Paris, captured in the film *The Red Balloon*, which was made here. Comprising the two former villages of Belleville and Ménilmontant, it is situated on a hilly site bounded roughly by the Rue des Pyrénées to the E, the *Père Lachaise* cemetery to the S, the Boulevards of Belleville and Ménilmontant to the W and the Rue de Belleville to the N.

The district has changed somewhat since Rousseau wrote in 1776: "After dinner I followed the boulevards as far as the Rue du Chemin-Vert by which I gained the heights of Ménilmontant, and from there, taking the paths through the vineyards and meadows, I made my way to Charonne, crossing the smiling countryside that separates these two villages."

Today the area presents a rather sad appearance, particularly S of the Rue de Ménilmontant, with a mixture of decay and brash new development. Fortunately, however, an urban renewal program has come just in time to save some fragments of this remarkable district before it is destroyed.

You will not find picture-postcard prettiness here, nor any elegant cafés or smart shops, but you will find some startling patches of a Paris that has long since vanished, shown in the little streets and alleys running N of the Rue de Ménilmontant. Off the Rue de l'Ermitage is a strange little rustic lane, the **Villa de l'Ermitage**, with dilapidated cottages and overgrown gardens. In a nearby street, the **Rue de la Mare**, is a doorway, **no. 32**, leading to a hidden street of row houses.

The streets in the angle between the Bd. and Rue de Belleville have, for the most part, held out against redevelopment, and this part of the district has become a stronghold for North African Jews, with kosher food shops much in evidence. There is also a thriving Arab population, and the two races live in total harmony. You can get excellent couscous and other North African food here at very reasonable prices.

To chart the full extent of this district, start at Ménilmontant metro and walk in a semicircle around to Belleville metro, or vice-versa.

Bibliothèque Nationale 🏛 ☆
*58 Rue de Richelieu, 4e ☎ 261-82-83. Map **4**G8*
Medallions and Antiques Gallery open noon–5pm, Mansart Gallery open noon–6pm, Photography Gallery (4 Rue Louvois) open Mon–Sat 1–5pm. Metro Bourse, Palais-Royal, Quatre-Septembre, Pyramides.
As befits one of the world's greatest collections of books, manuscripts, prints, maps, medallions and other treasures, the

Bibliothèque is housed in a splendid mansion, the main entrance of which is in the Rue de Richelieu, reached via a fine courtyard. The building was created by Cardinal Mazarin in the 17thC out of two adjacent houses, the Hôtel Tubeuf and the Hôtel Chivry, and the resulting complex covers an entire block. After Mazarin's death the mansion was split between different owners. Part of it, which had come into the hands of the crown, became the repository of the royal library, later the National Library, which ultimately took over the whole of Mazarin's mansion. Since 1537, a copy of every French book published has, by law, been kept in the library.

Accredited scholars have access to the Bibliothèque's service departments, and members of the public can view the **medallion collection** on the first floor, the temporary exhibitions in the ground floor **Mansart Gallery** and the superb **Mazarin Gallery** at the top of the imposing stairway, and those in the **Photographic Gallery** (*4 Rue Louvois*). Through a glass door, the magnificent Second Empire reading room, with its domed ceiling and cast-iron columns, gives the impression of a Byzantine cathedral.

Bois de Boulogne

*Map **18**C3.*

"I will not describe the Bois de Boulogne. It is simply a beautiful, cultivated, endless, wonderful wilderness."

This was Mark Twain's reaction in *The Innocents Abroad* to the 900ha(2,224 acre) park on the western outskirts of Paris, which was once a royal hunting forest. Today he might be slightly less fulsome in his praise for the Bois could no longer be described as a wilderness – there are too many roads. Furthermore, it is, in places, rather monotonous and much of it is haunted by libidinous characters, especially at night.

However, there are many spots of great beauty, and you must be prepared to seek these out. The most delightful of all is the **Bagatelle** (▣ *open daily 8:30am – 7:30pm*). It is a small park within a park where in the 18thC the Count of Artois, the future King Charles X, built himself an enchanting little villa (constructed in less than 70 days on a bet with Marie-Antoinette) surrounded by a romantic garden with artificial waterfalls, grottoes, Gothic ruins and other follies. Later, a second building, the Trianon, was added near the villa. Today the Bagatelle (the word means trifle) is a place of potent magic with a renowned flower garden. There is also an elegant restaurant, **La Roseraie de la Bagatelle**, where you can sip afternoon tea languidly and dream.

Another appealing oasis in the Bois is the **Pré Catalan** (▣) also a self-contained park. Its attractions include a majestic copper beech with a wider span of branches than any other tree in Paris. In addition, the Pré has a Shakespeare Garden containing plants mentioned in the master's works (▣ *guided tours at 11am, 3pm, 4:30pm*).

If you have children with you, the spot to head for is the **Jardin d'Acclimatation** (▣) an amusement park on the N side of the Bois (*open daily 10:30am – 6:30pm*). Here you will find, among other things, a zoo, a go-kart track, merry-go-rounds, a miniature golf course and a café, **La Ferme du Golf**, where youngsters can sit in a farmyard and eat an ice-cream or pizza while goats, sheep and ducks mill around their tables. Within the Jardin d'Acclimatation is the *en Herbe* museum and just near it the *Arts et Traditions Populaires* museum.

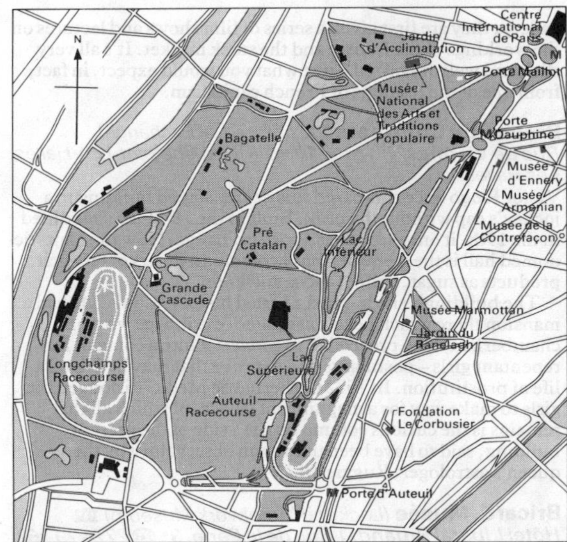

Other attractions of the Bois include lakes (one of which, the **Lac Inférieur**, has boating facilities), two racecourses (**Auteuil** and **Longchamp**) and the **Municipal Floral Garden** of Paris.

One of the best and most enjoyable methods of travelling about in the Bois is on two wheels (bicycle rental near Pavillon Royal). There is also a bus (no. 244) which goes diagonally through the park from Porte Maillot. However, you may prefer, like the famous Englishman who broke the bank at Monte Carlo, to "walk along the Bois de Boulogne with an independent air."

Bourdelle, Musée

16 Rue Antoine-Bourdelle, 15e ☎ 548-67-27
on Sun. Open 10am–5:40pm. Closed Mon. Metro Falguière, Montparnasse-Bienvenue.

This charming oasis in *Montparnasse* was for 45yr the home and studio of Antoine Bourdelle (1861–1929), a sculptor of genius who, along with his friend Rodin, helped to give sculpture a new lease on life. Where Rodin's work has the fluidity of emotion, Bourdelle's is characterized by the thrusting, harnessed power of the will in such creations as his *Héracles Archer* and *Tête d'Apollon*. These and other works are displayed in a series of light, spacious rooms and leafy courtyards. Part of the museum is used for temporary exhibitions by other sculptors.

Bourse *(Stock Exchange)* ☆

4 Pl. de la Bourse, 2e ☎ 261-85-90. Map ***9*** *F8*
Open Mon–Fri 11am–2pm. Metro Bourse.

Outwardly a serene, 19thC Classical building surrounded by Corinthian columns, inwardly a scene of apparent bedlam with brokers in the main dealing room gesticulating wildly and yelling *"J'ai!"* or *"Je prends!"*. To enable visitors to make sense of this puzzling spectacle, which they can witness from a gallery, they are first given a series of film shows and lectures on the workings of the Bourse and the stock market. It's all very slick and well organized – just what you would expect, in fact, from one of the bastions of French capitalism.

Bourse du Commerce *(Commercial Exchange)*
Rue de Viarmes, 1er. Map ***10****H8. Metro Châtelet-Les-Halles, Les Halles.*
Victor Hugo once compared this drum-shaped building to a jockey's cap without the peak. Built in the 18thC and modified in the 19th, it once served as a corn exchange. Now the majestic domed hall is the scene of a busy commodity market for such products as sugar, coffee, cocoa and grain.

The building's site has had a varied history. Louis XII had a mansion there which he lost at a game of cribbage with his chamberlain, who proceeded to convert it into a convent for repentant girls – postulants had to prove that they had lived a life of prostitution. In 1572 Catherine de Medici dislodged the girls to make way for a magnificent palace, of which all that remains is the curious column on the S side of the present building, said to have been used as an observatory by the queen's astrologer, Ruggieri.

Bricard, Musée *(Lock and Metalwork Museum)* 🏛
Hôtel Libéral Bruand, 1 Rue de la Perle, 3e ☎ 277-79-62. Map ***11****H11* *Open 10am–noon, 2–5pm. Closed Tues and Aug. Metro St-Paul, Chemin-Vert.*
Created by the Bricard company of lock manufacturers, this museum covers locksmithing and ancillary crafts from the early Christian era to the 20thC. Apart from locks galore, there are beautiful examples of related craftsmanship, from door handles to ornamented chests. The museum is housed in a graceful and well-restored *Marais* mansion designed and inhabited by Libéral Bruand, architect of *Les Invalides.*

Buttes Chaumont, Parc des
Rue Manin, 19e *Open daily, summer 6.30am–11pm, winter 7am–9pm. Metro Buttes-Chaumont.*
This park is totally unlike any other in Paris and has a strongly romantic appeal. Brilliantly landscaped by Haussmann on a disused quarry site, it has steeply undulating wooded contours and a lake with a rocky island rising dramatically from the center, spanned by two high bridges. On the island one path leads up a flight of steps through a grotto-like tunnel to the summit which is crowned by a small Classical temple with an open colonnade. From here there is a superb view over the city to the N, E and W, with *Montmartre* and the *Sacré-Coeur* standing out against the horizon.

This is one of the few Parisian parks where one can actually sit on the grass. There are rides in a donkey cart for children, and on the W side is an inviting restaurant called the **Pavillon du Lac** (open for lunch and tea) with tables overlooking the lake.

Carnavalet, Hôtel et Musée 🏛 ☆
23 Rue de Sévigné, 3e ☎ 272-21-13/278-60-39. Map ***11****I11* *on Sun* *Open 10am–5:40pm. Closed Mon. Cabinet of drawings, etc, open Mon–Fri 2–5pm, Sat 10am–noon. Metro St-Paul, Chemin-Vert.*
If you visited no other building in Paris but this one you would still come away with a good understanding of the spirit of the

city. Here, every phase of Parisian history, from the early Renaissance onwards, is illustrated, in painting, sculpture, models, furniture and decoration – all on view in a series of splendid rooms. One of the most pleasing displays is of old tradesmen's signs, including the entire front of a druggist's shop. Another section deals with the Revolution, and here you will find models of the guillotines, portraits of Revolutionary leaders, placards, pictures of the royal family in captivity, and other mementoes.

The building itself, situated at the heart of the *Marais*, tells its own part of the story. Built in the 1540s and later modified by Mansart, it possesses a gracious entrance courtyard with allegorical reliefs of the four seasons and a statue of *Louis XIV* anachronistically dressed as a Roman general wearing a wig. From 1677–96 the house was occupied by Mme de Sévigné, who immortalized herself by a series of lively and witty letters and who played hostess to distinguished writers and thinkers of her time. Her apartments are preserved as part of the museum, and she still casts her benign spell over the building.

Catacombs

2 bis Pl. Denfert-Rochereau, 14e ☎ 321–58–00. Map ***14****M7 ▣ ▣ Open first and third Sat of each month from Oct 16–June 30, every Sat from July 1–Oct 15. Visit starts 2pm. Metro Denfert-Rochereau.*

Here is a creepy experience: a walk of three-quarters of an hour through a subterranean necropolis. These are not ancient catacombs like the ones in Rome but former stone quarries which were filled with the bones cleared from many Parisian cemeteries during the 18th and 19thCs. They have been open to the public since 1874. The tunnels leading to the ossuary pass a representation of a fort, carved out of the rock by an 18thC tunnel worker in his leisure time. Then a chamber with black and white painted pillars leads off to a doorway over which are the words: *"Arrete! C'est ici l'empire de la mort."* ("Stop! This is the empire of death."). Beyond it stretches tunnel after tunnel, lined on each side with neatly-piled bones interspersed with rows of grinning skulls and enlivened by plaques bearing inscriptions of death. There are between five and six million skeletons here. The whole place is a *memento mori* of the most dramatic kind, a veritable temple of death.

On visiting days there is often a long line, so be prepared for a wait.

Cernuschi, Musée

7 Av. Velasquez, 8e ☎ 563–52–75. Map ***2****D5 ▣ ▣ on Sun. Open 10am–5:40pm. Closed Mon. Metro Villiers, Monceau.*

Paris possesses this interesting museum of Chinese art thanks to a colorful Milanese financier named Cernuschi. A disciple of Garibaldi, Cernuschi was once condemned to death for his Revolutionary activities but reprieved by Napoleon III, later becoming a French citizen. Before his death in 1896 he bequeathed his house and magnificent collection of Chinese objects to the city of Paris. Not as large or impressive as the collection in the *Guimet* museum, this exhibition nevertheless gives a very informative picture of the development of Chinese art from prehistoric times. It includes a selection of paintings by modern Chinese artists, but perhaps the most evocative picture is a 13thC ink-and-brush drawing of a bird on a twig which combines humor and simplicity with sophistication.

The museum is situated in a fine house just near the E gate of the *Monceau* park.

Champ-de-Mars

7e. Map 12I3. Metro Trocadéro, École-Militaire.

The Champ-de-Mars is the back garden of the *Eiffel Tower*. It was originally laid out in the 1760s as a parade ground for the *École Militaire*, which is why it is named after Mars, the god of war. These days it is anything but martial – just a typically tranquil Parisian park with a symmetrical pattern of treelined avenues and some pleasant little corners in which to sit and read or contemplate the wonders of Eiffel's engineering.

Champs-Élysées, Avenue ★

8e. Map 6&7. Metro Étoile, George-V, Franklin-D-Roosevelt, Champs-Élysées-Clemenceau, Concorde.

If there is one Parisian street that is known throughout the world it is this one. It forms a great triumphal, treelined sweep from the *Place de la Concorde* to the *Arc de Triomphe*. At its lower end, as far as the intersection known as the **Rond-Point**, it is bounded by strips of park. Then, along the stretch that climbs in a shallow ramp towards the Arc de Triomphe, it is lined by imposing buildings: offices, smart shops, cinemas and numerous restaurants and sidewalk cafés.

The lower part of the avenue was laid out by Louis XIV's gardener, Le Nôtre, in 1670, and the upper part some 40yr later. However, the road remained a muddy and insalubrious thoroughfare until it acquired an element of fashion and style in the 18thC with the building of the grand houses in the Rue du *Faubourg St-Honoré*. From very early in its history it was frequented by ladies of pleasure. In 1778, for example, a Swiss guard apprehended a priest there in the company of a young black woman to whom he claimed to be giving religious instruction. Half a century later Balzac wrote of the "dark-eyed houris" who frequented the avenue. Their successors are still operating here today.

The street is an obvious route for processions. It was down the Champs-Élysées that the victorious German troops marched in 1940, and 4yr later the same street witnessed the triumphant return of de Gaulle. Walk down it and you will feel a swell of exultation, but curiously, despite its many cafés, it is not the most inviting place to linger. The ghosts of all those marchers seem to hurry you on.

Charles-de-Gaulle, Place

8e. Map 6. Metro Étoile.

The great intersection encircling the *Arc de Triomphe* was given its present name after de Gaulle's death in 1970, but most Parisians still call it by its apt former name, the Pl. de l'Étoile (star). The Arc de Triomphe was built between 1806–36, but it was not until 1854 that Haussmann was commissioned by Napoleon III to create the grand townscape that we see there today.

Twelve great avenues radiate from Étoile. They include the *Champs-Élysées*, which plunges down to the *Place de la Concorde*, the gracious, park-lined **Av. Foch** with its luxurious apartment buildings stretching towards the *Bois de Boulogne*, and the **Av. de la Grand Armée**, which points to Neuilly and *La Défense*.

The Pl. Charles-de-Gaulle is one of the most photographed parts of Paris – especially from the air where its layout looks particularly dramatic.

Chasse, Musée de la *(Museum of Hunting)* ☆

Hôtel Guénégaud, 60 Rue des Archives, 3e ☎ 272-86-43. Map 11H11 Open 10am–6pm (5pm in winter). Closed Tues. Metro Rambuteau, Hôtel-de-Ville.

Everything you ever needed to know about hunting is assembled in an attractive old *Marais* mansion: hunting weapons of all kinds, stuffed animals, paintings of famous hunters and huntresses such as *Diana*, by Breughel and Rubens, and *St Eustache*, by Cranach.

The building, the **Hôtel Guénégaud**, with its well-mannered courtyard and dignified design, was built by François Mansart between 1648–51 and was in a dilapidated condition when François Sommer took it over in the early 1960s – his own big game trophies are among those on display. Now the building stands beautifully restored to delight architectural as well as hunting enthusiasts.

Cinéma, Musée du ☆

Palais de Chaillot, Place du Trocadéro, 16e ☎ 553-74-39. Map 12H2 Guided visits 10:30, 11, noon, 2:30, 3:30, 4:30. Closed Mon. Metro Trocadéro.

The modest entrance to this museum (allied to the *Cinémathèque Française*) at the bottom of a flight of steps in the *Palais de Chaillot* does not prepare the visitor for the riches within. The museum's eloquent curator, Alain Gabet, or one of his staff, takes visitors first through the early technology of cinematography, then through a series of galleries full of the trappings that have enabled filmmakers to create a world of make-believe. There are sets from famous films like *The Cabinet of Doctor Caligari*, costumes, such as the tunic worn by Rudolph Valentino in *The Sheik*, and Garbo's robes, papier-mâché monsters, a robot from Fritz Lang's *Metropolis* . . . and much more. The conducted visit takes about an hour and a quarter.

Cinémathèque Française

Palais de Chaillot, Jardin du Trocadéro, Av. Albert-de-Mun, 16e ☎ 704-24-24. Map 12H2 Closed Mon. Metro Trocadéro.

The film library in the *Palais de Chaillot* is a national institution for the screening of distinguished films from all periods of cinema history. A different film is shown at every performance, so between this and the other auditorium in the *Pompidou Center* there is always a rich choice for the connoisseur. Subscribers pay a lower entrance fee, but the Cinémathèque is open to everyone.

Details of program are available at the box office and in the press.

Cité Universitaire

Bd. Jourdan, 14e. Metro Cité-Universitaire.

This sprawling student community on the S perimeter of Paris, with its pavilions for different nationalities, is an excellent place to study contrasting styles of architecture. Each building reflects some aspect of its country's architecture: the Greek pavilion is a Hellenic temple, and the Indo-Chinese building resembles a pagoda. Admirers of Le Corbusier will be interested in the Swiss and Brazilian halls which he designed. Inaugurated in 1925.

Clémenceau, Musée

*8 Rue Franklin, 16e ☎ 520-43-51. Map **12**H2 ✗ Open Tues, Thurs, Sat, Sun 2-5pm. Metro Passy, Trocadéro.*

The apartment where the statesman Georges Clémenceau lived from 1895 until his death in 1929 is preserved exactly as he left it, down to the quill pen with which he wrote. The atmosphere has the stamp of an exceptionally powerful and many-faceted personality.

Cluny, Musée de ☆

*6 Pl. Paul-Painlevé, 5e ☎ 325-62-00. Map **10**J9 Open 9:45am-12:30pm. Closed Tues. Metro St-Michel, Odéon.*

This outstanding museum in the *Latin Quarter* is a remarkable archeological site housing a great collection of ancient and medieval objects. It comprises two buildings: the remains of the Gallo-Roman baths, the **Thermes de Lutèce** (c.200); and the medieval **Hôtel de Cluny**, constructed in the 14th and 15thC for the rich abbots of Cluny as their Parisian residence.

Everything that exists elsewhere exists in Paris.
Victor Hugo, *Les Misérables*, 1908

The museum owns one of the finest collections of medieval tapestry work in existence and its most famous exhibit is the set of six tapestries known as the *Lady with the Unicorn* ★ woven in lovely muted colours in lively detail. The tapestries were made in the late 15thC for a lawyer named Jean Le Viste. Five of the tapestries symbolically illustrate the five senses and the sixth is thought to illustrate mastery of them.

The museum's rooms contain many other treasures, including everyday objects from the Middle Ages. On the first floor is a small **chapel** containing some impressive Gothic tracery. Passing into the Roman building, one is overwhelmed by the vast room of the thermal baths, with its great vaulted roof, one of France's most impressive relics from the Roman period. In this and in adjacent rooms, Roman artifacts are exhibited.

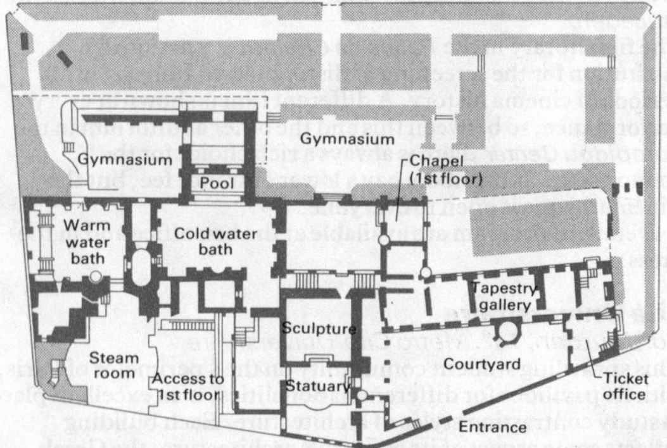

Cognacq-Jay, Musée

25 Bd. des Capucines, 2e ☎742-94-71. Map ***8****F7* ▣ ▣ *on Sun. Open 10am–5:40pm. Closed Mon. Metro Opéra, Madeleine.*

Founded in the 1920s by Ernest Cognacq, creator of the Samaritaine chain of shops, and his wife, Louise Jay, this is an elegant museum of 18thC art, housed in the premises of a former Samaritaine shop. Paradoxically, Cognacq was no art-lover – he boasted that he had never entered the Louvre – and he became a collector purely for status reasons. However, with the help of experts he succeeded in acquiring many works of the highest rank, such as Boucher's *Le Retour de Chasse de Diane*, Tiepolo's *Le Festin de Cléopatre* and Reynolds' portrait of *Lord Northington*. Watteau, Fragonard, Rembrandt and Gainsborough are among other artists represented.

There is also a remarkable collection of porcelain ornaments, gold and silver boxes and other small objets d'art. Some of the rooms have lovely 18thC woodwork and furniture, and the entire museum is a pleasing mixture of intimacy and quiet luxury – a place of beauty and repose contrasting with the hectic hustle of the *Opéra Quarter* that surrounds it.

Collège de France

Pl. Marcellin-Berthelot, 5e. Map ***15****J9. Metro Maubert-Mutualité.*

This great institute of learning in the *Latin Quarter* was founded in 1529 by François I at the instigation of the scholar Guillaume Budé, whose statue now stands in the W courtyard. The college was founded to counteract the hidebound dogmatism of the neighboring *Sorbonne* and was for a time known as the 'Three-Language College' because Hebrew, Greek and Latin were taught there. Subsequently, its syllabus expanded to include many other academic disciplines from Arabic to physics, and today it maintains a high reputation.

Smaller and less bombastic in architecture than the Sorbonne, it has something of the intimate atmosphere of a small Oxford or Cambridge college.

Comédie Française 🏛

2 Rue de Richelieu, 1er ☎296-10-20. Map ***9****H8. Metro Palais-Royal.*

After it was founded in 1680 by Louis XIV this famous company of actors moved house several times but finally settled on the present site at the end of the 18thC. The theater, which has evolved over the years into the grand colonnaded building that we see today, is set in a prime position next to the *Palais-Royal*, facing a busy intersection with attractive fountains, the **Pl. André Malraux.**

Despite its name, the company does not necessarily perform comedies. Traditionally the repertoire has emphasized classical French dramatists such as Molière, Corneille and Racine, but lately it has been widened to include modern and foreign playwrights.

Conciergerie

1 Quai de l'Horloge, Ile de la Cité, 4e ☎354-30-06. Map ***10****I9* ▣ ▣ *Open 10–11:25am, 1:30–5:25pm (4:25 in winter). Closed Tues in winter. Metro Cité.*

The Conciergerie has a gloomy atmosphere that matches its gloomy history as a place of imprisonment, death and torture.

Part of the great palace which was built on the N side of the *Ile de la Cité* by King Philippe le Bel (1284–1314), it is now incorporated into the *Palais de Justice* complex. The name is derived from the title of a royal officer called the Concierge (*'Comte des Cierges'*, 'Count of the Candles') who was superintendent of the palace and who also had the right to administer justice in its environs. Increasingly the Conciergerie took on the functions of a prison, especially after the building became for a time the seat of parliament which was also the country's supreme court.

It was here that such malefactors as Ravaillac, assassin of Henry IV, and Damiens, who attempted to kill Louis XV, were brought and hideously tortured before being executed. However, it was during the Revolution that the Conciergerie received its real baptism of blood. Its most famous prisoner was Marie-Antoinette, who was kept here before being taken to the guillotine. Her **cell** is now a chapel to her memory, but her name is only one of a list of many who passed through the Conciergerie on their way to execution in a gory chain of death. The Revolutionary leader Danton condemned 22 *Girondins*, Robespierre condemned Danton, the Thermidor Convention condemned Robespierre . . . . In all, nearly 2,600 prisoners were sent for execution from the Conciergerie between the winter of 1793 and summer of 1794. You can still see the grim little room where they were shaved and relieved of their possessions before being taken to the tumbrils. In 1792, 288 prisoners were murdered in the prison itself.

Despite the unpleasant vibrations created by this history, the building does, in fact, possess some beautiful features: the **Salle des Gardes**, the first room you enter, with its elegant vaulting and carved bosses; the magnificent **Salle des Gens d'Armes** – 69m(226ft) long and 27m(88ft) wide – with its three rows of eight pillars, is sometimes used as a setting for concerts; and the **kitchen**, with its four fireplaces, each big enough to roast an entire ox, is an interesting feature – in the 14thC it provided food for 5,000 people. Also of interest is the **chapel**, which housed the 22 condemned *Girondin* deputies. It now contains a depressing but intriguing little collection of mementoes, including a guillotine blade, Marie-Antoinette's crucifix and two portraits of her from life.

Concorde, Place de la ★

*8e. Map **8**G6. Metro Concorde.*

The largest square in Paris is also arguably the most striking and beautiful townscape in the world, but to appreciate the square fully you must brave the whirling blizzard of traffic and cross the road to the center.

This vantage point provides stately vistas in all directions: W up the *Champs-Élysées* to the *Arc de Triomphe*; E through the *Tuileries* to the *Louvre*, with the *Jeu de Paume* museum and the *Orangerie* on either side; S across the **Pont de la Concorde** to the *Palais-Bourbon* and N up the **Rue Royale** to the *Madeleine* between the matching colonnaded facades of the **Hôtel Crillon** (see *Hotels*) on the left and the **Hôtel de la Marine** on the right.

There once stood in the middle an equestrian statue of *Louis XV* in whose reign the square was laid out. This was removed during the Revolution and replaced briefly by an allegorical statue of *Liberty*. Now the site is occupied by the 3,300yr-old **obelisk of Luxor**, given to King Louis-Philippe by Mohammed

Ali, Viceroy of Egypt, and erected in 1836, thus putting an end to political arguments over the question of which monument should stand there. A few yards from this spot stood the guillotine which, during the Revolution, claimed over a thousand victims including Louis XVI and Marie-Antoinette. Two **fountains** resplendent with water nymphs and sea gods stand to the N and S of the obelisk.

Marking the octagonal perimeter of the original square are eight **statues** allegorically representing the towns of Lyon, Marseille, Bordeaux, Nantes, Lille, Strasbourg, Rouen and Brest. The curious pavilions on which they rest were once let out as tiny dwelling houses with just two rooms, one above the other. Other statues of note are the **Marly horses** sculpted by Guillaume Coustou in the 1740s, which flank the E end of the Champs-Élysées, and the statues of *Fame* and *Mercury* on winged horses by Coysevox, which stand on either side of the entrance to the Tuileries.

The Place de la Concorde is the magnificent pulsating heart of Paris, as breathtaking by day as it is by night, when floodlight transforms its buildings, obelisks, fountains and statues into a stunning *tableau vivant*.

Conservatoire National de Musique

14 Rue de Madrid, 8e ☎ 292–15–20. Map 3E6 Open Wed, Sat 2–4:30pm. Closed Aug. Metro Europe.

For music enthusiasts, this museum has an impressive collection of instruments, including some exquisite harpsichords and spinets. Here we find Marie-Antoinette's harp, Beethoven's clavichord, Paganini's guitar, and no less than five Stradivarius violins. Concerts are given frequently, sometimes using instruments from the museum.

Crypte Archéologique ☆

Pl. du Parvis Notre-Dame, 4e. Map 16J9 Open 10am–noon, 2:30–6:30pm. Closed Mon. Metro Cité.

Opened in Aug 1980, this splendid addition to Paris' museums consists basically of an important archeological site in front of *Notre-Dame* which was roofed over following its excavation. The resulting vault is the largest structure of its kind in the world. Descending a stairway from the square, one literally steps down into the Paris of an earlier age, finding an underground chamber where Gallo-Roman ramparts jostle the cellars of medieval houses. The remains are superbly presented, with information on the early history of Paris, illustrated by detailed models of the city at various stages. An object lesson in the imaginative use of an archeological site.

La Défense

Map 18C3.

This vast commercial and residential complex, lying beyond the river to the W of Paris, has been nicknamed 'Manhattan-sur-Seine'. Unfortunately it has all of the brutality and none of the style of 'Manhattan-sur-Hudson'. Begun in the 1960s, it dominates the western horizon of the city with its growing cluster of skyscrapers.

The main zone of La Défense focuses on a long podium running approximately E–W and descending towards the Seine in a series of terraces laid out with trees. On the S side, the bleak prospect is far from enhanced by a Joan Miró sculpture resembling two monstrous wilting pieces of fungus that are garishly and unattractively painted bright blue, red and yellow.

The forest of glass and concrete which surrounds the podium includes such buildings as the **Grande Braderie**, a vast three-cornered hall filled with small shops and stalls of every description, and the **Quatre-Temps**, the largest commercial center in Europe with a floor space twice the area of all the shops in the *Champs-Élysées*. There are also hotels, restaurants, cinemas, a skating rink and a station for the RER railway.

At the western end of the podium there is a view of an outlying zone of La Défense and the bizarre apartment buildings are painted in splotches of gray, blue, brown and green as though they had been camouflaged.

La Défense is a symbol of the aggressive prosperity that has overtaken France in the past 20yr. Despite its multitude of amenities, it is a place that dwarfs and crushes the spirit, but at least in Paris modern man's desire to build such structures has been concentrated into one area well away from the center.

Delacroix, Musée

*6 Rue de Furstenberg, 6ᵉ ☎ 354–04–87. Map **9**I8 🎫 Open 9.45am–5:15pm. Closed Tues. Metro St-Germain-des-Prés.*

Eugène Delacroix (1798–1863) was one of the great romantic painters of the 19thC, a Wagner among artists. His vivid canvasses of battle scenes, lion hunts and other stirring subjects have a controlled fire to them, like Delacroix himself, whom Baudelaire described as "a volcanic crater artistically concealed beneath bouquets of flowers".

In his last years, Delacroix lived a life of almost monastic seclusion in a charming Left Bank apartment with a studio overlooking a little garden. This apartment, in the *St-Germain Quarter*, is now preserved as a museum, full of photographs, letters, portraits and other mementoes of the artist.

Dôme church A masterpiece by Hardouin-Mansart containing the tomb of Napoleon. See *Les Invalides*.

École Militaire

*Pl. Joffre, 7ᵉ. Map **13**J4. Not open to public except by special arrangement. Write to: Général Direction, École Militaire, 1 Pl. Joffre, 75007. Metro École-Militaire.*

Where its neighbor, *Les Invalides*, is an officer in ceremonial dress, the École Militaire is a sergeant major bawling out across the *Champ-de-Mars* to the *Eiffel Tower*. The long Classical facade has a great central-domed portico, and the vast courtyard facing the Pl. de Fontenoy is imposing. It still serves as a military academy as it did when it was built by Gabriel in the reign of Louis XV, and when Napoleon was sent there at age 15 in 1784 – when he passed out he was told he would go far given the right circumstances!

Égouts *(Sewers)*

*Entrance at corner of Quai d'Orsay and Pont de l'Alma, 7ᵉ ☎ 705–10–29. Map **13**H4 🎫 ℹ Open Mon, Wed, last Sat of month 2–5pm. Metro Alma-Marceau.*

"Below Paris", wrote Victor Hugo in *Les Misérables*, "is another city". He was referring to the sewer network, the existence of which is vital to the gracious city above. Its tunnels would stretch from end-to-end as far as Istanbul, and a small section of this labyrinth has been equipped for public viewing. Visitors are shown an exhibition of documents on the history of the sewers, followed by an audio-visual display about the workings of the system. A guided tour takes visitors through dripping tunnels, past waste-collection pits and along the edge of a murky gray river. Instructive but smelly. Once you know the odor of the sewers you will catch whiffs of it occasionally from grates as you walk through the city.

Eiffel Tower

See *Tour Eiffel*.

d'Ennery, Musée

*59 Av. Foch, 16e ☎ 553–57–97. Map **6**F1 ⊡ ✗ Open Sun only 2–5pm. Closed Aug. Metro Dauphine.*

Ming vases, netsuke, images of Buddha, porcelain dogs, Chinese furniture – these and other oriental objects collected by the 19thC dramatist Adolphe d'Ennery and his wife are displayed in part of their opulent house in the Av. Foch. They bought indiscriminately, and only about one in ten of the objects are of any real value. However, the museum has a curious, musty charm. The house is also shared by the *Arménian* museum.

Etoile

See *Place Charles-de-Gaulle*.

Faubourg St-Honoré, Rue du

See *St-Honoré, Rue du Faubourg*.

Flea Market

See *Marché aux Puces*.

Forum des Halles ☆

*1er. Map **10**H9. Metro Châtelet-Les-Halles, Les Halles.*

Opened in 1979 as part of *Les Halles* redevelopment. This complex is a commercial counterpart of the *Pompidou Center*, but, where the latter thrusts boldly up, the Forum goes down. Built on four descending levels, it has concave glass and aluminium walls which plunge down to a sunken courtyard, frequently used by open-air performers, which displays a curiously stirring sculpture by Julio Silva entitled *Pygmalion*, consisting of a group of dreamlike mythological figures in polished stone.

The overall design of the center has a spare, crisp elegance and avoids the harsh, plastic colors that mar so many modern shopping precincts. The Forum has 200 shops (including clothes boutiques, jewelers, booksellers and furniture shops), 10 movie theaters and 12 restaurants, one of which has a terrace overlooking the courtyard. It also houses, on level minus-one, a branch of the *Grévin* museum, which contains an imaginary reconstruction of a Parisian street of 1885. From the lowest level there is access to the metro and RER, and there are two large underground parking lots. The place encourages a young and lively crowd.

Gare d'Orsay

*Rue de Lille, 7e. Map **8**H7. Metro Solférino, Gare-d'Orsay.*

A small suburban line still runs underground, beneath the Gare d'Orsay, but the main station above has long since ceased to function. Escaping demolition in 1973, the station housed a theater and auction rooms before it was decided to convert it into a **museum of the 19thC**, which is due to open in 1983.

The building itself is a good example of the steel architectural style of the late 19thC.

Gobelins (Tapestry Factories)

42 Av. des Gobelins, 13e ☎570-12-60. Map ***16****M10* *Open Wed, Thurs, Fri 11am–4pm; tour lasts 75min. Metro Gobelins.*

If you have ever struggled with a home tapestry kit and found that it tried your patience, you should visit the Gobelins factory to find out what patience really means. Here, skilled weavers, carefully chosen and trained from the age of 16, work their way millimeter by millimeter across huge upright looms at the rate of as little as one square meter a year. Thus it often takes 3–4yr to complete a single tapestry with two or three people working on it full time.

The techniques used are essentially the same as when the Gobelins was founded as a royal factory under Louis XIV, but the tapestries are now worked in a far wider range of colors (14,920 all together), and the subjects are no longer scenes of royal occasions and the like but copies of modern paintings or designs.

The Gobelins is a state enterprise, and its products are never sold. They are either made use of by the government or given as gifts. The atmosphere of the factory complex in the SE of Paris is rather like an old university college, with a cobbled quadrangle, garden and apartments for the employees.

A guided tour of the factory is given, which incorporates the two other state workshops of **Savonnerie** (carpets) and **Beauvais** (tapestries made on a horizontal loom). In an era of mass-production, here is craftsmanship of the highest standard.

Grand Orient de France, Musée du *(Freemasonry Museum)*

16 Rue Cadet, 9e ☎523-20-92. Map ***4****E9* *Open 2–6pm. Closed Sun. Metro Cadet, Richelieu-Drouot.*

What did Lafayette, Garibaldi and Franklin D. Roosevelt have in common? Answer: they were all Freemasons, as you will discover from this intriguing museum of Masonic documents, mementoes and regalia, mainly but not entirely related to French Masonry. In the same building there is a bookshop selling material of Masonic and esoteric interest.

Grand Palais, Galéries Nationales du ☆

Av. du Genéral-Eisenhower, 8e ☎256-09-24. Map ***7****G5* *Open 10am–8pm, Wed 10am–10pm. Closed Tues. Metro Champs-Élysées-Clémenceau.*

The Grand Palais and the *Petit Palais*, built for the Universal Exhibition of 1900, echo each other like two thunderous fanfares across the Av. Winston-Churchill, which runs from the *Champs-Élysées* to the *Pont Alexandre III*. Some people would call them fussy and pompous, but it would be fairer to call them joyous and exuberant pieces of architectural rhetoric, though the Grand Palais oversteps the mark perhaps with its gargantuan porticoes, its frescoes and its mass of cartouches and swags of carved stonework.

The western part of the building is now given over to the *Palais de la Découverte*, a science museum. The rest is used for temporary art exhibitions and other large-scale shows. The interior is as imposing as the exterior, particularly the main hall with its domed and vaulted roof in glass and iron. The N section of the building, fronted by a pleasing little garden with a fountain, contains a good self-service restaurant and a movie theater showing free films on subjects related to the arts.

Grands Boulevards

9e and 10e. Map ***8****F7–****11****G11. Metro Madeleine, Opéra, Rue Montmartre, Bonne-Nouvelle, Strasbourg-St-Denis, République.*

This is the name given to the string of boulevards extending roughly from the *Madeleine* to the Pl. de la République – Bds. Capucines, Italiens, Montmartre, Poissonière, Bonne-Nouvelle, St-Denis and St-Martin. They were constructed under Louis XIV to replace an obsolete line of fortifications, and soon became known just as 'The Boulevard'. In the middle of the 18thC The Boulevard became elegant and fashionable, but the main stretch from the Bd. Montmartre to the Pl. de la République has long since become rather tawdry.

The Boulevard is the source or distributive centre of all the flitting fancies of France.

Richard Whiteing, *The Life of Paris*

Grévin, Musée

16 Bd. Montmartre, 9e ☎ 770–74–72. Map ***9****F9* *Open 2–7pm, Sun and hols 1–8pm. Metro Richelieu-Drouot, Rue Montmartre.*

Cabinet fantastique are the words over the doorway, and fantasy is certainly what one experiences on entering this museum. As an appetizer, the visitor passes through a grotto with distorting mirrors, then through a series of ornate rooms filled with waxworks of contemporary personalities. Down in the basement are more waxworks arranged in a sequence of fascinating historical tableaux. Upstairs there is a conjuring show in a delightful little theater, followed by a ***spectacle d'illusion*** in a ***palais de mirages***, where visitors are miraculously transported into a variety of exotic environments, including a jungle. Founded in 1882 by the caricaturist Grévin.

Guimet, Musée

6 Pl. d'Iéna, 16e ☎ 723–61–65. Map ***6****G3* *Open 9.45am–noon, 1:30–5:15pm. Metro Iéna, Boissière.*

If the Far East holds any appeal for you, then this treasure house of oriental antiquities is a must. Its nucleus is a collection formed by the 19thC industrialist Émile Guimet, whose intention was to gather together objects illustrating the civilizations and religions of the orient. Since the museum became a national one, it has been greatly enriched by the addition of other oriental collections. It is renowned for its Cambodian sculptures and for its Tibetan and Nepalese banners and ritual instruments reflecting the richly colorful world of Tantric Buddhism. Some new galleries of Chinese ceramics and Central Asian paintings have been added. An annex to the museum (***19 Av. d'Iéna***) is devoted specifically to Asiatic religions with the objects arranged by religion.

The Musée Guimet is also a research and study center, housing a library, a photographic archive and an auditorium.

Gustave Moreau, Musée

14 Rue de la Rochefoucauld, 9e ☎ 874–38–50. Map ***4****E8* *Open 10am–1pm, 2–5pm. Closed Mon, Tues. Metro Trinité.*

"His sad and scholarly works," writes the novelist Huysmans about the symbolist painter Gustave Moreau (1826–98), "breathed a strange magic, an incantatory charm which stirred you to the depths of your being."

The artist's house on the edge of *Montmartre*, where he lived a reclusive life, is now filled with his strange, dreamlike works, such as his paintings of *Salome*, "the symbolic incarnation of undying Lust, the goddess of immortal Hysteria", as Huysmans described her in his novel *À Rebours (Against Nature)*.

Halles, Les ☆

*1er. Map **10**H9. Metro Châtelet-Les-Halles, Les Halles.*

This area is bounded roughly by the Rue Étienne-Marcel and the *Rue de Rivoli* to the N and S, with the *Bourse du Commerce* and the *Pompidou Center* marking the W and E boundaries. In the 12thC it became a food market (Zola called it "the belly of Paris") and remained so until 1979 when the traders moved to a huge new site at Rungis near Orly Airport, taking the atmosphere with them and leaving the city of Paris with the problem of deciding what to do with the area. The years since then have seen a total transformation which is still far from complete. The graceful old glass and iron market hall, built under Napoleon III, has been torn down and replaced by a commercial complex called the *Forum des Halles*, and in front of the Bourse du Commerce is a vast hole in the ground, plans for which include a park with a series of underground levels housing a swimming pool, auditorium, aquarium and other amenities.

The changes have been radical, but slowly Les Halles is adjusting to a new role as a center of entertainment, shopping and culture. Parts of it have taken on a brash seediness, with sex shops much in evidence. However, some of the old buildings have been renovated, the 16thC **Fontaine des Innocents** has been restored, and much of the area has been pedestrianized.

The old market has mostly, though not completely, disappeared. There remain a few semi-wholesale food merchants and a number of restaurants and bars of character: a particularly striking example is the **Les Halles Bar** (*15 Rue Montmartre*) with its tiles depicting scenes of the market in its heyday. When all the scars have finally healed, Les Halles promises to emerge as one of the liveliest districts in Paris.

Hébert, Musée 🏛

*Hôtel Montmorency, 85 Rue du Cherche-Midi, 6e ☎ 222-23-82. Map **14**J7 Open 2–6pm. Closed Tues. Metro St-Placide, Sèvres-Babylone.*

Housed in a small and gracious 18thC mansion on the Left Bank, this museum is devoted mainly to temporary exhibitions of the works of society painter Ernest Hébert (1850–1900) and his contemporaries. There is also a small permanent display downstairs. Visitors hear gentle tape-recorded music, chosen to relate to the theme of the exhibition.

Henner, Musée

*43 Av. de Villiers, 17e ☎ 763-42-73. Map **2**D4 Open 2–5pm. Closed Mon. Metro Malesherbes.*

This collection contains about 700 paintings, drawings and sketches by the Alsatian artist Jean-Jacques Henner (1829–1905), one of the great individualists among painters. Following no school but inspired by the old masters, he created canvases of a delicate luminosity and haunting grace.

En Herbe, Musée
Jardin d'Acclimatation, Bois de Boulogne, 16e
☎ 747-47-66 Open to individuals Wed, Sat, Sun during school term time, daily during school holidays 2-6pm; open for groups of children Mon, Thurs, Fri 9:30am-4:30pm. Metro Sablons.
Situated on the N side of the *Bois de Boulogne* within the **Jardin d'Acclimatation**, this museum exists "to enable children to discover art while having fun." The museum mounts lively temporary exhibitions on such subjects as 'Masks and Masquerades' and 'The Eiffel Tower', and there is a supervised studio in which children can paint or draw impressions of what they have seen.

For location, see map in *Bois de Boulogne*.

Histoire de France, Musée de l' Displays important historical documents. See *Archives Nationales*.

Histoire Naturelle, Museum d' Galleries concerning paleontology, paleobotany, mineralogy and entomology. See *Jardin des Plantes*.

Homme, Musée de l' *(Museum of Mankind)*
*Palais de Chaillot, Pl. du Trocadéro, 16e ☎ 505-70-60. Map **12**H2 Open 10am-6pm, Oct-Mar 10am-5pm. Metro Trocadéro.*
Occupying the W wing of the *Palais de Chaillot*, this museum contains one of the world's most important collections devoted to anthropology, ethnology and prehistory. The objects are, for the most part, arranged according to geographical region and include all manner of intriguing objects, from a Navajo sand painting to Japanese costumes. The excellent South American section includes a shriveled Inca mummy in a fetal position which inspired Munch's painting *The Scream*. There is an interesting room devoted to the arts and technologies of different world regions, and another labeled 'Anthropology' dealing with the biology and physical characteristics of man.

The museum holds film shows three or four times a week and special exhibitions are staged periodically. There is an attractive restaurant, **Le Totem**, commanding a superb view across the river to the *Eiffel Tower*.

Hôtel Biron 18thC mansion by Gabriel the Elder. See *Rodin, Musée*.

Hôtel des Monnaies *(Mint)* ☆
*11 Quai Conti, 6e ☎ 329-12-48 (shop 297-40-57). Map **9**I8 on Mon, Wed 2:15pm. Open Mon-Fri 11am-5pm; shop open Mon-Fri 9am-5:45pm, Sat 9-11:45am. Metro Pont-Neuf, Odéon, St-Michel.*
This simple but dignified mansion, which overlooks the Seine, was once the home of the Princess de Conti, but was taken over by Louis XV in the 18thC and remodeled by Jacques Denis Antoine to serve as the Royal Mint. In a set of sumptuous rooms on the first floor there is a **museum of coins and medallions** and equipment for making them. As the making of coins has been transferred elsewhere, the workshops in the building now concentrate on the manufacture of medallions of all kinds. There is a **sales counter** in the building (***also at 10, Rue du Quatre-Septembre, 2e***) where a rich selection of these medallions

is available. The medallions are not necessarily solemn objects – one has the cancan as its theme and shows a high-kicking leg. The Mint will even make you your own medallion – if you can afford it.

Hôtel de Rohan 18thC mansion built for the bishops of Strasbourg. See *Archives Nationales*.

Hôtel de Sens
*2 Rue du Figuier, 4ᵉ ☎ 278-14-60/278-13-34. Map **10**I11. Forney Library open Tues–Fri 1:30–8:30pm, Sat 10am–8:30pm. Metro Pont-Marie, St-Paul.*
This mansion at the S edge of the *Marais* is such a perfect specimen of medieval architecture, with its pepper-pot turrets and pointed arches, that if you came upon it without prior knowledge you might think it was 19thC imitation Gothic or perhaps a stray building from a Hollywood movie about the Middle Ages. In fact it is one of the oldest houses in Paris and was built by Tristan de Salazar, Archbishop of Sens, between 1475–1507. It was an anachronism for its day, since the archbishop, who came from a military family, could not resist adding a few touches to create the illusion of a fortified castle: a dungeon, watch-tower and watchwalk. The building was a late burst of Gothic feudalism at the dawn of the French Renaissance. It is now owned by the City of Paris and houses the Forney Library, a library of science, technology, arts and crafts. Admire the building's fine **courtyard**.

Hôtel de Soubise 18thC mansion with superb courtyard. See *Archives Nationales*.

Hôtel des Ventes 🏛
*9 Rue Drouot, 9ᵉ. Map **4**F8 ▣ Open Mon–Sat 11am–6pm. Closed Sun and April 16–20. Metro Richelieu-Drouot.*
The Parisian equivalent of Christie's, or Sotheby Parke Bernet, the Hôtel des Ventes has, like auction rooms everywhere, an atmosphere of glamor and excitement. In France, auctioneering is a more strictly regulated business than in most countries, and is controlled by the *Compagnie des Commissaires Priseurs*, the auctioneers' professional body, whose members can display gold plaques outside their doors.

The old Hôtel des Ventes, known as the Hôtel Drouot which stood on this site, was demolished in the 1970s, and the auctions moved temporarily to the *Gare d'Orsay*. However, in 1980 they moved back into the new Hôtel Drouot, a stylish building of steel, dark-tinted glass and concrete with traditional touches such as a high-pitched, vaulted roof and dormer windows.

Inside there are several floors of auction rooms where all kinds of objects – French tapestries, Italian drawings, autographed letters, Chinese vases – change hands under the eye of a *commissaire priseur* perched behind a high desk.

An amusing place to visit even if you are not bidding.

Hôtel de Ville *(Town Hall)* 🏛 ☆
*Pl. de l'Hôtel-de-Ville, 4ᵉ ☎ 276-40-40. Map **10**I10 ▣ 🅸 to salons, Mon 10:30am. Open Mon–Fri 8:45am–6:30pm, Sat 9am–6pm. Closed Sun. Metro Hôtel-de-Ville.*
There has been a town hall on this site ever since 1357, the year when one of the earliest mayors of Paris, Étienne Marcel,

moved the city council there. His equestrian statue now stands facing the river by the S side of the building.

The first town hall was replaced by a more imposing one in Renaissance style which was burned down by the *Communards* in 1871. The present edifice (1874–82) is a fairly convincing copy of its Renaissance predecessor, but has a ponderous 19thC touch to the ornate facade with its numerous statues of Parisian dignitaries ensconced in niches.

Before 1830, the **Pl. de l'Hôtel-de-Ville** formed part of the riverside and was called the Pl. de Grève (meaning foreshore). It was there that unemployed Parisians gathered – hence the term *faire la grève* (to strike). It was also the scene of numerous executions over the centuries.

For many years Paris had no mayor and was governed by a prefect of the city, but as recently as 1977 the office of mayor was re-established, and today the Hôtel de Ville is his headquarters. The 109 councilors meet in a spacious wood-paneled chamber which can be viewed during sessions from a public gallery.

Other rooms in the town hall can be visited by conducted tour on Mon mornings. A feast of visual extravagance, Paris must have kept an army of artists and craftsmen employed here for many years. For those interested in *fin-de-siècle* decor and painting, they are, perhaps, of particular interest.

The public relations department of the Hôtel de Ville is housed at 29 *Rue de Rivoli*. Here you can find out any information relating to the municipality; interesting exhibitions on Paris are also held here.

Hugo, Victor, Musée 🏛 ☆

*6 Pl. des Vosges, 4ᵉ ☎ 272-10-16. Map **11**I11 ▣ ▣ on Sun. Open 10am–5:40pm. Closed Mon. Metro St-Paul, Chemin-Vert, Bastille.*

This is the house where Victor Hugo, author of *Notre-Dame de Paris* (*The Hunchback of Notre-Dame*) and other famous novels, lived from 1832–48. By the time of his death, Hugo had attained the status of national hero. He was given a spectacular public funeral and buried in the *Panthéon*. Many people do not realize that Hugo, as well as being a great writer and distinguished public figure, was also an artist of genius, and the house is full of his drawings, paintings and lithographs – mostly dreamlike or surrealistic works depicting eerie landscapes with curious vegetation and sombre castles. There are also many portraits, documents and other mementoes of Hugo's public and private life.

One room is devoted mainly to illustrations of *Notre-Dame de Paris* by various artists and also contains Rodin's powerful bust of *Hugo*. (Hauteville House in Guernsey, where Hugo lived in exile from 1856–70, is also run as a museum by the City of Paris.)

Ile de la Cité and Ile St-Louis ★

*1ᵉ and 4ᵉ. Map **10**&**11**. Metro Cité.*

The Ile de la Cité floats in the Seine like a graceful galleon carrying over 2,000yr of history as its cargo, for it was here that Paris began when the tribe known as the *Parisii* settled on the island in the 3rdC. Trailing behind it is the smaller and less heavily laden Ile St-Louis.

A visit to the *Crypte Archéologique* in the square in front of *Notre-Dame* takes the visitor back to the Ile de la Cité's earliest times, and the different stages of settlement can be seen in layers. Another good place to begin is the little garden on a spit of land at the NW end of the Iles, approached by a stairway from the *Pont-Neuf*. On the other side of the bridge, where the island begins to widen out, is a charming little triangular square called the **Pl. Dauphine**, which André Breton describes in his novel *Nadja* as "one of the most profoundly secluded places I know." Further on, straddling the width of the island and bounded by the Bd. du Palais, is the vast historic complex containing the *Palais de Justice*, the *Sainte Chapelle* and the *Conciergerie*. Across the Bd. du Palais is the rather forbidding Préfecture de Police, headquarters of the immortal Inspector Clouseau, which is offset by the gay **flower market** in the Pl. Louis Lépine near the entrance to the metro station. On Sun the flower market becomes a colorful **bird market**.

The focal point of the island is the **Pl. du Parvis Notre-Dame**, crowned by Notre-Dame cathedral and bounded on the N side by the Hôtel-Dieu hospital, the foundation of which dates back to the 7thC. A riverside walk leads round the S side of the cathedral to the garden of the **Sq. de l'Ile de France**, at the E tip of the island. At the very end is the **Mémorial de la Déportation**, an underground vault commemorating the French victims of Nazi concentration camps. Its stark simplicity conveys solemnity, dignity and compassion.

Immediately to the N of the cathedral lies a little cluster of streets, including the **Rue Chanoinesse**. The name of this street derives from the canons of Notre-Dame whose houses used to line the street. Only two of these, nos. 22 and 24, remain, dating from the 16thC, but there are many fine facades belonging to later periods.

Off the Rue Chanoinesse is the Rue de la Colombe where the line of the old Gallo-Roman wall is traced in the cobblestones. Continue N to the **Quai aux Fleurs**; there are no flowers here, but of interest are two **stone heads** over the doorways of nos. 9 and 11. These represent the ill-fated lovers Abelard and Héloise who lived in a house on the site in the 12thC. The Quai aux Fleurs leads E from here to the **Pont St-Louis**, linking the two islands.

The Ile St-Louis, named after the canonized Louis IX of France, has a totally different atmosphere from its neighbor, being quieter, more private and more picturesque. Georges du Maurier in *Peter Ibbetson* writes graphically of the island "with its stately old mansions *entre cour et jardin*, behind grim stone portals and high walls, where great magistrates and lawyers dwelt in dignified seclusion – the nobles of the robe; and where once had dwelt, in days gone by, the greater nobles of the sword – crusaders, perhaps, and knight templars . . . ."

Many of these houses have remained intact. Two of the finest are the **Hôtel de Lauzun** ☆ (*17 Quai d'Anjou*) and the **Hôtel Lambert** ☆ (*1–3 Quai d'Anjou*) both designed by Louis XIV's architect Le Vau. The former can be visited by application to the Town Hall (☎ *277–15–40*).

The island is an architectural feast and also the town's first real estate development, built as a unit in the 17thC. All along the riverfront are houses with stately porticos and interesting stone carving, many of them also bearing plaques commemorating the distinguished men who lived there – aristocrats, politicians, artists, poets. No. 6, Quai d'Orléans, was, in the 19thC, a meeting place of expatriate Polish artists and writers and today is the **Adam Mickiewicz museum**, named after the man who is considered to be the Polish Dante. It contains the mementoes of his life and of other famous Poles such as Chopin. There is also a library and a fine collection of pictures by French as well as Polish artists (🎫 *open Thurs 2–5pm; closed July 14–Sept 15*).

The spine of the island is the **Rue St-Louis-en-l'Ile**, with its **church** ☆ of the same name, built between 1664–1725 and marked by a curious pierced spire and an ornate wrought-iron clock. The street is full of little shops and restaurants, many with old and interesting frontages. At no. 35 is the travel bookshop **Librairie Ulysse**, the doorway of which is full of notices offering or asking for lifts to faraway places – India, Katmandu, Morocco, Sri Lanka. Two doors away, at no. 31, is **Berthillon**, one of the best ice-cream shops in Europe, with a constant queue outside to prove it. For those who prefer a cup of tea there is the **Salon de Thé St-Louis** at no. 81 where no fewer than 54 varieties are served. Devotees of beer might be interested in the **Brasserie de l'Ile St-Louis**, beside the Pont St-Louis. It is much frequented by rugby-playing types, especially Englishmen, and has the boisterously convivial atmosphere of an Alsatian beer hall.

The Ile St-Louis is, however, mostly a peaceful place with its quiet streets, its little park, **Sq. Barye**, at the E end, and the treelined riverside walk which runs around most of the island.

The **quays** ☆ which line the banks of the Seine on either side of the Ile de la Cité and Ile St-Louis afford some superb views of the islands and of Notre-Dame. Particularly magnificent are the views from Pont des Arts, Sq. René Viviani, Pont de l'Archevêché, Pont de la Tournelle and the Pont de Sully on the Left Bank, and Quai Mégisserie and Quai des Celestins on the Right Bank. The parapets of many of the quays are lined with little second-hand bookstalls, *bouquinistes*, especially along the Left Bank.

Institut Catholique de Paris

21 Rue d'Assas, 6ᵉ. Map ***14****J7. Metro Rennes, St-Placide.*

This is both a Carmelite seminary and a college of high repute offering courses in a wide variety of subjects. It was here that in the years 1888–90 Edouard Branly discovered radio waves. The Institute now contains the **Branly Museum**, illustrating his work (🎫 *open Mon–Fri 9am–noon, 2pm–6pm; closed Sat, Sun, Aug, Christmas and Easter university hols*). It also houses a **Museum of the Bible and the Holy Land** (🎫 *open Sat only 3pm–6pm; closed Christmas, Easter and summer university hols*). The museum contains significant archeological finds from Palestine.

Institut de France

21–25 Quai de Conti, 6ᵉ. Map ***9****I8. Not open to public except cultural groups by arrangement. Metro Pont-Neuf, St-Germain-des-Prés.*

"There is no venerable forest", wrote Zola in *L'Oeuvre*, "no mountain road, no prairie or plain where the sun sets so triumphally as behind the dome of the Institut. This is Paris going to sleep in her glory."

The institute is indeed a majestic building, with a concave semi-circular facade facing the Seine. It was founded as a college and library with money bequeathed by Cardinal Mazarin, and was built by the ubiquitous architect Le Vau in 1663–4 on the site of the Nesle gate and tower, part of the medieval city wall of Philippe Auguste, no longer extant.

The college was suppressed after the Revolution and in 1805 the building became the seat of the recently created Institut de France, which it remains to this day. Of the five learned academies which make up the institute, the best known is the Académie Française comprising 40 distinguished literary figures, approved by the head of state, whose main task is to protect the interests of the French language. Alas, they are fighting a losing battle against the rising tide of *franglais*.

Zola, even though he wrote with such reverence of the building, was one of many famous Frenchmen, including Balzac, Maupassant, Proust, and Molière, who were refused admission to the Académie Française. Most of the honored members have attained total obscurity.

Invalides, Les 🏛 ☆

*7ᵉ. Map **13**I5. Metro Invalides, Latour-Maubourg, École-Militaire, Varenne.*

When Louis XIV's architects designed this building in the 1670s as a home for his invalided soldiers, they poured into it all the architectural rhetoric of the Sun King's era. The 196m (645ft) long **facade** overlooks a wide **esplanade** stretching down to the *Seine*; the great portico is guarded by statues of *Mars* and *Minerva*; the dormer windows in the roof are framed by huge stone suits of armor; the **courtyard** with its double colonnade is worth seeing; and the **Dôme church** (opposite) dominates the whole edifice. Most of the building is the work of Libéral Bruand, but the Dôme church was designed by Jules Hardouin-Mansart and the esplanade by Robert de Cotte.

Once this building housed nearly 6,000 old soldiers. Now the number has dwindled to around 100 and Les Invalides has taken on a new role as the home of four museums and as the resting place of Napoleon Bonaparte.

Musée de l'Armée *(Army Museum)*

☎ 551–92–84 Tickets also valid for other museums on two consecutive days. Open Apr 1–Sept 30, 10am–6pm, Oct 1–Mar 31, 10am–5pm.

This collection of militaria, one of the largest in the world, is divided into two sections, one housed on the E side of the courtyard, the other on the W. The E side tells the story of the French Army, illustrated by pictures, models and military mementoes of all kinds. Two large rooms on the ground floor, the **Salle Turenne** and the **Salle Vauban**, were once refectories for the inmates of the building. Now the former contains a fine collection of flags and standards, including those from the First World War, while the latter is devoted mainly to exhibits relating to the cavalry, among them a row of lifesize dummies of dashing uniformed men on horseback.

Upstairs, on the second floor, is a series of rooms covering different periods of French military history, dealing with defeat as well as victory. Predictably, Napoleon I features prominently. His death mask is here, and a reconstruction of the room at Longwood House, St Helena, where he died on May 5, 1821.

On the third floor, where there were once craft workshops manned by the invalids, there are now exhibits relating to the Second Empire and the Franco-Prussian War.

On the W side of the courtyard are two more former refectories, the **Salle François I** and the **Salle Henri IV**, which return to the era when suits of armor were worn. Presented here are soldiers standing at attention in glass cases or mounted on dummy horses.

The two rooms at the rear are filled with offensive weapons from the 15th to the 17thC, and there are also rooms dealing with prehistoric and oriental weaponry. Upstairs, on the first and second floors, the exhibits are from the First and Second World Wars. In addition there is a room full of model artillery guns; look out of the window into the **Cour de la Victoire** and you will see an impressive collection of the real thing.

Musée des Plans-Reliefs *(Museum of Relief Maps and Plans)*

☎ 705-11-07 Same ticket for Musée de l'Armée. Open Apr 1-Sept 30, 10am-12:15pm, 2-6pm; Oct 1-Mar 31, 10am-12.15pm, 2-4:45pm. Closed Tues, Sun morning.

Housed on the fourth floor, this museum owes its origin to Louvois, Louis XIV's Secretary of State for War, who suggested to the king that scale models be made of fortified frontier and maritime towns in France. This was done, and the practice was continued by subsequent regimes up to the end of the 19thC. Here are miniature versions of Mont Saint-Michel, Neuf-Brisach, Metz, Strasbourg and numerous other towns; detail is fine.

Musée des Deux Guerres Mondiales *(Museum of Two World Wars)*

☎ 551-93-02 Open summer 10am-6pm, winter 9am-5pm. Closed Sun, Mon.

This museum, not part of the Musée de l'Armée, has a small collection of posters, documents and relics from the First and Second World Wars and holds temporary exhibitions on related subjects. The entrance is in the NW corner of the **Cour d'Honneur**.

Musée de l'Ordre de la Libération *(Museum of the Order of Liberation)*

51 bis Bd. de Latour-Maubourg ☎ 705-04-10 Open 2-5pm. Closed Sun.

The Order of Liberation was created by de Gaulle to honor those who gave outstanding service in the freeing of France. The museum, separate from the Musée de l'Armée, has photographs, documents and mementoes related to the themes of the Free French, the Resistance, the Deportation and the Liberation.

St-Louis-des-Invalides †

This church, with its cool, light, barrel-vaulted interior, was where soldiers of Les Invalides worshipped. Its main entrance faces the Cour d'Honneur. When the Dôme church was added, the two opened into one another and shared a common altar, but a glass barrier now separates them.

Berlioz's *Requiem* was played for the first time in 1837 on the superb 17thC organ.

Dôme church 🏛 † ★

Same ticket as for Musée d'Armée.

When the rest of Les Invalides had been completed, Louis XIV decided that it needed an added touch of splendor, so he commissioned Hardouin-Mansart to add the Dôme church to the S side of the building. It was begun in 1677 and completed by Robert de Cotte after Mansart's death in 1708. With its high, slender, gilded **dome** and its **portico** with two rows of columns (Doric below, Corinthian above), it is considered one of the great masterpieces of its era.

However, the church is less visited for its architecture than for the fact that it contains one of the most prestigious tombs in the world, the **tomb of Napoleon Bonaparte**, whose body was brought here from St Helena in 1840 and entombed amid lavish funeral celebrations. The Emperor now lies encased in six coffins, one inside the other, which in turn are placed in a red porphyry sarcophagus. This rests in an open circular **crypt** surrounded by a gallery in which are reliefs commemorating his achievements. His son, the King of Rome, also lies here.

Appreciate the rest of the interior: the altar with its elaborate baldachin supported on twisted columns; the **cupola** with its vivid paintings by La Fosse; and the side chapels containing the tombs of Maréchal Foch and other military heroes.

Napoleon would have been pleased with his final resting place. "I wish my remains," he said, "to repose on the banks of the Seine among the people of France whom I have loved so much."

Jacquemart-André, Musée ☆

*158 Bd. Haussmann, 8ᵉ ☎ 562–39–94. Map **7**E5 ▣ ✿ Open 1:30pm–5:30pm. Closed Mon, Tues. Metro St-Philippe-du-Roule, Miromesnil.*

Like several other Paris museums such as the *Marmottan* and the *Nissim de Camondo*, this was originally a private house and collection. It was created by the banker Edouard André and his wife, the portraitist Nélie Jacquemart, who continued to add to the collection after André's death in 1881 and left it in her will to the *Institut de France*, along with the grand Neo-Classical house which her husband had built in 1875. Its opulent interior forms a pleasing setting for art of the 18thC and the Italian Renaissance which the Andrés collected voraciously and with great discernment.

Among the collection of Italian art you will find sculpture by Donatello, paintings by Botticelli, Titian and Uccello – see the magnificent *St George Slaying the Dragon*. French 18thC art is represented by Watteau, Fragonard, Greuze and Boucher, and foreign schools by Rembrandt, Reynolds, Murillo and others. There are frescoes by Tiepolo, a Savonnerie carpet, four *Gobelins* tapestries depicting the seasons, and a wealth of furniture and objets d'art. Notice too, the *Boucicaut Book of Hours*, which belonged to Diane de Poitiers.

Jardin des Plantes: Museum d'Histoire Naturelle

(Botanical Gardens: Natural History Museum)
*5ᵉ. Map **16**K11 ▣ ☕ ✱ Open summer 9am–6pm, Sun 9am–7pm; winter 9am–5:30pm, Sun 9am–6pm. Metro Jussieu, Monge, Gare d'Orléans-Austerlitz.*

"This morning," writes Henry Miller in *Tropic of Cancer*, "having nothing better to do, I visited the Jardin des Plantes. Marvelous pelicans here from Chapultepec and peacocks with studded fans that look at you with silly eyes."

He might have added that there are llamas, bison, tigers, bears, baboons, a round animal house built under Napoleon in the shape of a Legion of Honor cross, an open-air café and more. The Jardin des Plantes, lying near the Seine to the E of the *Latin Quarter*, is much more than a park and encompasses not only a botanical garden but also a **menagerie** and a Natural History Museum. The menagerie, the oldest public zoo in the country and dating back to the Revolution, is very popular despite its rather antiquated installations.

Near the menagerie, the **botanical garden** was established in the 17thC as a medicinal herb garden and now contains a wide variety of European and tropical plants as well as a maze and a tunnel-like avenue of plane trees.

Along the SE side of the garden is a row of buildings housing four departments of the Natural History Museum.

Paleontology: Passing the skeleton of a mammoth you enter a room full of bones and pickled organs, human and animal. Upstairs there are more skeletons as well as casts of alarming prehistoric monsters.

Paleobotany: A small collection of plant fossils, petrified tree trunks and other such recondite objects. A museum for the specialist.

Mineralogy: Fossils, precious stones, crystalline growths, some in lurid colours.

Entomology: A tiny collection of brightly colored beetles and other insects with maps of their habitats.

The Natural History Museum also holds frequent temporary exhibitions relating to its various departments.

Jeu de Paume, Musée de ★

*Pl. de la Concorde, 1er ☎ 260–12–07. Map **8**G6 ✉ Open 9:45am–5:15pm (tickets sold until 4:45). Closed Tues. Metro Concorde, Tuileries.*

The movement loosely known as Impressionism burst forth in 1874, bringing to painting a new world of naturalness, joyful colour, shimmering light, living shadow and liberated brushwork. The Jeu de Paume gallery, housed in a Second-Empire pavilion in the *Tuileries* gardens, owns one of the finest and most comprehensive Impressionist collections in the world. Here one can perceive not only the essence of the movement but also its great diversity.

In the entrance hall are two panels by Toulouse-Lautrec of the dancer *La Goulue.* Entering the ground floor galleries you will see some of Degas' sharply disciplined canvasses of racehorses and ballet dancers and his melancholy painting *l'Absinthe.* At the E end you will come to a room full of Manets, including his *Le Déjeuner sur l'Herbe* showing a naked woman reclining on the grass with two men – a picture which caused considerable scandal when it was first shown.

Mounting to the first floor you will find many Van Goghs – feverish, brilliant canvases. Seurat, Gauguin, Sisley, Pissarro, Monet and Renoir are among the other artists represented on this floor. Look out for Renoir's *Le Moulin de la Galette,* showing a carefree scene at an open-air café with a merry throng of dancers and revelers spattered by sunlight streaming through the leaves overhead. It embodies the sense of freedom and vitality that pervades the Impressionist movement.

The **Orangerie** in a matching pavilion on the other side of the Tuileries houses temporary exhibitions, and Monet's *Nympheas* (*Waterlilies*) series (closed for alterations).

Latin Quarter ★

*5e. Map **15**. Metro St-Michel, Maubert-Mutualité, Cardinal-Lemoine.*

The name *Quartier Latin* carries with it the image of a way of life: colorful, vibrant, intellectual, rebellious, Bohemian and, above all, cosmopolitan. It lies at the heart of the Left Bank and comprises most of the 5e and a sliver of the 6e districts, taking in the streets immediately to the W of the **Bd. St-Michel**.

Its name derives from the presence of the *Sorbonne*

university and other colleges in the district, the scholars of which formerly spoke Latin. The area is still full of students, not only from the Sorbonne but also from the neighboring *Collège de France*, the university of Jussieu a little further to the E and the École Normale Supérieure to the S.

There is another reason why the term 'Latin Quarter' is appropriate. The area now called the **Montagne Ste-Geneviève**, around the *Panthéon*, was once the focal point of the Roman colony. Although the governor had his palace on the *Ile de la Cité*, it was here that the forum, temple and baths were built. Virtually the only Roman remains that can be seen in Paris now are the great thermal baths in the *Cluny* museum and in the *Arènes de Lutèce.*

The main artery of the Latin Quarter is the Bd. St-Michel or **Boul'Mich** as it is known by all. This busy treelined thoroughfare full of bookshops and cafés rises near the Luxembourg gardens and descends southwards into the Pl. St-Michel by the Seine, which is dominated by the huge St-Michel fountain.

The Boul'Mich is intersected by the other great artery of the Left Bank, the **Bd. St-Germain**. At their junction is the *Cluny* museum, one of many architectural riches in the district. Turn up the Rue Soufflot and you will be confronted by the massive facade of the Panthéon standing on the Montagne Ste-Geneviève. Nearby are the church of *St-Etienne-du-Mont*, the **Ste-Geneviève library**, built in the mid-19thC on the site of the medieval Montaigu college, and the **Lycée Henri IV**, the buildings of which incorporate the refectory and belfry of the old abbey of Ste-Geneviève. There are three other important churches in the area, *St-Séverin*, *St-Julien-le-Pauvre* and

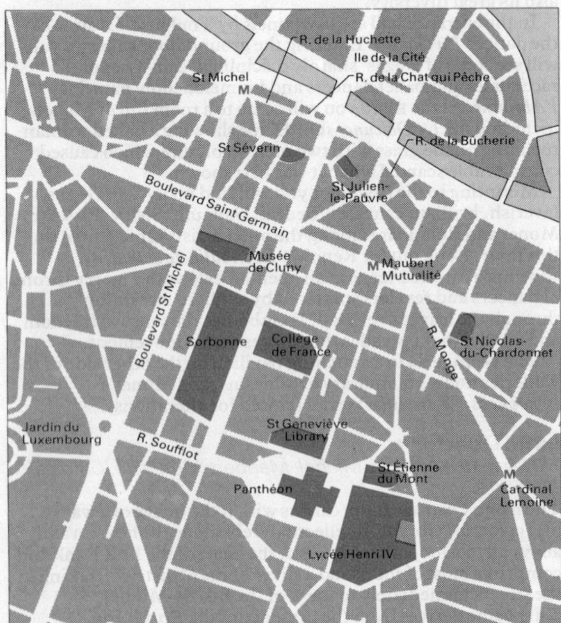

St-Nicholas-du-Chardonnet. The last named is the stronghold of traditional Catholics and mass is said here in Latin.

The district's main attraction, however, lies not so much in its monuments as in the tortuous side streets that twist around each other along the bank of the Seine. The strongest impression of the cosmopolitan Bohemian life is gained in the streets around St-Séverin and St-Julien-le-Pauvre. Here are restaurants of many nationalities, small bookshops, intimate little cafés, nightclubs and experimental cinemas. The pedestrian zone of the **Rue de la Huchette** and its tributaries is particularly full of color and atmosphere. Leading off the Rue de la Huchette is the amusingly named **Rue du Chat-qui-Pêche** (Street of the Fishing Cat), said to be the narrowest street in Paris. A stone's throw to the E (*at 37 Rue de la Bûcherie*) is one of the most enticing bookshops in the city, **Shakespeare and Co**, which specializes in English-language material, both new and secondhand. Between the wars, under the ownership of Sylvia Beach, it was the meeting place of expatriate literati such as Joyce, Pound, Miller and Hemingway. After the Second World War it was taken over by a genial American, George Whitman, who still runs the place with great verve and still accommodates penniless writers in rent-free rooms above the shop.

In the Latin Quarter one senses fewer barriers than in many other districts; the area seems to invite anyone who goes there to participate in its life. No doubt this is because of the presence of so many nationalities and so many students; certainly the student riots of 1968, whatever harm they did, kept alive the feeling of youthful restlessness that characterizes this colorful district.

Le Corbusier Foundation

8 Sq. du Docteur-Blanche, 16e ☎ 288-41-53 ✉ Open Mon–Fri 10am–1pm, 2pm–6pm. Closed Sat, Sun. Metro Jasmin.

The name Le Corbusier is synonymous with modern French architecture. This foundation, the purpose of which is to present Le Corbusier's work to the public, occupies two villas designed by the master himself in the 1920s. It encompasses a library, a photographic archive and a small collection of paintings and sculptures by the architect.

Temporary exhibitions are held on various aspects of his work.

Légion d'Honneur, Musée 🏛

Hôtel de Salm, 2 Rue de Bellechasse, 7e ☎ 555-95-16. Map ***8H6*** *✉ ✗ by prior arrangement. Open 2–5pm. Closed Mon. Metro Solférino.*

The museum is housed in the **Hôtel de Salm**, a fine 18thC mansion backing on to the Seine and built in Palladian style, resembling the White House in Washington. Its occupants included the writer Mme de Staël and Napoleon. The house was acquired by the Grand Chancellery of the Legion of Honor, soon after the Order's creation by Napoleon in 1802. It was burned down during the *Commune* but rebuilt in 1878.

The museum is devoted to the history of chivalric orders and other awards for distinction, including many from foreign countries such as Britain's Victoria Cross and Order of the Bath. There is a rich selection of insignia, regalia and documents. In the section on the Legion of Honor itself, we learn that Rodin, Utrillo and Colette were among the recipients.

Les Halles See *Halles, Les.*

Les Invalides See *Invalides, Les.*

Louvre, Musée du 🏛 ★
Palais du Louvre, 1er ☎ 260–32–14. Map ***9****H8* [symbols] *on Sun* [symbols] *Open 9:45am–5:15pm (certain rooms open until 6:30). Closed Tues. Metro Palais-Royal, Louvre.*

"I never knew what a palace was until I had a glimpse of the Louvre," wrote the 19thC American author Nathaniel Hawthorne.

Long before it became one of the great art museums of the world the Louvre was a royal residence. Built originally as a fortress in 1200, it housed its first royal inhabitant, Charles V, in the 14thC. However, it was François I who, in the 16thC, began a rebuilding program which was subsequently added to by every important French monarch up to Napoleon III.

The oldest part of the building is the SW corner of the **Cour Carré** ☆ which was designed by Pierre Lescot for François I in the Renaissance style. In the 17thC, Louis XIII commissioned Le Mercier to extend the W facade of the Cour Carré in the same style, and the remainder of the court was built by Louis XIV. Particularly noteworthy is the majestic **colonnade** ☆ of 52 Corinthian columns along the outside E facade of the court. This was the work of Claude Perrault and is one of the outstanding examples of the Classical style in Paris. From the Cour Carré the Louvre grew haphazardly westwards in two gigantic wings as successive monarchs added pavilion after pavilion until it finally linked up with the now vanished Tuileries palace. Today the Louvre is so vast that it can only be encompassed in a single sweep of the eye if one observes the building from the air or from one of the city's high vantage points.

The art collection grew in a similar piecemeal way. Begun by François I, it was built up by his successors and continued to expand after it was opened to the public in 1793. It was the fifth museum in the world to be opened in this way. The greatest leaders were the greatest collectors: François himself, then later Louis XIV and Napoleon. As the collection has grown, more and more of the palace has been opened up to accommodate it, and today the museum takes up most of the Cour Carré and the S wing, the N wing being occupied by the Ministry of Finance and the *Arts Décoratifs* museum.

The museum can be divided into seven sections: Greek and Roman Antiquities, Oriental Antiquities, Egyptian Antiquities, Sculpture, Objets d'Art, Painting, and Drawing. There are so many exhibits that if you were to spend half a minute in front of each one it would take three months, night and day, to see the whole collection. So clearly anyone visiting the Louvre must ration their time carefully (and wear comfortable shoes).

If possible, try to make more than one visit. A good idea for the first-time visitor is to take one of the general guided tours of the Paintings and Classical Antiquities. Then, having obtained a bird's-eye view of the museum, return later to explore individual parts in greater detail. Here is a brief guide to the departments and their highlights.

Greek and Roman Antiquities

This heading encompasses every chapter in the history of Classical art from early Hellenic times to the end of the Roman

Empire. The department occupies the ground floor galleries near the main entrance and also part of the Cour Carré including the 16thC **Galérie des Caryatides**, once used as a ballroom, with its row of caryatids looking curiously like some of the exhibits. The armless *Venus de Milo* ★ was found in 1820 by a peasant on the Greek island of Milos and is one of the most prized items. Dating from the 3rd–2ndC BC, she embodies all the idealized beauty and dignity that the Greeks invested in their portrayals of the human form. Notice that her face is rather masculine, a reminder that the Greeks of that time particularly exalted male physical beauty.

Another famous exhibit in this section is the headless *Winged Victory of Samothrace* ★ dating from about 200 BC and dominating the grand staircase which was built especially for her display. The statue commemorates a naval victory and stands upon the prow of a ship, symbolizing victory with far more impact than any arch of triumph. She stands proudly and defiantly, draped in whirls of cloth, her powerful wings spread out behind her.

Belonging to a much earlier period (6thC BC) is the *Hera of Samos* ☆ In this work and the other statues nearby you will notice the stiffness and frontal emphasis often found in ancient Egyptian statues – so different from the *Venus de Milo*. Hera, in

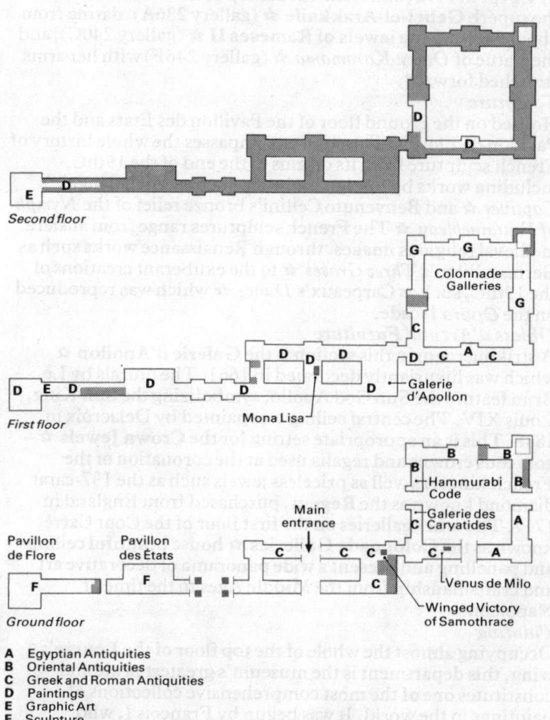

her enclosed roundness, recalls statuary made from tree-trunks. To the left of Hera you will see the *Rampin Horseman* ☆ He has an archaic smile, and his beard and hair are stylized, geometrical approximations of reality. Notice also the bronze *Apollo of Piombino* ☆ with copper inlaid lips, eyebrows and nipples (5thC BC).

Oriental Antiquities

Occupying the ground floor rooms in the N half of the Cour Carré, this section is, in fact, devoted mainly to the civilizations of Mesopotamia, the Far Eastern section of the collection being in the *Guimet* museum. Among the most impressive items here are the black basalt stele bearing the *Code of Law of King Hammurabi of Babylon* ☆ (found in gallery 4), the *Stele of the Vultures* ☆ and the *Stele of Naram-Sim* ☆ (gallery 1).

Egyptian Antiquities

This is one of the finest Egyptian collections in the world, thanks to long-standing French prominence in this field. Founded in 1826, its first curator was the great Egyptologist Champollion, decipherer of the Rosetta stone, now in the British Museum in London. Situated on the ground floor in the SW corner of the Cour Carré and in a first-floor gallery along the S side, it contains such masterpieces as the great sandstone bust of *Amenophis IV* (*Akhenaton*) ☆ which was presented to France by Egypt in 1972, and stands at the top of the stairs. Notice too the superb **Gebel-el-Arak knife** ☆ (gallery 236A), dating from about 3400 BC, the **jewels of Rameses II** ☆ (gallery 240C), and the statue of *Queen Karomama* ☆ (gallery 246F) with her arms stretched forward.

Sculpture

Housed on the ground floor of the Pavillon des États and the Pavillon de Flore, this section encompasses the whole history of French sculpture from its origins to the end of the 19thC, including works by foreign sculptors such as Michelangelo's *Captives* ☆ and Benvenuto Cellini's bronze relief of the *Nymph of Fontainebleau* ☆ The French sculptures range from austere medieval religious images, through Renaissance works such as German Pilon's *Three Graces* ☆ to the exuberant creations of the 19thC, such as Carpeaux's *Dance* ☆ which was reproduced on the *Opéra* facade.

Objets d'Art and Furniture

A striking room in this section is the **Galérie d'Apollon** ☆ which was luxuriantly decorated in 1661. The murals by Le Brun feature the Sun God Apollo, symbolizing the Sun King, Louis XIV. The central ceiling was painted by Delacroix in 1848. This is an appropriate setting for the **Crown Jewels** ☆ – gorgeous crowns and regalia used at the coronation of the French kings, as well as priceless jewels such as the 137-carat diamond known as the **Regent**, purchased from England in 1717. The other galleries on the first floor of the Cour Carré, known as the **Colonnade Galleries** ☆ house beautiful ceilings and panelling and present a wide panorama of decorative art and craftsmanship from the Middle Ages to the time of Napoleon.

Painting

Occupying almost the whole of the top floor of the Louvre's S wing, this department is the museum's greatest pride and constitutes one of the most comprehensive collections of paintings in the world. It was begun by François I, who acquired the Louvre's most famous exhibit, Leonardo da Vinci's *Mona Lisa* ★ with other Italian masterpieces. The

Mona Lisa now hangs in the Salle des États on the first floor of the Pavillon Denon (unfortunately behind glass) along with five other Leonardos. This is the richest collection of Leonardos possessed by any museum in the world, and includes *Bacchus*, a *John the Baptist*, the *Virgin of the Rocks*, a small portrait of a lady, *La Belle Ferronnière*, the *Virgin and Child with St Anne* and the lady with the mysterious and haunting smile, the *Mona Lisa* herself (also called *'La Gioconda'*). In each of Leonardo's paintings you will see how he has suppressed two-dimensional line in favor of mass and tone value, creating three-dimensional illusion. This part of his technique is called *chiaroscuro*, Italian for 'light-shadow.' Further, by use of very thin coats of glaze, hard outlines are obscured giving the subject a hazy look. This technique is called *sfumato*, Italian for haze. Leonardo also strove to reveal the intention of the soul through gestures. In the *Virgin of the Rocks* ★ the group is held together by various significant gestures: pointing, praying, blessing and protecting. In the *Virgin and the Child with St Anne* ★ Mary is shown sitting on the lap of her mother St Anne and reaching out towards the baby Jesus, who, in turn, reaches towards his future sacrifice for mankind symbolized by a lamb. Notice too that the *Mona Lisa* is not the only one smiling. The mysterious smile is found elsewhere, for instance in the *John the Baptist* ☆

In addition to the Leonardos, this room contains a wealth of paintings by Titian, Raphael, Veronese and other artists of the Italian Renaissance. Earlier and later Italian works are to be found in other rooms.

A small but distinguished Spanish collection is housed at the end of the Pavillon de Flore and includes such masterpieces as El Greco's *Christ Crucified* ☆ and Murillo's *The Young Beggar* ☆ as well as works by Goya and Velasquez. English works are also not numerous, but include portraits by Gainsborough and Reynolds. The Flemish, Dutch and German masters are well represented. Notice particularly the series of Rembrandts, including several self-portraits and a curiously haunting little picture called *Philosopher in Meditation*.

French paintings form the bulk of the collection and range from the 14th–19thC. Many of them are displayed along the **Grande Galérie**, one of the world's longest rooms. Here you will find Poussin's limpid canvases of mythological and allegorical subjects, La Tour's religious paintings with their striking effects of light and shadow, and Watteau's delicate scenes of gaiety touched with a nuance of melancholy.

If it is size and splendor you want, then move round into the 19thC rooms (galleries 5, 6, 7 and 8) where you will find David's vast painting *The Coronation of Napoleon* ☆ In the same section are works by other 19thC painters such as Delacroix, Corot and Courbet.

Drawing

Only a small part of the drawings collection, mainly pastels, is on permanent display on the second floor of the Flore Pavilion, but other parts of the collection are brought out frequently for temporary exhibitions on specific themes.

Luxembourg, Palais et Jardin ☆

15 Rue de Vaugirard, 6e ☎ 329–12–62. Map ***15****J8* *Open for tours Sun 9:30–11am, 2–4pm. Metro Luxembourg.*

The Luxembourg Palace was built between 1612–24 by Marie de Medici, widow of Henry IV. Finding the Louvre boring as a place of residence, she bought the house and grounds of the Duc de Piney-Luxembourg, then standing in a semi-rural position on the S edge of the city. Beside the duke's house (now known as the **Petit Luxembourg**) she built a grandiose mansion designed by Salomon de Brosse in the style of the Pitti Palace in Florence, but keeping the traditional French layout around a grand courtyard. However, her stay was short-lived for in 1630, 5yr after she had moved in, she was banished for life to Cologne.

During the Reign of Terror (1793–4) the palace became a prison, but after 1795 it housed the higher parliamentary assemblies, and the building underwent a series of alterations and enlargements.

Apart from the richly Italianate **Cabinet Doré**, with its masses of gold leaf, little remains of the original interior. Most of the rooms are decorated in a heavy 19thC idiom, typified by the **Salle des Conférences** with its painted cupola depicting the *Apotheosis of Napoleon* and its *Gobelins* tapestries illustrating Ovid's *Metamorphoses*. This room was originally the assembly chamber, but in the mid-19thC the assembly moved to its present chamber, the **Salle de Séances**, a large, semi-circular room like its counterpart in the *Palais-Bourbon* and equally ornate. Brass plaques on some of the senators' desks mark the places where famous members sat – one, for example, bears the names of Georges Clémenceau and Victor Hugo. Another imposing room is the **library**, which possesses paintings by Delacroix and an arresting view over the gardens towards the *Observatoire*. Notice also the great **stairway**, the **ceiling** of which has 400 rosettes, each of a different design.

The Petit Luxembourg next door is now the residence of the Senate's president.

The gardens, like the palace, are French with Italian touches such as the Baroque **Medici fountain** ☆ which stands at the end of a long pool filled with goldfish and flanked by shaded walkways. The focal point of the gardens is a large octagonal pool, surrounded by formal terraces and parterres and usually filled with a fleet of toy sailing boats. The rest is an engaging mixture of formality and intimacy, with plenty of little secret corners as well as broad, straight avenues. One of the great delights of this park is its statues. Here you will find, among others, *Delacroix*, *Paul Verlaine*, *George Sand*, *Stendhal* and *Flaubert*. In the **Av. de l'Observatoire**, which forms an extension to the gardens, is an exuberant fountain with an armillary sphere held up by female figures representing the four quarters of the globe.

The gardens also have tennis courts, donkey rides, a marionette theater (the Théâtre du Luxembourg), a school of bee-keeping and arboriculture, and an open-air café under the trees which reminds one of a Renoir painting. In fact the Luxembourg Gardens have just about all the ingredients for a good day out, except that you cannot sit on the grass.

Madeleine 🏛 ✝ ☆

*Pl. de la Madeleine, 8ᵉ. Map **8**F6 ✗ Open 8.30am–7pm. Metro Madeleine.*

Built to look like a Roman temple, this edifice, with its simple lines and colonnade of soaring Corinthian columns, stands at the hub of one of the most prosperous districts of Paris, confident of its architectural splendor, yet oddly uncertain of its role as a Christian church. Begun as a church in 1764, during the reign of Louis XV, it never seems to have quite thrown off the image of the bank that it nearly became in the early 19thC – other ideas included a theater, a banqueting hall, a Temple of Glory to Napoleon's army and a railway station. After many changes of design and plans for its use, it was finally consecrated as a church in 1842.

Contrasting with the rather austere exterior, the sensual beauty of the interior comes as something of a surprise – a feast of softly colored marble, gilt Corinthian columns, rich murals and some fine sculpture, including the *Baptism of Christ* by Rude, and the *Ascension of the Magdalen* by Marochetti which dominates the high altar.

The church possesses a superb organ, played in the past by Camille Saint-Saëns, among others, and concerts are held here once a month. By the E side of the church is an attractive little flower market.

Le Marais ★

*3e and 4e. Map **10&11**. Metro Hôtel-de-Ville, St-Paul, Chemin-Vert, St-Sébastien-Froissart, Filles-du-Calvaire, Temple, Arts-et-Métiers.*

This fascinating district has a grave beauty that is haunting, powerful and peculiarly un-Parisian. The stamp of the Middle Ages is still firmly imprinted on the narrow, huddled streets, lined by venerable houses built in the 16th, 17th and 18thC.

The name means 'marshland,' and this is what the area was, until in the 12thC it was drained by the Knights Templar and became the site of many other religious communities which have since disappeared but bequeathed their names to certain streets: Rue des Blancs-Manteaux, Rue des Filles-du-Calvaire, Rue St-Croix-de-la-Bretonnerie.

In the 15thC the Marais had begun to be a fashionable residential district for the aristocracy, and by the 17thC it had reached its heyday, abounding in gracious mansions of the kind that became the model for the traditional French *hôtel*, with a courtyard at the front and formal garden at the back. There are still more mansions left in the Marais than in any other district of Paris. By the early 18thC the nobility began to move W to the Faubourg St-Germain. The Marais became less favored and thereby began a gradual decline which lasted until de Gaulle's Minister of Culture, André Malraux, made it a conservation area in 1962 just in time to save it from wholesale redevelopment. Since then an enthusiastic restoration program has uncovered many treasures.

Not surprisingly, the Marais possesses what is claimed to be the oldest house in Paris, **no. 3 Rue Volta**, built in about 1300, and also the second oldest, **no. 51 Rue de Montmorency**, built in 1407 as a charitable lodging house by Nicholas Flamel, who is said to have made a fortune through alchemy. The house is now a restaurant. Near the Rue Volta is the Temple Quarter which includes the *Conservatoire des Arts et Métiers* technological museum, and the church of *St-Nicolas-des-Champs*.

This northern part of the Marais also boasts, to the W, the *Archives Nationales*, housed in the outstanding **Hôtel de Soubise** and **Hôtel Rohan**, and, to the E, the *Carnavalet* museum. Just to the N of the Archives Nationales, in the Rue des Archives, is another notable feature, the **Hôtel Guénégaud**, now housing the *Chasse* museum, a quietly harmonious Mansart building. Around the *Carnavalet* are a wealth of beautiful *hôtels*. Best known are the **Hôtel Libéral-Bruand** in the Rue de la Perle, now the *Bricard* museum, and the **Hôtel Salé** in Rue de Thorigny, shortly to be the home of the *Picasso* museum. Also worth seeing in nearby Rue de Turenne are the **Hôtel de Montresor**, now a school, and the **Hôtel de Grand-Veneur**, former home of the master of the royal hunt. The facade is adorned with a boar's head and other symbols of hunting and, inside, the impressive staircase is decorated with trophies (ask the caretaker to visit). Farther along the street is **St-Denys-du-Sacrement**, built in 1835 in the Roman style, which contains a *Deposition* by Delacroix.

Beginning at the Seine, a short itinerary takes in some of the southern part of the Marais' most interesting features. Just E of the *Hôtel de Ville* is the church of **St-Gervais-St-Protais** ☆ A Gothic building with a superb Classical facade, the interior contains some fine works of art, including lovely stained glass, and, in the N transept, a Flemish *Passion* painted on wood. Walk down to the river and along to the *Hôtel de Sens*, one of the oldest mansions in the city. Continue E for a short distance, then turn up the Rue des Jardins-St-Paul, leading into the **Village St-Paul**, a charming collection of craft studios and antique shops.

Twisting N, turn left at the Rue St-Antoine to visit the church of **St-Paul-St-Louis**, built in the Jesuit style in the 17thC. Return down Rue St-Antoine to the 17thC **Hôtel de Béthune Sully** at no. 62, now the headquarters of the administration of national monuments which holds temporary exhibitions on architecture and conservation. The *hôtel* has a particularly fine inner courtyard and the interior contains paneling and painted ceilings (■ ■ *Wed, Sat, Sun 3pm*). Turn up the Rue de Birague into the graceful red brick expanse of the *Place des Vosges*. Leave it by the NW corner and walk W down the **Rue des Francs-Bourgeois** to the corner of Rue Pavée and the **Hôtel de Lamoignon** ☆ which is now the Paris Historical Library, with its curious little corner tower jutting out over the pavement. The courtyard and building are of majestic proportions, the facade divided by tall Corinthian pilasters. Opposite is the Carnavalet museum and beyond it, up the Rue Payenne, a magical little oasis called **Sq. Georges-Cain**, a garden full of intriguing fragments of sculpture. In the same street are two interesting buildings, the **Hôtel de Chatillon**, at no. 13, and **Hôtel de Polastron-Polignac**, next door.

Returning to the Hôtel de Lamoignon, walk S down the Rue Pavée and immediately right into the area which for centuries has been a **Jewish quarter** ☆ In this street, the Rue des Rosiers, Rue des Écouffes, and in the surrounding streets, synagogues, kosher food shops and Hebrew booksellers abound. For good kosher food try **La Bonne Boucherie** (*Rue des Hospitalières-St-Gervais*).

Not far away, in the street of the same name, is the graceful little church of **Notre-Dame-des-Blancs-Manteaux** ☆ with its ornate Flemish wooden pulpit. Opposite is the attractive **Rue Aubriot**, dating from the Middle Ages, and to the left, the Rue des Guillemites, from which lead the tiny inner courts of the **Passage des Singes**. The passage leads to the Rue Vieille du Temple and to the left is the **Hôtel des Ambassadeurs de Hollande** ☆ one of the finest mansions in the Marais (not open to public), once the home of Beaumarchais who wrote the *Marriage of Figaro* there.

Just to the NW lies the Archives Nationales. Here also, at the corner of Rue Rambuteau and Rue des Archives, is a delightful bookshop-café called **Les Milles-Feuilles** where salads are served at lunch, and tea or coffee with delicious cakes at all

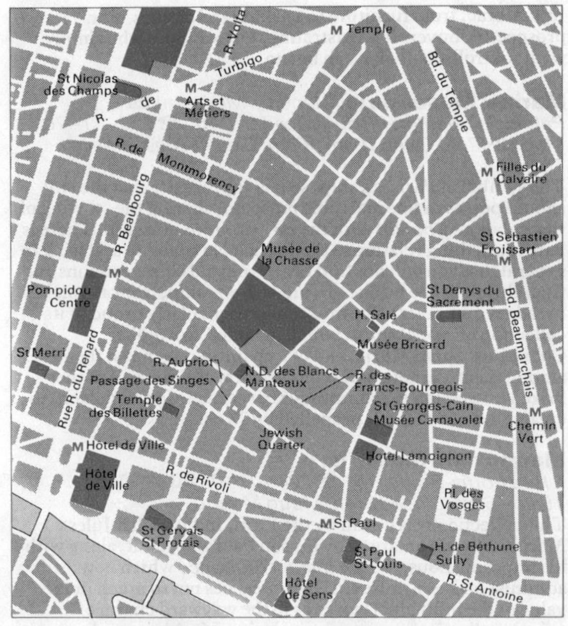

other times, in a chintzy inner sanctum behind the bookshelves.

The lower half of the Rue des Archives has the curious nickname of 'the street where God was boiled' dating from 1290 when a money lender was said to have cut up a host (communion bread) with a knife. To his surprise the host began to bleed whereupon he threw it into boiling water which immediately turned red. The unfortunate man was apprehended and burned at the stake and soon after a church was built on the site of his house to commemorate the miracle. Around this a monastery called Carmes-Billettes grew up in the 14thC. The **Church of Billettes** was rebuilt in the 18thC and is now Lutheran, but the charming little **cloister** still survives, the only complete medieval cloister in Paris.

A little distance to the W lies another interesting church, that of **St-Merri**, completed in 1612, but anachronistically built in the Flamboyant Gothic style. It has a richly decorated W front, and the oldest bell in Paris, made in 1331.

A block to the N of this church, up the Rue St-Martin, lies the *Pompidou Center*, taking the visitor with a jolt from some of the oldest architecture in Paris to a building that points uncompromisingly to the future.

Marché aux Puces *(Flea Market)*

Map ***19****C4. Metro Porte-de-Clignancourt.*

There were once spectacular bargains to be had at this sprawling bazaar lying in a seedy area to the N of the Périphérique. Alas, this is no longer the case, and the only cheap stalls are the ones selling tawdry modern goods. Most of the market consists of a maze of alleys lined with booths selling an intriguing but over-priced variety of antiques and bric-à-brac, from furniture to secondhand clothes. For prospective buyers it is frustrating, but for those who simply want to stroll and look it can be fun.

Marine, Musée de la *(Maritime Museum)* 🏛

*Palais de Chaillot, Pl. du Trocadéro, 16ᵉ ☎ 533-31-70. Map **12**H2 Open 10am–6pm. Closed Tues. Metro Trocadéro.*

The symbol of Paris is a ship, so it is appropriate that the city should possess a fine maritime museum, sharing the SW wing of the *Palais de Chaillot* with the *de l'Homme* museum. There is hardly anything relating to the French Navy and to seafaring in general that you will not find here, from old ship's cannons and figureheads to the bridge of a modern warship, from astrolabes to radar equipment. The museum is particularly proud of its collection of model ships, which include Christopher Columbus' *Santa Maria*, and of its paintings on naval themes, among them Vernet's series on the ports of France. Another prized possession is a sumptuous barge made for Napoleon, in cream, green and gold, propelled by 28 oars.

Marmottan, Musée 🏛 ☆

2 Rue Louis-Boilly, 16ᵉ ☎ 224-07-02 Open 10am–6pm. Closed Mon. Metro Muette.

This collection was begun by the 19thC industrialist Jules Marmottan and enlarged by his son Paul who left it, along with his imposing house, to the *Institut de France* which now administers it as a museum. Its appeal lies not so much in the value of the individual works as in the wayward charm of a private collection, comprising paintings, furniture and ornaments, displayed in a series of beautiful rooms.

Although there are works of many periods, there are three groups of items which are given pride of place: a series of rooms devoted to works of art and furniture of the Napoleonic era; a collection of medieval illuminated manuscripts; and a collection of works by Monet and his contemporaries. These include Monet's *Impression, Soleil Levant*, from which the term Impressionist is derived, and also many of his paintings of water lilies.

Mint Now contains a museum of coins and medallions. See *Hôtel des Monnaies*.

Mode, Musée de la *(Fashion Museum)* 🏛

*Palais Galliéra, 10 Av. Pierre 1-de-Serbie, 16ᵉ ☎ 720-85-23/720-85-46. Map **6**G3 Open 10am–5:40pm. Closed Mon. Metro Iéna, Alma-Marceau.*

To many people, Paris and fashion are synonymous. Visit this stylish museum and you are sure to learn something new about the art of dressing. The museum has no permanent collection but plays host to a continuous series of well-mounted temporary exhibitions on various aspects of clothing and its history.

Even if fashion does not interest you it is worth taking a look at the building. The **Palais Galliéra** was built in a striking Neo-Classical style by the Duchesse de Galliéra in the decade 1878–88. The S front gives on to a charming public **garden** where, on clear days, the sun splashes down on to the colonnaded facade and over the park with its fountains, statues and shaded benches, creating the impression that one has been transported to a little corner of Italy.

Monceau, Parc de

*Entrance in Bd. de Courcelles, 8e. Map **2**E4. Metro Monceau.*

This is an unusual and rather poetic place. The entrance is a gateway in a tall railing along the Bd. de Courcelles, revealing a picturesque garden in the English style. Beside a little lake there is a semicircular Roman colonnade, and dotted about among the chestnuts, acacias and plane trees are curious objects: a pyramid, a stone archway, some Classical columns. These are all follies remaining from the garden designed for the Duke of Orléans by the writer and painter Carmontel in the late 18thC.

Montagne St-Geneviève Area of university buildings and famous colleges on the Left Bank. See *Latin Quarter*.

Montmartre ★

*18e. Map **4**. Metro Abbesses, Pigalle, Blanche, Anvers, Barbès-Rochechouart, Château-Rouge, Marcadet-Poissoniers, Jules-Joffrin, Lamarck-Caulaincourt.*

In AD 250 the martyred St Denis is said to have picked up his severed head and walked up and over a hill to the N of the city. Since then millions of people have made the journey in more conventional style up through the winding streets of what is now called Montmartre or simply the **Butte** (hillock). Montmartre is a district full of contrasts. By turns quiet, raucous, quaint, sordid and hauntingly beautiful, it is a must on the itinerary of anyone who wishes to absorb the spirit of Paris.

For centuries Montmartre was a country village, bristling with windmills that supplied flour to the city below. Then in the 19thC it became part of Paris and its picturesque charm and atmosphere and low rents attracted painters, sculptors, writers and musicians. The late 19thC was the heyday of Bohemian Montmartre, when Toulouse-Lautrec drew the cancan girls at the **Moulin Rouge** in Pl. Blanche, when Picasso, Braque and others created Cubism at the **Bateau-Lavoir** studios (burned down in 1970 but since rebuilt) in the **Pl. Emile-Goudeau**, and when artists' models hung about the Pl. Pigalle looking for

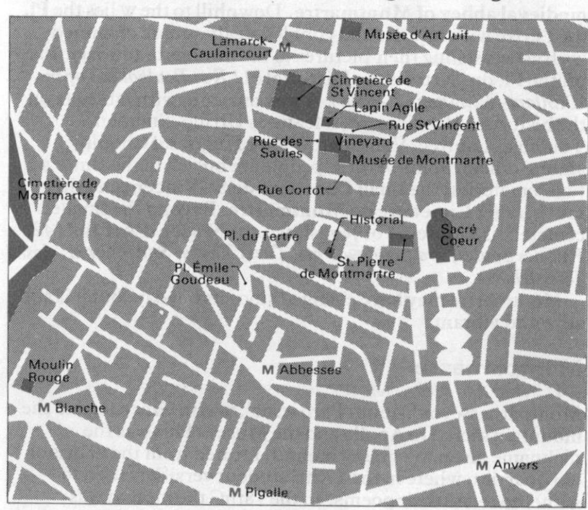

work. By 1914 most of the artists had migrated to the Left Bank, and the great tourist influx had begun.

Today Montmartre has a number of different faces. The garish nightlife which Toulouse-Lautrec loved to portray has now spread all along the Bd. de Clichy and the surrounding streets. Pigalle today has become decidedly sleazy, the artists' models now replaced by numerous members of an older profession. This is the Montmartre of neon lights, strip clubs and cheap glitter. Further up the hill in the area around the *Sacré-Coeur*, the ghost of the old Montmartre still lingers, but strictly for the tourists' benefit. Yet behind the facade of fake Bohemianism, Montmartre is still a village, an ordinary community with a strong sense of its own history. This aspect is most evident on the N side of the hill, an area of quiet residential streets turned symbolically away from Paris.

One of the best ways to begin a visit to Montmartre is to take the metro to Lamarck-Caulaincourt and go to the **Musée de Montmartre** ☆ (*17 Rue St Vincent* ▣ *open 2:30–5:30pm, Sun 11am–5:30pm*). A house inhabited by many artists in the past, it contains interesting mementoes of the district. This route passes another famous meeting place of the Bohemian days, the café **Lapin Agile** at the pretty, countrified crossroads of the **Rue des Saules** and the **Rue St-Vincent** ☆ On the slope to the right of the terraced garden in front of the museum there is a little **vineyard**. This is the last surviving vineyard within the Parisian boundaries and every year, on the first Sat in Oct, the vintage is celebrated by festivities and a procession.

The lights winking up at a pallid moon, the slender painted ladies, the wings of the Moulin Rouge, the smell of petrol and perfume and cooking . . . . The Place Blanche, Paris, Life itself . . . .

Jean Rhys, *Quartet*, 1969

Behind the museum is the pretty **Rue Cortot**, within a short walk of the Butte's most prominent feature, the magnificent church of *Sacré-Coeur*. Beside this landmark is the **great medieval abbey of Montmartre**. Downhill to the W lies the **Pl. du Tertre** with its cafés and cobbled, leafy square crammed with artists selling their pictures to the throngs of tourists. Just off the Pl. du Tertre is the **Historial** (*11 Rue Poulbot* ▣ *open 10:30am–12:30pm, 2–6pm*). A wax museum with tableaux on the history of Montmartre, it features Utrillo, Steinlen, Toulouse-Lautrec, Van Gogh, Victor Hugo and Chopin, among others. Some of these people are buried in the Butte's two cemeteries, the small **Cimetière de St-Vincent** and the much larger **Cimetière de Montmartre**. Beyond the smaller cemetery is a museum of Jewish art, the **Musée d'Art Juif** (*42 Rue des Saules, 3rd floor* ▣ *open Tues, Thurs, Sun 3–6pm; closed Jewish hols*).

Montmartre may have changed since its heyday, but it is still alive and vibrant.

Montparnasse

14ᵉ. Map ***14***. *Metro Montparnasse-Bienvenue.*

Montparnasse, or 'Mount Parnassus', was in Greek legend the mountain sacred to Apollo and the Muses. This was the nickname given to a grassy mound, formed from the debris of old quarries, where in the 17thC student versifiers used to gather to recite their poems. In the 18thC the mound was leveled off, but the name stuck, and so did the carefree, pleasure-loving image. By the time of the Revolution, cafés and pleasure gardens had sprung up in Montparnasse, and it was here that the cancan was first performed.

In many ways Montparnasse is to the Left Bank what Montmartre is to the Right. Both are situated on hills, both have been in their heyday Bohemian haunts of artists and literati, and both have since undergone a change of image. Montmartre now thrives on its picture-postcard quaintness, whereas Montparnasse has, in recent years, become the victim of a brutally insensitive policy of redevelopment, exemplified by the *Tour Montparnasse*, the new railway station and the rash of new buildings around it. The opulently modern **Sheraton Hotel** overlooks an area of condemned and boarded-up buildings; the once charming **Rue de la Gaîté**, whose little theaters are now down-at-heel, is swamped by an increasing number of sex shops.

Yet the old Montparnasse struggles valiantly to survive, and there are still glimpses of it here and there along the Bd. Montparnasse, once the center of flourishing artistic endeavour. Among those drawn to the boulevard and its surrounding streets were artists Rousseau, Van Dongen, Modigliani, Chagall and Whistler, writers Apollinaire, Rilke, Max Jacob and Cocteau, musicians Satie and Stravinsky, and political exiles including Lenin and Trotsky. Between the wars the district was particularly popular with American expatriates, most notably Ernest Hemingway.

The crowd of artists and intellectuals thronged the new cafés of the boulevard: La Coupole, Le Sélect, Le Dôme, La Rotonde and Le Closerie des Lilas, which was one of Hemingway's favorite retreats. In *A Moveable Feast* the author recalls seeing the English occultist, Aleister Crowley at the café, "a rather gaunt man wearing a cape." Crowley was another of the eccentric and colorful characters who used to frequent the district, and he appears pseudonymously as Oliver Haddo, the villain of Somerset Maugham's novel, *The Magician*, in which a Montparnasse café scene is vividly described.

Those were the days when Montparnasse was one mad continuous party, a period that is vividly described by Michel Georges-Michel in his novel *Les Montparnos* (1924). It was this writer who coined the word 'Montparno' to refer to an inhabitant of the district.

Today the sparkling café life of Montparnasse has declined. Only La Coupole, Le Sélect and Le Closerie des Lilas keep alive something of the atmosphere. The writers have dispersed, although there are still many artists' studios in the area.

Montparnasse enjoyed a brief moment of glory during the Liberation of Paris in 1944 when the **Gare Montparnasse** was used as the headquarters of General Leclerc. It was there that the German military governor signed his surrender. In 1967 it was demolished to make way for the present station complex which incorporates huge blocks of offices and apartments.

The station is the point of arrival from Brittany, so Montparnasse is traditionally a Breton area, especially the Rue Montparnasse where there are still excellent restaurants serving pancakes and Breton cider.

The streets to the NW of the station are relatively unspoiled. Here you will find the *Postal* museum in the Bd. de Vaugirard and the *Bourdelle* museum in the street named after the sculptor Antoine Bourdelle. The sculptor himself is buried in the tranquil **Montparnasse cemetery** which also contains the graves of writers such as Baudelaire and Maupassant, composers César Franck and Saint-Saëns, and other distinguished figures. One of the graves has a bronze effigy of a couple sitting up in bed – no doubt very daring for its time. Another is decorated with Brancusi's sculpture, *The Kiss*, a tender and moving piece of work.

Montsouris, Parc de

14e. Metro Cité-Universitaire.

The most striking feature of this appealing park, with its hills, lake and rambling paths, is a Moorish-looking building with onion domes which is a replica of the Bey of Tunis' palace, given by the Bey for the Paris Exhibition of 1867. Sadly it is now derelict.

The park also contains the Paris meteorological observatory and a tower marking the S bearing of the former Paris meridian.

Monuments Français, Musée des ☆

*Palais de Chaillot, Pl. du Trocadéro, 16e ☎ 727-97-27. Map **12**H2 Open 9:45am–12:30pm, 2–5pm. Closed Tues. Metro Trocadéro.*

Try to imagine part of the facade of Chartres cathedral standing right next door to a tympanum from Reims, a pair of gargoyles from Nantes and some sculptures from Notre-Dame, and you will get some idea of what you will see when you enter this museum. You might well think for a moment that you had wandered by accident into the *Cinéma* museum, also housed in the *Palais de Chaillot*, and were looking at relics of a Hollywood film studio's props department – except that the replicas here are better made than on any film set. They are so well made in fact that, even close up, it is hard to tell that these are not stone or wood carvings but plaster copies. The same skill is seen in the department devoted to mural painting, where you may suddenly find yourself apparently inside a 12thC Romanesque church, painted with biblical scenes in flat ochres, browns and reds.

The original idea behind the museum was to restore French sculpture to its rightful place among the arts by showing casts of distinguished works. Formerly called the Museum of Comparative Sculpture, it was given its present title in 1937 and widened to include mural painting and a small amount of stained glass. For the student of sculpture it is a treasure house, for the lay visitor an enjoyable feast of make-believe.

Mosquée de Paris, Institut Musulman

*Pl. du Puits-de-l'Ermite, 5e ☎ 535-97-33/34/35. Map **16**L10 Open 10am–noon, 2–6:30pm (5pm in winter). Closed Fri. Metro Monge.*

Lending an exotic touch to a somewhat drab district of Paris near the *Jardin des Plantes* is this little corner of the Middle East, built in the 1920s. It incorporates fine craftsmanship from all over the Islamic world and one of its most pleasing features is a central courtyard with a traditional Moorish garden. If you tour the building with a guide, you will be given a fascinating introduction to the Muslim religion (in French). You can also refresh yourself in a traditional Arab café with divan seats and dim lights. Sipping a glass of sweet mint tea here you might imagine yourself in Cairo or Marrakesh.

Mouffetard, Rue ☆

*5ᵉ. Map **15**K10. Metro Monge.*

This "wonderful, narrow, crowded market street", as Hemingway described it, begins at the **Pl. de la Contrescarpe**, one of those little leafy village squares which bring a feeling of rusticity to so much of Paris. From here the Rue Mouffetard descends S in a haphazard fashion. It is lined with charming old houses and shop fronts with interesting signs, such as at **no. 122**, which reads 'At the Sign of the Clear Spring' and which has a well carved on the facade, and **no. 134** with its swirling pattern of birds, foliage and wild boar. **Nos. 101** and **104** mark the entrances to two tiny undisturbed passages, **Pge. des Patriarches** and **Pge. des Postes**. The street itself remains a bustling shopping area, the food shops bursting with mouth-watering cheeses, fruit and delicacies.

At its lower end is the little church of **St-Médard**. Here in the 1720s there grew up a curious cult in which groups of people assembled in the charnel house and took part in orgies of convulsion, hysteria and self-mortification in the hope of attaining miraculous cures or visions. These meetings of *convulsionnaires* were stopped by a royal order in 1732.

The Rue Mouffetard and its tributaries constitute one of the few authentic Parisian 'villages' that survive and flourish.

Nissim de Camondo, Musée 🏛

*63 Rue de Monceau, 8ᵉ ☎563-26-32. Map **7**E5 Open 10am–noon, 2–5pm. Closed Mon, Tues. Metro Villiers.*

Like the nearby *Cernuschi* museum, this consists of a private house and contents bequeathed to the nation. Its creator, Count Moïse de Camondo, was a rich collector with a passion for 18thC decorative art. In 1910 he built a house in the style of the Petit Trianon at Versailles where he set out to re-create the atmosphere of an 18thC interior. Thanks to his discrimination and finely tuned visual sense, the effect is one of harmony combined with the highest quality. The furniture is by such master cabinet-makers as Jacob, Riesener and Saunier, and the tapestries come from the great workshops of *Gobelins*, Beauvais and Aubusson – one particularly fine set depicts the famous fables of LaFontaine.

The museum is sumptuous, though it is hard to imagine such objects ever being approached other than on tiptoe.

Notre-Dame de Paris, Cathédrale de 🏛 † ★

*Pl. du Parvis Notre-Dame 4ᵉ ☎354-22-63. Map **16**J10. Church ✗ open 8am–7pm. Treasury open 10am–5pm. Towers open 10am–4:45pm winter, 10am–5:45pm summer. Museum 10 Rue du Cloître Notre-Dame, open Nov 1–June 30 Sat, Sun, 2:30–6pm. Metro Cité.*

One of the world's great architectural masterpieces, the cathedral of Notre-Dame dominates the skyline of central Paris with its lacy facade and its two solid rectangular towers. It has fascinated artists and writers over the centuries and was made the setting for Victor Hugo's famous novel, *Notre-Dame de Paris* (*The Hunchback of Notre-Dame*), whose hero, the bell-ringer Quasimodo, has become a figure of legend. "A vast symphony in stone" Hugo called the building in the novel.

For 800yr the history of Paris has revolved around the cathedral. Its towers have looked down upon wars, revolutions, executions, pilgrimages and, today, a virtually unceasing stream of tourists. It is one of the symbols not only of Paris but of France itself, and appropriately just in front of the main doorway is a brass plaque set into the ground marking the zero point from which all distances from Paris are measured.

The site of Notre-Dame has been a place of worship since pagan times, when a temple to Jupiter stood there. Later came two adjacent Christian churches, one to the Virgin Mary and the other to St Stephen. These were removed in the 12thC and the building of Notre-Dame was begun – a process that was to take nearly 200yr. By 1330 the cathedral stood complete in its essential form, though in the 17th and 18thC sweeping alterations were carried out in the interior. In the Revolution most of the statues of the portals and choir chapels were destroyed, the bells were melted down, the treasures plundered, and the cathedral became a Temple of Reason. In the mid-19thC a magnificent restoration was carried out by Viollet-le-Duc, who replaced hundreds of destroyed carvings. During the *Commune* of 1871 the whole cathedral very nearly perished when the *Communards* made a bonfire of chairs in the choir. Luckily the building was saved by the lack of air and the dampness of the walls.

An unusual feature of the cathedral is that its floor is absolutely level with the street, so that it seems to welcome passers-by to enter without formality.

Before going into the building, spend a while taking in the abundant sculptures on the **facade** ★ remembering that most are skilful copies or restorations by Viollet-le-Duc and his pupils. It was he who carved the 28 kings of Israel who stand in a row, known as the **King's Gallery**, across the facade as ancestors of Jesus Christ. The heads of the originals of these are now in the *Cluny* museum. The three doorways are known as the **portals of the Virgin Mary**, **of the Last Judgement**, and **of St Anne**, and the stonework is richly carved with appropriate figures, such as Christ sitting in judgement (over the central doorway) flanked by the Virgin Mary and St John as intercessors. Notice some of the smaller carvings, such as the zodiacal signs on the left-hand portal and the curious medallions on the central one, representing virtues and vices: purity is a salamander and pride is a man being thrown from a horse – these have also been given an alchemical interpretation. The other facades also have some fine carving; the most famous sculpture of all is that of the ***Virgin*** ☆ by the door of the N transept, carved in the 13thC and unscathed in the Revolution, but for the loss of the Child.

I listened to Vespers and watched the sounding nave grow dusky and the yellow light turn pale in the eastern clerestory . . .

Henry James, *Parisian Sketches*, 1875–76

Go inside the cathedral and, before looking at individual features, take in the majestic construction of the building, with its walls rising in the traditional Gothic manner, through three tiers of arches to a ribbed, vaulted ceiling that seems infinitely far away. Stand in the center of the transept and you will feel the full impact of the architecture. From here you will also get a good view of the **rose windows** ☆ – three great shimmering pools of light and color to the N, S and W. Only the N rose, made in 1270, retains most of its original glass. The S window

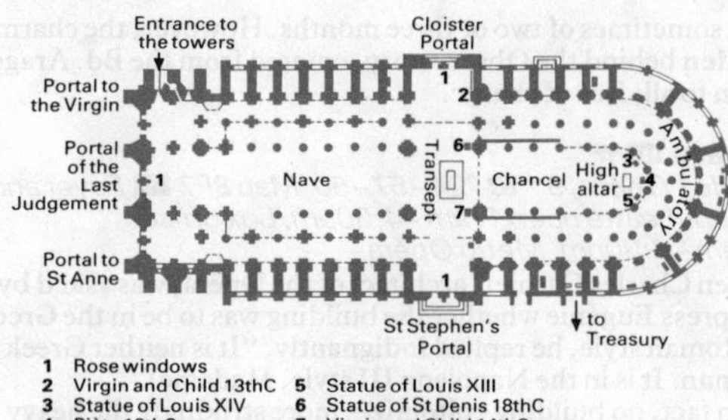

was extensively restored in the 18thC and the W window in the 19th. It is partly hidden by the largest organ in France. Features of the transept that are worth seeing include the lovely 14thC statue of the *Virgin and the Child* ☆ against the S pillar flanking the entrance to the chancel, and the 18thC statue of *St Denis* against the opposite pillar.

Around the nave are a series of chapels containing many fine sculptures and paintings, mostly from the 17thC. In the St Peter chapel on the S side there is some beautiful woodwork of the 14thC, carved with representations of saints. In the ambulatory there are more chapels, filled with the mausoleums of various bishops of Paris.

The high altar in the chancel was made in the 19thC to a design by Viollet-le Duc. Behind it is an 18thC *Piéta,* to the right a statue of *Louis XIII* who, in 1638, consecrated his kingdom to the Virgin. To the left is a statue of *Louis XIV*.

On the S side of the ambulatory a door leads to the **treasury**, where a collection of plate and other treasures can be seen including a reliquary said to contain a fragment of the Cross.

No visit to Notre-Dame would be complete without climbing the **towers**. You ascend via the N tower, then cross over to the S one, passing a series of splendid gargoyles and carved monsters, including the **striga** (a kind of vampire) who gazes, chin resting on his hands, over the city. In the S tower you can visit, with a guide, the belfry containing the great 13-ton bell which is rung only on special occasions.

The S tower can be climbed to the top and on the descent you pass a room containing a **museum of the cathedral's history**. If you want a more detailed presentation of the building's history go across the road to the **cathedral museum**, housing a small but interesting collection of objects, pictures and documents which illustrate the life story of this remarkable building.

Observatoire 🏛

*61 Av. de l'Observatoire, 14^e. Map **15**M8 ✉ ✗ Open first Sat in month. Apply in writing to Secretariat at above address. Metro Port-Royal, Denfert-Rochereau.*

This chaste building, with its two-domed octagonal towers, was built between 1667–72. No iron was used in the construction because it might have affected the instruments, and wood was also avoided for fear of fire. The S wall of the building marks the latitude of Paris.

Today the Observatory is the headquarters of the International Time Bureau which sets universal time. In theory the building and its small museum can be visited by guided tour on the first Sat of every month, but there is usually a waiting list, sometimes of two or three months. However, the charming **garden** behind the Observatory, entered from the Bd. Arago, is open to all, free of charge.

Opéra 🏛 ☆

*Pl. de l'Opéra, 9e ☎ 724-57-50. Map **8**F7 ✉ Foyer and amphitheatre open 11am–4:30pm, box office 11am–6:30pm. Metro Opéra.*

When Charles Garnier, architect of the Opéra, was asked by the Empress Eugénie whether the building was to be in the Greek or Roman style, he replied indignantly, "It is neither Greek nor Roman. It is in the Napoleon III style, Madame!".

In fact, no building epitomizes more strikingly the heavy opulence of that era. During its construction between 1862–72 the builders encountered an underground lake which now lies beneath the cellars of the building, where the 'Phantom of the Opéra' had his dwelling in the horror film of that name. Above, however, all is brightness and gaiety.

If the world were ever reduced to the dominion of a single gorgeous potentate, the foyer (of the Opéra) would do very well for his throne room.

Henry James, *Parisian Sketches*, 1875–76

The ornate facade with its multitude of columns, friezes, winged figures and busts of famous composers is the architectural equivalent of Offenbach's music: lighthearted and irresistible. Inside the building the tone changes. The richly colored marble staircase with its caryatids holding up elaborate candelabra evokes the setting for Belshazzar's Feast.

As for the auditorium, it has all the right ingredients: red velvet, gold leaf and an abundance of plaster nymphs and cherubs. The only discordant element is the domed ceiling painted by Chagall – exquisite but out of key.

During the day you can walk around the building in return for a small fee, but really the only way to see the Opéra is to attend a performance there – always a great experience.

Opéra Quarter

*9e and 2e. Map **8**&**9**. Metro Madeleine, Opéra, Havre-Caumartin, Chaussée-d'Antin, Richelieu-Drouot, Quatre-Septembre, Pyramides, Tuileries, Palais-Royal.*

This distinctive area surrounding the magnificent *Opéra* falls roughly between the Bd. Haussmann and the *Rue de Rivoli* to the N and S, and the Rue de Richelieu and the *Madeleine* to the E and W. More than any other district of Paris, it bears the stamp of Baron Haussmann, Napoleon III's energetic Prefect of the Seine, who re-planned much of central Paris in the years 1853–70 and whose signature was the wide boulevard and spacious townscape. It was he who carved out the **Pl. de l'Opéra**, which many considered unnecessarily large at the time, as well as the **Av. de l'Opéra**, the Rue Auber and the Rue Halévy, which clasp the ornate Opéra building as in a forked stick.

The **Bd. des Italiens** and its extensions were already a fashionable area for rich pleasure-seekers, but with Haussmann's developments and the Gare St-Lazare near at hand, the quarter also became a thriving commercial and financial center. This transformation was accelerated by the building of the metro at the beginning of the century (four lines now converge at Opéra metro station).

The district today preserves both of these aspects. Everywhere you look there seem to be palatial banks, such as the frothy pile of the Crédit Lyonnais building in the **Bd. des Italiens**, and huge stores – Trois Quartiers in the **Bd. de la Madeleine**, Printemps and Galéries Lafayette in the **Bd. Haussmann**. There are also many smaller but often more expensive shops, some bearing anglophile names like 'Old England', others inimitably French, such as the couturiers in the elegant **Rue St-Honoré**, which becomes the even more elegant *Rue du Faubourg St-Honoré*. The most luxurious street of all, however, is the **Rue de la Paix** ☆ leading from the Opéra to the *Place Vendôme* and lined with sumptuous couturiers and jewelers, including **Cartier**.

Theaters in the district, apart from the Opéra itself, include the **Olympia** auditorium in the Bd. des Capucines (mainly for pop concerts), the experimental **Opéra Studio** and the *Comédie Française*, the seat of Classical French drama (see *Nightlife*).

One of the Comédie's greatest (and funniest) dramatists, Molière (1622–73), is commemorated by the **Molière fountain**, near the site of his house in the Rue de Richelieu. The fountain is a grand affair with a bronze statue of the playwright sitting on a pedestal supported by two languid female figures – a somewhat solemn monument for so humorous a writer.

Another appealing **fountain** lies a short distance further up the Rue de Richelieu in the **Sq. Louvois**, a small park beside the *Bibliothèque Nationale*. Podgy cherubs on dolphins support a great bowl decorated with the signs of the zodiac, surmounted by four buxom women representing four great rivers of France, the Seine, Saône, Loire and Garonne. The park, with its chestnut trees, is one of the few intimate little

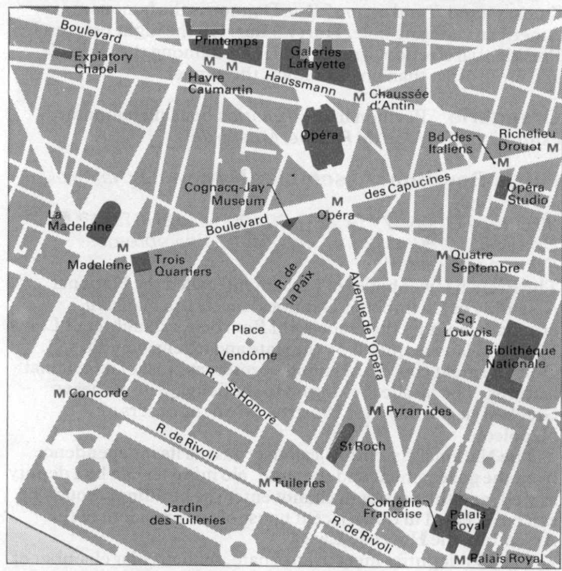

retreats in the district. Near the entrance is a *colonne Morris*, one of those charming onion-domed advertisement pillars which, alas, are disappearing almost as fast as the *pissotières*.

If you are looking for imposing architectural riches you need only cross the road to the *Bibliothèque Nationale* or go W to the *Place Vendôme* and the *Madeleine*, or S to the *Palais-Royal* or the church of *St-Roch*. There are not many museums in this quarter, but the *Cognacq-Jay* museum, in the Bd. des Capucines, has a superb collection of paintings and objets d'art.

One rather curious monument lies on the NW fringes of the quarter. This is the **Expiatory Chapel**, built by order of Louis XVIII to the memory of his brother and sister-in-law, Louis XVI and Marie-Antoinette. It stands in the **Sq. Louis XVI**, now another tranquil little garden off the Bd. Haussmann, but formerly a cemetery where lie victims of the guillotine from the Revolution. Louis XVI and Marie-Antoinette were also buried here, until Louis XVIII had their bodies removed to *St-Denis*. The chapel itself looks rather like a glorified waterworks from the outside. Inside it is a frostily Classical mausoleum, somewhat like a miniature *Panthéon*, with statues of the unfortunate couple and a gloomy little crypt below (*open 10am–noon, 2–5pm or 6pm*).

Across the road in the Rue d'Anjou, the beheaded king is commemorated in more mundane fashion by the **Pub Louis XVI**, one of the many so-called 'pubs' which have sprung up all over Paris in recent years. A more convincing imitation of the English variety is the **Stock Exchange Tavern**, at the corner of the Rue de Richelieu and the Rue du Quatre-Septembre, with its frosted glass, dark paneled interior and beer taps. Another is the **Pub Haussmann** in Rue Taitbout.

Despite these English touches the district remains, as Henry James called it, "the classic region" for Americans. **American Express** has its offices in Rue Scribe, described by James as "most sacred," and at no. 5 Rue Daunou is the famous American watering hole, **Harry's Bar**. On the night before a US Presidential election, a mock poll is held among the clientele – and more often than not it predicts the winner.

Orangerie Pavilion in the *Tuileries* housing temporary exhibitions. See *Jeu de Paume, Musée de*.

Palais-Bourbon: Assemblée Nationale *(National Assembly)*
*33 Quai d'Orsay, 7e ☎ 297-60-00. Map **8**H6*
Open Sat 10:30am, 2pm, 3pm. Metro Chambre-des-Députés, Invalides.

The French lower house of parliament (called the National Assembly or Chamber of Deputies) meets in a mansion originally built by the Duchess of Bourbon, a daughter of Louis XIV, and later acquired by the state and extensively altered. Only the great courtyard facing S preserves most of its original features. The facade looking on to the Seine, with its heavy Greek-style portico, was constructed on the orders of Napoleon.

The National Assembly jealously guards its independence from the government and the state. No minister can be a deputy as well, and the president cannot enter the building, though he can be received in the adjacent house of the president of the Assembly, the **Hôtel de Lassay**.

The 491 deputies meet in an ornate, semicircular chamber of

red, white and gold. The marble speaker's tribune was originally adorned with a Napoleonic eagle, tactfully changed into a cock when republicanism finally triumphed, but the room retains an aspect of imperial splendor.

During sessions you can watch from a public gallery, but seats are limited. The first ten people in the line on any given day are admitted on showing a passport or identity card. The remainder must have a pass signed by a deputy (*apply in writing to the Quaestor's Office, 126 Rue de l'Université, 75007 Paris*).

Other parts of the building which visitors are allowed to see include the **library**, a discreetly grand room with a ceiling decorated by Delacroix depicting a **history of civilization**.

The Palais-Bourbon has the atmosphere of an exclusive London club; the deputies even have their own barber shop.

Palais de Chaillot 🏛 ☆

Pl. du Trocadéro, 16ᵉ. Map ***12****H2. Metro Trocadéro.*

The commanding height on the Right Bank of the Seine, known as the Chaillot, has been occupied by a series of buildings beginning with a country house built by Catherine de Medici in the 1580s. After the Restoration, Charles X wanted to build a monument to commemorate the French capture of the Trocadéro fort near Cadiz in Spain. This was never built, but the name stuck and was given to an elaborate palace created on the site for the Paris Exhibition of 1878. Its successor, built for the Exhibition of 1937, was called the Palais de Chaillot, and the name Trocadéro was kept for the square on to which the N side of the building faces. The whole complex is aligned with the *Eiffel Tower* and the *Champ-de-Mars* across the river, creating a dramatic townscape.

With its simple lines, Neo-Classical colonnades and heroic sculptures, the palace is reminiscent of the monumental Nazi and Soviet architecture of the period. But it has aged well, and its sandstone facade has a crisp elegance.

From a spacious piazza with a magnificent view of the Eiffel Tower, two curving wings reach out, embracing a garden that slopes down toward the Seine, the central axis of which is laid out in a descending series of fountains and pools.

The Palais de Chaillot is now occupied by the following museums: *Cinéma*, *de l'Homme*, *Marine* and *Monuments Français*. Also housed here are the film library of the *Cinémathèque Français* and the **Theâtre National de Chaillot** with its two auditoriums.

Palais de Congrès: Centre International de Paris

Pl. de-la-Porte-Maillot, 17ᵉ ☎ 758-27-01. Map ***6****D2. Metro Porte-Maillot.*

A streamlined, multi-purpose building, opened in 1974, dominates the chaotic spaghetti crossroads by the NE corner of the *Bois de Boulogne*. It comprises the Palais de Congrés and a vast hotel. The palais itself is a low-rise block which houses exhibition halls, shops, restaurants, cinemas, conference rooms, a discotheque, an air terminal and the huge and impressive **Main Conference Hall**, home of the Paris Symphony Orchestra and also used for conferences (no admittance unless attending a performance or a participant). Beside this is the high-rise Hôtel Concorde La Fayette, with 1,000 rooms. The whole complex, known as the Centre International de Paris (CIP), is a planners' dream with every facility – except charm.

Palais de la Découverte *(Palace of Discovery)*
Av. Franklin-D-Roosevelt, 8e ☎359-16-65. Map ***7****G5* ▣ ▣ *in Grand Palais. Open 10am–6pm. Planetarium lectures Tues–Sat 11am, 2pm, 3:15pm, 4:30pm; Sun 12:45, 2pm, 3:15, 4:30pm. Closed Tues. Metro Champs-Élysées-Clemenceau.*
The imposing W wing of the *Grand Palais* with its huge domed entrance hall is a place in which to wonder at the properties of the symbol Pi, the structure of the atom, the nature of laser beams or the fundamentals of genetics. These and many other branches of discovery are imaginatively presented and kept up to date.

The museum has a **planetarium** where different aspects of the universe are projected on to a hemispherical dome. There are regular temporary exhibitions, film shows and lectures.

Palais de l'Élysée
55 Rue du Faubourg St-Honoré, 8e. Map ***7****F5. Metro St-Philippe-du-Roule, Champs-Élysées-Clemenceau.*
Built in 1718 for the Comte d'Evreux and later lived in by Madame de Pompadour and Napoleons I (who signed his abdication here) and III, among others, this palace with its extensive garden has been since 1873 the official residence of the French president and the meeting place of the Council of Ministers. The public is not allowed in but can glimpse the elegant facade and courtyard beyond a gateway heavily guarded by police.

Palais Galliéra 19thC Italian Renaissance-style building. See *Mode, Musée de la.*

Palais de Justice *(Law Courts)*
Bd. du Palais, 1er ☎329-12-55. Map ***10****I9* ▣ ▣ *Open Mon–Fri 8:30am–7pm. Closed Sat, Sun. Metro Cité.*
Together with *Sainte Chapelle* and the *Conciergerie*, the Palais de Justice forms a vast complex of buildings running the whole width of the *Ile de la Cité*, with an imposing courtyard and entrance on the Bd. du Palais. There was a palace here in Roman times, and later the site was occupied by a magnificent royal residence which in the 14thC became the seat of parliament. Since the Revolution, the buildings have been occupied by civil and criminal law courts.

Shining gates, ascending flights of steps, *Liberté, Egalité, Fraternité* in golden letters, *Tribunal de Police* in black. As it were, a vision of heaven and the Judgement.

Jean Rhys, *Quartet*, 1929

The most impressive room in the complex of courts and galleries is the **Lobby** (Salle de Pas-Perdus), formerly the great hall of the palace which was twice destroyed by fire and rebuilt in its present form in the 1870s. The royal courtiers are now replaced by lawyers and litigants scurrying about the "cathedral of chicanery" as Balzac called it. If you want to see them in action you can drop into any of the courts with the exception of the juvenile court.

Palais-Royal
Pl. du Palais-Royal, 1er. Map ***9****H8. Metro Palais-Royal.*
Few buildings in Paris have played as many different roles as

the Palais-Royal. Built by Cardinal Richelieu in the 17thC as his private palace, it later came into the hands of the Orléans family, one of whom was the dissolute regent Philippe II of Orléans who turned the palace into a scene of frenzied orgies. His descendant, the so-called 'Philippe Égalité,' in order to raise money built matching terraces of apartment houses around the garden, with an arcade at the ground level in which there were premises for tradesmen. These buildings form the splendid quadrangle that one can enter today to the N of the palace itself.

In the heated period before the Revolution, this quadrangle was the scene of rallies and demonstrations – the "nucleus of the Revolution" Marat called it. Then, after the execution of Philippe Égalité, the palace, its gardens and cafés became a center of gambling and prostitution.

Returned to the Orléans family at the Restoration, the palace was sacked during the Revolution of 1848 and set on fire by the mob during the *Commune* of 1871. Soon afterwards it was restored, and today it has settled down to a more tranquil existence. The palace is now occupied by administrative offices and the garden is a public park with the buildings around it given over to apartments and small shops, selling a variety of goods from stamps to handbags.

The Palais-Royal (now the office of the Council of State and closed to the public) finally seems content after its hectic past. The fountain plays drowsily in the middle of the courtyard, and the sunlight filters lazily through the trees – a fine spot for a midday siesta.

Palais de Tokyo Built for the 1937 World Exhibition. See *Art Moderne de la Ville de Paris, Musée d'*.

Panthéon 🏛 ☆
*Pl. du Panthéon, 5e ☎ 354-34-51. Map **15**K9 ▣ ✗ but ▣ for crypt. ▣ in crypt, fee elsewhere. Open 10am–6pm. Closed Tues. Metro Luxembourg, Cardinal-Lemoine.*
For half of its life this building has led a schizophrenic existence. It was initiated by Louis XV in thanksgiving for his recovery from an illness, and was intended as a more magnificent shrine to Paris' patroness Saint Geneviève than the old abbey church of that name (later demolished). Situated in a commanding position on the Montagne St-Geneviève, it was built in the form of a Greek cross, with a **dome** at the intersection and a massive portico with Corinthian columns. Hardly had it been completed than the new Revolutionary government decided to change it from a church into a mausoleum for the bodies of great Frenchmen. For this purpose many of the windows were removed and blocked up, hence the rather bald and forbidding appearance that the building now presents. Twice it was to revert to its role as a church and then changed back to a secular mausoleum. The last occasion was in 1885 when it was finally secularized to provide a suitable resting place for Victor Hugo. Did they consider that there was not enough room for God *and* Hugo?

When you enter the building it strikes a chill, with its pale, diluted light that filters down from the high windows and through the clerestory in the dome, seeming to freeze as it falls on the chaste stonework and the great empty expanse of floor. However, as you look around, there is much to please the eye, particularly the series of **paintings** by the 19thC symbolist Puvis de Chavannes depicting scenes from the lives of St Geneviève and St Germain d'Auxerre. His deliberately flat, pale colors harmonize well with the building. There is also a horrifying painting showing the newly decapitated St Denis reaching out to pick up his head while an astonished executioner looks on.

The **crypt**, which runs in a series of vaulted corridors beneath the whole building, holds the remains of countless illustrious Frenchmen. The tombs are housed in gloomy little rooms looking for all the world like prison cells. Hugo shares one with Zola – a curious pair of cell-mates. Rousseau's tomb is like a dog kennel, out of which reaches a hand holding a torch. Others buried here include the building's architect, Soufflot, the chemist Berthelot and the Resistance leader Jean Moulin. A distinguished assembly but one that the visitor is glad to escape from into the light of day.

Paradis, Rue de

*10e. Map **5**E10. Metro Château-d'Eau, Poissonière.*

Unexpectedly situated in the rather characterless hinterland between the *Grands Boulevards* and the Gare du Nord, this street is monopolized by retailers of glass and ceramic tableware. The goods displayed in these shops range from the breathtakingly vulgar to the stunningly beautiful. At no. 30 is the **Musée des Cristalleries** (Glassware Museum), run by the firm of Baccarat and containing a dazzling collection of glass objects dating from the early 19thC to present day (*open Mon–Fri 9am–5:30pm, Sat 10am–noon, 2–4pm; closed Sun*).

Another interesting museum on the street is the **Musée de l'Affiche** (Poster Museum) at no. 18, which holds temporary exhibitions. It is housed in the former premises of a ceramics manufacturer with a superbly tiled entrance way (*open noon–6pm; closed Tues*).

Pasteur, Musée

*25 Rue du Docteur-Roux, 15e ☎541–52–66 ext. 523. Map **13**L5 by prior arrangement. Open 2:30–5pm. Closed Sat, Sun, and Aug. Metro Pasteur, Volontaires.*

The name of Louis Pasteur (1822–95) has been immortalized in the word 'pasteurization'. His development of immunization and other disease-controlling methods has become legendary and saved innumerable lives. Pasteur's house, now surrounded by the buildings of the Pasteur Institute, is a museum affording an interesting glimpse of both the scientific and private life of this great man. His remains rest in a magnificent tomb in the basement built in the form of a small Byzantine chapel with rich mosaics illustrating different aspects of his work.

Père Lachaise, Cimetière

20e. Open Mon–Sat Mar 16–Nov 5, 7:30am–6pm; Nov 6–Jan 15, 8:30am–5pm; Jan 16–Mar 15, 8am–5:30pm; Sun and hols 9:30am to seasonal closing time. Metro Père-Lachaise.

Like many old cemeteries, this one, the largest in Paris, has a powerfully romantic appeal. Named after Louis XIV's confessor, this cemetery was originally the site of a Jesuit house of retreat, and its hilly ground was laid out in 1804. The closely huddled graves encompass a wide variety of sepulchral art. It is easy to lose one's way among the twisting, treelined lanes that wind up and down between the main avenues, but in return for a small tip the custodian will provide a map of the cemetery which marks the graves of the many celebrities buried here. These include Molière, Balzac, Chopin, Rossini, Colette, Edith Piaf and Oscar Wilde. The monument to Wilde is a massive block by Jacob Epstein, adorned with a winged Egyptian figure. One of the most visited graves is that of the spiritualist Allan Kardec, whose followers can sometimes be seen communing with his spirit by passing their hands over his statue.

Petit Palais 🏛

*Av. Winston-Churchill, 8ᵉ ☎ 265-12-73. Map **7**G5 ▣ ▣ on Sun. ✗ by prior arrangement. Open 10am–5:40pm. Closed Mon. (Hours of temporary exhibitions vary.) Metro Champs-Élysées-Clemenceau.*

Completed in 1900 along with its neighbor, the *Grand Palais*, this building has rather more harmonious proportions and a less obtrusive personality. Lying a stone's throw from the *Champs-Élysées*, it houses the **Musée des Beaux Arts de la Ville de Paris** whose galleries divide into two groups.

In the galleries facing the outside of the building, you will pass from ancient Egyptian and Classical sculptures, through medieval and Renaissance art, to paintings, furniture and porcelain of the 18thC. The inner galleries are devoted to French art of the 19th and early 20thCs. This is a wonderfully rich collection including works by Delacroix, Courbet, Corot, Manet, Monet, Cézanne, Pissarro, Sisley, Redon and Bonnard. Among famous individual works are Courbet's painting of two sleeping women, *Le Sommeil*; and Bonnard's vibrant *Nu dans le Bain*. Bonnard's palette is here on display as well – a riot of color like his paintings. The museum also has often superb temporary exhibitions.

These galleries are surrounded by a courtyard which, with its Roman-style colonnade, pool and garden, is a charming place in which to take a break.

Picasso, Musée

*Hôtel Aubert-de-Fontenay (Hôtel Salé), 5 Rue de Thorigny, 3ᵉ. Map **11**H11. Metro St-Sébastien-Froissart. Museum due to open in 1983.*

Picasso was rare among major artists in that all his life he kept a significant proportion of his own paintings and sculpture for his personal collection. Much of this collection passed to the French government in lieu of tax after Picasso's death, and it was decided to create a new museum to house it. The Hôtel Salé (to use its familiar name) was chosen for the purpose. The gracious 17thC *Marais* mansion both emphasizes and complements the modernity of Picasso's work.

Although the artist's most famous paintings are already in other museums, this collection gives a unique personal view of the whole span of Picasso's long, creative life. The works range from his astonishing childhood creations such as *Girl with Bare Feet*, painted when he was only 14, through his blue, rose and Cubist periods to the inimitable style of his later years. The joy, anguish and turbulence of his private life are brought out in these works, for Picasso was an unusually self-revelatory artist.

The museum contains works by other artists from Picasso's collection, including paintings by Cézanne, Renoir, Matisse and Rousseau.

Place Charles-de-Gaulle See *Charles-de-Gaulle, Place*.

Place de la Concorde See *Concorde, Place de la.*

Place Vendôme See *Vendôme, Place.*

Police, Musée de la Préfecture de
*1 bis Rue des Carmes, 5e ☎ 033-81-61. Map **10**J9 ☒*
Open Wed, Thurs 2–5pm. Metro Maubert-Mutualité.
A sober but fascinating collection of documents and objects is housed in this little museum in the heart of the *Latin Quarter*. It presents a panorama of police and criminal activity in Paris from the *ancien régime* to 20thC. It includes a frightening display of criminal tools and weapons, as well as orders for the arrest of prominent figures, such as Danton and Charlotte Corday (who killed Marat in his bath) from the Revolution.

Pompidou Center (Centre National d'Art et Culture) ★
*Plateau Beaubourg, 4e ☎ 277-12-33. Map **10**H10 for museums ☒ on Sun. Day passes available. Open Mon, Wed, Thurs, Fri noon–10pm; Sat, Sun 10am–10pm. Closed Tues. Metro Hôtel-de-Ville, Rambuteau, Châtelet.*
Like the *Eiffel Tower* nearly a century ago, the Georges Pompidou Center (or **Beaubourg** as it is informally called) has aroused both shock and admiration. It is now one of the major attractions of the city and a place that pulsates with energy. Shaped like a giant matchbox on its side, brightly painted as though in a child's coloring book and enveloped in a cat's cradle of gleaming steel girders, it looks like a crazy oil refinery. Even if you are a die-hard opponent of modern architecture, it will take your breath away, especially if you come upon it at night when, confronted by its glittering expanse, you might think you had wandered on to the set of a science-fiction movie.

It is one of the most revolutionary buildings of its age. Built on the initiative of President Georges Pompidou as part of the redevelopment of *Les Halles* and opened in 1977, it was designed by the British architect Richard Rogers and the Italian Renzo Piano. The building is turned, as it were, inside-out, so that its intestines – pipes, shafts, escalators, etc – are festooned around the outside, thus liberating large areas of space within. The main escalator runs in a transparent tube up the front of the building, so that the visitor can see a changing panorama of the city while ascending the five stories.

The Beaubourg radiates a sense of celebration that spills over into the surrounding area. As a foretaste of the building itself the visitor crosses a huge sloping piazza which is the scene of perpetual 'happenings.' Here one may come across a poet, a juggler, a fire-eater or a group of street actors.

The function of the Beaubourg is to provide a multi-media center in which modern art and culture are made accessible to the public in a new and exciting way. Its four main departments are listed here.

Art Moderne, Musée Nationale de ☆ has the largest collection of its kind in the world, illustrating all the main schools of the 20thC.

Bibliothèque Publique d'Information (Public Information Library ☒) which is essentially a library of the 20thC with some half a million books, planned to reach a million.

Centre de Création Industrielle (Industrial Design Center) has a gallery on the ground floor presenting exhibitions on all aspects of our planned environment.

Institut de Recherches Contemporaines Acoustiques Musicales (Institute for Contemporary Acoustic and Musical Research), the underground studios of which are closed to the public, but lectures and demonstrations are held here. On the top floor there is a large gallery for temporary exhibitions.

Other features of the Beaubourg include a **library** and supervised **play center** for children, a reconstruction of the **studio of the sculptor Brancusi**, a branch of the *Cinémathèque Française* (Film Library) with its own movie theater, an auditorium for lectures, concerts and theatrical performances, and a top-floor self-service restaurant with a superb view over Paris.

Pont Alexandre III ☆

7e and 8e. Map 7H5. Metro Champs-Élysées-Clémenceau, Invalides.

The broadest bridge in Paris and also one of the most beautiful, it forms part of a great triumphal way leading down the Av. Winston-Churchill, past the *Grand Palais* and *Petit Palais*, across the *Seine* and down the esplanade to *Les Invalides*. It was built for the World Exhibition of 1900 and named after Tsar Alexander III of Russia (1845–94). It is flanked by two massive pillars at each end, the decorations of which represent, on the Right Bank, medieval and modern France, and, on the Left, Renaissance France and the era of Louis XIV. All along the bridge are cast-iron lamp standards with the ornate, prosperous look that characterized the *Belle Epoque*.

Pont-Neuf ☆

1er. Map 9I8. Metro Pont-Neuf.

"Of all the bridges which were ever built, the whole world who have passed over the Pont-Neuf must own that it is the noblest, the finest, the grandest, the lightest, the longest, the broadest that ever conjoined land and land together upon the face of the tremendous globe."

Thus wrote the 18thC English novelist Laurence Sterne about the bridge which spans the *Seine* in two sections, divided by the W spike of the *Ile de la Cité*. He might have added that, despite its name, it is also the oldest. Completed in 1607 under Henry IV, whose equestrian statue stands at the center, it has 12 arches, all of slightly different sizes. The cornices overlooking the river are carved with a row of amusing caricatured faces of Henry IV's ministers and courtiers, and there are comic carvings of stall-holders, pick-pockets and tooth-drawers.

The bridge, the two halves of which are not quite in line, was designed by Androuet du Cerceau.

Paris is the throne of . . . . sensuality and godless frivolity.

King Ludwig II of Bavaria

Portes St-Denis et St-Martin

10e. Map 10F10. Metro Strasbourg-St-Denis, St-Martin.

These two triumphal arches, situated close to each other on the *Grands Boulevards*, were built in the 1670s to commemorate Louis XIV's military victories, and they replaced two fortified gates which had disappeared along with the old perimeter wall. Both bear reliefs glorifying the Sun King, but the Porte St-Denis is the grander and more elaborate of the two. They now overlook the seedy environment that has grown up around them, with its garish movie theaters and fast-food stalls.

Postal, Musée ☆
*34 Bd. de Vaugirard, 15e ☎ 320–15–30. Map **13**L5 ✉ on request. Open 10am–5pm. Closed Thurs. Metro Montparnasse-Bienvenue, Pasteur, Falguière.*
Did you know that during the Siege of Paris, in 1870, microfilm messages were carried out of the city by pigeons whose wings were stamped with a postmark? This is one of many snippets of information one gleans from a visit to the Postal Museum. Here on four floors is an imaginative display on philately and the history of postal communication – everything relating to the subject from postmen's uniforms and mailboxes, to modern sorting machines and stamp-making equipment. And, of course, there are stamps galore for the philatelist. On the ground floor is a gallery showing temporary exhibitions of postage-stamp art and related work.

The Musée Postal is an unexpectedly lively and well-laid-out museum; worth a visit.

Quatre-Saisons, Fontaine des *(Four Seasons Fountain)*
*57–59 Rue de Grenelle, 7e. Map **8**I6. Metro Rue-du-Bac.*
When this fountain was built by Bouchardon in the 1730s to supply water to the district, Voltaire complained that such a splendid monument should not have been erected in so narrow a street. He had a point, for the facade cannot be seen properly unless you are standing right in front of it. A central portico with a seated figure representing Paris is flanked by reclining personifications of the Seine and Marne; and on either side are curved walls adorned with statues of the four seasons and reliefs of their corresponding labors.

Radio France, Maison de 🏛
116 Av. du Président Kennedy, 16e ☎ 524–24–24/ 230–29–07 ✉ in museum Open 9am–5pm. Studios closed Mon. Metro Ranelagh, Passy, Mirabeau.
This huge glass and aluminum edifice, shaped like a giant cylinder, is the nerve center of French radio. It is a statistician's delight – ½ km (⅓ mile) in circumference, with 3,500 personnel, 58 studios and 1,000 offices. Architecturally, it may leave the visitor cold.

Its main attractions for the public, however, are the extensive **museum of the history of radio and television**, well worth a visit, and the concerts and shows which are held here on a regular basis.

Rivoli, Rue de ☆
*1er and 4e. Map **8**, **9**, **10**&**11**. Metro Hôtel-de-Ville, Châtelet, Louvre, Palais-Royal, Tuileries, Concorde.*
Like so many long Parisian thoroughfares, the Rue de Rivoli begins with one personality and ends with another. It starts at the *Place de la Concorde* and runs down beside the *Tuileries* and the *Louvre* in a long, uniform colonnade with many smart shops and an elegant café or two – a place for promenading in style. This section was laid out between 1800–35, and it was stipulated that the facades must not be disfigured by any placards or signs.

Beyond the Louvre, the street becomes progressively less formal as it wends its way past the *Hôtel de Ville* and on into the *Marais*. It ends, however, not with a whimper but with a bang, with the marvelous facade of the church of **St-Paul-St-Louis** (see *Marais*).

Rodin, Musée ★

*Hôtel Biron, 77 Rue de Varenne, 7e ☎ 705-01-34. Map **13**I5 to garden if with children Open 10am–6pm. Closed Tues. Metro Varenne.*

Auguste Rodin (1840–1917) is widely considered to be the greatest sculptor of the 19thC. You will see why when you visit this museum, housed in a splendid 18thC mansion near *Les Invalides*. It is impossible not to marvel at the way in which Rodin magically transformed stone, clay or bronze into the living tissue of human emotion and experience. Take, for example, his famous work, *Le Baiser* (*The Kiss*), which powerfully evokes in white marble the tenderness of love between man and woman; or his *Homme qui Marche* (*Walking Man*), which embodies all the urgency and thrust of human aspiration; or *La Cathédrale*, where a pair of hands speaks of piety and contemplation.

In many of Rodin's sculptures the figures emerge from the crude marble as though surfacing from the foam of the sea. This effect is particularly striking in such works as *Adam and Eve*, *L'Aurore* and *La Pensée*. These are all to be found on the ground floor. The exhibits on the first floor include busts of famous contemporaries and studies for such monumental works as *Balzac* and *La Porte de l'Enfer* (*The Gate of Hell*).

The delightful garden surrounding the museum makes an ideal setting for many of Rodin's works. Here we find, among others, casts of his *Balzac*, *Le Penseur* (*The Thinker*), *La Porte de l'Enfer* and *Les Bourgeois de Calais* (*The Burghers of Calais*).

Temporary exhibitions of work by other artists are held in a separate building, formerly a chapel, to the right of the entrance.

The lovely **Hôtel Biron** was built by Gabriel The Elder for a rich wig-maker in 1728 and was subsequently lived in by, among others, Marshal Biron, who was beheaded in 1793. Later the building became a convent and much of the painted and gilt paneling was ripped out by the mother superior, though some has been restored.

At the beginning of this century the building was bought by the state and made available for artists. Rodin himself occupied a ground floor studio from 1907 until his death.

Rue de Rivoli See *Rivoli, Rue de*.

Sacré-Coeur, Basilique † ☆

*35 Rue du Chevalier-de-la-Barre, 18e ☎ 251-17-02. Map **4**C9. Church Dome and crypt Open 6am–10:45pm. Metro Abbesses, Lamarck-Caulaincourt.*

Subject of countless travel posters and paintings, the Sacré-Coeur has acquired the status of a visual cliché. However, seen afresh, in its superb setting on *Montmartre*'s hill, the Butte, it has stunning impact and beauty, whether glimpsed from a train drawing into one of the northern stations or revealed suddenly around a corner in one of the old streets that surround it.

The church rose, like a phoenix, from the ashes of the Franco-Prussian War of 1870. As a reaction to the despair aroused by France's defeat, a national vow was adopted in 1873 by parliament to erect a church in Paris as a symbol of contrition and a manifestation of hope. A competition was held and there were 78 entries. The winner was an architect named Abadie, with a Romano-Byzantine design. The first stone was laid in

1875 and the cathedral was completed by 1914, but the First World War delayed consecration until 1919. Since 1885, worshippers have kept up perpetual adoration before the high altar, continuing night and day even through the Nazi occupation.

The material used for the church was Château-Landon stone, which hardens and whitens with age – notice how much grayer the stonework of the interior is compared with the gleaming exterior. The design is not to everyone's taste, but many find the outline of its five beehive-like domes pleasing.

Approach the church by the long flight of steps from the S (you can go part of the way by funicular railway). This way you get the full impact of the main facade with its great portico surmounted on each side by equestrian statues of *St Louis* and *Joan of Arc*. The bell-tower to the N, higher than the rest of the church, contains one of the largest bells in the world, weighing over 17 ton.

The inside is light and elegantly proportioned. The eye follows the great rounded arching sweeps of stonework, up to the cupola with its clerestory and its two encircling balconies and down again to the nave, coming to rest on the natural focal point of the interior, the great mosaic in the alcove above the high altar. This **mosaic**, one of the largest in the world, depicts Christ with outstretched arms exposing a golden heart, while around him are grouped worshippers including the Virgin, St Michael and Joan of Arc.

The crypt, entered by a stairway from the W aisle, is somewhat gloomy and severe. It contains the church treasury and a number of chapels, the central one possessing a *Pièta* on the altar. By the same stairway one ascends to the dome, with dizzying views down into the church and out over Paris.

St-Denis, Basilique 🏛 ✝ ☆

Pl. de l'Hôtel-de-Ville, St-Denis ☎ 243–00–71. Map ***19****B4*
Open Apr 1–Sept 30 Mon–Sat 10am–6pm, Sun 1pm–6pm; Oct 1–Mar 31 Mon–Sat 10am–4pm, Sun 1pm–4pm. Metro St-Denis-Basilique.

Visitors on their way to Paris from Charles de Gaulle Airport are often surprised to see an imposing cathedral rising out of grim industrial surroundings. It is the Basilica St-Denis, necropolis of the kings of France and precursor of Gothic architecture, which was soon to sweep over Europe.

It was in the 12thC that the learned Abbot Suger, friend of Louis VII, decided to rebuild his church dedicated to the Apostle of France, St Denis. Having been beheaded in Montmartre by the ungrateful Gallo-Romans for trying to bring them Christianity, St Denis walked northwards with his head tucked under his arm until he fell down, on the spot where his church was later founded. The prestige of being buried near the relics of a saint made the church a natural choice for a royal necropolis for all but a handful of French kings and their queens, starting with Dagobert in the 7thC. The tombs and statuary of the kings are as good a reason for visiting St-Denis as the church itself. The tombs are empty however – during the Revolution, 800 royal bodies were pitched into a communal grave in the crypt under the N transept. Luckily the tombs were saved from destruction: the archeologist Lenoir had the foresight to remove them to safety some time earlier.

In the late 13thC Louis IX (St Louis) ordered purely symbolic effigies to be made of all his ancestors back to the

7thC, but, from the death of Philippe The Bold in 1285, likenesses were taken from real portraits. Notice particularly the Renaissance mausoleums of François I and Henry II. Unfortunately, all the tombs are chained off and close inspection is difficult.

The beginnings of lightness, harmony and rational disposition of the elements in the church itself proclaim the spirit of a new age, and the close of the Dark Ages. Elements which had been developed separately were now combined for the first time: the Latin cross plan with radiating pilgrimage chapels, the pointed arch, the ribbed groin vault – look for these facets of Suger's original plan in the ambulatory, apse and facade. The latter has an air of dissymmetry with its pointed Gothic and rounded Romanesque arches and its missing N tower. The facade boasts the first-ever rose window, a feature which was soon to become standard.

Within the church, a further progress toward lightness was made in the next century when the architect Pierre de Montreuil gave the nave, side aisles and chancel an architectural lift that recalls his masterwork, *Sainte Chapelle*.

St-Étienne-du-Mont 🏛 ✝ ☆

Pl. St-Geneviève, 5ᵉ ☎ 354-11-79. Map ***15****K9. Open Mon–Fri 8am–noon, 2–7:30pm, Sun 8am–noon, 3pm–7:30pm. Metro Cardinale-Lemoine.*

Built between 1492–1626, the church is a mixture of styles which defy all the rules of architectural purity. The result is rather like a crazy composite photograph, amalgamating elements from contrasting buildings. Take the main **facade** ☆ for example, with its three pediments piled one on top of the other and combining Classical motifs with a Gothic rose window stuck in the middle. The belfry is similarly eclectic, begun in the medieval style and topped with a little Renaissance dome. Nevertheless, the whole effect is pleasing.

I . . . . bent my steps to the curious church of St-Étienne-du-Mont – the church that hides its florid little Renaissance facade behind the huge Neo-Classic drum of the Panthéon . . . .

Henry James, *Parisian Sketches*, 1875–76

The interior, which preserves greater consistency of style, has some remarkable features, notably the 16thC **roodscreen** ☆ with its delicately pierced stonework and its two flanking spiral stairways. This is the only surviving roodscreen in Paris. Notice also the flamboyant vaulting over the transept, the 5.5m(18ft) hanging keystone, the splendidly ornate organ loft (1630) and the richly carved wooden pulpit (1650). At the W end of the nave is a slab indicating where the Archbishop of Paris, Mgr. Sibour, was assassinated by an unfrocked priest in 1857. Those buried in the church include Pascal and Racine, commemorated by plaques on either side of the entrance to the Lady Chapel.

There is also a chapel to St Geneviève, created in 1803 and containing the stone on which her body had rested in the former abbey church of St Geneviève before her remains were destroyed during the Revolution. All that is left of her body is a bone or two, now preserved in an elaborate reliquary.

Although the church was badly plundered and damaged during the Revolution, it was later skilfully restored and today contains some valuable works of art. Particularly striking is the series of **stained-glass windows** in the cloister.

St-Eustache 🏛 † ☆

*2 Rue du Jour, 1er ☎ 236–31–05. Map **10**H9. Open 8am–6pm. Metro Halles.*

This lovely church, the largest in Paris after *Notre-Dame*, deserves to be better known than it is. For centuries it has stood at the focal point of Parisian history and, until recently, was the local church of the *Les Halles* market. Now it surveys the new *Forum des Halles* and the chaotic building site around it with the solid equanimity of the Middle Ages confronting the transcience of the present day. The site was originally occupied by a small 13thC chapel to St Agnes, which was later rededicated to St Eustace, the 2ndC Roman who, like St Hubert later on, is said to have seen a vision of the Cross between the antlers of a stag. The building as we see it today, with its elegant flying buttresses, took shape between 1532–1640 and is a curious mixture, the form being Gothic, the details Classical.

Many famous names crop up in the history of this church. Cardinal Richelieu, Madame de Pompadour and Molière were baptized in it, and Louis XIV celebrated his first communion here. During the Revolution the church was pillaged, then made a Temple of Agriculture. In 1844 it suffered a worse fate when it was devastated by a fire. Subsequently, it was completely restored by Baltard and today stands as one of the finest of Paris' architectural monuments.

The interior is thrilling, with its exhilarating vertical emphasis. Everything thrusts upwards to the ceiling with its delicate network of ribbed vaulting and elaborately carved bosses. The stained glass is luxurious, and there are some important works of art here, including an early Rubens *Pilgrims at Emmaus* and a sculpture of the *Virgin* by Pigalle on the altar of the Lady Chapel.

One of the church's proudest possessions is its organ, one of the finest in the city, and concerts are held here periodically, carrying on a well-established musical tradition. It was here in 1855 that Berlioz conducted the first performance of his *Te Deum*.

St-Germain l'Auxerrois 🏛 †

*2 Pl. du Louvre, 1er ☎ 260–13–95. Map **9**H9. Open Mon–Sat 8am–5pm, Sun 8:30am–12:30pm, 3pm–5:30pm. Metro Louvre.*

Opposite the E end of the *Louvre* stands this church which embodies a fascinating resumé of medieval architecture. There has been a church on this site since the 6thC when an oratory dedicated to St Germanus was built. The present building is the fourth on the spot and is a combination of five centuries of architectural design.

12thC: the oldest part of the building is the Romanesque belfry behind the transept crossing. It played a somber role during the Wars of Religion when, in 1572, Catherine de Medici ordered the bells to ring out to signal the start of the Massacre of St Bartholomew. Three thousand Huguenots, in town to celebrate the marriage of Henri de Navarre to his cousin Marguerite de Valois, were slaughtered in their beds and thrown from the windows.

13thC: the Gothic ambulatory and chancel, the Lady Chapel on the right and the central portal were all added.

14thC: St-Germain l'Auxerrois became the royal parish church when Charles V transformed the Louvre from fortress to a medieval palace. The nave dates from this century.

15thC: the unusual and Flamboyant Gothic **porch** was built, with its lovely multi-ribbed vaulting.

16thC: the Renaissance came and left its mark on the doorway N of the choir. The late Gothic transept portals were added.

In the 17thC, Versailles was built, the court abandoned the Louvre to the court artists who made their studios there, and St-Germain became their parish church. Many artists, sculptors and poets are buried here: Chardin, Boucher, Nattier, Van Loo, Coysevox, Le Vau, de Cotte, Gabriel, Soufflot, Jodelle, Malherbe. Even today artists and show people come here on Ash Wednesday to celebrate a special mass. Royalists have not been forgotten: every year on Jan 21, the anniversary of his execution in 1793, a mass is said for Louis XVI.

St-Germain-des-Prés 🏛 †

*Pl. St-Germain-des-Prés, 6ᵉ ☎ 325-41-71. Map **9**I8. Open 8am–7:30pm. Closed Mon until 12:30pm. Metro St-Germain-des-Prés.*

The oldest church in Paris stands passively at the hub of the lively *St-Germain Quarter*. Its origin dates back to AD 542 when the Merovingian King Childebert I, son of Clovis, brought back from Spain the tunic of St Vincent and a golden cross said to have been made by Solomon. To receive these relics he built a monastery and church which was at first called the Basilica of St Vincent and St Croix but later came to be named after St Germanus, the Bishop of Paris, who consecrated the church in AD 558 and was buried there. As the burial place of the Merovingian kings and a seat of the great Benedictine order, it became virtually a miniature state in its own right, possessing 17,000ha(42,000 acres) of land, its buildings fortified by towers and a moat fed from the Seine. For centuries it stood in meadows called the Pré aux Clercs.

The church was destroyed twice by the Normans, and its present form dates from the 11thC. During the Revolution the abbey was dissolved and the property subjected to an orgy of vandalism in which the royal tombs and most of the buildings were destroyed, the church itself being turned into a saltpeter factory. Of the once splendid complex of buildings only the church, minus its transepts, and the abbot's palace on the NE side remain.

Except for a few capitals and columns, nothing that can be seen in the church is earlier than 11thC. The interior is an interesting mixture of different periods, with its Romanesque arches, Gothic vaulting and polychrome wall painting by the 19thC artist Hippolyte Flandrin. The works of art in the church include a 14thC Virgin and Child known as *Notre-Dame de Consolation*, and a number of fine tombs, including that of John Casimir, a 17thC king of Poland who became abbot of St-Germain. There are also tombs to two Scottish noblemen, William Douglas and James Douglas, courtiers of Henry IV and Louis XIII respectively.

Beside the church, facing S, is a little garden shaded by chestnut trees, a tranquil refuge from the busy Bd. St-Germain.

St-Germain Quarter

*6ᵉ and 7ᵉ. Map **8**&**9**, **14**&**15**. Metro St-Germain-des-Prés, Rue-du-Bac, Solférino, Mabillon, Odéon.*

The St-Germain district is really made up of two adjacent quarters: St-Germain-des-Prés, consisting roughly of the northern half of the 6e; and the Faubourg St-Germain, comprising the NE section of the 7e. These two areas have their own distinct personalities, complementing each other well.

The former community first grew up around the great medieval monastery and church of *St-Germain-des-Prés*, but for centuries it lay outside the Paris boundaries and remained cut off from the life of the city. Its only link with the Right Bank was a ferry (*bac*) which was reached by what is now called the Rue du Bac. This remained the case until the 17thC when Louis XIV began to extend the *Louvre*, for which purpose stone had to be brought from the quarries at Denfert-Rochereau to the S. The ferry was too slow a means of bringing it across the river, and so the **Pont-Royal** was built, ending the isolation of St-Germain and putting it firmly on the map of Paris. It was, incidentally, also Louis XIV who established the *École des Beaux Arts*, across the river from the Louvre. Later, after the Louvre had become a museum, the bridge known as the Passerelle des Arts (now **Pont des Arts**) was built so that the students could cross the river to look at the works of art. The construction of the Pont-Royal turned St-Germain-des-Prés into a thriving community which soon became a favorite haunt of writers and intellectuals of all kinds.

The Faubourg (suburb) St-Germain is, as the name implies, of more recent origin. During the reign of Louis XIV the aristocracy had been concentrated around the court at Versailles, but under the more relaxed regime of Louis XV they felt able to take up residence in Paris again and chose the plain to the E of *Les Invalides* as the place to build their homes. The result can be seen today in the gracious houses that line such streets as the **Rue de Lille**, the **Rue de l'Université**, the **Rue de Grenelle** and the **Rue de Varenne**. Most of the larger ones have now become government buildings or embassies. The **Hôtel de Matignon** ☆ (*no. 57 Rue de Varenne*) is now the residence of the Prime Minister, while the **Hôtel de Courteilles** ☆ (*at no. 110 Rue de Grenelle*) has become the Ministry of Education. The Rue de Grenelle is also the site of the lovely *Quatre-Saisons* fountain. A few well-heeled families, however, remain in the area, and the atmosphere retains the privileged, inward-looking quality that it has always possessed, whether dominated by aristocrats or civil servants.

The buildings belong to a felicitous period when French architecture had thrown off the Italian influence and blossomed into a light but restrained elegance that was typified by the **Hôtel Biron** ★ at the western end of the Rue de Varenne, which is now the *Rodin* museum and one of the few houses in the area which the public can enter.

Edward Bulwer-Lytton described the Faubourg St-Germain vividly in his novel, *Pelham*: "I love that *quartier*! If ever I go to Paris again I shall reside there . . . . *there*, indeed, you are among the French, the fossilized remains of the old régime – the very houses have an air of desolate, yet venerable grandeur . . . . You cross one of the numerous bridges, and you enter another time – you are inhaling the atmosphere of a past century; no flaunting *boutique*, French in its trumpery, English in its prices, stares you in the face. . . . Vast hotels, with their gloomy frontals and magnificent contempt for comfort; shops, such as shops might have been in the aristocratic days of Louis Quatorze . . . . all strike on the mind with a vague and nameless impression of antiquity; a something solemn even in gaiety, and faded in pomp, appears to linger over all you behold."

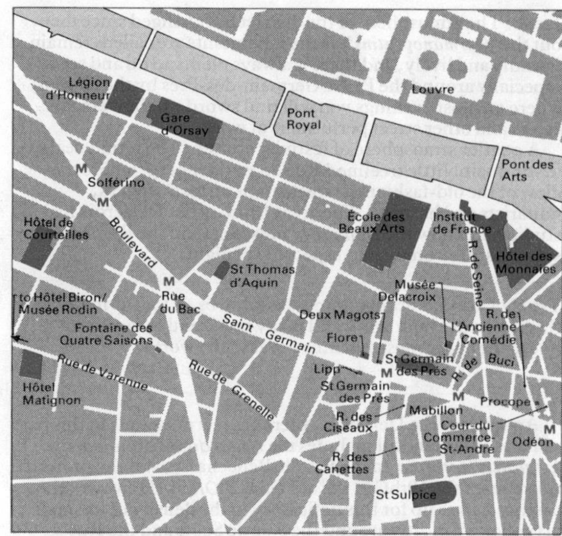

The link between these two areas is the Bd. St-Germain, a great bow-shaped thoroughfare which touches the Seine at each end. Begin a stroll down the boulevard perhaps somewhere near the secluded little Jesuit-style church of **St Thomas d'Aquin**, which lies just off the route to the N. This is still the Faubourg St-Germain, but, approaching the church of *St-Germain-des-Prés* itself, everything becomes busier, more colorful and more cosmopolitan. Turn right opposite the church into the **Rue des Ciseaux** and a little Italian enclave with many pizzerias. This spills over into the **Rue des Canettes** (Duckling St.) which runs up to *St-Sulpice* – notice the ducklings over the doorway of no. 18. Farther E the **Rue Grégoire de Tours** is full of Greek restaurants. This street leads into the **Rue de Buci**. Here and in the neighboring **Rue de Seine** is one of the best food markets in the city of Paris.

Nearby is the church of St-Germain-des-Prés, dominating the intersection of the Bd. St-Germain, the Rue de Rennes and the Rue Bonaparte. This is the heart of the district that has come to be known as the *'Capitale des Lettres'* (Literary Capital), a role which it began to take on in the 17thC when the Comédie Française played in what is now the Rue de l'Ancienne Comédie. The café **Procope**, at no. 13, as popular now as ever, was the haunt of Molière, Corneille, Racine and, in later centuries, Voltaire, Balzac, Verlaine and Anatole France.

Between the wars the quarter was fueled by an influx of writers from *Montmartre* and *Montparnasse* who met habitually in the three great cafés in front of St-Germain-des-Prés: **Flore**, **Lipp** and **Deux Magots**. Publishers, booksellers, painters and art dealers also set up shop there in increasing numbers. After the Second World War, St-Germain became the headquarters of a new generation of intelligentsia, revolving around Jean-Paul Sartre and the Existentialists. In those days they crowded into jazz cellars such as the Tabou in Rue Dauphine, and small bars, such as the Bar Vert in the Rue

Jacob. The atmosphere of the district has changed since then, but the *'Germanopratins'*, as the inhabitants are called, remain friendly and lively, and there is always plenty to do and see, especially around the Pl. St-Germain-des-Prés by the church, where on most evenings you will find sword-swallowers, fire-eaters and other street performers at work.

A gentler atmosphere of festivity is often to be found nearby in the quaint little treelined Rue de Furstenberg, where the glow of the old-fashioned street lamps attracts singers, guitarists and harpists. The great 19thC artist Delacroix had his studio here (now the *Delacroix* museum) and the Romantic spirit is still strongly felt, especially at night.

Truely Paris, comprehending the suburbs, is for the material the houses are built with, and many noble and magnificent piles, one of the most gallant cyttyes in the world.

John Evelyn, *The Diary*

Apart from the Delacroix, there are few museums in this part of Paris – the handful includes the *Hôtel des Monnaies*, the *Légion d'Honneur* in the Rue de Bellechasse, and the projected museum of the 19thC in the old *Gare d'Orsay*. However, the district makes up for this deficiency in the density of its small art galleries (mostly around the Rue de Seine and the Rue Mazarine) and its second-hand bookshops. If you like to be able to drink coffee while you browse try the bookshop-café **Un Moment . . . . en Plus** (*1 Rue de Varenne*). Another cozy retreat for tea or coffee and cakes is the **Salon de thé Tsara** (*11 Rue Bernard Palissy*), just around the corner from Watney's London Tavern, a fairly convincing imitation of an English pub.

There are many little pockets in St-Germain where history can be found. One of them is the **Cours du-Commerce-St-André**, an alley off the Rue St-André-des-Arts. If you look through the windows of **no. 4** you will see part of one of the towers of the medieval city wall built by Philippe Auguste. **No. 9** was the site of the workshop of a German carpenter called Schmidt, who built the first guillotine and tested it out on unfortunate sheep.

Much of the attraction of St-Germain lies in unexpected moments of visual delight: an old shop front, a flourish of carved stonework above a well-proportioned doorway, the glimpse of a cobbled courtyard through an arch. It is an area to be seen at leisure if its many attractions are not to be missed.

St-Honoré, Rue du Faubourg

*8e. Map **7&8**. Metro Ternes, St-Philippe-du-Roule, Madeleine.*

The Parisian equivalent of Fifth Avenue or Knightsbridge, or the Via Tornabuoni, this glossy shopping thoroughfare runs parallel to the *Champs-Élysées*. It is full of gracious houses once occupied by the aristocracy after the district took over from the *Marais* as the fashionable place to live. Today few people, apart from the president (see *Palais de l'Élysée*), actually live here, and the old mansions have found new uses. No. 35 houses the **British Embassy** and no. 96 the **Ministry of the Interior**. Another mansion, at no. 112, disappeared in the 1920s to make way for the discreetly opulent **Hôtel Bristol** (see *Hotels*). For the rest, the street is mostly occupied by smart shops with such famous names as Heim, Hermès, Lanvin, Yves

St Laurent, Courrèges and Helena Rubinstein. Beside the window of the Hermès shop is a jet spurting clouds of perfume at the passers-by, filling the air with the aroma of high living.

St-Joseph-des-Carmes 🏛 †

*70 Rue de Vaugirard, 6ᵉ. Map **14**J7. Metro Rennes, St-Placide.*

This elegant little church forms part of the *Institut Catholique de Paris* complex which stands on the site once occupied by a great Carmelite monastery with vast gardens, many treasures and a priceless library. During the Revolution the monastery was closed, its treasures confiscated and the buildings turned into a prison where, in September 1792, 115 priests and three bishops were massacred. Their bones are buried in the crypt of the church which today possesses a gloomy atmosphere despite its fine works of art including, to the left of the transept, a marble *Virgin and Child* after a model by Bernini.

St-Julien-le-Pauvre 🏛 † ☆

*1 Rue St-Julien-le-Pauvre, 5ᵉ ☎ 354–20–41. Map **10**J9. Open 8:30am–1pm, 2pm–6:30pm. Metro St-Michel, Maubert-Mutualité.*

This enchanting little building, set in a charming garden, **Sq. René Viviani**, facing *Notre-Dame* from the Left Bank, is the oldest complete church in Paris, built between 1170–1240. Only parts of *St-Germain-des-Prés* are older. The beauty of the interior, with its elegantly foliated **capitals**, is all the more potent for its modesty. The **wooden screen** (iconostasis) across the choir is a reminder that this is now a church of the Melchite (Greek Catholic) rite.

From the square there is also an attractive view across the Rue St-Jacques to *St-Séverin*.

St-Martin Canal

*19ᵉ and 10ᵉ. Map **5**&**11**. Metro Jaures, J. Bonsergent, Goncourt.*

Built in the early 19thC, the St-Martin Canal links the *Seine* with the Canal de l'Ourcq and runs through a tunnel for about half its length. It is a working canal, plied by many barges and lined by warehouses and depots, but it has its picturesque moments, when it shakes off the dust and stops work for a pause. Particularly romantic is the stretch between the Sq. Frédéric Lemaître and the Rue Bichat, with its tree-lined banks and hump-backed bridges. Here the atmosphere is not unlike Amsterdam. (You can take a boat trip up the canal with **Quiztour**, *19 Rue d'Athènes, 9ᵉ ☎ 674–75–30/31.*)

St-Michel, Boulevard Called the Boul 'Mich, this is the main artery of the Left Bank. See *Latin Quarter*.

St-Nicolas-des-Champs 🏛 †

*254 Rue St-Martin, 3ᵉ ☎ 272–92–54. Map **10**G10. Open 7am–7pm. Metro Arts-et-Métiers.*

Begun in the 12thC, this church boasts distinguished features from different periods: a Flamboyant Gothic facade and belfry, a fine Renaissance **doorway** on the S side and many paintings of the 17th, 18th and 19thCs. In the St-Michel chapel, a pudgy archangel steps daintily on a pitiful bald-headed devil. The high altar is curiously like a stone bath complete with lion's feet. In short, the church is a mixture of beauty and bathos.

St-Roch 🏛 † ☆

*296 Rue St-Honoré, 1er ☎ 260–81–69. Map **8**G7. Open Mon–Fri 7am–7:15pm, Sat 11am–6:30pm, Sun 7am–noon. Metro Pyramides, Tuileries.*

As Paris grew towards the W in the 17thC, the need arose for a new parish church in the vicinity of the *Palais-Royal*. St-Roch was created, and the author of the *Grand Siècle*, Louis XIV himself, laid the first stone in 1653. The interior is marked by some of the great creative personalities which make Louis' century alive to us today. There is the tomb of *André Le Nôtre*, a kind old man, friend to Louis XIV and the first gardener to make history with the park of Versailles. He also created the nearby *Tuileries*. Other tombs include those of the playwright Corneille and the philosopher Diderot.

The church itself was designed by some of the most important architects of the 17thC, notably Jacques Lemercier, and work was prolonged into the 18thC, making it a combination of Classical and Baroque elements, with a Jesuit-style facade designed by de Cotte in 1736.

Unlike the Gothic churches of Paris, the church is not orientated E–W but N–S because of the terrain. It is also unusually long, with one chapel following another beyond the chancel.

In the nave, one can admire the vaulting which has penetrating arches. This part of the building was financed in 1719 by John Law, the Scottish wheeler-dealer of the Mississippi Bubble. Notice the pulpit in the highly theatrical Baroque style by Challe, 1755. The round domed room after the chancel, the Lady Chapel, was designed by Jules Hardouin-Mansart. Its ceiling portrays the cloudscape of the *Triumph of the Virgin* by J.B. Pierre, 1750; and above the altar, with its nativity group, is a mass of clouds in gilded stucco. Behind the Lady Chapel is the small round Holy Communion Chapel, and behind this, a Calvary Chapel which is under restoration. The church has three organs and excellent acoustics, making it a splendid musical auditorium, and concerts are given here about once a week.

On leaving, one should pause by the facade in which bullet holes can be seen. These are a reminder of a terrible battle which took place in front of the church in 1795. The Republican Convention was under attack by royalists and anarchists, but thanks to the technical skill of the leader of the Republican forces, the Revolution was saved. The leader: a 27-year-old general, Napoleon Bonaparte.

St-Séverin 🏛 † ☆

*Rue des Prêtres St-Séverin, 5e ☎ 325–96–63. Map **10**J9. Open Mon–Fri 11am–1pm, 3:30–7:30pm, Sat 11am–11pm, Sun 9am–8pm. Metro St-Michel.*

Tucked away among the labyrinth of narrow streets in the *Latin Quarter* to the E of the Bd. St-Michel, St-Séverin is one of the best cherished medieval churches in the city, possessing a quiet magic all of its own. The church is named after two saints named Séverin: a hermit who once lived on the site in an oratory dedicated to St Martin, and a namesake of the same era who was Abbot of Agaune. The present building was begun in the early 13thC and much altered and enlarged in the 15thC when it was stamped with the so-called 'Flamboyant' (flame-like) style which can be seen in the shape of the stonework in the **stained-glass windows**. The double **ambulatory** ☆ with its forest of columns, one of them with twisted veins, is particularly fine.

What the church lacks in size it makes up for in the perfection of its proportions and the delicacy of its decoration. Every arch, column, piece of ribbed vaulting and lozenge of stained glass sings out in joyful harmony. Perhaps this is why it is such a wonderful place in which to listen to music – don't miss a concert here if you get the chance. The only discordant note is the ungainly Baroque touch given to the chancel in the 18thC when part of the arcade was rounded and faced with false marble – the effect is that of a nun wearing an ostrich-feather hat.

Adjoining the church to the S is a little garden shaded by trees and bordered on two sides by the arcades of the former charnel house. Standing in the garden (possible during concerts), one feels one is in a time warp as beyond its cloistered calm stands the neon-lit front of a brash restaurant in the street outside.

St-Sulpice 🏛 ✝ ☆
*Pl. St-Sulpice, 6ᵉ ☎ 633–21–78. Map **15**J8. Open Mon–Fri 6:30am–7:30pm, Sat, Sun 6.30am–8pm. Metro St-Sulpice.*

Unlike many of the other great churches of Paris, this one does not form part of an imposing townscape. It looms unexpectedly out of the maze of narrow streets to the N of the *Luxembourg, Palais et Jardin*. Starting life as a modest medieval church dedicated to St Sulpicius, the 16thC Archbishop of Bourges, it was reconstructed in a piecemeal fashion between the years 1655–1788 by six different architects, the essential Classical form being the work of the Florentine Giovanni Servandoni. The result is not the hodge-podge that one might expect, but a grand and harmonious whole, apart from the unmatching towers over the portico with its two tiers of columns.

During the Revolutionary period the church became a Temple of Reason, then of Victory. In November 1799 it was the scene of a sumptuous banquet in honor of Napoleon.

Its interior houses vast recesses of space and the stillness is trapped beneath a great weight of stone. There are many interesting objects in the church, including two enormous shells serving as holy-water stoups, with rock-like bases sculpted by Pigalle. Another feature worth noticing is the bronze meridian line running from a plaque set into the floor of the S transept to a marble obelisk in the N transept. The sunlight, passing through a window in the S transept, strikes the line at different points to mark the equinoxes and solstices. The **Lady Chapel**, at the E end of the church, is heavily ornate, with a *Virgin and Child* by Pigalle floating above a cascade of plaster clouds. Don't miss the **murals** by Delacroix in the side chapel immediately to the right of the main door. The one depicting Jacob struggling with the Angel is particularly compelling. The splendid organ, with its 6,588 pipes, is one of the largest in the world, and organ recitals are given here frequently.

Sainte Chapelle 🏛 ✝ ★
*4 Bd. du Palais, 4ᵉ ☎ 354–30–09. Map **10**I9 ✗ Open Apr 1–Sept 30, 10am–6pm, Oct 1–Mar 31, 10am–5pm. Metro Cité.*

It is hard to describe the beauty of this church without hyperbole; its interior is one of the most thrilling visual experiences that Paris affords. Formerly adjacent to a palace of the medieval kings, it now stands hidden away in a side courtyard of the *Palais de Justice* on the *Ile de la Cité*. It was built by Louis IX (St Louis) in the 1240s to house relics believed to be the Crown of Thorns and a portion of the True Cross – these cost the king more than the church itself. They were kept in a tabernacle on a platform over the high altar, and on feast days St Louis would take out the Crown of Thorns and hold it up before his courtiers and the public. The relics are now kept in *Notre-Dame*.

When the Revolution came, the church suffered the indignity of being turned into a flour shop, then a club and finally a storage place for archives. Under the *Commune* in 1871 it narrowly escaped destruction by fire.

The building has an unusual 'double-decker' construction with two chapels, one above the other. The upper one, dedicated to the Holy Crown and the Holy Cross, was intended only for the king and his retinue. The lower one, dedicated to the Virgin Mary, was for the staff of the chapel and certain officials of the court.

Enter by the rather dark **lower chapel**, its low ceiling supported by columns painted in the 19thC. From here mount a spiral staircase to the **upper chapel** ★ and emerge into a soaring chamber where one is dazzled by the jeweled light that pours through the enormous **stained-glass windows** ★ on every side. The remarkable effect of lightness was achieved by the then revolutionary technique of supporting the roof on buttresses.

The window to the left of the entrance depicts scenes from Genesis. The remainder, taken clockwise, show more Old Testament events as well as the story of Christ. The next to last window is devoted to St Helena and the True Cross, together with St Louis and the relics of the Crucifixion. Finally, the splendid Flamboyant rose window on the W shows scenes from the Apocalypse.

Sainte Chapelle and its neighbor, the *Conciergerie*, present a striking contrast. The latter represents the baseness and cruelty of the Middle Ages; the former embodies all that was God-seeking in the medieval world.

Salpêtrière, Hôpital

Bd. de l'Hôpital, 13ᵉ. Map ***16****L11. Metro St-Marcel.*

'*Les Invalides* with a gentler voice' could be the description of this sprawling hospital in SE Paris. It stands on the site of a former factory for gunpowder – which is 75 percent saltpeter, hence the name. Built by Louis XIV to a design by Le Vau as a refuge for beggars, it became a hospital, an asylum for the insane, a house of correction for prostitutes and a prison. The inmates were often treated brutally, but towards the end of the 18thC the Salpêtrière pioneered a more humane treatment of the insane, and today it has a justifiably distinguished reputation in the field of neurology and neuro-psychiatry (Freud's teacher Charcot did research there), and as a general hospital.

The main **facade**, with its central domed **St-Louis chapel** which was designed by Libéral Bruand, is one of the most majestic in Paris.

Sculpture, Musée en Plein Air *(Open Air Sculpture Museum)*

Quai St-Bernard, 5ᵉ. Map ***16****K11* 🎫 *Open daily. Metro Jussieu, Gare d'Orléans-Austerlitz.*

If you are tired of the *Venus de Milo* and the like and want to see sculpture that is aggressively modern, you will find plenty of it at this open-air museum, opened in 1980 and situated in a riverside park near the *Jardin des Plantes*. There is a permanent display, and temporary exhibitions are also held here.

Seine

Lovers, painters and songwriters have for so long made the Seine their own that it is easy to forget the vital role that the river has played in Paris' history as an artery of trade and a strategic route since Roman times. In fact, without the Seine there would be no Paris. It is not for nothing that the badge of Paris depicts a boat, for the men who operated the river trade were for centuries the leading citizens of the town, and it was their corporation that formed the municipal administration in the Middle Ages.

Parisians often measure the river's waterlevel by looking at the statue of the *Zouave* (an Algerian soldier of the Second Empire) which stands at the E side of the Pont de l'Alma. When the Zouave has his feet in the water it is a sign that the river is getting dangerously high. In the notorious floods of 1910 the water reached his chin.

The Seine provides some of the most beautiful riverscapes in the world. To get to know the river at close hand, walk along the riverside path (see *Walks* in *Planning*) or take a trip on one of the famous Bateaux-Mouches which leave regularly from the Pont de l'Alma.

Sewers See *Égouts*.

Sorbonne

Rue Sorbonne, 5e. Map ***15****J9. Metro Maubert-Mutualité, Luxembourg.*

The imposing buildings of the Sorbonne, which dominate the center of the *Latin Quarter*, testify to the long and distinguished history of this world-famous university. Founded in 1253 by Louis IX's (St Louis) confessor Robert de Sorbon, it started life as a college for 16 poor theological students but rapidly grew into a powerful body which had its own government, laws and jurisdiction – virtually a state within a state. In the 17thC its chancellor, Cardinal Richelieu, commissioned the architect Jacques Lemercier to reconstruct the college buildings and add the magnificent domed Jesuit-style **church**, the interior of which can, unfortunately, be seen only during temporary exhibitions.

The university was closed during the Revolution and then re-opened by Napoleon in order to enter a new lease of life as the premier university of France. Alas it no longer exists as a university in its own right. After the student riots of 1968, in which it played a key role, the Sorbonne became merely part of the University of Paris with its multitude of buildings scattered over the city.

However, the glory of the past still clings to the buildings: the great courtyard with its **superb sundial** surmounted by a relief of Apollo in his chariot; the Baroque library possessing over 1.5 million volumes; and the ornate lecture rooms with their numerous murals.

It is amusing to walk around and rub shoulders with the students. They no longer talk Latin, as they did in the days when the name 'Latin Quarter' was born, but they are heirs to an illustrious tradition.

Tour Eiffel *(Eiffel Tower)* 🏛 ★
7ᵉ. Map ***12****H3* 🎫 *stages 1 and 2* 🎫 *stage 3 to top* ☕ *Stages 1 and 2 open Mon–Sat Nov 1–Mar 31, 10:30am–11pm, 6pm Sun; Apr 1–Oct 31 daily 10am–11pm. Stage 3 open summer 10am–6pm; closed mid-Nov to mid-Mar. Metro Trocadéro, École Militaire.*

The controversy which once raged over this world-famous tower has long since died down, and it has become universally accepted as the unofficial symbol of Paris. The reason why it was built has been almost forgotten: to commemorate the centenary of the French Revolution in 1889. Those who think that Gustave Eiffel's design is bad enough should remember that it was one of 700 submitted for a competition in which rival proposals included a gigantic lighthouse capable of illuminating the entire city, and a tower shaped like a guillotine to honor the victims of the Reign of Terror. Fortunately Gustave Eiffel's design was unanimously accepted, and the iron tower was completed in time for the centenary and the World Exhibition of the same year. It rose 300m(984ft) and was a miracle of engineering, comprising 9,700 tons of material. Today its height, including aerials, is 320.75m(1,052ft).

Whenever we think of the city, we do well to remember Mirabeau: "Paris is a sphinx; I will drag her secret from her", but in this neither he nor any man has succeeded.

Hilaire Belloc, *Paris*

At first it was widely reviled. The writer Huysmans scornfully called it a "hollow candlestick," and a group of distinguished Parisians published a manifesto declaring it a "dishonor to Paris." Many advocated its demolition, but it was saved by the First World War when it became an important military radio and telegraphic center. In 1964 it was classified as a national monument.

The journey to the summit is made in three stages. The first and second platforms of the tower, which can be reached by elevator or stairs, support restaurants and souvenir shops. The third and top platform, which can be reached only by elevator, has a bar, souvenir shops and the office in which Eiffel worked, recently restored. The superb **panorama** ★ over the city can be viewed from behind glass or from a balcony.

The tower has witnessed some strange scenes in its history. One man died trying to fly from it with artificial wings; in 1923 a daredevil journalist succeeded in riding a bicycle down from the first floor; and in 1954 it was scaled by a mountaineer. However, most people climb it for the view or simply to be able to say that they have been right up to the top of the famous Eiffel Tower. (Presently undergoing reorganization.)

Tour Montparnasse *(Montparnasse Tower)*
Centre Maine-Montparnasse, 37 Av. de Maine, 14ᵉ ☎ *538-52-56. Map* ***14****L6* 🎫 ☕ *Open Oct 1–Mar 31, 10am–10pm, Apr 1–Sept 30, 9:30am–11:30pm. Metro Montparnasse-Bienvenue.*

Opened in 1973, this 200m(656ft) high tower, with its adjacent shopping center, is regarded as one of the worst atrocities ever inflicted on Paris, a sad relic of Pompidou's misguided attempts to 'modernize' the French capital.

It rises like a vast black tombstone from the center of *Montparnasse*, dominating the skyline from almost every part of the city and creating a discordant element in the otherwise human scale of central Paris. Fortunately the law has now been changed to prohibit buildings of this and similar height in the city.

It must be admitted, however, that the view from the top of the tower is spectacular and interestingly different from the one afforded by the *Eiffel Tower*. The fifty-sixth floor has a viewing gallery with a bar and a good restaurant. You can also go right up on to the flat roof of the building.

The adjacent **Maine-Montparnasse** shopping center is a multi-level complex containing shops, restaurants and squash courts. It is linked to the tower by a vast bleak podium, which makes a good place for roller-skaters.

Tour St-Jacques *(St Jacques Tower)*
*Sq. St-Jacques, 4ᵉ. Map **10**I9. Metro Châtelet.*
This curiously haunting edifice, rising out of a little park off the *Rue de Rivoli*, is all that remains of the medieval church of St-Jacques-la-Boucherie, once a starting point for pilgrims setting out for the shrine of St James of Compostella in Spain. The church was demolished in 1802, but the bell-tower was spared to be used for dropping globules of molten lead in the manufacture of shot. It was later bought by the City of Paris and restored and now serves as a meteorological station. At the base sits a statue of *Blaise Pascal* who, in 1647, carried out the first meteorological experiment with a barometer at the summit.

Transports Urbains, Musée des *(Urban Transport Museum)*
*60 Av. de Sante-Marie, 94160 St Mandé ☎374-73-63. Map **19**D5 ▣ ✗ for groups. Open Sat, Sun, Apr 15–Oct 31, 2:30–6pm. Closed weekdays. Metro Porte-Dorée.*
What are a Glasgow corporation tram and a London trolley bus doing in a Paris suburb? Answer: they are part of an intriguing museum devoted to urban public transport vehicles, from horse-drawn buses to metro carriages, housed in a former RATP bus depot and run entirely by an amateur association. Its members are very willing to share their enthusiasm with any visitors. You will find plenty here to stir nostalgia, including the old Parisian buses with platforms at the back.

Tuileries ☆
*1ᵉʳ. Map **8**H7. Metro Tuileries.*
If you want to see French formal gardening at its most elegant, you need go no further than the Jardin des Tuileries, laid out by Louis XIV's gardener, Le Nôtre, and occupying a splendid site bounded by the *Louvre*, the *Seine*, the *Place de la Concorde* and the *Rue de Rivoli*, with the *Jeu de Paume* and *Orangerie* museums on raised terraces at the western end. The central avenue, with its two ponds, is dramatically aligned with the *Champs-Élysées* and the Louvre.

There seem to be almost as many statues in the gardens as there are trees: ancient gods and goddesses, allegorical figures of rivers and the seasons, and a bust of *Le Nôtre* himself.

However, contrasted with the gaiety of the gardens is the tragic specter of the vanished Tuileries palace, which once ran N–S between the two projecting western pavilions of the Louvre, with the *Arc de Triomphe du Carrousel* forming the entrance to its courtyard. Queen Catherine de Medici built the palace in the 16thC but never lived there because her astrologer warned her not to, and subsequently an evil spell seemed to afflict the building. It witnessed violent and dramatic events, such as the escape of Louis XIV and his family across the gardens in 1792, the massacre of the Swiss Guards at the same time, and the riots which led to the departure of Charles X in 1830 and of Louis-Philippe in 1848. Finally, it was sacked and burned by the *Communards* in 1871.

At Paris I took an upper apartment for a few days in one of the hotels on the Rue de Rivoli; my front windows looking into the garden of the Tuileries (where the principal difference between nursemaids and the flowers seemed to be that the former were locomotive and the latter not).

Charles Dickens, *The Uncommercial Traveller*, 1861

A well-known legend stated that on the eve of each catastrophe the occupier of the palace would see an apparition known as the 'Red Man of the Tuileries,' said to be the ghost of a skinner who had been murdered on the orders of Catherine de Medici and had vowed to haunt the building until its destruction. Today, however, the spirits that haunt the Tuileries are entirely benevolent, and riotous mobs have given way to pram-pushing mothers, children with toy boats and strolling couples.

UNESCO Building

*7 Pl. de Fontenoy, 7e ☎ 577-16-10. Map **13**J4 for exhibitions for performances for groups by prior arrangement Closed Sat, Sun. Metro Ségur.*

This Y-shaped structure must have seemed daringly modern when it was opened in 1958, but now it has a rather old-fashioned look. In the grounds the black metal Alexander Calder mobile and Henry Moore's *Figure in Repose* add to the period flavor, as does the rather unattractive Picasso mural in the interior. They are security-conscious here, so one cannot just walk in and look without being organized, but there are regular exhibitions which the public can attend, and the main assembly chamber is often used for spectacles ranging from circuses to piano recitals. The atmosphere is lively and international.

Val-de-Grâce † ☆

*1 Pl. Alphonse-Laveran, 5e ☎ 329-12-31. Map **15**L9. Church open 8am-6pm; museum 10am-noon, 2pm-5pm, 4pm on Fri. Closed Sat, Sun. Metro Port-Royal.*

One of the great architectural treasures of Paris, the Val-de-Grâce hides its light under a bushel, tucked away as it is down the Rue St-Jacques. Anne of Austria, wife of Louis XIII, installed a Benedictine convent here in 1622 which she used as a retreat. The buildings still remain, including the superbly proportioned **cloister**. Later she added the church in thanksgiving for the birth of a son, the future Louis XIV, after 23 childless years of marriage; the young king himself laid the first stone of the building.

The church, in the Jesuit style, has many beautiful features including a **cupola** ☆ painted with frescoes by Mignard, an unusual six-columned baldachin over the altar, and an attractive sculpted ceiling, the pattern of which is reproduced in the floor tiles.

In the Revolution the convent was turned into a military hospital, which it remains to this day. The museum in the cloister displays documents and objects relating to great French military physicians, and shows, by means of models and equipment, the various ways in which wounded soldiers were treated before the Second World War. The Val-de-Grâce stands in an area devoted to medicine, with its large hospital and various medical institutions.

Vendôme, Place 🏛 ★

*1er. Map **8**G7. Metro Tuileries.*

Few squares in the world convey such an impression of effortless opulence and wealth as this one. Built under Louis XIV to a design by Jules Hardouin-Mansard, it presents a uniform facade of the utmost beauty of proportion: an arcade at ground level, then Corinthian pilasters rising through two stories, topped by a roof with dormer windows. The keystones over the arches are carved with Bacchanalian faces, each one bearing a different expression like a ring of revelers at some expensive feast. This jolly throng has witnessed many dramatic events in the square. The statue of *Louis XIV*, which stood in the center, was destroyed during the Revolution and later replaced by a bronze column commemorating Napoleon's victories in Germany and modelled on Trajan's column in Rome. This monument was pulled down during the *Commune* in 1871 but later re-erected. It is surmounted by a statue of *Napoleon*.

Besides numerous financiers and aristocrats, the square housed such colorful characters as the Austrian F.A. Mesmer, inventor of mesmerism, who held sessions of 'animal magnetism' at **no. 16**, and Chopin, who died at **no. 12**. Today the square is occupied mainly by offices and expensive shops. The **Ministry of Justice** is at nos. 11 and 13, and the luxurious **Ritz** (see *Hotels*) at no. 15. You will also find here banks, jewelers and art dealers. Like a beautiful woman grown used to riches, the Place Vendôme has an aloofness that does not invite closer acquaintance – unless, of course, you happen to be very well-heeled.

Victor Hugo Museum See *Hugo, Victor, Musée*.

Vincennes

*Map **19**D5 ✉ ☎ keep and chapel. Open 10–11:15am, 1:30–5:15pm, 4:30pm in winter. Closed Tues. Metro Château-de-Vincennes, RER Vincennes.*

The Château de Vincennes is made up of a series of buildings of different periods, parts of which have served at various times as a royal residence, prison, porcelain factory and arsenal. The main entrance is approached across a vast moat, now overgrown with grass, and the whole place has a rather forbidding aspect which mirrors its grim history. Henry V of England died of dysentery here in 1422, and in 1944 it was the scene of the execution of 26 members of the Resistance by the Nazis who, for good measure, blew up part of the castle and set one of the pavilions on fire. The **keep** ☆ or *donjon* is the only medieval one in the environs of Paris and houses the **museum of the Château**.

Opposite the keep is a Gothic chapel, the **Sainte Chapelle**, modeled on the one of the same name on the *Ile de la Cité*. It has some fine stonework and **stained-glass windows**. Both chapel and keep can only be seen with a guide. To the S of the keep and chapel are two 17thC **pavilions** facing each other across a courtyard. Louis XIV spent his honeymoon in one of these buildings in 1660, but evidently this did not endear the château to him for he subsequently preferred to spend his time at his other residences.

The restoration of the château was begun on the order of Napoleon III and continued spasmodically for a century. It is now complete.

Bois de Vincennes ★

This great open space of woodland to the SE of Paris is one of the most important of the city's lungs. Enclosed in the 12thC as a royal hunting ground, it was made into a park for the citizens of Paris by Louis XV and was given to the town by Napoleon in 1860. Since then, many inroads have been made into it, and much of the greenery has been lost. In recent years, however, the municipality has started to reclaim some of the lost parkland; thousands of trees have been planted and new avenues laid out.

If you are lucky enough to have lived in Paris as a young man, then wherever you go for the rest of your life, it stays with you, for Paris is a moveable feast.

Ernest Hemingway to a friend, 1950

Though not as fashionable as the *Bois de Boulogne*, this park contains just as many features of beauty and interest. Starting at the château and traveling clockwise, you come first to the **floral garden** (*open 9:30am–6 or 7:30pm*), an attractively laid out garden, which is planted with an interesting variety of flora and including a small lake, riding stables, a children's play area and restaurant. Flower shows are held in the Bois de Vincennes regularly.

Nearby are the **Minimes Lake** with three islands, a restaurant and boating facilities, and the garden of the **School of Tropical Agronomy**, with its oriental touches and its **temple** commemorating the Indo-Chinese killed in the First World War.

Turning S you come to the **Breuil School of Horticulture**, with more lovely gardens and an arboretum, and beside it the

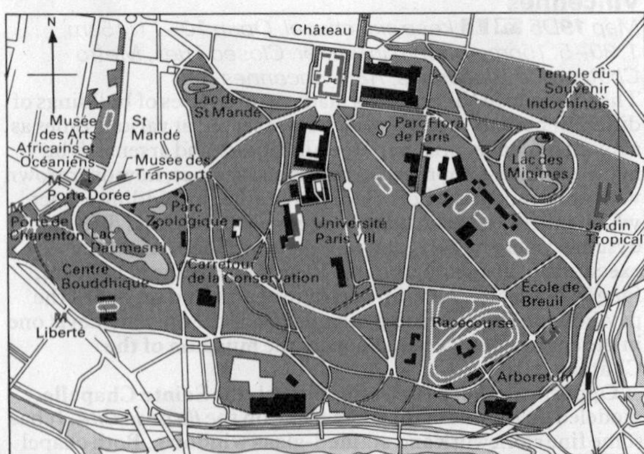

Vincennes **trotting and cycling tracks**.

A walk E through the woods will bring you to the **Daumesnil Lake**, a popular boating place with a plush café-restaurant on one of its two islands. Near the lake is the **Buddhist Center**, the temple of which contains the largest effigy of Buddha in Europe, made of fiberglass and impressively covered with gold leaf.

On the opposite side of the lake is the **zoological park**, the largest of the Paris zoos (*open 9am–5:30 or 7pm*). Here you can see elephants, bison, kangaroos, peacocks and many other animals and birds roaming in natural-looking surroundings. There are two cafés and a huge artificial rock from the top of which you have an excellent view over the Bois to the E and Paris to the W.

Don't try to see the whole of the Bois de Vincennes in one day. It would be a better idea to see the château and the eastern part in one trip, and reserve the zoo and the Daumesnil Lake for another occasion.

See also the *Arts Africains et Océaniens* and *Transports Urbains* museums, which are close by and worth a diversion.

Vosges, Place des 🏛 ★

*4ᵉ. Map **11**/11. Metro St-Paul, Chemin-Vert.*

The oldest square in Paris is also arguably the most beautiful. It was built on the orders of Henry IV who wished to create a square suitable for fêtes and ceremonial occasions, but was not finished until 1612, 2yr after his death. Planned as a single unit of matching facades, it was begun with the **King's Pavilion** on the S side, which is counterbalanced to the N by the **Queen's Pavilion**. The buildings are constructed of red brick and pale gold stone, with an arcade at ground level in which are a number of shops and cafés – try **Ma Bourgogne** at the NW corner, with its tables under the arches.

My Paris is a land where twilight days
Merge into violet nights of black and gold;
Where, it may be, the flower of dawn is cold:
Ah, but the gold nights, and the scented ways!

Arthur Symons, *Poems*

• The Place des Vosges, like the rest of the *Marais* in which it is situated, is rather uncharacteristic of the city of Paris in its solid, quiet elegance. The poet Gérard de Nerval left behind him a vivid description of the houses in the square at sunset which captures the atmosphere beautifully.

"When you see their high windows and brick facades, interspersed and framed with stone, at the moment when they are lit up by the splendid rays of the setting sun, you feel the same veneration as you do before a parliamentary court, assembled in red robes trimmed with ermine."

The square had many distinguished residents. Mme de Sevigné was born at **no. 1 bis**, Richelieu lived at **no. 21**, and Victor Hugo at **no. 6**, now a museum (see *Victor Hugo, Musée*).

In the garden enclosed by the square, where summer fêtes and duels once took place, children now play together and lovers stroll. Fashionable Paris has long since moved westwards, but the Place des Vosges retains an aristocratic patina.

Introduction

Hotel life in Paris can be a mixed delight: it has its hazards, but on the whole it is full of pleasant surprises. Few cities have such a rich and varied choice of hotels, and many of them preserve an old-fashioned style of management that is rapidly dying out elsewhere, as well as cleanliness, courtesy, a high ratio of staff to guests, and often a quintessentially French atmosphere. On the debit side, however, Paris has its share of sleazy hotels and smallness of rooms is a common characteristic, so it is wise to choose carefully and reserve well in advance.

Reservations

Though Paris boasts some 1,300 hotels from the French grade of one star and up, the problems of getting a room on short notice are manifold: it is best to book at least a month in advance (see *Sample reservation letter* in *Words and phrases*). If last-minute booking is unavoidable, you can use the services of the tourist offices found at Orly and Roissy-Charles-de-Gaulle airports, the Gare du Nord, Gare d'Austerlitz, Gare de Lyon and Gare de l'Est; and at the main Tourist Office at 127 Av. des Champs-Élysées, 8e – July and Aug, by the way, are two of the least heavily booked months.

Price

The price categories quoted for each hotel in this book are a rough guide to what you can expect to pay. There are five of these: cheap, inexpensive, moderate, expensive, and very expensive. (See *How to use this book* for the approximate prices these correspond to.) In Paris, 'very expensive' means some of the best hotels in the world, whereas 'cheap' signifies the bare essentials; in the latter, cleanliness, relative comfort and atmosphere are what count. Prices in the intervening categories are dependent on the lavishness of the fittings and amenities, the size of the room and the quality and quantity of the service. Nearly all the hotels listed here have the standard amenities of toilet, bath and/or shower, and bidet. In France, two people occupying one room will pay little more than one.

Tipping

Hotel prices now always include all service and taxes, and sometimes breakfast. If you are particularly pleased with the service you can slip a few more francs into the palm of the chambermaid and/or receptionist.

Meals

French hotel breakfasts are the one blot on the nation's gastronomic copybook: too often individually packed portions of butter and jam, and cardboard croissants are served up, except in topnotch establishments, which charge a fortune for good breakfasts. A breakfast is not usually included in the price, and unless you give priority to breakfasting in bed, you'll probably find better value round the corner from the hotel at a nearby café or *salon de thé*.

Choosing

Apart from price, a convenient location is usually the most important factor in choosing a hotel, so it is best to decide on where you want to stay first and then to pick the most suitable hotel in the area (see list of hotels by *arrondissement*).

In Paris, the two most popular areas are St-Germain and the Champs-Élysées/Rue St-Honoré district. Both are central, and the former is one of the liveliest, yet most historic parts of the city, whereas the latter is the most sophisticated and business-orientated. Becoming increasingly popular since renovation was begun in the 1960s is the *Marais* – the lovely old town houses make ideal small hotels. *Montparnasse*, once Bohemian, has attracted the giant luxury hotels such as the **Sheraton** and **P.L.M. St-Jacques** since the redevelopment began.

If you are booking at the last minute through the Tourist Office's booking service, do not be too put off if all you are offered is hotels in one of the less central of Paris' 20 *arrondissements* – the capital is small (it can be walked across in $1\frac{1}{2}$ hr), and has an excellent metro and bus system.

The selection in this book has been made not only to give a wide choice of price and area, but also with other various priorities in mind: atmosphere, relative quiet and space. Addresses, telephone numbers (telex where appropriate), and nearest metro stations are given, as well as symbols showing which hotels are particularly luxurious or simple and which represent good value. Other symbols show price categories, and give a resumé of the facilities that are available. See *How to use this book* for the full list of symbols. You can deduce the *arrondissement* in which the hotel is situated from the last two numbers of the postcode. When hotels and restaurants are described elsewhere in the book, they appear in bold type.

Hotels classified by arrondissement

1er
Ducs d'Anjou to
Family Hotel
France et Choiseul
Inter-Continental
Lotti
Meurice
Montana-Tuileries
Montpensier to
Ritz
St-James et Albany to
Tuileries to

3e
Parc-Royal to

4e
Deux Iles
Fauconnier
Maubuisson
Vieux Marais to

6e
L'Abbaye St-Germain to
L'Hôtel to
d'Isly
Marronniers to
Pas-de-Calais
Perreyve to
Relais Christine to
St-André-des-Arts
Scandinavia

7e
Lenox to
Montalembert
Pont Royal
Quai Voltaire to
St-Simon
Solférino to
Suède to
Université to

8e
Bradford
Bristol
Crillon
George V
Lancaster
Nova-Park
Plaza-Athénée
Résidence Lord Byron to
Royal Monceau
San Regis

9e
Chopin
Cité Trévise to
Grand Hôtel

10e
Terminus Nord to

14e
P.L.M. St-Jacques to
Sheraton

15e
Hilton
Nikko to

16e
Raphael
Résidence Foch to

17e
Étoile
Regent's Garden to

18e
Central
Résidence Charles-Dullin
Terrass' to

L'Abbaye St-Germain
10 Rue Cassette, 75006 Paris ☎ 544-38-11. Map **14***J7 to 45 45 Metro St-Sulpice.*
Location: In a short, quiet street close to St-Germain-des-Prés and the Luxembourg Gardens. This extraordinary converted 17thC convent shows just what results can be obtained when the ancient and modern are skilfully combined. Contemporary sofas are surrounded by 18thC antiques in the downstairs lobby, while the rooms themselves, some of which have original beams and alcoves, are decorated with successfully unusual color schemes and fabrics. Furthermore, the courtesy and helpfulness of the staff are exemplary. With so much to recommend it, however, it is hardly surprising that it can be extremely difficult to find a room here in peak periods, so be sure to book well in advance.

Bradford
10 Rue St-Philippe-du-Roule, 75008 Paris ☎ 359-24-20. Map 7F4 48 48. Metro St-Philippe-du-Roule.
Location: Next to the Rue du Faubourg St-Honoré, with the Champs-Élysées nearby. Friendliness is one of the best features of this unassuming hotel. The rooms are large and pleasantly furnished, the bathrooms brand new. Also most welcome in an area blighted by heavy traffic is the almost total quiet of the Rue St-Philippe-du-Roule.

Bristol
112 Rue du Faubourg St-Honoré, 75008 Paris ☎ 266-91-45 280961. Map 7F6 211 211 Metro Champs-Élysées-Clémenceau.
Location: In a prime part of one of the most expensive streets in Paris. Heads of government and high-flying diplomats who have an appointment with the President at the Élysée Palace like to stay at the Bristol, which is conveniently situated just down the road. It is also one of Paris' finest hotels – both traditional and luxurious, it is richly decorated with original oil paintings, antiques and oriental carpets. Bathrooms are sumptuous and several are in the Art Deco style. There is a hairdressing salon and massage parlor, conference room, and an excellent restaurant which bears the same name. The private parking lot and swimming pool are marks of distinction shared with very few hotels situated in the centre of the city of Paris.

Central
110 Rue Damrémont, 75018 Paris ☎ 264-25-75. Map **4***B8 43 6. Metro Lamarck-Caulaincourt.*
Location: Near the Rue Ordener behind the Butte de Montmartre. A honeycomb of a hotel, with small and rather noisy rooms and fairly basic facilities, but nevertheless good value in a place that is clean and where the prices are rock-bottom. Not very central, despite the hotel's name, but only a quarter-of-an-hour's stroll from Montmartre.

Chopin
46 Passage Jouffroy, 75009 Paris ☎ 770-58-10. Map **9***F9 38 38. Metro Rue Montmartre.*
Location: In one of Paris' distinctive arcades, close to the Opéra Quarter. It must have occurred to anyone who has wandered through the area of delightful arcades, which branch unobtrusively off the noisy Grands Boulevards, that this would be an ideally traffic-free place to stay in Paris (or live in, for that matter). The charming mid-19thC Hôtel Chopin, in the Passage Jouffroy, fills the bill perfectly, even if the majority of its rooms are rather small and cramped.

Cité Trévise
16 bis Cité de Trévise, 75009 Paris ☎ 770-42-07. Map **9***E9 to 23 6 Closed Jan 15–Feb 5. Metro Cadet.*
Location: Between Rue Bleue and Rue Richer, near the Folies Bergère and close to the Grands Boulevards. As quiet as the arcades (see **Chopin** above), and in the same area of Paris are the *cités* (mews), fascinating and mostly unspoiled relics of a more leisurely age. The delightful Cité Trévise is a haven of tranquillity centered on a leafy little square. Overlooking it is this simple, friendly and cozy hotel, enlivened by bright floral wallpaper.

Crillon
10 Pl. de la Concorde, 75008 Paris ☎ *296–10–81* *290204. Map* **8**G6 *201* *201* *Metro Concorde.*

Location: Overlooking one of the most famous townscapes in the world, at the hub of the Right Bank. The Crillon has long been established as one of the great classic hotels of the world. Its air of quiet excellence is symbolized by the fact that it displays no ostentatious signs, only its name in discreet letters over the entrance to its magnificent 18thC premises in one of the best positions of any hotel in Paris. Formerly an aristocratic mansion, it was turned into a hotel in 1907, and the sumptuous decor and formal inner courtyard were preserved. Here you will find the last word in elegance and controlled good taste along with a good restaurant, a famous bar and a clientele that includes official guests of the French government and the occasional film star shunning the company of other film stars. The only drawback is that traffic noise, albeit muffled, from Pl. de la Concorde creeps insidiously into many of the bedrooms.

Deux Iles
59 Rue St-Louis-en-l'Ile, 75004 Paris ☎ *326–13–35. Map* **10**J10 *17* *17. Metro Cité.*

Location: On the Ile St-Louis, the smaller and quieter of the Seine's two islands, in the heart of Paris. The Hôtel des Deux Iles occupies a 17thC building in the quiet street that runs the length of the Ile St-Louis. The rooms could not by any stretch of the imagination be described as large, but they do have delightfully tiled bathrooms; the bar in the cellar, with its open fire and comfy sofas, is the ideal place for a *rendezvous galant* on a cold winter's evening.

Ducs d'Anjou
1 Rue Ste-Opportune, 75001 Paris ☎ *236–92–24. Map* **10**H9 *to* *38* *33. Metro Les Halles.*

Location: In the Halles/Beaubourg area. This hotel is a pleasant if unremarkable base from which to explore the vicinity which includes the Forum des Halles, that curious cross between a mega-shopping center and a meeting place for people of every description. The rooms are very quiet, if somewhat dark, and the hotel is situated on the very pretty Pl. Ste-Opportune.

Étoile
3 Rue de l'Étoile, 75017 Paris ☎ *380–36–94* *642028. Map* **6**E3 *25* *25* *Metro Ternes.*

Location: Close to the Arc de Triomphe. A small, intimate hotel where you can live like a prince, almost for a song, with color TV, minibar, direct-dial telephone, thick wall-to-wall carpets and functional modern furniture in your room, plus a bar and a mini-library in the lobby.

Family Hotel
35 Rue Cambon, 75001 Paris ☎ *261–54–84. Map* **8**G7 *25* *10. Metro Madeleine.*

Location: In the fashionable area between the Rue St-Honoré and La Madeleine. Surprisingly for such a luxurious area, this hotel is just what its Anglified name suggests – a *hôtel familial*. Run by a friendly and courteous husband and wife, it has a tranquil air and simply furnished but attractive bedrooms. If you want a room with a bathroom, book well in advance.

Fauconnier
11 Rue du Fauconnier, 75004 Paris ☎ *274–23–45. Map* **11**I11 *100 beds. Metro St-Paul.*

Location: In a small street by the Seine, opposite the Ile St-Louis. Like the nearby **Maubuisson**, this is a government-subsidized hotel-hostel, in theory for young people, in a superb 17thC former private house, with beams, original floor tiles, stone flagging and antique furniture. Rooms have anything from two to six beds in them, and although there used to be an upper age limit of 30, anyone willing to share a room with a stranger – or strangers – of the same sex is now welcome. Spotless, friendly, and of course very cheap.

France et Choiseul
239 Rue St-Honoré, 75001 Paris ☎ *261–54–60* *680959. Map* **8**G7 *141* *141* *Metro Tuileries.*

Location: In the smart, fashionable area of the Rue St-Honoré and Pl. Vendôme. An unhurried, timeless air and a courtly, old-fashioned style of management mark out this traditional Paris hotel with its upright Louis XV-style furniture. The rooms are small, but have been carefully modernized, each with its own up-to-date bathroom. There's a pretty patio at the rear.

George V

31 Av. George-V, 75008 Paris 723-54-00 290776. Map 7F4 395 395 Metro George-V.

Location: Just off the Champs-Élysées, in the city's principal business area. Unlike the equally luxurious **Crillon**, with its discreet elegance, the George V is grand and unashamedly lavish. Flemish tapestries, sculptures, ormolu clocks and original paintings (including Renoir's *Le Vase des Roses*) complement the gracious 18thC-style furniture. The hotel has a delightful bar and a lovely inner courtyard, where in summer meals are served amid red umbrellas and masses of potted plants as part of the excellent restaurant, **Les Princes**.

Grand Hôtel

2 Rue Scribe, 75009 Paris 260-33-50 220875. Map 8F7 600 600 Metro Opéra.

Location: On Pl. de l'Opéra. Paris' largest old hotel was designed by Charles Garnier, architect of the Paris Opera House which dominates the view from the front windows. It was recently refurbished, along with the celebrated Café de la Paix adjoining it. The hotel is too vast to have a sharply defined clientele, though because of its location it is naturally a favorite with visiting musicians and singers who are performing at the Opéra. As well as a delightful, centrally placed winter garden, the establishment has well-appointed rooms, a sauna, a sun lounge, a gymnasium, and 17 air-conditioned conference rooms.

Hilton

18 Av. de Suffren, 75015 Paris 273-92-00 200955. Map 12I3 487 487 Metro Champ-de-Mars.

Location: Close to the Seine and the Eiffel Tower. The Paris Hilton, considerably more luxurious and expensive than many others in the Hilton chain, was the first modern hotel built in Paris after the war. By the late 1970s it seemed to be dated, and redecoration was carried out. No expense is spared to provide home comforts for Americans in Paris, from movies on closed-circuit color TV to sweet corn and T-bone steaks flown in from the States.

L'Hôtel

13 Rue des Beaux-Arts, 75006 Paris 325-27-22 270870. Map 9I8 to 27 27 Metro St-Germain-des-Prés.

Location: In the heart of the St-Germain-des-Prés Quarter. A top-notch hotel with the cozy, human proportions of a small 18thC town house – there are antiques everywhere, pink Venetian marble in the bathrooms, and velvet on virtually every surface, from the elevator to the uniforms. The facilities include a winter garden with restaurant and resident pianist, and an intimate cellar bar. You may be given the room containing Mistinguett's own Art Deco furniture, the bedroom (and bed) that Oscar Wilde died in, or one of the two top-floor suites with flower-decked balconies and a view over the church of St-Germain-des-Prés. Fellow guests may include Mick Jagger, Julie Christie or any number of personalities (both real and aspiring) from showbiz, fashion or advertising. This extravaganza is the brainchild of Guy-Louis Duboucheron, who converted it in 1967 from the cheap, sleazy hotel that Oscar Wilde knew. Although he has been accused of charging inflated prices, it is, perhaps, fairer to say that he has merely a shrewd understanding of what his assets are worth.

Inter-Continental

3 Rue Castiglione, 75001 Paris 260-37-80 220114. Map 8G7 500 500 Metro Tuileries.

Location: Close to Pl. Vendôme. The hotel was built in 1878 by Charles Garnier, architect of the Paris Opera House, and also of the **Grand Hôtel**. Several of its amazingly ornate *salons* are now listed as historic monuments. It was completely and intelligently renovated about 10yr ago and, while keeping its original atmosphere almost intact, it now has all the trappings of a modern luxury hotel: air conditioning throughout, color TV in all rooms, 24hr room service, a bar, a discotheque and conference rooms complete with secretaries and interpreters. The Inter-Continental also has a beautiful patio, which is a highly fashionable spot for outdoor eating when the **Rôtisserie Rivoli** serves its meals there in summer. The top-floor rooms afford a majestic view over the Tuileries Gardens.

d'Isly
29 Rue Jacob, 75006 Paris 326-32-39. Map ***9****I8* *37* *26. Metro St-Germain-des-Prés.*
Location: An attractive street on the Left Bank. A St-Germain hotel which caters well to its guests. Converted from a lovely old townhouse it has fresh, well-equipped and comfortable, if small, rooms, new bathrooms and a modern lobby that doubles as a lounge. The d'Isly has smooth and attentive service and a friendly atmosphere.

Lancaster
7 Rue de Berri, 75008 Paris 359-90-43. 640991. Map 7E4 *67* *67* *Metro St-Philippe-du-Roule.*
Location: In a fairly quiet street just off the Champs-Élysées. This haunt of American movie stars and big-time journalists looks and feels more like a smart private house than a hotel. Most of its rooms overlook a charming, flower-filled, statue-studded courtyard. The less fortunate ones on the street side have double-glazing, so a good night's sleep is guaranteed despite the proximity of the 24hr traffic on the Champs-Élysées.

Lenox
9 Rue de l'Université, 75007 Paris 296-10-95. Map ***8****I7* *to* *34* *34. Metro Rue-du-Bac.*
Location: Three minutes' walk from the Bd. St-Germain and the Seine. One of those rare hotels that stands out, not only in its class, but by any standards, because of a special thoroughbred quality. All the bedrooms and the reception area have been furnished and decorated with excellent taste, and the whole atmosphere has a warm elegance. What's more, the staff are extremely friendly, and the service is willing. Light meals will be provided in your room at any time of the day.

Lotti
7 Rue Castiglione, 75001 Paris 260-37-34 240066. Map ***8****G7* *132* *132* *Metro Tuileries.*
Location: Only moments from the Pl. Vendôme and Rue St-Honoré. A luxury hotel of manageable proportions with a subdued, but regal air, the Lotti caters to the high society of many countries, but particularly Britain, Italy and France. The decor is traditional and extremely tasteful, with no two bedrooms the same. The service is quick, efficient and unobtrusive, and an air of calm and sophistication pervades the whole establishment.

Marronniers
21 Rue Jacob, 75006 Paris 354-91-66. Map ***9****I8* *to* *37* *37. Metro St-Germain-des-Prés.*
Location: In the heart of the St-Germain-des-Prés Quarter, on the Left Bank. Mother Nature has a strong hold on this tall hotel, from the profusion of leaves, flowers and birds on the wallpaper and carpets, the fruit on the crockery, and the flower-filled vases to the delightful little garden at the back, with its veranda, white garden furniture, and horse-chestnut trees (which give the hotel its name). There are two cozy lounges in the very old vaulted cellars. To top it all, the prices are as soothing as the service.

Maubuisson
12 Rue des Barres, 75004 Paris 272-72-09. Map ***10****I10* *92 beds* *Metro Hôtel-de-Ville.*
Location: In a tiny street behind St-Gervais-St-Protais church by the Hôtel-de-Ville. This hotel-hostel with dormitories is, in every respect, like the **Fauconnier** (a couple of minutes' walk away) from the 17thC building, original flooring and quiet location to the rock bottom prices.

Meurice
228 Rue de Rivoli, 75001 Paris 260–38–60 230673. Map 8G7 226 226 Metro Tuileries.

Location: Opposite the Tuileries Gardens. Opened in 1816, the Meurice used to receive almost all the crowned heads of Europe. During the German occupation, the governor of Paris, General Von Choltitz, set up his headquarters here. More recently the hotel has been patronized by Salvador Dali, Gulf State Arabs, and other wealthy members of the international set. Recent renovation naturally spared the gilded paneling, tapestries and huge chandeliers, but installed beautiful pink marble bathrooms and air conditioning in every room.

Montalembert
3 Rue Montalembert, 75007 Paris 548–68–11 200132. Map 8I7 61 61. Metro Rue-du-Bac.

Location: On the Left Bank, between the Seine and the Bd. St-Germain. A slightly less expensive alternative to the **Pont Royal** in the same street, the Montalembert is an old school house, converted to make a large, somewhat soulless hotel in the heart of the literary Left Bank. The literary crowd who used to patronize it have, however, decamped in recent years to the **Pont Royal** and other nearby hotels, but it remains a reasonably priced, functional base from which to explore the area. All the rooms have been modernized and have well-equipped bathrooms.

Montana-Tuileries
12 Rue St-Roch, 75001 Paris 260–45–10 210311. Map 8G7 25 25 Metro Pyramides.

Location: Just off the Rue de Rivoli and Rue du Faubourg St-Honoré. If you feel like giving yourself a treat but can't afford the luxury hotels that line the Rue de Rivoli (**Meurice, St-James et Albany, Inter-Continental**), take a few steps down a side-street and try this small but spacious hotel. It has almost all the facilities of its more illustrious neighbors, from color TV and direct-dial telephone to minibar in each room, but it won't cost the earth.

Montpensier
12 Rue de Richelieu, 75001 Paris 296–28–50. Map 9F8 to 43 32. Metro Richelieu-Drouot.

Location: Close to the Palais-Royal and Comédie Française. Occupying a 17thC building that was once the home of a baroness on whom Louis XV bestowed his favors, this hotel has plenty of atmosphere, a grand staircase, and some rooms of quite regal proportions. Others are much more modest, which explains the wide price range. Most rooms overlook a quiet inner courtyard. Another secluded courtyard, but on a totally different scale, awaits the curious visitor at the back of the hotel, where the vast and superbly proportioned courtyard of the 18thC Palais-Royal can be seen.

Nikko
61 Quai de Grenelle, 75015 Paris 575–62–62 260012. Map 12J1 to 784 784 Metro Bir-Hakeim.

Location: On the quais overlooking the Seine, opposite Maison de Radio France. With admirable efficiency, the Japanese moved into the Paris hotel scene and within a mere 4yr the Nikko's restaurant, Les Célébrités, had earned a much-coveted reputation for its excellent foods. The management has changed recently, however, and it remains to be seen whether the standards are maintained. The hotel itself offers all the amenities of a smoothly run international hotel, from streamlined accommodation (with Japanese or western decor), to a clutch of bars, a sauna and a swimming pool. There is also a good Japanese restaurant, the Benkay.

Nova-Park
51 Rue François-1er, 75008 Paris 562–63–64 643–189. Map 7G4 73 73 Metro George-V.

Location: On the corner of Rue Françoise-1er and Rue Pierre-Charron, close to the Champs-Élysées. Paris has been agog at the unrivaled facilities of this recently opened hotel which boasts all the businessman's needs, plus swimming pools, a health and beauty centre, live music, a bridge club and three restaurants run by expert chef Jacky Fréon. All very nice if, like the oil sheiks, you can afford it.

Parc Royal
17 Rue du Parc-Royal, 75003 Paris 887–84–50. Map **11**H11 to 13 10 *Metro Chemin-Vert.*
Location: In the heart of the Marais. In summer one can mistake this tiny Alice-in-Wonderland establishment for a restaurant, as its own pocket-size restaurant opens onto the street, and the hotel entrance itself is unobtrusive. The friendly proprietress has a smile of Carrollian ambiguity, and the dark, twisting stairs and corridors leading to sometimes minuscule rooms resemble a rabbit warren. Perfectly situated for exploring the Marais.

Pas-de-Calais
59 Rue des Sts-Pères, 75006 Paris 548–78–74. Map **8**I7 41 41. *Metro St-Germain-des-Prés.*
Location: On the Left Bank, just off Bd. St-Germain. This labyrinthine hotel was recently given a face-lift, but much of the downstairs furniture, though modern, looks amusingly passé. The best of the rooms (which are more stylishly decorated) overlook a small courtyard notable for its *trompe-l'oeil* trelliswork.

Perreyve
63 Rue Madame, 75006 Paris 548–35–01. Map **14**J7 to 30 30. *Metro Rennes.*
Location: A quiet street near the Luxembourg Gardens. The Jardin du Luxembourg, a pocket of relaxing greenery in the hurly-burly of the Left Bank, is just round the corner from this charming hotel, which was recently renovated with admirable good taste. The rooms are comfortable and the bathrooms, though small and rather cramped, are sparkling clean.

Plaza-Athénée
25 Av. Montaigne, 75008 Paris 723–78–33 650092. Map **7**G4 216 216 *Metro Franklin-D-Roosevelt.*
Location: Near the Seine and the Champs-Élysées, but away from the noise and bustle. Perhaps the most glamorous and elegant hotel of all in Paris, attracting a galaxy of stars, and a particular favorite of wealthy South Americans and Greeks. Afternoon tea can be taken in the elegant long gallery, and there is a beautiful inner patio. Gorgeous period-style suites and attractive bedrooms, superb service (albeit slightly cool toward mere mortals), two celebrity-studded bars and an excellent restaurant, the **Régence-Plaza**.

P.L.M. St-Jacques
17 Bd. St-Jacques, 75014 Paris 589–89–80 270740. Map **15**M8 to 797 797 *Metro Denfert-Rochereau.*
Location: A leafy boulevard near Denfert-Rochereau on the Left Bank. This bustling modern four-star hotel is very convenient for air travelers (and is therefore much appreciated by executives) because it is one of the few places where the Air France bus stops on its way to and from Orly Airport. The vastness of the hotel itself contrasts with the smallness of the rooms, but they are not at all cramped and have all the usual luxury facilities. The P.L.M.'s building also contains three restaurants, a piano bar where the barman specializes in exotic cocktails, a club for parlor games (chess, bridge, backgammon, scrabble, and the like), a hairdressing salon, an Air France bureau and even a movie theater.

Pont Royal
7 Rue Montalembert, 75007 Paris 544–38–27 270113. Map **8**I7 75 75 *Metro Rue-du-Bac.*
Location: In a small street between the river and the Bd. St-Germain. Close to the famous literary publishing house of Gallimard and conveniently situated for the restaurants and charms of the Left Bank, yet only a short walk to the river, Notre-Dame and the Louvre, this hotel – named after the nearby bridge – provides a consistent standard of comfort for visiting publishers and a good base for the tourist who wants a genuinely middle-of-the-road hotel. The rooms, if a little small, are pleasantly furnished and comfortable, each with TV, mini-bar and even safe; the bathrooms

reflect the style and standard of the typical chain (Mapotel) hotel. Service is prompt and straightforward, and reflects the general style. The restaurant, Les Antiquaires, is a safe bet for a business lunch, though there is plenty of more interesting competition nearby. There is an underground parking lot close to the front of the hotel.

Quai Voltaire
19 Quai Voltaire, 75007 Paris 261–50–91. Map ***8****H7 to 32 25. Metro Solférino.*
Location: On the Left Bank overlooking the Seine, opposite the Tuileries Gardens. Twenty-nine of the rooms in this light, bright and unfortunately rather noisy little hotel afford a superb view over the Seine – a view enhanced by the tall French windows. The establishment has a literary past – it was patronized by Charles Baudelaire and Oscar Wilde in their time – and its small, unostentatious bar is a choice meeting place for the lions of modern French literature.

Raphael
17 Av. Kléber, 75016 Paris 502–16–00 610356. Map ***6****F2 90 90 Metro Kléber.*
Location: On one of the avenues radiating from Étoile and the Arc de Triomphe. The smallest of the Parisian *palaces* (luxury hotels), the Raphael has a curiously unreal atmosphere heightened by dark wood paneling, heavy tapestries, thick carpets, and a huge painting of a seascape by Turner. This and its discreet location may be what appeals to the international film stars and producers who stay here regularly. It's also located conveniently close to the film-world's offices, which are clustered round the Étoile and the Champs-Élysées.

Regent's Garden
6 Rue Pierre-Demours, 75017 Paris 574–07–30 640127. Map ***6****D3 to 41 41 Metro Ternes.*
Location: A quiet street in a residential area. The Regent's Garden lives up to its name by possessing a real garden, as opposed to the courtyard found in so many Parisian hotels, complete with statues and fountains. The building itself is typical of the showy *grand bourgeois* architecture of the mid-19thC. Its cavernous rooms, the lofty ceilings of which sport decorative mouldings, are furnished in appropriate style, with brass bedsteads and large mirrors. The bathrooms, on the other hand, are equipped with thoroughly 20thC conveniences. The 17ᵉ may seem a little far from the hub of things, but the Rue Pierre-Demours is in fact only a few minutes' walk from the Arc de Triomphe.

Relais Christine
3 Rue Christine, 75006 Paris 326–71–80 202606. Map ***9****I8 to 51 51 Metro Mabillon.*
Location: A tiny backwater in the heart of the Latin Quarter, close to Pl. St-Michel. The Rue Christine not only boasts an excellent cinema and the **Photogalerie** restaurant, but one of the area's most distinguished and fashionable hotels, the Relais Christine. The 16thC building, once a monastery, became a publisher's book depot among other things before being transformed into a hotel in 1979. Its comfortable, spacious and tastefully decorated rooms, several of which are split-level apartments, are individually furnished with period pieces. Those on the lower floors are a trifle dim although Rm 1 on the ground floor has a stone wall and a fine carved door. Other features include parking in the hotel courtyard, automatic shoe-cleaning machines, and color TV, minibar and direct-dial telephones in all the rooms – which will strike you as only fair when you come to peruse the bill.

Résidence Charles-Dullin
10 Pl. Charles-Dullin, 75018 Paris 257–14–55 290532. Map ***4****D9 74 74 Metro Anvers.*
Location: A quiet little square in Montmartre. The recently-opened Résidence Charles-Dullin, where you can rent one-, two- and three-room flats by the week, is not strictly speaking a hotel. Nevertheless it is an ideal place for the couple or family, for instance, who want to try out the joys of French cooking for themselves: each flat has a fully-equipped

kitchen. Otherwise, the services provided are those of any good quality hotel.

Résidence Foch
10 Rue Marbeau, 75016 Paris 500–46–50 250303 to 16 16 Metro Porte-Maillot.

***Location: In the expensive residential area of the 16*[e]**. This small and exclusive luxury hotel is tucked away in the secluded calm of a tiny street near Paris' millionaires' row, Av. Foch, a minute or two's stroll from the Bois de Boulogne, and very near the excellent **Le Petit Bedon** restaurant. It is furnished with pleasant antiques, has an intimate bar, and includes, among its attractive rooms, a large and brightly lit split-level suite on the top floor.

Résidence Lord Byron
5 Rue de Châteaubriand, 75008 Paris 359–89–98 250302. Map **7**F4 to 26 26. Metro Étoile.

Location: Close to the Arc de Triomphe and Champs-Élysées. One of the quietest and most pleasant places to stay near the Champs-Élysées, which is a minute's walk away, and a must for anyone shunning the sometimes over-fussy service of the area's bigger hotels in the same high class. The furniture and decor are discreet and relaxing. There is an attractive inner courtyard with trelliswork, which many of the rooms overlook.

Ritz
15 Pl. Vendôme, 75001 Paris 260–38–30 220262. Map **8**G7 163 163 Metro Pyramides.

Location: Superbly situated in the exclusive and beautiful Pl. Vendôme. Arguably the most famous hotel in the world, the Ritz lives up to its reputation, seeming to exude luxury, attentiveness and just the right amount of old-fashioned charm. Nor has it rested on its laurels like many other long-famous hotels, but has, in recent years, been carefully and sensitively renovated: the huge and splendid original baths remained, while the telephones were computerized. The benefits of staying at the Ritz are many: kind and unobtrusive service, beautiful period furnishings, a lovely inner garden, several chic bars, and an excellent restaurant, **L'Espadon.**

Royal Monceau
35 Av. Hoche, 75008 Paris 561–98–00 650361. Map **2**E4 200 200 Metro Courcelles.

Location: Between the Arc de Triomphe and the attractive Monceau Park. The best rooms in the quiet, distinguished and pleasantly passé Royal Monceau are, as in many Paris hotels, those that overlook the patio – in this case, a fine, multilevel blue mosaic garden with fountains, trelliswork and striped awnings. In summer the **Royal Monceau** restaurant is one of the most attractive places for outdoor eating. Despite its old-fashioned atmosphere and old-fashioned (that is to say high) standards of service, the Royal Monceau is run along very businesslike lines, and provides numerous facilities for seminars and conferences.

St-André-des-Arts
66 Rue St-André-des-Arts, 75006 Paris 326–96–16. Map **9**I8 35 16. Metro St-Michel.

Location: On the Left Bank, between the St-Germain-des-Prés and Latin Quarters. Fun-loving, amusing clientele and a friendly welcome are what make this establishment memorable; the accommodation itself, unfortunately, is nothing special. The hotel is remarkably well located for exploring the Left Bank.

St-James et Albany
202 Rue de Rivoli, 75001 Paris 260–31–60 213031. Map **8**G7 to 142 142 Metro Tuileries.

Location: Overlooking the Tuileries Gardens. For years, the Hôtel St-James et Albany, parts of which date from the time of Louis XIV, chugged along in its old-fashioned way with its own select band of aristocratic habitués (as one would expect of a hotel with a name so wonderfully redolent of London's clubland). Then, after a long period of closure for alterations, it reopened in 1981, revealing an unusually successful combination of the old and the new in fittings and furniture. The refurbished and well-managed hotel, with its two excellent restaurants, **Le Noailles** and the **Lafayette Bistrot**, is now giving its prestigious neighbors on the Rue de Rivoli some stiff competition.

St-Simon
14 Rue de St-Simon, 75007 Paris ☎ 548-35-66. Map 8I6 34 34. Metro Rue-du-Bac.
Location: In a calm street just off the Bd. St-Germain. Quiet, cozy, intimate, welcoming, discreet and lived-in are all adjectives that have been liberally applied to this 19thC hotel, and there is no reason to dispute these assessments. The St-Simon, which was always remarkable for its period furnishings, was taken over in 1976 by a Swedish couple, the Lindqvists, whose hobby is antiques; since then, they have been gradually adding new pieces to the rooms. A delightful and consequently very popular hotel.

San Regis
12 Rue Jean-Goujon, 75008 Paris ☎ 359-41-90 260717. Map 7G4 42 42. Metro Champs-Élysées-Clémenceau.
Location: Between the Champs-Élysées and the Seine. This very exclusive hotel, tucked away in a mercifully calm side street near the Champs-Élysées, is frequented by big movie stars – Lauren Bacall, Raquel Welch and Gene Kelly, to name but three – business tycoons, and minor European royalty, who appreciate its beautiful decor, original antiques, bibelots and paintings and, above all, its discretion. Reasonably priced in view of its class.

Scandinavia
27 Rue de Tournon, 75006 Paris ☎ 329-67-20. Map 15J8 22 22. Closed Aug. Metro Mabillon.
Location: Between the Luxembourg Gardens and Bd. St-Germain. For those who prize a historic setting above modern fittings, this small hotel is the answer. The lack of an elevator, or of TV, minibar and direct-dialing in the rooms, is amply offset by the building itself – the fine early 17thC Auberge des Scandinaves, where Casanova once lived – with its 17thC paintings, antique furniture, more carefully chosen than the unlovely Louis XVI pieces found in most luxury hotels, the suits of armor, and, in some of the rooms, the carved baldachins over the beds. These features combine with the warm and generally rather dark colors used in decoration, which lend the Hôtel Scandinavia a quite unique atmosphere.

Sheraton
19 Rue Cdt-Mouchotte, 75014 Paris ☎ 260-35-11 200432. Map 14L6 962 962 AE CB VISA Metro Montparnasse-Bienvenue.
Location: In the center of Montparnasse. The Paris branch of the luxury, worldwide chain of Sheraton hotels has chosen to become part of the Montparnasse redevelopment scheme, dominated by the controversial Maine-Montparnasse Tower. The Sheraton building itself, by Pierre Dufau, who also designed part of La Défense, is an elegant white giant, rising 35 stories, and contrasting strongly with its unlovely surroundings. With the benefit of the Gare Montparnasse and metro at its side, the Sheraton caters with renowned efficiency to its guests – mainly tour groups and business travelers who appreciate its many facilities, including several bars and restaurants.

Solférino
91 Rue de Lille, 75007 Paris ☎ 705-85-54. Map 8H7 to 35 27. Metro Solférino.
Location: In St-Germain, tucked between the Seine and the Bd. St-Germain. A charming, old-fashioned and modest hotel with prettily decorated, high-ceilinged bedrooms, a delightful little *salon* and a veranda for breakfasting. The faithful, mainly English, clientele are especially appreciative of the warm welcome extended by the friendly proprietress.

Suède
31 Rue Vaneau, 75007 Paris ☎ 705-00-08 200596. Map 14J6 to 41 37. Metro Varenne.
Location: In a plush area between Rue de Varenne and Rue de Babylone. Cool elegance

distinguishes this hotel, which is just as it should be since it backs on to the gardens of the Prime Minister's official residence, the Hôtel Matignon. If you want to try to glimpse the man, or simply admire the towering plane trees that grow here, ask for a room on the second or third floor. The hotel also has a large, gently lit lounge in the Directoire style and a pretty little inner courtyard where morning or afternoon refreshment may be taken.

Terminus Nord
12 Bd. Denain, 75010 Paris 280–20–00 660615. Map 5E10 to 230 196 Metro Gare du Nord.
Location: Opposite the Gare du Nord. Prices vary considerably in this large and completely renovated hotel – which, by the way, has nothing to do with the adjoining restaurant of the same name – depending on whether or not you choose to have a private bathroom. If you do, you get a TV set as well. Rooms facing the street are insulated from noise. As a special bonus, the management does not charge for local telephone calls. Extremely convenient location for anyone in transit to or from the capital via the Gare du Nord.

Terrass'
18 Rue Joseph-de-Maistre, 75018 Paris 606–72–85 280830. Map 4C8 to 108 102 Metro Blanche.
Location: On the edge of Montmartre. The hotel rooms with the best views in Paris are undoubtedly to be found in this first-class establishment, which is perched on one of the outcrops of the Butte de Montmartre. From the hotel you can see the Panthéon, the surprisingly tall Opéra, Les Invalides, the Arc de Triomphe and, of course, the Eiffel Tower. Otherwise the Terrass', built in 1912 but modernized more than once since then, and being the only four-star hotel in Montmartre, provides all the services one would expect to find in a good hotel – though it does manage to charge marginally less for them than its rivals situated in other parts of the city.

Tuileries
10 Rue St-Hyacinthe, 75001 Paris 261–04–17 240744. Map 8G7 to 28 28 Metro Pyramides.
Location: Close to Pl. Vendôme and within easy reach of Av. de l'Opéra and the Tuileries Gardens. You won't find a much quieter street in the center of Paris than the tiny Rue St-Hyacinthe: it is scarcely used by vehicles at all except those looking for a parking space. The Hôtel des Tuileries, which occupies a late 18thC building with a superb carved wooden front door, was recently modernized with care, and each room was decorated differently. Downstairs, though, there is still plenty of warm, old-fashioned velvet.

Université
22 Rue de l'Université, 75007 Paris 261–09–39 260717 Map 8I7 to 28 28. Metro Rue-du-Bac.
Location: On the Left Bank, between Bd. St-Germain and the Seine. Despite its rather steep prices, this hotel is booked up well ahead by people who want to stay in style in the antique-dealing and publishing end of St-Germain-des-Prés. The establishment, which occupies a 17thC *hôtel particulier* (private house), has been completely refurbished, and is filled with antiques and tapestries. The rooms are decorated with individual style and the breakfast lounge, hall, and tiny courtyard are charming.

Vieux Marais
8 Rue du Plâtre, 75004 Paris 278–47–22. Map 10H10 to 30 30 Metro Rambuteau.
Location: On one of the less picturesque streets in the Marais. This charming quarter was a virtual slum 25yr ago. Now in the process of renovation, it contains some of the priciest property in town, but it does not yet have its fair share of hotels, so the Vieux Marais, modernized in 1979, is a welcome addition. The amiable Rumiel family have done a good job of decorating it, brightening up the five-floor building with flowery wallpaper, matching curtains (made by Madame Rumiel herself), and light-colored bathrooms. The direct-dial telephones are rare for the price.

Eating in Paris

French cuisine is renowned as the finest in the world; the superb standard of cooking in the average French household is matched by the unequalled quality of France's restaurants. Whereas provincial restaurants reflect local produce and traditions, those of Paris act as a focus for the rest of the country, bringing together the individual and varied regional cuisines, being continually interested in change and innovation, and constantly striving for new limits of perfection. In Paris, with a little judicious choosing, you can quite simply have the gastronomic experience of a lifetime, whether it is a perfectly smoked Auvergne ham in a crowded wine bar, or a five-course extravaganza in one of the city's revered establishments.

Cooking in France is regarded not as a necessity but as an art, and its leading exponents, such as Paul Bocuse, Michel Guérard and Roger Vergé, are held in god-like esteem. They are the modern day successors of the immortalized 19th and early 20thC chefs Carême and Escoffier; but whereas Escoffier, for all his technical brilliance, put many strictures on French cuisine, many of today's great chefs are breaking free from his rules and regulations and seeking entirely new directions.

This new style of cooking, pioneered in France since the war by such chefs as Alexandre Dumaine, André Pic and Fernard Point, is termed just that: *nouvelle cuisine*. In keeping with the modern trend away from rich, heavy food, and with the emphasis on absolute freshness, *nouvelle cuisine* at its best is lighter and tastier than traditional French cuisine, and is often characterized by unusual combinations of high quality ingredients, and carefully presented, smaller and more manageable portions. *Nouvelle cuisine* is not a total culinary revolution, because although the ideas are different the methods remain the same, but it is a far-reaching adaptation to today's requirements of classic French cooking.

It must not be thought, however, that *nouvelle cuisine* has entirely swept traditional French cookery aside. On the contrary, the classic dishes will always remain, as will the excellent and more than ever popular *cuisine bourgeoise* that is the root of all French cooking. Regional cookery too, the individual cuisines of every part of France, still flourishes, as a visit to Normandy or Nice, Alsace or the Auvergne or to many of the regionally-inspired restaurants of Paris will tell you.

In Paris, all these varieties can be sampled. For a good insight into *nouvelle cuisine* try **Les Semailles** or **Daniel Tuboeuf**; for a Provençal fish soup try **Pierre Vedel**; for food from the Auvergne try **L'Ambassade d'Auvergne**; from Normandy try **Chez Fernard**; from the Landes try **Le Repaire de Cartouche**; for mushrooms try **Au Quai d'Orsay**; for *choucroute* try **Baumann**; for a *cassoulet* try **Le Cabécou**; for classic cuisine try **Lasserre**; or for good plain *cuisine bourgeoise* try **L'Annexe au Quai** or **Le Trumilou**. (See *Restaurants*.)

Of course, it's not just French cuisine that can be sampled in Paris. Like all major capital cities, Paris is cosmopolitan, and although in our selection of the city's restaurants we have concentrated almost solely on French cooking, the food of many different nations is also to be found. Some parts of Paris have a remarkably ethnic flavor, such as the Belleville/Ménilmontant quarter where you can find North African dishes, or the Marais, which is packed with Jewish restaurants.

Some of the best foreign restaurants in town are: for

Chinese/Vietnamese, **Délices de Szechuen** (*40 Av. Duquesne, 7e ☎306–22–55*); **Pagoda** (*50 Rue de Provence, 9e ☎874–81–48*); for Indian, **Anarkali** (*4 Pl. Gustave-Toudouze, 9e ☎878–39–84*); **Indra** (*10 Rue Cdt-Rivière, 8e ☎359–46–40*); for North African, **Abel** (*15 Rue St-Vincent-de-Paul, 10e ☎878–41–88*); **Timgad** (*21 Rue Brunel, 17e ☎574–23–70*); for Japanese, **Nikko Hotel** (Benkay), (*61 Quai de Grenelle, 15e ☎575–62–62*); for Italian, **Au Châteaubriant** (*23 Rue Chabrol, 10e ☎824–58–94*); **Gildo** (*153 Rue de Bourgogne, 7e ☎551–54–12*); for Russian, **Daru** (see *Restaurants*); **Dominique** (*19 Rue Bréa, 6e ☎372–08–80*).

A resumé of cooking styles in Paris restaurants

Grande cuisine

Though the simpler classic dishes will survive no matter what, *grande cuisine* (also known as *haute cuisine*) on a grand scale has gone into irreversible decline as labor costs have risen and people have become fussier about their digestions and waistlines. The cooking may necessitate 50 or more scullions in the kitchen preparing rich and complicated dishes. Definitely food for a treat rather than for every day.

Nouvelle cuisine

The four main tenets of France's most recent school of cookery are that produce should be: fresh and of the highest quality; under- rather than over-cooked whenever possible; undisguised by rich, indigestible sauces; and often imaginatively combined with other ingredients. Particularly in Paris, however, one must beware of chefs who have exploited the cult of *nouvelle cuisine* by serving badly thought-out and often outlandish combinations of ingredients in amounts so tiny that they do not even cover the exiguous centers of the basketweave-patterned crockery that in such places seems to be *de riguer*. Less unscrupulous and more dedicated chefs tend to re-interpret the well-established favorites of *cuisine bourgeoise* while retaining the better elements of *nouvelle cuisine*.

Cuisine bourgeoise

This can be classical, traditional or mainstream cooking, often with a regional flavor. It is the alchemy that turns a tough old bird or gristly cut of meat into a dish that melts in your mouth. *Cuisine bourgeoise* has never been more popular; an increasing number of Paris restaurants that once served nothing but *grande cuisine*, then tried pure *nouvelle cuisine*, now offer lighter versions of such stalwarts as *coq au vin, blanquette de veau, civet de lièvre*, and so on.

Regional cookery

One of the great fountainheads of mainstream French cooking, regional dishes have as their keynote extraordinary variety, and the ingenious use of mundane ingredients. Languedoc's *cassoulet* is an example, being made from white haricot beans, sausages, pork and preserved goose. Regional cookery lends character to some of Paris' best restaurants.

Ethnic cookery

Chinese (usually Vietnamese in disguise), unashamed Vietnamese, Italian, Russian and Jewish are the main non-French cuisines to be found in Paris, as well as North African food, from the former French colonies of Morocco, Tunisia and Algeria, which is specific to France.

Choosing a restaurant

There is little doubt that in Paris practically any mood or gastronomic whim can be catered to. Apart from the restaurants proper, upon which the selection on the following pages concentrates, there are many other types of eating houses providing snacks and lighter meals. Since few people can even eat, let alone enjoy, two full-blooded French meals a day, it is a good idea if eating out to try a place of this sort for lunch, and visit a restaurant in the evening, or vice versa.

Brasseries are restaurants-cum-cafés, often with a long bar, which serve both large and light meals; some of the most famous, including **Lipp** and **La Coupole**, are included in our selection of restaurants. So-called drugstores (little like their American originals) are popular too and, like *brasseries*, provide continuous service throughout the day. The ordinary café, always close at hand, is an excellent place for anything from a huge French bread sandwich or a *croque monsieur* (toasted ham and cheese sandwich) to a midday *plat du jour*, often scrawled in whitewash on the window.

The more prestigious *salons de thé* and their recent offshoots, sometimes called *tarteries*, specialize in tarts, quiches and pizzas, and also serve wine. Hamburger chains are firmly established in Paris, but a more indigenous and imaginative version of fast food is the *croissant* in various unorthodox guises (stuffed with anything from cheese to raspberries and bananas). *Crêpes*, too, make delicious take-out food.

Perhaps the very best place for a gourmet snack, however, is one of the cafés that serves excellent wine by the glass with sandwiches (often open ones) of equally high quality. Six of these are described in detail in Restaurants: **Café de la Nouvelle Mairie, La Cloche des Halles, L'Écluse I and II, Au Rubis** and **Le Val d'Or**.

Choosing somewhere for a pleasant snack is unlikely to prove problematic or disappointing, but taking pot-luck with restaurants is more hazardous, though it can just as easily turn out to be a real find as a disaster. Look carefully at the menu in the window of the restaurant. If the chef takes any trouble there will be a few *plats du jour, specialités* or unusual dishes; a drab list of easily refrigerated escalopes, chops and steaks bodes ill. A packed restaurant is always a good sign, but this is no golden rule, as some good and less expensive restaurants are half-empty in the evening, while fashionable establishments do not fill up until 9pm. Bear in mind that if you have chosen a restaurant in advance, particularly if it is a well-established one, it is always worth making a reservation.

The menu

At first sight, a French menu can be a mystifying document. But, particularly if you are trying to estimate the likely cost, there are several things for which you should look. Does the set menu (*menu à prix fixe* or *menu conseillé*), if available, include drink (*boisson comprise* or *b.c., vin compris* or *v.c.*) and/or service (*service compris, s.c.* or *prix nets*), and is it free of *suppléments* on the dishes you want? If not, you may find yourself paying substantially more than the basic price.

The set menu is often very good value at more expensive restaurants. The choice of dishes may be rather limited, but the difference in price compared with the same fare *à la carte* is often considerable, even if portions are occasionally smaller.

The menu at a restaurant which offers only *à la carte* fare needs careful scrutiny too, because service may not be included, and sometimes normally inexpensive dishes such as side salads, may be offered at a disproportionately inflated price.

Restaurants that offer both set price and *à la carte* menus often keep the former on a separate card and you may find you have to ask specifically for this.

A full five-course meal in France begins with hors-d'oeuvre, then continues with an *entrée* (often a fish dish), main course (often a *plat du jour*) and sometimes salad, before cheese, and finally a dessert. A true feast, but if all that sounds too much, you can order a main course with either a starter or dessert from the *à la carte* menu. See *Menu decoder p209.*

As you are handed the menu, you will probably be asked if you want an aperitif. The French prefer not to knock out their taste buds with a whisky or dry Martini (the properly mixed version of which is unknown outside a few deluxe hotel bars). Instead they order a *kir* (blackcurrant liqueur, *cassis*, with white wine) or a *kir royal* (with champagne).

Wine in Paris

The wine you choose when eating out depends very much on your choice of restaurant and in Paris you can find the richest variety in the world. Among these you will also find differing degrees of seriousness about wine, ranging from the establishments that push the wine with the highest profit margin to some like **L'Écluse** where their primary interest is featuring 15 Bordeaux, and offering light meals to match.

Although there is much talk about asking the advice of a wine-waiter (*sommelier*), in fact there are hardly two dozen Paris restaurants that have one who is properly qualified.

A restaurant need not have a *sommelier* to keep a good wine list, however. It is often worthwhile asking advice from the owner, who is not infrequently the person who greets and seats the customers, and is probably also the one who buys the wines.

There are two methods a helpful waiter may use when suggesting wine. The professional, with good experience in judging and serving people, will pick up numerous hints about the customer that will help determine the category of wine to recommend. Others will suggest wines within a moderate price range, await the customer's reaction, then recommend something of greater or lesser price accordingly.

You should always look at the wine list for an idea of the price range and qualities offered before asking advice. There are invariably some bargains, but they are not always easy to find. On average the mark-up is about three times higher.

French wines are classified into *Appellation Contrôlée*, VDQS (*Vins Délimités de Qualité Supérieure*), *Vin de Pays* or *Vin de Table*. None of these are a guarantee of quality, but simply mean that each category must conform to certain criteria of origin, vinification and grape variety. The criteria are more strict for *Appellation Contrôlée* than VDQS, and so on down the scale, and prices reflect this. Good value, however, can be found in each category.

In choosing wines, the so-called *Réserve du Patron* should be avoided. In nearly all Paris restaurants it is of very poor quality and simply not worth the risk. You should also be wary of ordering a '*petit Bordeaux*', for similar reasons.

The reputation of the grower, château or *négotiant* is another extremely important criterion, particularly with Burgundies. If a name is not familiar, it is often wiser to choose according to the year because a good vintage VDQS can often be better quality, and value, than a mediocre vintage of an *Appellation Contrôlée*. Most wine in the lower categories is blended by the shippers and does not carry vintage dates. *Vin de Table* is commonly served in carafes or jugs called '*pichets*'.

Wine and food

Choosing wine to go with food is primarily a matter of common sense. A meal is a progression of tastes, and for this reason a dry white wine is often chosen at the beginning of a meal to accompany the more simple-tasting first course. This progression may also be a cause of difficulties with cheese: some are too fatty or strong-tasting for the delicate old red that was drunk with the main course. Ordering a white or young red would be an anticlimax and, consequently, it is rare that a wine is specifically ordered to go with the cheese.

It is often worthwhile to be adventurous, however, following the guidance of your palate. And to this end it is interesting that the Lyonnais sometimes drink a light chilled Beaujolais with oysters; and one of Paris' best wine waiters dispels the myth that no wine goes with salad vinaigrette, suggesting that a young Chinon or Beaujolais agree perfectly well.

Vintage chart

A guide to the major areas and the general qualities of recent vintages. See key below.

	1973	1974	1975	1976	1977	1978	1979	1980	1981
Red Bordeaux									
Médoc/Graves	◑ *	◑ *	●	◑ *	○ *	●	●	◑	●
Pomerol/St-Emilion	◑ *	○ *	●	● *	○ *	●	●	◑	●
White Bordeaux									
Sauternes & sweet			●	● *	○ *	◑	◑	◑	●
Graves & dry	○ *	◑ *	● *	◑ *	◑ *	● *	◑ *	◑ *	●
Red Burgundy and neighbours									
Côte d'Or	◑ *	○ *	○ *	●	○ *	●	◑	◑	○
Beaujolais				● *	○ *	● *	◑ *	○ *	●
White Burgundy and neighbours									
Côte d'Or	● *	○ *	◑ *	● *	◑ *	●	◑	◑	○
Chablis	● *	● *	● *	● *	◑ *	● *	◑ *	◑	○
Alsace	○ *	◑ *	● *	● *	○ *	● *	●	◑ *	◑
Rhone	○ *	○ *	○ *	● *	◑ *	● *	●	◑	●

Above-average vintages of other white wines

Mâcon-Villages, 1978, 1979, 1980, 1981; **Loire** (sweet – Anjou, Touraine), 1976, 1978, 1979, 1981; **Upper Loire** (dry – Pouilly-Fumé, Sancerre), 1978, 1979, 1981; **Muscadet**, the newest vintage is best.

Key: ● above average to outstanding ◑ average
○ acceptable * for drinking now

Restaurants listed by arrondissement

1er

André Faure
Baumann-Baltard
Bistro de la Gare-I
La Cloche des Halles
L'Espadon
Gérard Besson
Le Grand Véfour
Le Lafayette Bistrot
Le Noailles
Pharamond
Pierre Traiteur
Rôtisserie Rivoli
Au Rubis
Willi's

2^e^

L'Assiette au Boeuf-I
Le Petit Coin de la Bourse
Le Vaudeville

3^e^

L'Ambassade d'Auvergne
Daniel Tuboeuf
Plats du Jour

4^e^

La Ciboulette
Le Trumilou

5^e^

L'Ambroisie
Atelier Maître Albert
Le Balzar
La Bûcherie
Café de la Nouvelle Mairie
Chez Toutoune
Dodin Bouffant
Au Pactole
La Tour d'Argent

6^e^

L'Assiette au Boeuf-II
L'Assiette au Boeuf-IV
Bistro de la Gare-II
Le Cabécou
Claude Sainlouis
La Closerie des Lilas
L'Écluse-I
La Hulotte
Lipp
Le Muniche
Le Petit Zinc
La Photogalerie
Polidor
Le Procope

7^e^

L'Annexe du Quai
L'Archestrate
Bistrot de Paris
Chez Françoise
La Chope d'Orsay
Au Quai d'Orsay
Relais Saint-Germain
Le Sancerrois
Thoumieux

8^e^

L'Assiette au Boeuf-III
Bateaux-Mouches
Baumann-Napoléon
Bistro de la Gare-III
Boulangerie St-Philippe
La Boutique à Sandwiches
Le Bristol
Chez Edgard
Daru
L'Écluse-II
Germain
Les Jardins d'Edgard
Lasserre
Laurent
Le Lord Gourmand
Lucas-Carton
La Marcande
Maxim's
Le Moulin du Village
Au Petit Montmorency
Les Princes
Régence-Plaza
Royal Monceau
Taillevent
Le Val d'Or
Au Vieux Berlin

9^e^

À l'Annexe
L'Auberge
Bistro de la Gare-IV
Chartier
Le Grand Café
Le Petit Riche

10^e^

Brasserie Flo
Julien
Terminus Nord

11^e^

Le Repaire de Cartouche

12^e^

Le Morvan
Le Trou Gascon

14^e^

L'Auberge de l'Argoat
Chez Fernand
Chez Julie
La Coupole
Le Duc
Le Jardin de la Paresse
Léni-Olympic Entrepôt
Le Pouilly

15^e^

L'Aquitaine
Chez Ribe
Morot-Gaudry
Pierre Vedel
Le Restaurant du Marché

16^e^

Le Petit Bedon
Le Pré Catalan
Quéré
Le Vivarois

17^e^

Baumann-Ternes
Le Bernardin
Chez Gorisse
L'Étoile Verte

18^e^

Beauvilliers
Le Maquis

Neuilly-sur-Seine

Jacqueline Fénix

L'Ambassade d'Auvergne
22 Rue du Grenier-St-Lazare, 3e
*☎ 272-31-22. Map **10**H10 Last orders 11pm. Closed Sun. Metro Arts-et-Métiers.*
The vast majority of café owners in Paris hail from the Auvergne. When they have something to celebrate, they will, as often as not, head for this invitingly rustic 'embassy' of Auvergnat tradition to savor the dishes of their – or their parents' – childhood. It's the only place in Paris that regularly serves such specialities as *mourtayrol* and *estofinado*. The Auvergnat cheeses, which owner Joseph Petrucci obtains direct from his wife's relations, are quite superb. Recently, one or two dishes of a less hearty, more *nouvelle cuisine* character have appeared on the menu, so there's something for everyone. ***Specialties:** Boudin aux châtaignes, falette, aligot.*

L'Ambroisie
65 Quai de la Tournelle, 5e
*☎ 633-18-65. Map **16**J10 to Last orders 9:30pm. Closed Sun evening, Mon, Aug 15–Sept 15. Metro Maubert-Mutualité.*
This restaurant had just opened when François Mitterrand, who lived around the corner in the Rue de Bièvre, was elected President; and for several weeks the area crawled with police blocking off the street, joined by TV cameramen, journalists, and prospective ministers – some of whom dropped in for a meal. However, this is not why almost all French food writers immediately hailed l'Ambroisie as the great new Parisian restaurant – it simply lived up to its name (*ambroisie* meaning ambrosia).

Bernard Pacaud was well trained by Claude Peyrot and has included some of **Le Vivarois'** dishes on his menu; others he has invented. All of them are executed with a perfect sense of balance and seasoning that matches the pleasant ultra-modern furnishings. ***Specialties:** Salade de légumes à la coriandre, trois poissons à la nage, bavarois de poivrons.*

André Faure
40 Rue du Mont-Thabor, 1er
*☎ 260-74-28. Map **8**G7 Last orders 10:30pm. Closed Sun, Aug. Metro Concorde.*
This conveniently situated restaurant (just by Pl. de la Concorde) offers two set menus: a lighter one at lunchtime for office workers, and a gargantuan five-course 'farmer's meal' in the evening, with unlimited wine, for hungry, thirsty tourists. They are both, without doubt, bargains, although the emphasis is on straightforward *cuisine bourgeoise* rather than on great subtlety. ***Specialties:** Coq au vin, lapin sauté.*

À l'Annexe
15 Rue Chaptal, 9e
*☎ 874-65-52. Map **4**D8 to Last orders 10:30pm. Closed Sat (June–Oct), Aug, week of Christmas and New Year. Metro St-Georges.*
Habitués of this atmospheric bistro range from office workers to the elderly residents of the quiet and respectable little streets surrounding it, only a minute or two from the glitter and glare of Pigalle. The food is hearty home-cooking, served by a waitress of the old school – once you're on the right side of her, you're firm friends. ***Specialties:** Salade frisée aux lardons, raie au beurre noir, pommes au four.*

L'Annexe du Quai
3 Rue Surcouf, 7e
*☎ 551-48-48. Map **13**H5 to Last orders 10:30pm. Closed Sat, Sun, Aug. Metro Invalides.*
The 'Quai' of which this is the annex is the fashionable restaurant **Au Quai d'Orsay** (not the Foreign Ministry, which is also popularly known as Quai d'Orsay). Seated at its old-fashioned horseshoe bar or at a table, you can tuck in to *cuisine bourgeoise* in a lively, almost party-like atmosphere, surrounded by attractive Second Empire decor. Cheaper but no more down-market than the Quai itself. ***Specialties:** Ragoût de veau aux pleurotes, palette de porc aux choux, civet de lapin de garenne.*

L'Aquitaine
54 Rue de Dantzig, 15e
☎ 828-67-38 to Last orders 11:30pm. Closed Sun, Mon. Metro Convention.
There are few pleasures greater than eating on the first-floor terrace of L'Aquitaine, overlooking La Ruche, the '*cité des artistes*' where Soutine, Modigliani and Chagall worked. Sample the superb cuisine of winsome Christiane Massia, a deceptively

fragile-looking feminist, who has publicly crossed swords with that self-confessed king of *phallocrates*, Paul Bocuse. With the help of an all-female team of assistant cooks – and her husband Michel, for the fine selection of wines and Armagnacs – she treats typically southwestern ingredients with an idiosyncratically light touch. *Confits* come with sorrel purée; a discreet Roquefort and butter sauce is served with steamed turbot. ***Specialties:** Salade de haddock aux épinards, bouillabaisse de maquereaux aux petits pois.*

L'Archestrate
84 Rue de Varenne, 7e
*551-47-33. Map **8**I6 Last orders 10:30pm. Closed Sat, Sun, Aug 3-25, Dec 23-Jan 5. Metro Rue-du-Bac.*
Alain Senderens has joined the pantheon of jet-setting star chefs (others include Paul Bocuse, Michel Guérard and the Troisgros brothers). His restaurant is regarded by many (including influential food writers Henri Gault and Christian Millau, who have placed it on a pinnacle of perfection in their Paris guide) as the capital's finest restaurant. It also happens to be one of the most expensive. Beware of the wine waiter, who has an odd idea of what constitutes "*un petit bordeaux*" (a 14yr-old vastly expensive *cru bourgeois*). However, the highly imaginative cooking is very, very good – as it most certainly ought to be at the price. ***Specialties:** Salade de langouste aux mangues, escalope de ris de veau à la crème de poivrons, turbot aux fèves.*

L'Assiette au Boeuf-I
Bd. des Italiens, 2e
*297-49-55. Map **9**F8 to Last orders 12:30am. Metro Richelieu-Drouot.*
L'Assiette au Boeuf-II
*22 Rue Guillaume-Apollinaire, 6e 260-88-44. Map **8**I7 to Last orders 12:30am. Metro St-Germain-des-Prés.*
L'Assiette au Boeuf-III
*123 Av. des Champs-Élysées, 8e 720-01-13. Map **7**F4 to Last orders 12:30am. Metro George-V.*
L'Assiette au Boeuf-IV
*103 Bd. du Montparnasse, 6e 325-25-25. Map **14**K7 to Last orders 12:30am. Metro Montparnasse-Bienvenue.*
The four Paris restaurants of this name are all part of Michel Oliver's empire (see **Bistro de la Gare I–IV** and **Bistro de Paris**). The unique decor (a feast of mirrors and moldings) at **l'Assiette au Boeuf-I** was bequeathed by the former Poccardi restaurant. **L'Assiette au Boeuf-II** is often the scene of high-jinks among less well-heeled St-Germain habitués. **L'Assiette au Boeuf-III** was, in fact, the first of Michel Oliver's successful chain (its modern decor is just beginning to look dated), while **L'Assiette au Boeuf-IV** is the latest addition. ***Specialties:** Steak, desserts.*

Atelier Maître Albert
1–5 Rue Maître-Albert, 5e
*633-13-78. Map **16**J10 Last orders midnight. Closed for lunches and Sun. Metro Maubert-Mutualité.*
When a formula works, it's a good idea to stick to it, which is precisely what M. Crouzier has done at his maze-like, low-lit restaurant. For years, contented Left Bankers have flocked back for the very reasonably priced set dinner (no lunch) offering plenty of choice: five starters, seven main dishes, two cheeses and seven desserts, washed down by, perhaps, a well-chosen Gamay de Touraine. In summer there's air conditioning, and in winter the superb old fireplace springs to life with a blaze of logs. ***Specialties:** Jambon persillé, daube de canard au gamay.*

L'Auberge
164 Rue Montmartre, 9e
*236-71-09. Map **9**F9 to Last orders 10:30pm. Closed Sat lunch, Sun, Aug. Metro Rue Montmartre.*
Despite its pretty-pretty half-timbered front, this is not a tourist trap (although located in an area that abounds in them). The excellent cuisine is vaguely *nouvelle* (steamed fish, duck with peaches), the decor cozy, and the service friendly if a trifle slow – but then with staff costs being high, a leisurely pace is often the price that has to be paid for inexpensive food – in this case, a bargain set menu. ***Specialties:** Terrine de poisson, poulet au vinaigre façon Troisgros.*

L'Auberge de l'Argoat
27 Av. Reille, 14e 589-17-05 Last orders 10pm. Closed Sun, Mon, Aug. Metro Porte-d'Orleans.
Marcel Goareguer is a very inventive cook who makes and

flavors his own vinegars (with an assortment of fresh fruits – blackberries, tangerines, peaches) and blends them into his marvelous fish sauces. He gets consignments of butter, cream and farm eggs direct from his native Brittany every week; he knows how to choose the best and freshest fish at Rungis market; he has an unusual and interesting wine list; and he offers good value for money. So why his pseudo-rustic, family-run restaurant in a Paris backwater is not more popular than it is remains a mystery. A younger and trendier chef would probably have blown his own trumpet a little more loudly: we prefer to take this unassuming stickler-for-quality as he is. ***Specialties:** Andouillette à la vapeur de cidre, terrine de poisson au pamplemousse, lieu au velouté d'écrevisses.*

Le Balzar
49 Rue des Écoles, 5e
354-13-67. Map ***15**J9*
Last orders 12:30am. Closed Tues, Aug. Metro Maubert-Mutualité.

Solid, traditional fare is served here by expert waiters in waistcoats and long aprons. But people eat at this old-fashioned Latin Quarter brasserie (or have a drink in its small café section) not so much for the food as to watch – or be watched by – famous actors and actresses, television personalities, talent-spotters and members of the literary world. ***Specialties:** Cervelas rémoulade, cassoulet, choucroute.*

Bateaux-Mouches
Pont de l'Alma, 8e
225-96-10. Map 7G4
Closed Mon, Nov 15–March 1 except Fri (dinner), Sat (lunch, dinner), Sun (lunch). Metro Pont-de-l'Alma.

Eating on a Bateau-Mouche cruiser as it chugs up and down the River Seine may not appeal to everyone, but it is a romantic and remarkably neat way (particularly for those with little time on their hands) to combine traffic-free sightseeing with good classical food. The two formulas available – a moderately priced lunch trip and a more expensive and lavish dinner outing (tie and jacket are required) – are both very good value, considering that they include the price of the very pleasant river trip. ***Specialties:** Coulibiac de saumon, fricassée d'escargots, lotte à l'armoricaine.*

Baumann-Baltard
9 Rue Coquillière, 1er
236-22-00. Map ***10**G9*
Last orders 2am. Metro Les Halles.

Baumann-Napoléon
38 Av. de Friedland, 8e
227-99-50. Map ***7**E4 to Last orders 1am. Metro Étoile.*

Baumann-Ternes
64 Av. des Ternes, 17e
574-16-66. Map ***6**E3 Last orders 1am. Closed Sun, Mon, three weeks over Easter, two weeks at Christmas and New Year. Metro Ternes.*

Guy-Pierre Baumann owns three restaurants, and the food at all of them is predominantly Alsatian: many varieties of sauerkraut (with fish, with *pot au feu, à l'orientale*, etc.), shoulder of pork with red cabbage, and a good selection of wines and *alcools blancs* (fruit spirits) from Alsace. At the **Baumann-Napoléon**, the smartest of the trio, you can also try some interesting fish dishes and recipes from centuries gone by, such as Menon's *cuisses de canard à la moutarde* (1742). At **Baumann-Baltard** the atmosphere is that of a turn-of-the-century Halles brasserie, while at **Baumann-Ternes** the decor is engagingly kitsch and cozy, a nice place for late-night eating. ***Specialties, Baumann-Baltard:** Salades de tripes à la ciboulette, estomac de porc à l'ancienne.* ***Baumann-Napoléon:** Choucroute de crabe, sole aux courgettes, filets de barbue marinés.* ***Baumann-Ternes:** Salade de poireaux Adeline, chou farci doré au four.*

Beauvilliers
52 Rue Lamarck, 18e
254-19-50. Map ***4**D8*
Last orders 10:30pm. Closed Sun, Mon lunch, Sept. Metro Lamarck-Caulaincourt.

One has the sense, when dining at Beauvilliers, of being a guest in a calm and beautiful private house, and that is precisely the effect that owner Edouard Carlier has striven to create. The restaurant is filled with lovely things: antique silver, porcelain, flowers, and Carlier's own superb (and growing) collection of prints. The house itself stands on the hillside of Montmartre and has a delightful terrace. The food, served either indoors or on the terrace, matches the surroundings – Carlier aims for top quality, and almost invariably achieves it. ***Specialties:*** *Filets de rouget grillé au piment, terrines d'agneau à la fleur de thym, girolles au jus de truffe et noisette, salmis de cuisses de canette aux fruits de la passion.*

Le Bernardin
18 Rue Troyon, 17e
380–36–22. Map ***6****E3*
VISA *Last orders 11:00pm. Closed Sun, Mon, Aug. Metro Étoile.*

The brother-and-sister team, the beautiful Gilbert and Maguy Le Coze, moved recently from their tiny fish restaurant on the Left Bank to larger premises in a little street by the Arc de Triomphe, where they have enraptured the upper-crust *piscivores* of the area (businessmen and *grands bourgeois*). The emphasis is more on absolutely topnotch raw materials than on invention, and Gilbert's cuisine is what the French call *sage*. ***Specialties:*** *Rougets meunière, raie au beurre noisette, Saint-Pierre aux oignons blancs.*

Bistro de la Gare-I
30 Rue St-Denis, 1er
260–84–92. Map ***9****H9*
Last orders 1am. Metro Châtelet-Les-Halles.

Bistro de la Gare-II
59 Bd. du Montparnasse, 6e
548–38–01. Map ***14****K7*
Last orders 1am. Metro Montparnasse-Bienvenue.

Bistro de la Gare-III
73 Av. des Champs-Élysées, 8e
359–67–83. Map ***7****F4*
Last orders 1am. Metro George-V.

Bistro de la Gare-IV
38 Bd. des Italiens, 9e
246–15–74. Map ***9****F8*
Last orders 1am. Metro Richelieu-Drouot.

Raymond Oliver of **Le Grand Véfour** spawned a son, Michel, who combines an infectious love of food (as can be seen from his cooking programs on French TV) with business acumen. He has now built up an empire of eight restaurants (four Bistros de la Gare and four **Assiettes au Boeuf**) that have proved to be among Paris' best stand-bys for people who want a reliable, quick meal when going to a show or film. They provide – till 12:30 or 1am and every day of the year – limited but carefully balanced set menus of reasonable price. There is a slightly greater choice at the more expensive Bistros de la Gare than at the Assiettes au Boeuf; at both, the main qualities are good meat and interesting desserts.

The most interesting atmosphere in any of Michel Oliver's establishments is to be found at **Bistro de la Gare-II**. Formerly the Restaurant Rougeot, it boasts one of the finest Art Nouveau decors in Paris (mini-landscapes in *faïence*, mirrors, stained-glass ceiling). ***Specialties (at all four establishments):*** *Fruits de mer en cassolette, pavé aux deux poivres, desserts.*

Bistrot de Paris
33 Rue de Lille, 7e
261–16–83. Map ***8****H7*
VISA *Last orders midnight. Closed Sat, Sun. Metro Solférino.*

The fashionable gastronomic meeting place, Bistrot de Paris is the jewel in Michel Oliver's substantial crown (see also **Assiette au Boeuf I–IV** and **Bistro de la Gare I–IV**). Tables are packed, the conversation animated, the décor (Slavik, green and glittering) ravishing, and the food good. Service, though, can be a trifle slow and casual; and the bill undoubtedly reflects not only the food, but the famous faces at nearby tables. ***Specialties:*** *Charlotte d'écrevisses aux poireaux, la soupe de pêche, gâteau au chocolat amer.*

Boulangerie St-Philippe
73 Av. Franklin-D-Roosevelt, 8e
359–78–76. Map ***7****G5 to*
VISA *Closed for dinner and Sat. Metro Franklin-D-Roosevelt.*

Elbow your way through the crowds of gourmet shoppers and office workers buying snacks in this busy bakery, and you'll find a pleasant little lunch restaurant serving surprisingly sophisticated *plats du jour*. The butter and cream used in these dishes, and in the delicious desserts and pastries, comes from Echiré, which has an *appellation*, like a wine-producing area. Quality is commensurate. ***Specialties:*** *Bavarois d'écrevisses, flan chaud au haddock, foie de veau à la vapeur.*

La Boutique à Sandwiches
12 Rue du Colisée, 8e
359–34–32. Map ***2****F5*
Last orders midnight. Closed Sat, Aug. Metro St-Philippe-du-Roule.

This unalluringly named, two-floor restaurant/snack bar just off the Champs-Élysées offers not only an extraordinary range of excellent sandwiches, but good Alsatian *pickelfleisch*, Swiss *raclette* and pastries. A very useful stand-by for the film-goer as it stays open late. ***Specialties: Sandwiches, pickelfleisch, raclette.***

Brasserie Flo
6 Cour des Petites-Écuries, 10e ☎ 770-13-59. Map ***5****F10 to Last orders 1am. Closed Sun, Aug. Metro Château-d'Eau.*

One of Jean-Claude Bucher's four Paris restaurants (see also **Julien, Terminus Nord** and **Le Vaudeville**), Brasserie Flo reflects his Alsatian origins in its food and drink, and there is beer drawn from the barrel, a rarity in Paris. The turn-of-the-century decor, with its old brass luggage racks, and hat-stands, is equally reminiscent of France's most Germanic province. Despite, or possibly because of, the brasserie's rather cramped seating and very reasonable prices, it attracts a lot of well-known faces. ***Specialties:*** *Gendarmes, choucroute, foie gras au Riesling.*

Le Bristol
112 Rue du Faubourg St-Honoré, 8e ☎ 266-91-45. Map 7F6 Last orders 10:30pm. Metro Champs-Élysées-Clémenceau.

It's the decor and the clientele that are most distinctive and distinguished here (see also *Hotels*). The dining room, gently lit from above and lined with *régence* wood paneling, is one of the most elegant to be found in any luxury Paris hotel. Your neighbors at the next table are likely to be members of the more staid international jet-set (politicians, chief executives, elderly heiresses). If you don't care about the setting or the company, you can always fall back on Emile Tabourdiau's excellent *cuisine*, which is discreetly *nouvelle*. ***Specialties:*** *Huîtres chaudes au beurre de homard, veau à la graine de moutarde.*

La Bûcherie
41 Rue de la Bûcherie, 5e ☎ 354-78-06. Map ***10****J10 Last orders 12:30am. Open as salon de thé 3-7:30pm. Metro Maubert-Mutualité.*

This restaurant can be a bit cramped, but on a cold winter's evening, with the logs crackling in the grate and lots of convivial neighbors, few would object. Amiable, bear-like Bernard Bosque is an inventive cook: witness his interpretation of fish *à l'oseille*, in which he replaces sorrel with the equally tart but distinctive rhubarb. His desserts are light and delicious, and his wine list strong, featuring both well-known and less familiar vintages. ***Specialties:*** *Chou farci au crabe, sauté d'agneau au citron.*

Le Cabécou
151 Rue de Vaugirard, 6e ☎ 734-72-46. Map ***14****K6 to Last orders 9pm. Closed Sun, July 15-Aug 15. Metro Falguière.*

A good *cassoulet* is hard to come by outside Carcassonne, Castelnaudary or Toulouse, all of which have their own authorized versions. However, an excellent and inexpensive version (of the Castelnaudary school, i.e. without tomato) can be had at this minuscule restaurant. Chef Gérard Letrou is content to stay on a very short gastronomic wavelength: *cassoulet* aside, all his dishes, a mere dozen, are from the province of Quercy (next to the Dordogne), the dominant ingredients of which are duck, goose, *cèpes* (mushrooms), truffles and walnuts. ***Specialties:*** *Confit de canard or d'oie, magret de canard, gâteau de noix.*

Café de la Nouvelle Mairie
19 Rue des Fossés-St-Jacques, 5e ☎ 326-80-18. Map ***15****K9 Last orders 8pm. Closed Sat evening, Sun, Aug. Metro Luxembourg.*

A few minutes' walk from the Luxembourg Gardens is this attractively intact prewar café, kept spick and span by boyish owner Bernard Pontonnier. His small selection of good snacks and sandwiches is really only a pretext for cracking open a bottle (or two) from his succinct but excellent range of Beaujolais and Loire wines, or for trying his superb old rum. ***Specialties:*** *Charcuterie, fromage.*

Chartier
7 Rue de Faubourg-Montmartre, 9e ☎ 770-86-29. Map ***9****F9 Last orders 9:30pm. Metro Rue Montmartre.*

Hurry to get a last glimpse of Paris' sole surviving mid-19thC *bouillon* decor (*bouillons* were popular restaurants, or soup kitchens) before it becomes transmogrified, with taste of course, into a chic 'eatery'. The atmosphere is very much the same as it must have been 100yr ago (bustling and noisy), and prices don't seem to have risen much either. The Bohemian atmosphere, and not the food, is what going to Chartier's is all about. ***Specialties:*** ***Croustade au jambon, pièce de Charolais.***

Chez Edgard

4 Rue Marbeuf, 8e
*☎ 720-51-15. Map **7**F4 ▯▢ to ▯▯ ▢ ▢ ▢ ▢ ▢ ▢ Last orders 1am. Closed Sun. Metro Franklin-D-Roosevelt.*

Perhaps the most startling thing about this excellent, if rather noisy restaurant, which is located in the plush business quarter of Av. George-V and constantly bulges at the seams with personalities from politics, the cinema and commercial radio, is its wide spectrum of prices. You can eat a three-course meal for remarkably little or rather a lot, depending on what you choose from the *à la carte* selection. The fare is simple but imaginative, and the sweet whiff of the sea as you walk in bears witness to the extraordinary freshness of the shellfish displayed outside. ***Specialties:*** ***Aiguillette de boeuf en gelée, rouget au pistou et aux pâtes fraîches, pot-au-feu aux trois viandes.***

Chez Fernand

9-11 Rue Georges-Saché, 14e
*☎ 543-65-76. Map **14**M6 ▯▢ to ▯▯ ▢ ▢ ▢ ▢ Last orders 10:30pm. Closed Sat, Sun, Aug. Metro Mouton-Douvernet.*

Really good Camembert is very hard to come by, even in France, but farmer's son Fernand Asseline is too fond of his native Normandy to let the side down, and he matures Camembert to perfect ripeness in his cellar (and even includes it, most successfully, in a fish sauce). He also makes his own butter, brown bread, *charcuterie* and *confit de canard*, as well as smoking his own fish. (Everything is also available as takeout food.) Particularly well-represented on the menu are fish and duck in various guises. The place is packed with knowledgeable gourmets, who like to kick off the meal in style with a *hue cocotte!* (literally, gee up!), a cocktail of truly Norman robustness (Calvados, cider and Mandarine). ***Specialties:*** ***Mousseline de barbue au Camembert, joues de porc et civet, émincé de canard, cidre et pommes.***

Chez Françoise

Aérogare des Invalides, 7e
*☎ 705-49-03. Map **13**H5 ▯▢ ▢ ▢ ▢ Last orders 10:30pm. Closed Mon, Aug 9-31. Metro Invalides.*

Conveniently tucked away in the Invalides Air Terminal, this is a rather old-fashioned-looking buffet, with skylight and potted plants. However, it provides reliable and far from dull dishes, as well as inexpensive wines, for the air traveler wishing to leave the capital with a pleasant taste in his mouth. ***Specialities:*** ***Aiguillette de saumon sauce verte, boeuf à la mode en gelée, marquise au chocolat.***

Chez Gorisse ✿

84 Rue Nollet, 17e
*☎ 627-43-05. Map **3**C6 ▯▢ to ▯▯ ▢ ▢ ▢ ▢ Last orders 10pm. Closed Sun, Aug. Metro La Fourche.*

Rémy Pommerai, after winning the prestigious *Meilleur Ouvrier de France* award as an apprentice cook, worked as chef on the Left Bank for a restaurant specializing in game. Then he took over this bistro in the delightfully provincial quarter of Batignolles. By respecting its original cozy and old-fashioned atmosphere, reasonable prices and down-to-earth cooking, he managed to retain its original customers – bistro connoisseurs. ***Specialties:*** ***Lapin à la moutarde, pot-au-feu, petit salé aux lentilles.***

Chez Julie

8 Rue Jolivet, 14e
*☎ 320-70-34. Map **14**L6 ▢ to ▯▢ ▢ ▢ Open noon-3pm, 4-6:30pm. Closed Sun, Aug. Metro Edgar-Quinet.*

Lissome, suntanned, young mothers wearing Hermès scarves, who frequent the nearby branch of Habitat, mingle here amid Habitat-style furniture, with secretaries working in the Tour Maine-Montparnasse. There is a wide selection of very good salads, well-filled pizzas, tarts and ice creams at reasonable prices. The tarts and pizzas can also be bought to take out, indeed Chez Julie started out as a shop. A good place for a lunchtime or afternoon break if you are in the area. ***Specialties:*** ***Tarte aux fruits de mer, salade Julie, glace exotique.***

Chez Ribe
15 Av. de Suffren, 15e
566–53–79. Map ***12****I3 to Last orders 10:30pm. Closed Sat evening, Sun, Aug, week of Christmas and New Year. Metro Champ-de-Mars.*

Radio and TV people working in the area like this well-redecorated former *bougnat* (coal merchant's shop and café). Owner Antoine Pérès cooks most of the dishes, which are generously served, while his diet-conscious wife Mireille is in charge of starters and desserts. The style is fairly traditional with regional touches, though there are also more modern dishes such as raw marinated scallops (when in season) and veal with limes. ***Specialties: Oeufs en cocotte au foie gras, terrine de canard avec une confiture d'oignons, saumon frais en papillote à la julienne de légumes.***

Chez Toutoune
5 Rue de Pontoise, 5e
326–56–81. Map ***10****J10 Last orders 10.30pm. Closed Sun, Mon, Aug 15–Sept 15. Metro Maubert-Mutualité.*

Good food cuts across class divisions (in France at least), which probably explains Chez Toutoune's wide spectrum of customers, from casually dressed students to elderly *bourgeois* couples complete with pearls and Légion d'Honneur rosettes. The exceptionally friendly atmosphere is effortlessly created by the blonde Toutoune herself. The formula is a lavish five-course set menu chalked up each day on a blackboard: a soup, a good choice of *entrées* and main dishes, two cheeses in peak condition, and a battery of desserts. The *cuisine* is best described as sophisticated provincial. ***Specialities: Moules aux endives, rognonnade de veau, tian de morue, Brie.***

La Chope d'Orsay
10 Rue du Bac, 7e
261–21–89. Map ***8****G7 Last orders 10:30pm. Closed Sat, Sun. Metro Rue-du-Bac.*

Antique dealers and publishers are the mainstay of this rustic Left Bank bistro. They flock here, especially at lunch, for Jacques Cosnard's down-to-earth and delicious *cuisine bourgeois*, cooked with a great deal of care and using really fresh produce. ***Specialties: Andouillette au vinaigre fin, daube, pot-au-feu.***

La Ciboulette
141 Rue St-Martin, 4e
271–72–34. Map ***10****H10 to Last orders 1am (Rez de Chaussée), 10pm (restaurant). Closed Sat, Sun. Metro Châtelet.*

Owner Jean-Pierre Coffe used to work in advertising, an experience that has served him well. After expertly identifying his target group – chic, quietly intellectual – he set about attracting them. La Ciboulette, located in an early 18thC building opposite the Beaubourg, is, in fact, several eating places rolled into one: the **Rez de Chaussée** serves breakfasts and snacks on the terrace, and in the evening provides medium-priced meals (including an exceptional *andouillette*) in the winter garden inside; upstairs, more expensive and sophisticated fare, cooked by Claude Segal, is served in the elegant **restaurant** proper and in its three *salons particuliers* (superbly decorated in Art Deco, Directoire and Viollet-le-Duc styles). Coffe has ambitions for La Ciboulette to become the ***ne plus ultra*** of fashionable Paris eating, and we can give him top marks for a good start. ***Specialties: Salade de perdreau rouge aux chanterelles, ris de veau en papillote de salade cuite, glace à la menthe, écorces d'orange.***

Claude Sainlouis
27 Rue de Dragon, 6e
548–29–68. Map ***8****I7 Last orders 11pm. Closed Sun, Aug, Easter, Christmas, New Year. Metro St-Germain-des-Prés.*

When owner Claude Sainlouis (real name, Claude Piau) gave up his job as a stuntman and took up catering, he decided he wasn't going to take any more risks. For the last 20yr or so, he has been serving an immutable menu of salad, expertly grilled steak and chocolate mousse for (almost) a song. His caution paid off: the place is permanently packed with people out for an evening in St-Germain-des-Prés. ***Specialties: Steak grillé, mousse au chocolat.***

La Cloche des Halles
28 Rue Coquillière, 1er
236–93–89. Map ***10****G9 Last orders 9pm. Closed Sun, Aug. Metro Les Halles.*

Serge Lesage is keeping up the standards of previous owner Géraud Rongier (now at **Le Val**

d'Or) by continuing to lavish top-quality ham (raw, cooked on the bone, and *persillé*), quiches, pâtés, tarts, sandwiches of every description and, last but not least, excellent wines (Beaujolais and Burgundy in particular) on the happy habitués, many from the nearby Banque de France, of this bustling café. ***Specialties: Jambon persillé, terrine de foies de volailles.***

La Closerie des Lilas
171 Bd. du Montparnasse, 6e
☎ 326-70-50. Map ***15****L8 Last orders midnight. Metro Montparnasse-Bienvenue.*
La Closerie has always been, and is still, the haunt of literati, artists and plain hacks, though nowadays they tend to congregate in the bar and brasserie section. The restaurant proper, which has a pleasant terrace, accommodates an altogether more *bourgeois* gathering, and its food is suitably classical. ***Specialties: Chaud-froid de canard à l'orange, andouillette, pigeon de Bresse rôti.***

La Coupole
102 Bd. du Montparnasse, 14e
☎ 320-14-20. Map ***14****K7 Open noon–2am. Closed Aug. Metro Montparnasse-Bienvenue.*
La Coupole, a cavernous hall decorated with rather wan 1920s murals, is Paris's largest brasserie, and an institution. It probably serves the most motley crowd of customers to be found in any Paris eating place: they range from be-suited politicians, film-producers, painters and students to photographers and bevies of very attractive girls who appreciate the excellent exposure afforded by La Coupole's open plan with its long, broad aisles. The waiters are particularly hard-boiled, the food competent if undistinguished, and the noise, when the evening is in full swing (around 11pm), deafening. But it's worth it for the show. ***Specialties: Steak au poivre, oreilles de cochon grillées, soufflé au Grand-Marnier.***

Daniel Tuboeuf ✿
26 Rue de Montmorency, 3e
☎ 272-31-04. Map ***10****H10 to Last orders 10:30pm. Closed Sat lunch, Sun, Aug. Metro Rambuteau.*
Brass coat hangers, tiled floor, discreet prints, velvet bench seats, attentive service: this restaurant has all the ingredients of a typical cozy Parisian bistro. But there is a difference: the food is several cuts above average, in quality, imagination and value. Daniel Tuboeuf worked at **Pierre Traiteur** and with *nouvelle cuisine* exponent Gérard Pangaud (now in the suburbs of Paris) before moving to this rather forgotten corner of the Marais. Local habitués (craftsmen, jewelers) appreciate his delicious *foie gras de canard*, interesting fish dishes (anglerfish with saffron and avocado, scallops with morels, hot sea-bass terrine with sea-urchin sauce), and excellent desserts. ***Specialties: Foie de veau au vinaigre de framboise, aiguillette de canard aux grains de myrtilles, soufflé au praline accompagné de sa glace.***

Daru
19 Rue Daru, 8e ☎ 227-23-60. Map ***2****E4 to Last orders 11pm. Closed Sun, Mon, Aug. Metro Courcelles.*
White Russians, many of them taxi drivers, used to recall the 'good old days' over a glass of vodka and a *zakouski* in this grocery-snack bar opposite the Russian Orthodox Church. Although most of them have since departed this world, the Daru remains a repository of Russian tradition, boasting a score of Russian and Polish vodkas as well as a passable French brand, Tersa. There is also tasty food for every purse, from *tarama* and *borstch* to smoked salmon and caviar. ***Specialties: Luli kebab, krepkaya, smoked sturgeon.***

Dodin Bouffant ✿
25 Rue Frédéric-Sauton, 5e
☎ 325-25-14. Map ***15****J9 to Last orders 12:30am. Closed Sat, Sun, Aug, two days over Christmas and New Year. Metro Maubert-Mutualité.*
Jacques Manière, among Paris' most iconoclastic, outspoken and warm-hearted chefs, made Dodin Bouffant one of the finest – and certainly cheapest for the quality – restaurants in the capital. It was he who installed the saltwater tanks in the cellar, where oysters, mussels, clams, the rare *violet*, and other shellfish co-exist peacefully before expiring at your command. Before ill-health caused him to retire in 1981, Manière managed to find a worthy successor in the person of Jean-Marie Clément, who had

survived the blisteringly tough training he had been put through by Manière (an ex-army man). With the restaurant's former *maître d'hôtel*, Maurice Cartier, Clément has kept the Manière ensign flying: in other words, Dodin Bouffant still provides wonderful fish combinations, both as starters and as main courses, a sumptuous *plateau de fruits de mer* of utter freshness, unusual meat dishes, featherlight desserts, and wines that are nothing less than a gift. ***Specialties:*** ***Bar fumé aux endives, ragoût de clams aux asperges vertes, fricassée de tête de veau au romarin.***

Le Duc
243 Bd. Raspail, 14ᵉ
322-59-59. Map ***14****M7 to Last orders 10:30pm. Closed Sat, Sun, Mon. Metro Denfert-Rochereau.*

If, like Fats Waller, your favorite dish is fish, make a point of eating at Paul and Jean Minchelli's establishment, which is regarded by many as being the finest seafood-only restaurant in town. Paul, who has written an authoritative cookbook on the subject, was one of the first chefs to approach the preparation of fish with a completely fresh and inventive eye, and, among other things, to take his cue from the Japanese and explore the possibilities of raw fish. In his hot dishes, the fish is always cooked to perfection (just a second or two underdone), and never swathed in a strong sauce of the kind that destroys delicate flavors. ***Specialties: Palourdes au thym, tartare de loup, soupe de langouste et d'étrilles.***

L'Écluse-I
15 Quai des Grands-Augustins, 6ᵉ 633-58-74. Map ***9****I9 to Open 11:30am–2am. Closed Sun. Metro St-Michel.*

L'Écluse-II
64 Rue François-1ᵉʳ, 8ᵉ 720-77-09. Map ***7****G4 to Open 11am–2am. Closed Sun. Metro Franklin-D-Roosevelt.*

Georges Bardawil has been going from strength to strength: after opening **L'Écluse-I** and **La Photogalerie** on the Left Bank, he recently moved into the Champs-Élysées area with the more sophisticated **L'Écluse-II**, like its namesake a wine bar restricted to Bordeaux – open bottles of which are ingeniously topped up with nitrogen to stop them deteriorating so that the very best wines can be served by the glass. At off-peak hours **L'Écluse-I** is one of the most relaxing places in which to sit and read, work or chat. The good selection of vintages available at reasonable prices can be accompanied by excellent 'super-snacks': *carpaccio*, smoked salmon, *saucisson sec*, goat's cheese, and a superbly rich and sticky chocolate cake that connoisseurs cross Paris to sink their teeth into. **L'Écluse-II**, frequented by photographers, journalists and glamorous models, has a similar range of classy titbits to enhance the wines. ***Specialties: Carpaccio, gâteau au chocolat.***

L'Espadon
15 Pl. Vendôme, 1ᵉʳ
260-38-30. Map ***8****G7 Last orders 10:30pm. Metro Tuileries.*

The wonderfully atmospheric restaurant of the **Ritz** (see *Hotels*), with its gentle lighting and *trompe-l'oeil*, was presided over by Escoffier at the turn of the century, and until fairly recently it maintained standards worthy of the great man. In the last few years, however, there has been a slight decline, from superlative to just plain good. Unfortunately the prices are still as high as ever. ***Specialties: Oeufs pochés Benedictine, foie gras au porto, coquilles Saint-Jacques à la vieille Chartreuse.***

L'Étoile Verte
13 Rue Brey, 17ᵉ 380-69-34. Map ***6****E3 to Open 11am–midnight. Closed Aug. Metro Étoile.*

A faithful old stand-by (next to the Arc de Triomphe) that seems to extend almost endlessly into the recesses of the building. A very wide range of straightforward food is served by no-nonsense waitressses all day. A good place to know about when you are very hungry between the traditional eating hours. ***Specialties: Tournedos béarnaise, sauté de veau.***

Gérard Besson
5 Rue du Coq-Héron, 1ᵉʳ
233-14-74. Map ***10****G9 to Last orders 10:30pm. Closed Sat lunch, Sun, July. Metro Les Halles.*

The lunchtime menu served by Gérard Besson, owner-chef of easily the best restaurant in the Les

Halles area, is such good value it verges on the philanthropic. After things to nibble with your apéritif, you get a choice of three starters, such as a chunky *soupe de poissons* with saffron, four main courses, fromage blanc, and one of six desserts, such as pistachio profiteroles, washed down by, perhaps, half a bottle of Château Capbern (a Saint-Estèphe *cru bourgeois*). Coffee follows, with homemade *petits fours*, and a bill so light for the quality it almost flutters away. *À la carte* prices are higher.

Besson, who comes from Bourg-en-Bresse and has worked with Alain Chapel, has a classical yet very personal style that contrasts refreshingly with the striving-after-effect of which some *nouvelle cuisine* chefs are guilty. He also lays down his own wines (45,000 bottles of them), then offers them at bargain prices, especially the Bordeaux, when they are ready for drinking. ***Specialties:*** ***Game, ris et rognon de veau au vinaigre de malvoisie, tarte feuilleté et sa glace caramel.***

Germain
19 Rue Jean-Mermoz, 8ᵉ
359–29–24. Map ***7****F5 to Last orders 10pm. Closed Sun, Aug. Metro Franklin-D-Roosevelt.*

It's hard to grab a table here, and one can see why as the value for money is quite exceptional for the area. In a genuine bistro setting with imitation-leather seats and original paintings on the walls, habitués (art dealers, fashion designers and models, among others) enjoy straightforward cooking. If you're lucky or patient enough, you'll be able to join them. ***Specialties:*** ***Blanquette de veau, petit salé aux lentilles, potée auvergnate.***

Le Grand Café
4 Bd. des Capucines, 9ᵉ
742–75–77. Map ***4****F8 AE Φ VISA Open 24hr a day. Metro Quatre-Septembre.*

This is the best of the handful of Paris brasseries that serve full-blown meals 24hr a day. Its clientele are hungry local shift and night-workers (mainly journalists), topping up with solid or liquid nourishment, and others who are less easily pigeonholed. ***Specialties:*** ***Seafood of all types, depending on season and availability.***

Le Grand Véfour
17 Rue de Beaujolais, 1ᵉʳ
296–56–27. Map ***9****G8 Last orders 9pm. Closed Sat evening (Sept 1–May 1), Sun, Aug. Metro Pyramides.*

If you walk out of the Palais Royal at its N end, you will pass, under the arcade, a muskily-lit restaurant that looks like a rare fossil from another age. This is the world-famous Le Grand Véfour, home ground of much-traveled author and cook Raymond Oliver. Its decor, which dates from the Directoire, is, in fact, one of the oldest extant restaurant interiors in Paris, if not the oldest (it is classified as a historical monument). The excellent food is classical as you might expect, with the occasional touch of *nouvelle cuisine* and a distinct flavor of Oliver's native Bordeaux (for example, lampreys, when in season). Bordeaux are, of course, staggeringly well-represented on the wine list. ***Specialties:*** ***Ragoût de brochet et d'écrevisses à l'anis, poulet sauté au vinaigre de miel.***

La Hulotte
29 Rue Dauphine, 6ᵉ
633–75–92. Map ***9****I8 to AE Φ VISA Last orders 10:30pm. Closed Sun, Mon, Aug. Metro Mabillon.*

This restaurant's snug little upstairs dining room is a haven of reliability in the shark-infested waters of Quartier Latin catering. A basket of brown bread served, unusually for Paris, with a little dish of butter and a jug of good cheap wine, will keep your hunger and thirst at bay as you wait. One might mind the leisurely service if the food were not so good and the prices so reasonable. ***Specialties:*** ***Pintade aux choux, brandade de morue, veau à la berrichonne.***

Jacqueline Fénix
42 Av. Charles-de-Gaulle, Neuilly-sur-Seine
624–42–61 Last orders 10pm. Closed Sun, Mon, Christmas week, Aug. Metro Porte-Maillot.

This chic and inviting restaurant is only 5mins' walk from Porte Maillot. Much of its becoming decor is the work of the comely Jacqueline Fénix herself, who runs the establishment jointly with mustachioed chef Michel Rubod. Rubod, once a professional gardener, uses vegetables and herbs with imagination. A stickler for fresh ingredients, he is most at home in a *nouvelle cuisine* idiom (some of the dish titles sound rather too grandiose, as is often the case). Smart Neuilly clientele. ***Specialties:*** ***Moelleux de ris de veau au cresson de fontaine, salade de soles tièdes au buisson de feuilles vertes.***

Le Jardin de la Paresse
20 Rue Gazan, 14e
588-38-52 to Open noon-12:30am. Metro Cité-Universitaire.

Would you believe that cow's udder (*tétine*) could be delicious? Well, it can be when sautéed with chanterelle mushrooms, tiny onions and bacon in a cream sauce, as at this quaintly named (*paresse* means idleness) Belle Époque restaurant overlooking – and in summer opening on to – the attractive Parc Montsouris. Other specialities include the Provençal *anchoïade* and a mint-flavored moussaka. Habitués (of the **La Coupole** type, including Claudia Cardinale) like the restaurant's free-and-easy opening hours: you can eat, though not always *à la carte*, at any time between noon and half-past midnight. ***Specialties:*** ***Cassoulet de poisson, foie de veau à la vapeur, soupe de fraises à la menthe et aux pêches.***

Les Jardins d'Edgard
92 Rue La Boétie, 8e
359-08-20. Map ***7****F4 to Last orders 11:30pm. Closed Sat, Sun, Aug. Metro St-Philippe-du-Roule.*

Le Tout Paris goes for this restaurant's extravagant Art Deco fittings, winter garden, and clever mixture of cooking genres: *cuisine minceur* (apparently preferred by more male than female customers), *cuisine bourgeoise*, and straightforward, good seafood. The *arbiter elegantiae* is now none other than Guy-Louis Duboucheron, who also owns the ultra-fashionable **L'Hôtel** (see *Hotels*). ***Specialties:*** ***Gigot à la ficelle, navarin de lotte, foie de veau au vinaigre de framboise.***

Julien
16 Rue du Faubourg St-Denis, 10e 770-12-06. Map ***5****F10 Last orders 1am. Closed July. Metro Strasbourg-St-Denis.*

Jean-Claude Bucher, owner of four Parisian eating places, has single-handedly done more than anyone to save authentic restaurant decors from the modernizer's axe. Though both **Brasserie Flo** and **Le Vaudeville** are museum pieces in their own way, the jewel in Bucher's crown must be Julien, which sports some of Paris' most fabulous Art Nouveau designs – and is accordingly much favored by extrovert admen and showbiz people. The food is classical and straightforward, with a slight leaning towards Bucher's native Alsace. ***Specialties:*** ***Potages, foie gras frais, civet de sanglier.***

Le Lafayette Bistrot
6 Rue du 29-Juillet, 1er
296-57-11. Map ***8****G7 to Last orders 10:30pm. Metro Tuileries.*

This 'snack bar' of the classy **Hôtel St-James et Albany** (see *Hotels*) is, in fact, much more than that. It is an efficient, modern bistro which charges reasonable prices in this part of town for a succinct selection of dishes which curiously combine prewar, *nouvelle* and rustic *cuisine*. See also **Le Noailles**, the hotel's main restaurant. ***Specialties:*** ***Oeuf Bénédictine, pannequet normand.***

Lasserre
17 Av. Franklin-D-Roosevelt, 8e
359-53-43. Map ***7****F5 Last orders 10:30pm. Closed Sun, Mon, Aug. Metro Franklin-D-Roosevelt.*

The essence of Lassere, like that of the equally famous **La Tour d'Argent**, is found particularly in the decor, tableware and superlative service. The food is excellent and deeply traditional. It is a haven for the extremely rich, old-fashioned gourmets who almost seem to use it as their canteen. In Lasserre your caviar or *foie gras* is wheeled processionally to your table and each speck of cigarette ash, each empty oyster shell, is spirited away by a deft waiter. ***Specialties:*** ***Canard de Challans à l'orange, escalope de saumon sauvage à la crème de cerfeuil, coupelle des ducs de Bourgogne.***

Laurent
41 Av. Gabriel, 8e
359-68-07. Map ***8****G6 Last orders 11pm. Closed Sat, Sun. Metro Concorde.*

A few years back, this sumptuous restaurant was renowned less for its food than for its lovely garden, perfect service, superb wine list, and withering prices. The difference today is that the food is now on a par with the rest – an intelligent combination of the best in classical cooking (tempting trolley of old-fashioned hors-d'oeuvres), *nouvelle cuisine* (salad of raw red mullet with black radish), and provincial tradition (*soupe de grenouilles*, samphire). To help you decide how best to accompany such a symphony of styles is one of the capital's finest wine waiters, Philippe Bourguignon. ***Specialties: Consommé de poissons en gelée aux deux poivrons, papillotes de homard au caviar, caneton au cassis.***

Léni-Olympic Entrepôt
9 Rue Francis-de-Pressensé, 14e ☎ 541-06-17. Map ***14****M6 Last orders 11:30pm. Closed Tues. Metro Pernéty.*

This is one of the most popular places for younger intellectuals, photographers, actors and journalists. Even proprietress Léni herself and her squad of waitresses look as though they would be happier discussing the respective merits of Barthes and Levi-Strauss than feeding film-goers, for film-goers most of the customers are. The building's functional interior of steel girders and glass (it used to be a bookbinding workshop) also houses one of Paris' best revival cinemas, the **Olympic Entrepôt**. The set menu is competently cooked and usually centers on a hearty stew of some kind, with vegetables that sometimes could do with a little less cooking. The straightforward desserts are copious and tasty. Things begin to heat up at the Olympic's bar, **L'Eléphant Rose**, when the films are over. ***Specialties: Fromage blanc aux fines herbes, sauté de veau, mousse au chocolat.***

Lipp
151 Bd. St-Germain, 6e ☎ 548-53-91. Map ***8****I7 Open 8am (for breakfast) and noon–1am. Closed Mon, July, two weeks over Christmas and New Year. Metro St-Germain-des-Prés.*

This delightfully intact turn-of-the-century brasserie attracts the capital's intellectual, political and showbiz élite in far greater swarms than any other Parisian restaurant, however chic. Owner Roger Cazes decides at a glance where to place his customers: he avoids sending political opponents or, for that matter, close friends to adjoining tables, and likes to enliven a huddle of intellectual heavies by seating a bevy of pretty girls next to them. The unknown usually get sent up to the first floor (where the occasional celebrity is to be spotted) but they can, if so inclined, brave the small, crowded café section by the entrance. Impeccable service by long-aproned and long-serving waiters, reliable *plats du jour*, and the herd instinct explain Lipp's phenomenal success. ***Specialties: Pied de porc farci, boeuf à la mode, tête de veau.***

Le Lord Gourmand
9 Rue Lord-Byron, 8e ☎ 562-66-06. Map ***6****F3 to Last orders 10pm. Closed Sat, Sun, Aug, Christmas week. Metro Étoile.*

Daniel Météry offers some of the best food to be had in the vicinity of the Champs-Élysées. As one would expect of someone who once worked with Paul Bocuse, he is an expert at imaginative but basically simple gastronomic combinations. His other assets are his friendly wife and *maître d'hôtel*, Brigitte, and a welcoming beige decor with above-average pictures and pleasantly hushed acoustics – ideal for a tête-à-tête celebration. ***Specialties: Salade de gésiers et navets tièdes, ris de veau à la moelle, gâteau au chocolat et à la framboise.***

Lucas-Carton
9 Pl. de la Madeleine, 8e ☎ 265-22-90. Map ***8****F7 AE VISA Last orders 10pm. Metro Madeleine.*

Lucas-Carton is the grand old man of Paris restaurants. It used to be the haunt of politicians when on duty (when off duty they made for the less staid **Maxim's** down the road), and more than one Fourth Republic government is said to have been made or unmade in its august surroundings. Culinary standards may have slipped a bit in recent years, but its famous flambéed woodcock (only in season) is as good as ever – some of those fanatics who are willing to pay the price for it are reported to cover their heads with a napkin as though inhaling, so that not a whiff of aroma is lost. The regal wine list (rich in Burgundies) is as tempting as ever, and the decor is a delight (red velvet bench seats and superb Art Nouveau woodwork by

Majorelle). ***Specialties:*** ***Bécasse flambée, cassolette d'écrevisses, délices de sole Lucas.***

Le Maquis
69 Rue Caulaincourt, 18e
259–76–07. Map ***4C8*** *to* *Last orders 10:30pm. Closed Sun, Mon, two weeks in Aug. Metro Lamark-Caulaincourt.*
Montmartre – and in particular the streets bordering that center of kitsch art, the Place du Tertre – is not a good area for eating, as some of the bad habits of picture-vendors seem to have rubbed off on restaurant owners. Ten minutes' walk down the Butte, however, this attractively decorated bistro offers an inexpensive set lunch and interesting *à la carte* food – unfussy, up-to-date, colorful and light. Two other exceptions to the rule about the quality of food in Montmartre are **Beauvilliers** and Les Semailles. ***Specialties:*** ***Potage de potiron à l'oseille, filet de sandre au cidre, coquilles Saint-Jacques aux deux beurres.***

La Marcande
52 Rue Miromesnil, 8e
265–76–85. Map ***7F5*** *to* *AE* *VISA* *Last orders 10:30pm. Closed Sat, Sun, two weeks in Aug, two weeks over Christmas and New Year. Metro Miromesnil.*
Rugged Jean-Claude Ferrero's restaurant affords diners a view not only over a delightful courtyard garden, but also over part of his own kitchens. Behind the glass partition, he and his assistants prepare some of the most imaginative food to be had in this part of town (chiefly a business area), such as duck fillets in honey, smoked leg of lamb or veal sweetbreads with asparagus. ***Specialties:*** ***Hure de crêtes de coqs, volaille en vessie, confiture de lapereau au romarin.***

Maxim's
3 Rue Royale, 8e *265–27–94. Map* ***8G6*** *Last orders 1am. Closed Sun. Metro Concorde.*
The food and the clientele are not what they used to be at this world-famous restaurant, though they are both still in the luxury league. The only things that have not gone into decline are Maxim's marvelous Art Nouveau decor – and its prices. It remains to be seen what changes will be made by the restaurant's new owner, fashion designer Pierre Cardin. ***Specialties:*** ***Sole Albert, poularde aux concombres, crêpes Veuve Joyeuse.***

Morot-Gaudry
8 Rue de la Cavalerie, 15e
567–06–85. Map ***12J3*** *VISA* *Last orders 10pm. Closed Sat lunch, Sun, July. Metro La Motte Piquet-Grenelle.*
Majestically located, à **La Tour d'Argent**, on the top floor of a ship-like 1920s building with a wonderful view of the nearby Eiffel Tower, this restaurant is much favored by bigwigs from UNESCO (also nearby). French food gurus can't seem to decide whether Jean Pierre Morot-Gaudry's cuisine is *nouvelle* or not. No matter: his concoctions have the stamp of true originality (calf's liver with raspberries, crab *boudin*, red mullet with chanterelles). There is an excellent set menu of six dishes with six different wines, as well as a venerable collection of Calvados. ***Specialties:*** ***Salade tiède de langue et de fraise de veau aux kumquats, charlotte fondante de lotte, gâteau de riz au gingembre.***

Le Morvan
22 Rue Chaligny, 12e
307–47–66. Map ***17K14*** *to* *Last orders 9:15pm. Closed Sat, Sun, Aug. Metro Reuilly-Diderot.*
Although the recent addition of bright flowery wallpaper has somewhat dented the authentic charm of this constantly packed bistro, Denis Guyard's cooking has remained resolutely the same for years. It is still a mixture of *cuisine bourgeoise* and of specialties from his native Morvan, a wild, hilly region near Burgundy (such as excellent ham and black pudding). Regulars include doctors from a nearby hospital. ***Specialties:*** ***Rognons de veau dijonnaise, cervelle au beurre noir, omelette morvandelle.***

Le Moulin du Village
Cité Berryer, 23–25 Rue Royale, 8e *265–08–47. Map* ***8G6*** *VISA* *Last orders 11pm. Closed Sat, Sun. Metro Concorde.*
Probably the largest selection of little-known wines in Paris is to be found here. Englishman Steven Spurrier, who part-owns the place, runs a very well-stocked wine shop a little farther down the Cité Berryer. The restaurant is in a

mews, almost invisibly tucked away off the Rue Royale, a marvelously calm and unpolluted spot for outdoor eating in summer. *Nouvelle cuisine* is featured here. ***Specialties:*** ***Aspic d'écrevisses à l'aneth, soupe de moules à la fleur de thym, canard aux pêches.***

Le Muniche
27 Rue de Buci, 6e
633-62-09. Map ***9****I8. Last orders 3am. Metro Mabillon.*
This large, bustling, noisy and cramped brasserie, which serves hearty food (for example, *choucroute, charcuterie*), is the canteen of Left Bank literati, who can be seen exchanging pleasantries from table to table before, perhaps, drifting down to the live jazz club below, **Le Furstenberg** (under the same management, and well air-conditioned). ***Specialties:*** ***Queue de porc grillée, langue de veau sauce gribiche, andouillettes.***

Le Noailles
6 Rue du 29-Juillet, 1er
296-57-11. Map ***8****G7 Last orders 10:30pm. Closed Sun. Metro Tuileries.*
The most discreet of all good hotel restaurants in Paris (it adjoins the **Hôtel St-James et Albany**, see *Hotels*) and ideal for a low-profile business lunch or *dîner à deux* (with piano). In summer, food is also served in the pleasant courtyard overlooking the hotel's 17thC rear facade. Chef Daniel Soret offers a catholic range of excellent dishes (and a very reasonable set menu) that features both *cuisine régionale* and *nouvelle*. ***Specialties:*** ***Mesclum aux gésiers confits, saucisson de grenouilles au beurre nantais, lotte au vinaigre et au miel.***

Au Pactole
44 Bd. St-Germain, 5e
326-92-28. Map ***16****J10 to Last orders 11pm. Closed Sat lunch, Sun. Metro Maubert-Mutualité.*
Lunch is the best time to eat here because, with luck, the sun will be streaming through the windows of the attractive covered terrace (the brown decor inside and the clientele tend to be a bit gloomy in the evening). Roland Magne is an inventive yet unfussy cook with a penchant for unusual combinations (kid with mint, lamb with violets). His set menu is a bargain at this level of gastronomy. ***Specialties:*** ***Blanquette de baudroie à l'oseille, saumon à la chartreuse.***

Le Petit Bedon
38 Rue Pergolèse, 16e
500-23-66. Map ***6****E2 Last orders 10:15pm. Closed Sun, Mon lunch, Aug. Metro Argentine.*
The very well-heeled quarter of Av. Foch had no really good restaurant until recently, when one of Paris' most gifted and inventive young chefs, Christian Ignace, who was trained by Raymond Oliver (of **Le Grand Véfour**), took over Le Petit Bedon. His cuisine might loosely be called *nouvelle*, but it steers clear of the chi-chi terminology (e.g. *petits légumes*), contrast for contrast's sake, and the microscopic portions that are continuing to give the school a bad name. Ignace, a man drawn more toward ingredients like lamb's tongues, carp and teal than caviar or *foie gras*, has proved himself to be a master of subtle combination. ***Specialties:*** ***Barbue à la fondue de poivrons, méli-mélo de queues d'écrevisses au xérès.***

Le Petit Coin de la Bourse
16 Rue Feydeau, 2e
508-00-08. Map ***4****F8 Last orders 10pm. Open Mon-Wed lunch only, Thurs-Fri lunch and dinner. Closed Sat, Sun, Aug. Metro Bourse.*
The essence of Guy Girard's *cooking* is the inventive use of whatever the market or season has to offer. One day, when his eye has caught some particularly succulent-looking sea urchins at Rungis (Paris's main food market, on the outskirts), customers will be treated to a *soufflé aux oursins*; the next, they may be gorging on *petits gris* (a small variety of snail) *à la vinaigrette*, sent up in a consignment of thousands by Girard's father in southwest France. If Girard retires and steps aside for the talented restaurateur Claude Verger, high standards will continue. The decibels generated by the customers of this unspoiled Belle Epoque bistro – chiefly stockbrokers from the nearby Bourse, and journalists – are slightly more tolerable on the ground floor than upstairs. ***Specialties:*** ***Contrefilet à l'aveyronnaise, choucroute de poisson.***

Au Petit Montmorency
5 Rue Rabelais, 8e
☎ 225–11–19. Map ***7****E5 to VISA Last orders 10:30pm. Closed Sat, Sun, Aug. Metro Miromesnil.*
Daniel Bouché calls his cooking "*cuisine buissonnière*" ('truant cooking'), by which he means he follows no school but his own. That may sound pretentious but it's results that count. A faithful and rather chic clientele comes back again and again for such inventive delights as rabbit with sea urchins, beef cheek with calf's foot, or coffee and whisky ice cream. The decor is pleasantly old-fashioned (prints, flowers, bentwood chairs). ***Specialties:*** ***Lotte rôtie à la creme de bacon, foie gras de canard au caramel poivré.***

Le Petit Riche
25 Rue Le Peletier, 9e
☎ 770–68–68. Map ***4****E8 VISA Last orders 1am. Closed Sun, Aug. Metro Le Peletier.*
The new management of this restaurant has not, thankfully, tampered with its quite exceptional decor, which, with its decorated frosted windows, large mirrors and brass luggage-racks, is somewhat more Edwardian than Belle Epoque. Nor has the management changed the strong emphasis on Loire wines: a good selection is still available, and this must be one of the very few Paris restaurants serving Bourgueil in carafes. But not all is as it was; indeed, the reasonably priced food is a distinct improvement on previous offerings, which had become stuck in a deep rut. It cleverly combines ancient and modern, and is generously served. And Le Petit Riche now stays open till 1am, whereas before it would begin to empty by 9pm. ***Specialties:*** ***Gâteau de foie blond et son coulis, pied de porc à la Sainte-Ménéhoulde.***

Le Petit Zinc
25 Rue de Buci, 6e
☎ 354–79–34. Map ***9****I8 AE VISA Last orders 3am. Metro Mabillon.*
Probably the best restaurant in town open until 3am, Le Petit Zinc has a pleasant, old-fashioned bistro atmosphere, a short menu of *plats bourgeois*, and some unpretentious wines. A favorite haunt of insomniacs, it is under the same management as **Le Muniche**. ***Specialties:*** ***Poule au pot, confit de canard, gigot aux flageolets.***

Pharamond
24 Rue de la Grande-Truanderie, 1er ☎ 233–06–72. Map ***10****H9 AE VISA Last orders 10:15pm. Closed Sun, Mon lunch, July. Metro Châtelet-Les-Halles.*
This gem of a restaurant, with its Art Nouveau *faïence* and mirrors, was formerly in the heart of the vegetables section of Les Halles market (now banished to Rungis); it's now surrounded by a plethora of trendy, here-today-gone-tomorrow clip-joints that have proliferated in and around the Forum des Halles. Pharamond used to be famed mainly for its succulent tripe (simmered for 12hr in tomato sauce) and *andouillette*, but it now features some more modern dishes on its varied menu. ***Specialties:*** ***Tripes à la mode de Caen, coquilles Saint-Jacques au cidre, canette au citron.***

La Photogalerie
2 Rue Christine, 6e
☎ 329–01–76. Map ***9****I8 to VISA Open 12:15–11:30pm. Closed Sat evening, Sun. Metro Mabillon.*
In the evening, this photographic gallery-bookshop-restaurant-*salon de thé* is the haunt of *intellocrates* (a cult word in Paris, coined by the acerbic authors of the successful book *Les Intellocrates* to describe members of the trend-setting cultural establishment). During the day, you're more likely to see very pretty girls (usually models or aspiring actresses) accompanied by their Pygmalions. The food is elegant, as you would expect, and can be washed down by the excellent wines chosen by owner Georges Bardawil (also proprietor of the two **Écluses**). ***Specialties:*** ***Terrine chaude de poisson à l'oseille, turbot au céleri-rave, foie gras chaud au sauternes.***

Pierre Traiteur
10 Rue de Richelieu, 1er
☎ 296–09–17. Map ***9****F8 to AE VISA Last orders 10pm. Closed Sat, Sun, Aug. Metro Richelieu-Drouot.*
A rather noisy, up-market bistro that offers a tempting choice between Auvergnat food (such as the rare *estofinado*, made from wind-dried cod) and more sophisticated fare (raw sea bass with chives). There is a good selection of lesser-known wines. ***Specialties:*** ***Chou farci, feuilleté à la moelle.***

Pierre Vedel ✿
50 Rue des Morillons, 15ᵉ
☎ 828-04-37 Last orders 10:30pm. Closed Sat, Sun, July 15–Aug 15, week of Christmas and New Year.
Genuine Mediterranean restaurants are not particularly common in Paris, so all the more reason to be thankful for the existence of this welcoming bistro in a rather bleak backwater of the 15ᵉ. Vedel himself, who comes from the fishing port of Sète, naturally feels most at home with seafood (excellent fish soup, fillet of *rascasse* in saffron-flavored aspic), but he also has a talent for inventive vegetable dishes, for example, an unashamedly garlicky cold cucumber soup and a gamut of combined vegetable mousses. ***Specialties:** Bourride, ris de veau à l'orange, soupe de pêches à la menthe.*

Plats du Jour
60 Rue Rambuteau, 3ᵉ
*☎ 274-46-33. Map **10**H10 to Last orders 10:30pm. Closed Sat, Sun, Aug. Metro Rambuteau.*
The eponymous *plats du jour* served here are simple fare (two daily); also available are a handful of cheap starters and desserts. With its friendly service and spacious 1920s-style decor (formerly the premises of **La Ciboulette**, which has moved round the corner), the place is a boon in an area (Beaubourg) that bristles with cramped, amateurish and over-priced restaurants. ***Specialties:** Salade frisée aux lardons, navarin d'agneau, boudin aux coings.*

Polidor ✿
41 Rue Monsieur-le-Prince, 6ᵉ
*☎ 326-95-34. Map **15**J8 to Last orders 10pm. Closed Sun, Aug. Metro Odéon.*
Price has little to do with fashion, and the fact that Polidor gives away a three-course set meal for a ludicrously low price does not deter Claire Bretécher or Serge Reggiani from bestowing their custom on the place. Little has changed since the time of previous habitués such as Verlaine, Valéry and Joyce: there are still lace curtains, numbered napkin lockers (some in use), a spiral staircase, and even waitresses in turn-of-the-century dress. That this is so is due to owner Marie-Christine Kervella who, 5yr ago when still a law student, rescued Polidor from being turned into a Chinese restaurant. It's been packed ever since. Good *cuisine bourgeoise*. ***Specialties:** Potage au potiron, canard aux petits pois.*

Le Pouilly
96 Rue Daguerre, 14ᵉ
*☎ 322-60-18. Map **14**M7 to Last orders 9pm. Closed Sat, Sun, Aug. Metro Denfert-Rochereau.*
One of the places to which the people working in the 195m (650ft) Tour Maine-Montparnasse escape at lunchtime in order to restore their sanity and sate their appetites is this quiet, almost provincial bistro. Situated at the Montparnasse end of the equally provincial Rue Daguerre (home of the film maker Agnès Varda and subject of a documentary by her), it serves good uncomplicated food. ***Specialties:** Maquereaux au vin blanc, gigot aux flageolets, cassoulet.*

Le Pré Catalan
Route de Suresnes, Bois de Boulogne, 16ᵉ ☎ 524-55-58 Last orders 10:30pm. Closed Sun evening, Mon, Aug.
Most well-heeled Parisians abandon the capital during *le weekend*. Many of those who don't, and who hanker after tip-top food in an accessible pastoral setting, make for this establishment in the Bois de Boulogne. It was transformed a few years ago from an ailing eating place into a palatial summerhouse of a restaurant by the well-known caterer and pastry cook, Gaston Lenôtre. His nephew, Patrick Lenôtre, trained at no fewer than four three-star restaurants before being let loose by his uncle in the kitchens of Le Pré Catalan and turning it into Paris' finest outdoor restaurant. (In winter there's cozy, indoor dining in front of an open fire.) His cooking is stylish and very decorative – thus mirroring the clientele. ***Specialties:** Ris, pieds et mignons de veau aux primeurs, marinière de poisson et de crustaces.*

Les Princes
31 Av. George-V, 8ᵉ
*☎ 723-54-00. Map **7**F4 AE VISA Last orders 11pm. Metro George-V.*
That Les Princes, in the **Hôtel George V** (see *Hotels*), is the least starchy restaurant in a luxury Paris hotel is due, in large part, to its manager M. Frison, who is neither

stuffy, nor obsequious. The clientele here includes admen and film-producers with pretty women in tow. The food combines the aristocratic (truffles in champagne) with peasant food (salt pork with lentils), and with, for France, the exotic (angels on horseback). In summer you can eat in the George V's lovely flower-filled inner courtyard. ***Specialties:** Gratin de macaronis aux écrevisses Nantua, confit de canard aux cèpes.*

Le Procope
13 Rue de l'Ancienne-Comédie, 6e ☎ 326-99-20. Map 9I8 to Last orders 1am. Closed July. Metro Odéon.
No other restaurant in Paris has been going as long as the Procope, which opened in 1686 (as a café to start with). Previous customers include La Fontaine, Voltaire, Benjamin Franklin, Jean-Jacques Rousseau, Robespierre, Napoleon, Balzac, George Sand and Huysmans. Although recently renovated, its two floors have retained their warm, original atmosphere. But don't expect any great culinary prowess. ***Specialties:** Côte de veau Gorgonzola, boeuf bourguignon.*

Au Quai d'Orsay
49 Quai d'Orsay, 7e ☎ 705-69-09. Map 7H5 AE VISA Last orders 10:45pm. Closed Sun, Aug. Metro Invalides.
Mushroom freaks should make a beeline for this restaurant (or its smaller adjoining establishment, **L'Annexe du Quai**). Owner Étienne Bigeard prides himself on his selection of fungi, which includes (depending on the time of year) *cèpes, chanterelles*, hedgehog mushrooms, saffron milk-caps and oyster mushrooms. The very copiously served *cuisine bourgeoise* offered has recently made some concessions to 'modernity', perhaps to please the restaurant's very fashion-conscious clientele. ***Specialties:** Salade de pleurotes à l'huile de truffe, pain de veau farci aux rognons et zestes de citron.*

Quéré
125 Rue de la Tour, 16e ☎ 504-35-35 Last orders 10:30pm. Closed Sat, Sun, Aug. Metro Passy.
Amazingly, this cavernous restaurant, hidden away in the most exclusive part of the uppercrust 16e, is one of the very cheapest places to eat in Paris. The simple fare on offer is enjoyable, though hardly sophisticated. Frequented by workmen, students and the occasional sheepish aristocrat eking out his private income. ***Specialties:** Boeuf aux carottes, sauté de veau.*

Régence-Plaza
25 Av. Montaigne, 8e ☎ 723-78-33. Map 7G4 AE Last orders 10.15pm. Closed two weeks of Christmas and New Year. Metro Franklin-D-Roosevelt.
People go to the Régence-Plaza, the more expensive of the **Hôtel Plaza-Athénée's** two restaurants, to savor the glittering company as much as the food. Manager M. Roland uses the experience he gained at **La Tour d'Argent** to good effect: he is an expert at organizing the arrangement of diners so that the celebrities whom ordinary customers have come to see are sprinkled evenly over the whole dining room. In summer the inner courtyard is a marvelous, verdant jungle of plants. The cuisine is very good – a mixture of classical and new styles – and the wine list superb. ***Specialties:** Sole Reine Astrid, crêpes Montaigne.*

Relais Saint-Germain
190 Bd. St-Germain, 7e ☎ 548-11-73. Map 8I7 AE VISA Last orders 10:30pm. Closed Aug. Metro Rue-du-Bac.
The covered terrace of this restaurant is a good vantage point from which to observe the exotic parade that roves between the Café Flore at St-Germain-des-Prés and the Escurial at Rue du Bac. The cuisine is good (with the emphasis on fish) and excellent value for the money; and the chef makes excellent *profiteroles au chocolat*. Frequented by antique dealers and publishers working round the corner in the Rue des Sts-Pères. ***Specialties:** Terrine de rascasse, barbue au Sauternes sur lit d'épinard.*

Le Repaire de Cartouche
8 Bd. Filles-du-Calvaire, 11e ☎ 700-25-86. Map 11H12 VISA Last orders 10:30pm. Closed Sat, Sun, July 24–Aug 22. Metro Filles-du-Calvaire.
Raymond Pocous, a printer by trade, presides over this relaxed, two-level old restaurant. He may have a strong Paris accent, but his heart is in the Landes, in southwest

France, where he spent his early childhood. The menu is suitably atavistic, though without any of the heaviness that often mars the cuisine of that area. His smoked duck breast, *confits* of duck and goose (not only the best cuts, but gizzards and hearts), and renowned Chalosse beef are all eminently digestible. Pocous has a contagious enthusiasm for his superb selection of Bas-Armagnacs. ***Specialties:*** ***Faux-filet aux cèpes, ris de veau aux moules.***

Le Restaurant du Marché
59 Rue de Dantzig, 15ᵉ
828–31–55. Map ***9****D4 Last orders 10:30pm. Metro Convention.*
Under the same friendly management as **L'Aquitaine** down the road, this partly old-fashioned, partly modern establishment sets out, like the preceding restaurant, **Le Repaire de Cartouche**, to acquaint the customer with the hearty fare of the Landes, in southwest France, much of which revolves around goose and duck. This is one of the few places in Paris where you'll get a *garbure*, the soup that is a meal in itself (with ham, various vegetables including cabbage, and, if required, a sprinkling of Roquefort). ***Specialties:*** ***Salade de peaux de canard, cou et gésier d'oie confits aux haricots blancs, glace aux pruneaux.***

Rôtisserie Rivoli
Hôtel Inter-Continental, 3 Rue de Castiglione, 1ᵉʳ
260–37–80. Map ***8****G7 Last orders 11:15pm. Metro Tuileries.*
This restaurant is unusual for a luxury hotel (it's part of the **Hôtel Inter-Continental**, see *Hotels*) in that it offers a set menu which, in view of its copiousness and high quality, is very good value indeed – particularly in summer, when there is the additional bonus of eating on the hotel's celebrated and often celebrity-packed Italian-style patio. Chef Jean-Jacques Barbier shows a refreshing interest in the kitchen garden, and his two *plats du jour*, themselves traditional rather than inventive, are imaginatively served with two, and sometimes three vegetables. ***Specialties:*** ***Selle d'agneau avec mousseline de cèpes et pommes de terre Anna et coeurs de céleri braisés, mousseline de truite à l'oseille avec gâteau de carottes et brocoli.***

Royal Monceau
35 Av. Hoche, 8ᵉ 561–98–00. Map ***6****E3 Last orders 10:30pm. Metro Étoile.*
Hotel restaurants can often be disappointing, but not so the Royal Monceau (see also *Hotels*). Its restaurant offers an ultra-fresh and very varied lunchtime buffet, sophisticated *à la carte* cuisine in the evening, and, for eating out in fine weather, a delightful paved garden. The daily set lunch with unlimited wine, and the Thurs evening fish buffet with vodka and champagne available, are both excellent value. ***Specialties:*** ***Marinated fish, foie de veau rôti à la citronnelle.***

Au Rubis
10 Rue du Marché-St-Honore, 1ᵉʳ 261–03–34. Map ***8****G7 Open lunch only. Closed Sat, Sun, Aug. Metro Pyramides.*
Owner Léon Gouin has retired, but the success of his tiny wine bar has not abated. You still have to get there early to stake out your table for the lunchtime *plat du jour*; and if all you want is a glass of one of the many wines available and an excellent open sandwich, you still have to fight your way to the bar in true English-pub style. ***Specialties:*** ***Charcuterie, boeuf bourguignon, petit salé aux lentilles.***

Le Sancerrois
12 Rue du Champ-de-Mars, 7ᵉ 555–13–47. Map ***13****I4 Last orders 9pm. Closed Sat evening, Sun, Aug. Metro École-Militaire.*
People from the nearby TV studios appreciate the quiet atmosphere of this friendly, unpretentious cafe-restaurant. The food is Auvergnat, and the handful of wines (some available by the glass in the café section) mainly Loire and Beaujolais, and all impeccably chosen. ***Specialties:*** ***Confit de porc, tripoux, saucisses d'Auvergne.***

Taillevent
15 Rue Lamennais, 8ᵉ 563–39–94. Map ***7****F4 Last orders 10:30pm. Closed Sat, Sun, Aug. Metro Étoile.*
Taillevent, named after one of the first great French cooks who lived in the 14thC, is run by Jean-Claude Vrinat with all the skill you would expect of a business-school graduate, and he has made it one of the capital's top five or six restaurants. He follows new

cooking trends, and will occasionally send his chef off for a refresher course with the Troisgros brothers or Michel Guérard. Vrinat is also always on the look-out for excellent lesser-known wines to fill out his incredible wine list. He buys some of his cheeses direct from the farm, which is most unusual for this class of establishment. Taillevent is much frequented by politicians and top businessmen. The decor is suitably discreet, with gentle lighting and well-spaced tables. ***Specialties:*** ***Tête de veau en tortue, huîtres chaudes aux truffes et aux poireaux, coquilles Saint-Jacques à la vapeur d'algues.***

Terminus Nord
23 Rue de Dunkerque, 10e
☎ 285-05-15. Map ***5****D10 to Last orders 12:30am. Metro Gare-du-Nord.*

Cafés and restaurants near stations tend to treat their irregular, hurried and captive clientele in less than gentlemanly fashion. A notable exception is the Terminus Nord, the fourth restaurant in the stable of Jean-Claude Bucher (see **Brasserie Flo**, **Julien** and **Le Vaudeville**). An ideal place at which to eat before taking a train from the Gare du Nord opposite, this brasserie offers food that is good enough to attract swarms of gourmets who have no intention of leaving town. ***Specialties:*** ***Choucroute au jarret de porc fumé, pot-au-feu, lapin à la moutarde.***

Thoumieux
79 Rue St-Dominique, 7e
☎ 705-49-75. Map ***13****H5 to Last orders 10:30pm. Closed Mon, July 15-Aug 15. Metro Solférino.*

No one would claim that this spacious, vaguely Art Deco restaurant does what its name suggests in French – *tout mieux* (everything better); but it does do an honest job of serving good traditional food to office workers and genteel retired people who like dining out alone in the evenings. ***Specialties:*** ***Raie au beurre noir, boudin aux châtaignes, gâteau de pain et de raisins.***

La Tour d'Argent
15-17 Quai de la Tournelle, 5e
☎ 354-23-31. Map ***16****J10 Last orders 10:30pm. Closed Mon. Metro Maubert-Mutualité.*

This penthouse restaurant is world famous. Eccentric but shrewd ex-playboy Claude Terrail has, over the years, perfected the art of giving his customers what they want: the pleasure of a table overlooking the illuminated Notre-Dame (if they book well ahead); of dealing with a *sommelier* who looks delighted, not petulant, if they choose the cheapest wine on his list (the finest classical cellar in Paris); and the convenience and style of walking out of the elevator, after the meal, straight into their coats and out of the building to find their cars purring at the curbside. Service of this caliber and the very high quality of La Tour d'Argent's cuisine cost a great deal; it is Paris' most expensive restaurant. ***Specialties:*** ***Canard du Grand-Frédéric, crème Princesse Anne, pigeon au confit d'endives.***

Le Trou Gascon
40 Rue Taine, 12e
☎ 344-34-26 Last orders 10pm. Closed Sat, Sun. Metro Daumesnil.

Alain Dutournier's rather theatrical mustache of truly musketeer-like proportions (he comes from the Gers) conceals a very serious cook who is interested in the essence not the show of gastronomy. Hence his most unusual blend of new ideas and provincial (Gascon) tradition, and his equally rare selection of wines (some 450) ranging from prestigious Bordeaux to humble, little-known *crus*, all annotated in detail on the city's most compulsively readable wine list. Throw in his amazing collection of Armagnacs, and the restaurant's turn-of-the-century decor (a riot of mirrors and moldings), and you have the makings of a memorable meal. ***Specialties:*** ***Jambon d'oie, daurade aux oursins, persillé de lapereau en saupiquet.***

Le Trumilou
84 Quai de l'Hôtel-de-Ville, 4e
☎ 277-63-98. Map ***10****I10 to Last orders 9:30pm. Closed Mon, Sept. Metro Pont-Marie.*

Madame Rouby, who must surely incarnate everyone's ideal of the farmer's wife – sturdy, hospitable and just a little shy – was indeed born on an Auvergne farm. She runs an establishment that belongs to a fast-disappearing breed; the homely bistro, with potted plants and freshly cut flowers everywhere, and original paintings with no artistic pretensions all over the walls. Their quality does not matter, for the contented habitués who fill the Trumilou to bursting point have their attention glued to the food on their plates – good solid *cuisine bourgeoise*, generously served. ***Specialties:** Canard aux pruneaux, lapin à la provençale.*

Le Val d'Or

28 Av. Franklin-D-Roosevelt, 8ᵉ
*359–95–81. Map **7**F5 to Restaurant closed for dinner; snacks only served in evening till 9pm. Closed Sat evening, Sun. Metro St-Philippe-du-Roule.*

Youthful Géraud Rongier moved recently from his tiny **La Cloche des Halles** to this larger café near St-Philippe-du-Roule. On the ground floor he provides cold snacks (including, in many people's opinion, the very best sandwiches in town), and in the mirror-filled basement hot lunches of exceptional value are served. At both levels, a small but very reliable selection of wines is available (mainly Beaujolais and Burgundy). ***Specialties:** Gâteau de légumes, andouillette, salade de coquilles Saint-Jacques.*

Le Vaudeville

29 Rue Vivienne, 2ᵉ
*233–39–31. Map **9**F8 to VISA Last orders 1:30am. Metro Bourse.*

Once upon a time this was a dreary, half-empty Art Deco brasserie, haunted by tired journalists working nearby. In stepped Jean-Claude Bucher (see **Brasserie Flo**, **Julien** and **Terminus Nord**) with his magic wand to restore the establishment's Egyptian-style walls and opaque fittings to their former glory and put professionals in charge of the kitchens. It now offers very good classical cuisine at highly competitive prices – and open until 1:30am it is a boon for people wanting a bite after a show. As the quality of the Sylvaner wine has greatly improved since the Alsatian Bucher took over, the journalists have suffered less ferocious hangovers. ***Specialties:** Boeuf à la ficelle, pied de porc pané.*

Au Vieux Berlin

32 Av. George-V, 8ᵉ
*720–88–96. Map **7**F4 to AE VISA Last orders 11pm. Closed Sat, Sun. Metro George-V.*

Film and showbiz people (Serge Gainsbourg, Jacques Dutronc) appreciate the discretion and attentive service available at this accurate reproduction of a pre-war Berlin eating house (complete with pianist and candles in the evening). The food, though mainly German (plenty of game in season, pumpkin soup with bacon, knuckle of pork with pease pudding) has an attractively light and – dare it be said? – French touch. The less expensive bar section serves many of the same dishes in less snug surroundings. ***Specialties:** Filet de porc à la bière et au cumin, charcuterie allemande, wiener schnitzel.*

Le Vivarois

192 Av. Victor-Hugo, 16ᵉ
*504–04–31. Map **6**F2 Last orders 9:30pm. Closed Sat, Sun, July 14–Aug 31. Metro Victor-Hugo.*

This is the most unusual of the city of Paris' pantheon of first-class restaurants, run by a true eccentric, chef-patron Claude Peyrot, and frequented by well-heeled gourmands, often political. Peyrot is no disciple of *nouvelle cuisine*, rather a past-master at dishes that are traditional in the best sense (i.e. not overcomplicated or smothered in heavy sauces). His aim is not flashy inventiveness, but utter perfection of both raw materials and the end-product – and he usually succeeds. A very interesting wine list with a very interested wine waiter to explain it. ***Specialties:** Bavarois de poivrons, estragonnade de volaille, coq au vin au Pommard.*

Willi's

13 Rue des Petits-Champs, 1ᵉʳ
*261–05–09. Map **9**G8 to Open 11am–10pm. Closed Sat evening, Sun, Aug. Metro Bourse.*

Willi's (named after owner Mark Williamson) is a fairly faithful copy of a typical London wine bar, except that the number of wines (99, and many available by the glass) and the quality of the food served (Anglo-French) are much higher than one would normally expect in Britain. It is crowded with English expatriates and tweedy French Anglophiles, who doubtless appreciate being served by attentive and well-bred young ladies of quite impeccable manners. ***Specialties:** Salade de moules au curry, carré de porc au fenouil, gâteau au chocolat.*

Cafés

The café is one of the most civilized institutions ever invented. It is a living stage, a forum for debate, a club, a home away from home. Paris was among the earliest cities to establish a café society, and it remains one of the few where traditional café life still thrives; in fact the French capital without its cafés would be unthinkable. In them revolutions have been plotted, poems written, philosophies born. As literary and artistic circles have migrated from one district to another, so different cafés have had their spells as fashionable meeting places. Some of the famous ones have disappeared, others have been ruined by modernization, but many are still virtually intact.

In the Middle Ages young men went in search of the Grail; today the café is the quest of a young man in search of an artistic education.

George Moore, *Vale*, 1914

The more than 10,000 cafés in Paris cater, between them, to almost every need a Parisian might have. An often staggering range of alcoholic, soft and hot drinks is available; solid fare includes croissants, hard-boiled eggs and sandwiches, and sometimes hot snacks and even sit-down meals, especially at lunchtime. You can make local and sometimes trunk (*inter*) calls, though both will cost much more than from the public phone booths that have recently sprung up in increasing numbers in the streets of Paris. The main brands of French cigarettes can be found in most cafés, but *cafés-tabacs* (recognizable by their red lozenge sign) sell a wide range of cigarettes, cigars, pipe- and even chewing-tobacco, snuff, stamps, envelopes, postcards, pens and state lottery tickets (including the bingo-like *Loto*). If the letters PMU are displayed outside, it means the *café-tabac* turns into a betting shop on certain days, and you can have a flutter on the horses via the state tote system. Other café amusements may include pinball machines (known as 'flippers'), electronic games, juke-boxes, miniature soccer, American pool and French billiards. You can even use them for their public toilets (for the price of a coffee) and the standard of these has improved greatly over the last decade or so.

There are free attractions, too. You can read, write, work or just while away the time with or without friends for as long as you like (except in one or two cafés on the Bd. St-Michel, where notices fiercely warn you that your order will be automatically renewed every hour!). Cafés with terraces are good vantage points from which to observe the passers-by on, say, the Champs-Élysées or one of the busy boulevards like the Bds. Montmartre, des Italiens, des Capucines, Haussmann, Clichy, Pigalle, St-Germain, St-Michel and du Montparnasse. But expect to be asked to pay a stiffer price here: you're paying not only for the refreshment, the seat and the service, but for the prime location.

If you simply want to rest your feet, recharge your batteries or appease the children, look for a little side-street café, which will usually be quieter and cheaper, as well as often providing friendlier and more personal service.

Remember that most cafés have a two-tiered price system, depending on whether you drink at the bar or occupy a table. Usually, the price difference is not enormous. However, at some more expensive establishments the cement-stained building workers knocking back their *pastis* at the bar will pay up to 50% less than the well-heeled customers sitting on the terrace – cafés are democratic, too. Watch out for the price of certain drinks – non-French beer, bottled mineral water, Coca Cola, whisky and vodka, to name but a few.

A word about the different types of café you're likely to encounter. *Buvettes*, which are getting rarer every day, are grocery shops or wine merchants with a counter (*zinc*) but usually no tables; here, and at the almost extinct *bougnats* (tiny, Spartan cafés run by coal-and-wood merchants), you will find the authentic flavor of prewar Paris.

The already mentioned *cafés-tabacs* differ from other cafés in that their prices may be fractionally lower and their atmosphere a little livelier. Brasseries, 'drugstores' and 'pubs' (the last two bear little relation to the American or British originals) are large and generally serve hot meals throughout the day. Some cafés and brasseries specialize in high-quality wines and beers.

Lastly, at the more elegant end of the spectrum, there are *salons de thé*. When they double up as *pâtisseries* they tend to cater to maiden aunts and usually do not serve alcoholic drinks. Sometimes, however, run-of-the-mill cafés with social ambitions arrogate the title *salon de thé*. Genuine *salons de thé*, if you can afford them, are the best places for a good continental breakfast.

As in restaurants, tipping in cafés is no longer a problem: at the tables, the tip is clearly included on the ticket the waiter gives you, or else he will add it on himself. At the bar, there is generally a notice indicating whether it is included or not. If in doubt, ask.

Interesting cafés in Paris are far too numerous to list exhaustively, but here are a few favorites arranged according to area.

Left Bank

Montparnasse

Still the center of Bohemian life in Paris, though many of the café decors have been ruined. Genuine artists, intellectuals, writers, film people and hangers-on of every description gather in **La Coupole** (see *Restaurants*), or **Le Select** (*99 Bd. du Montparnasse*), which has hardly changed since it was frequented by Erik Satie, Francis Poulenc, Robert Desnos and Foujita. Across the way, **Le Dôme** (*108 Bd. du Montparnasse*) is still cashing in on its reputation as a favorite watering hole of Modigliani, Stravinsky, Picasso and Hemingway. Unfortunately, its hybrid 1920s redecoration has destroyed the charm of its former atmosphere. Five minutes' walk along the boulevard is the still lively **Closerie des Lilas** (see *Restaurants*). Behind Montparnasse station is **Les Mousquetaires** (*77 Av. du Maine*), a marvelous, cavernous café-cum-billiard hall.

St-Germain-des-Prés

Two of the most famous of all cafés, **Les Deux Magots** and **Le Flore** (*170 and 172 Bd. St-Germain respectively*), are to be found right in the heart of this district. The list of their customers past and present reads like a roll call of French *vie intellectuelle* over the last century: Rémy de Gourmont, Jarry, Huysmans, Barres, Maurras, Giraudoux, Sartre, de Beauvoir, Breton, Camus and the Prévert brothers, to name but a few. The Existentialist movement was born in one or other of them, or both, as were many of Sartre's philosophical and literary works – he preferred writing on a café table rather than on a desk.

Nowadays, however, times have changed and only the wealthier literati can afford to hold court regularly at the two cafés, and most of the cafés' day-to-day customers belong to the most trendy international set.

On the other side of the boulevard there is still plenty of action at **Lipp** (see *Restaurants*). The high priests of modern French intellectual life, such as *nouveau philosophe* Bernard-Henri Lévy and novelist Philippe Sollers, have retreated to the quieter waters of the English 'pub' round the corner, **The Twickenham** (*70 Rue des Sts-Pères*). Another 'pub' in the area is the vast **Pub St-Germain-des-Prés** (*17 Rue de l'Ancienne-Comédie*), which boasts an unrivalled range of draft and bottled beers, teas and whiskies, and is open all day and all night. Also in the Rue de l'Ancienne-Comédie is the famous **Procope**, the first-ever café in Paris, which opened its doors to the public as far back as 1686. Though it is open for a few hours in the afternoon, its prime function is now as a restaurant (see *Restaurants*).

The man regarded by many as the finest *pâtissier* in Paris, Christian Constant, has a *salon de thé* in his shop nearby (*26 Rue du Bac*).

St-Michel

The cafés on the Bd. St-Michel itself are no longer as interesting as they used to be, and two of them have been turned into MacDonalds, though **La Boule d'Or** (*4 Pl. St-Michel*) has retained some character. However, you can take refuge nearby at **L'Écluse-I, Le Balzar**, or **Café de la Nouvelle Mairie** (see *Restaurants*). There are also three afternoon-only *salons de thé* within easy reach: **La Photogalerie**, **La Bûcherie** (see *Restaurants*) and **The Tea Caddy** (*14 Rue St-Julien-le-Pauvre*), where you'll enjoy better scones, muffins and cinnamon toast than you're ever likely to encounter in a café or tea shop in Britain.

Right Bank

Champs-Élysées

There are only two cafés of any real interest actually on the Champs-Élysées: **Le Fouquet's** (*no. 99*) and **L'Alsace** (*no. 39*). At the first, you pay withering prices for the privilege of joining starlets on its terrace; the real film stars can be found in the hushed and old-fashioned (no unaccompanied ladies) bar within. L'Alsace is a brasserie which has the merit of serving genuine Alsatian beer, wine and food 24hr a day. Not far from the Champs-Élysées there are several good establishments which serve refreshments and snacks outside meal times, notably **Le Val d'Or**, the bar of **Aux Vieux Berlin**, **L'Écluse-II**, and **Boulangerie St-Philippe**. These are all described under *Restaurants*.

Opéra – Boulevard Haussmann

Once the hub of café society, this is now mainly a business quarter, and becomes pretty bleak after the early evening. But French office-workers being as demanding as they are, most cafés are reliable, particularly those that are found lurking down side streets.

One of the most celebrated establishments in Paris is, of course, the **Café de la Paix** (*12 Bd. des Capucines*). It emerged from meticulous restoration a few years ago with its deliciously ornate green and gold decor, designed by Charles Garnier, architect of the Opéra opposite, and with its clientele (wealthy tourists for the most part) unscathed. By way of contrast, the late 1930s interior and long sinuous bar of **La Boutique du Pâtissier** (*24 Bd. des Italiens*) was recently ripped out by its vandalous owners, though it still offers some of the best coffee, homemade croissants and other pastries in the area. They are equalled only by those at the smart but stark *salon de thé* of **Fauchon** (*26 Pl. de la Madeleine*), Paris' most famous food store. Here you proceed as in Italy; you decide whether you want a pastry or not, pay for it and/or for a coffee at the cash desk, hand over your ticket at the counter, collect your order and eat it standing up at one of the pedestal tables. Half-way down the Av. de l'Opéra is the **Royal-Opéra** (*no. 19*), a large and eventful *café-tabac* with more character than its rivals in the vicinity. A number of cafés serve good wines and snacks: as well as **Au Rubis** (see *Restaurants*), there is **Ma Bourgogne** (*133 Bd. Haussmann*), frequented by the less sophisticated kind of French businessman, and **Le St-Amour** (*4 Rue de Rome*), a friendly and often rollicking café usefully located near the big department stores on the Bd. Haussmann.

Les Halles

Now, sadly, only a shadow of its former self, '*le ventre de Paris*' is in such a state of ferment – with cafés and restaurants mushrooming overnight and disappearing without trace within a month or two – that it is safe to recommend only the gilt-edged stock.

Opposite the excellent **La Cloche des Halles** (see *Restaurants*) is a pleasant old-fashioned café with nothing extraordinary about it except its name, **La Promenade de Vénus** (*44 Rue du Louvre*), which resulted in its being selected by André Breton as the meeting place for fellow Surrealists. Round the corner, the best-known Les Halles restaurant, **Au Pied de Cochon** (*6 Rue Coquillière*), still serves fairly pricey but unexceptional food 24hr a day every day of the year, but the bar functions as a café, and you can go in and order anything from a coffee or a glass of robust house wine to a reasonably priced *plat du jour* or a traditional *gratinée* (onion soup), which you have to eat standing up.

Le Marais

If you wander round this fascinating old quarter, which has retained an almost provincial calm, you're bound to find several small cafés, filled with regulars and rich in character. On the beautifully intact 17thC Pl. des Vosges, there is the cozy and altogether trendier **Ma Bourgogne** (*no. 19*), which serves reasonably good wines. But for a really wide and reliable selection of vintages, try **La Tartine** (*24 Rue de Rivoli*) on the southern edge of Le Marais; this bustling, smoke-filled café has not changed much since Lenin and Trotsky drank there. Also on the periphery is a very good *pâtisserie/salon de thé* called **Clichy** (*5 Bd. Beaumarchais*).

Montmartre – Pigalle

All self-respecting painters have long since fled the Pl. du Tertre in Montmartre, crammed now with terrible paintings of sad-eyed children and dogs, and Pigalle has become a sex-shop jungle haunted by tough Brazilian transvestites. In both areas, cafés have turned the exploitation of tourists into a fine art, but as soon as you move away from the bright lights you may find a genuine Montmartrois café.

One such establishment is the delightful **Aux Négociants** (*27 Rue Lambert*), where excellent and inexpensive wines flow freely as regulars converse, conveniently gathered around the tiny, horseshoe-shaped bar.

Nightlife

From the panhandling mimes in the piazza at Beaubourg to the idolized divas at the *Opéra*, Paris remains a compelling magnet for performers and their followers from every French-speaking country, and much of the rest of Europe as well. The center of established culture is the monumental state Opéra, the glorious Baroque interior of which is accessible to even the most hard-up devotee, though the price of a good ticket can be exorbitant. Around it lie the Boulevard theaters. Just as plush are the grand cinemas along the Champs-Élysées, which sometimes even show French films with English subtitles. The Left Bank shelters most of the revival and avant-garde cinemas, and the ancient Marais quarter now thinks itself the home of the *café-théâtre*.

Although not cheap, most prices are fair, and many concerts are free. Informality is the rule for all but the grandest occasions. Beware of late summer, when almost all theaters close for a month or two. Many theaters require bookings a week or two in advance, but **SOS Théâtres** (☎*225–67–07*) or **Allo Théâtre** (☎*742–60–32*) provide last-minute assistance. For music bookings try **FNAC** (*Rue de Rennes, 6*[e] ☎*544–39–12 or Rue Pierre-Lescot, Forum des Halles, 1*[er] ☎*261–81–18*). Indispensable publications are *Pariscope* and *l'Officiel des Spectacles* published every Wed.

As for less serious nightlife, 'Gay Paree' still conjures up visions of cancan dancers, champagne and a cosmopolitan sophistication unique to the French capital. Since the Belle Époque, the combination of Bohemian artists, international café society and madcap expatriates has given Paris a slightly naughty but very glamorous after-dark reputation.

While a considerable bourgeois element has crept in and the favored nightlife among certain natives is eating out, Paris is still very lively indeed after dark. The chief and cheapest spectator sport, people-watching, can be accomplished in many cafés, particularly on the Left Bank (see *Cafés*). At the most expensive end of the scale, the spectacular revues with feathered and sequined scantily-clad beauties are flourishing as never before.

Parisians have always loved dancing, so clubs and discos are crowded and colorful. Like revues and cabarets, they tend to charge by the drink (*consommation*) rather than by the combination of admission fee plus drink. Prices can range from inexpensive at the more popular discos to vastly expensive at the most lavish nightclubs. Bar-hopping is not really a Parisian diversion, although many good bars welcome customers for the apéritif hour, and for a late-night drink. Cabarets and jazz clubs, with their echoes of the postwar era, are largely unchanged since the 1950s, and they can offer both nostalgia and entertainment.

Visible nightlife is concentrated in St-Germain and the Latin Quarter on the Left Bank, and in Pigalle, its side streets crammed with sex shows and tattoo parlors, on the Right Bank. While prostitution is not illegal, soliciting is. Thus, prostitutes displaying their charms in the Bois de Boulogne and around the Rue St-Denis meet with some indifference from the police. Though there are still plenty of prostitutes in evidence, the Rue St-Denis is now becoming chic, part of the transition catalyzed by the influx of trendy shops and restaurants around the *Forum des Halles*. Ladies of the night (and day) also hang out in more stylish districts, such as around the Opéra and along the Rue Daunou.

Ballet

In recent years, great efforts have been made to liberate the dance from the traditional gold standard of the Opéra. More informal space is offered to foreign and touring companies of every kind, especially during festivals. Every July, there is open-air ballet in the Cour Carrée of the Louvre.

Carré Sylvia Montfort
106 Rue Briançon, 15e
☎ 531-28-34. Metro Porte-de-Vanves.
Off the beaten boulevard perhaps, but worth an expedition south.

Espace Marais
22 Rue Beautrellis, 4e
*☎ 271-10-19. Map **11**J11. Metro Sully-Morland.*
Simple, unconventional and often exciting.

Opéra
Pl. de l'Opéra, 9e
*☎ 742-57-50. Map **8**F7. Metro Opéra.*
Home of French ballet, shared with the **National Opera**. Magnificent setting.

Théâtre de la Ville
2 Pl. du Châtelet, 4e
*☎ 274-22-77. Map **10**I9.*
Base for the larger visiting companies.

Bars

A night in a bar is not a Parisian habit. Bars are crowded before dinner for an apéritif, or very late after everything else has closed. They tend to open around 5pm and may stay open till dawn. Unlike many other cities, there are no legal closing hours in Paris.

Some of the more sophisticated bars are found in the smart hotels, notably **L'Hôtel**, the bar of which resembles an indoor garden, the **Plaza-Athénée**, the **Crillon**, the **Ritz** and the **George V** (for addresses see *Hotels*).

Prices are high for spirits or champagne, considerably less for pastis or a wine-based drink such as *kir*. Non-alcoholic drinks are just as popular among the French as the more intoxicating variety, such as the refreshing *citron pressé*.

Bedford Arms
*17 Rue Princesse, 6e. Map **15**J8. Metro St-Germain-des-Prés* AE Φ VISA
Based on the French idea of an English pub, very lively, popular with journalists and movie types.

Centreville
*9 Rue de la Grande-Truanderie, 1er. Map **10**H9. Metro Étienne-Marcel* AE VISA
Waiters used to wear roller-skates, now they sport running shoes and jeans. Huge bar, in a cozy room furnished with soft couches.

Closerie des Lilas
*171 Bd. Montparnasse, 6e. Map **15**L8. Montparnasse-Bienvenue* AE Φ VISA
The ghost of Hemingway lingers in the bar, which still attracts assorted artists and literati. (See also *Restaurants*.)

La Coupole
*102 Bd. Montparnasse, 14e. Map **14**K7. Metro Vavin* CB
A cultural landmark and watering hole for three generations of artists. Motley, crowded, noisy; politicians, beautiful girls, journalists, *cinéastes*, anybody. (See also *Restaurants*.)

Fouquet's
99 Champs-Élysées, 8e,
*☎ 723-70-60. Map **6**F3. Metro George-V* AE Φ
Liveliest bar on the Champs-Élysées, with a friendly mix of regulars and tourists. (See also *Cafés*.)

Harry's Bar
*5 Rue Daunou, 2e. Map **8**F7. Metro Opéra.*
"Sank Roo Doe Noo," as popular with Parisians as with visiting Anglophones, stocks 160 types of

whisky and harks back to the Lost Generation when such distinguished drinkers as Hemingway and Fitzgerald graced the stools. Good piano bar in the basement. Opened in 1911, it closes only on Christmas Day.

Kenz
*22 Rue Vernet, 8ᵉ. Map **6**F3.*
Metro George-V AE
Quiet, discreet and elegant piano bar.

Rosebud
*11 bis Rue Delambre, 14ᵉ. Map **14**L7. Metro Vavin.*
Once a rendezvous for Montparnasse artists and writers, such as Sartre and Simone de Beauvoir, now slightly run-down. Good chilli.

Le Village
*7 Rue Gozlin, 6ᵉ. Map **15**I8.*
Metro St-Germain-des-Prés.
A dim echo of prewar St-Germain.

Cabarets

Caveau des Oubliettes
11 Rue Galande, 5ᵉ
*☎ 354–94–97. Map **10**J9.*
Metro St-Michel.
Fake decor and costumed waiters but a real Latin Quarter atmosphere with old French songs of love and life.

Chez Félix
23 Rue Mouffetard, 5ᵉ
*☎ 707–68–78. Map **16**K10.*
Metro Cardinal-Lemoine.
Candle-lit 14thC cellar with Brazilian music; dancing in the basement.

Club des Poètes
30 Rue de Bourgogne, 7ᵉ
*☎ 705–06–03. Map **8**H6. Metro Invalides* VISA
Totally Parisian idea – selected poems are sung, acted, danced and mimed.

Crazy Horse Saloon
12 Av. George-V, 8ᵉ
*☎ 723–32–32. Map **7**F4. Metro George-V* AE Φ VISA
Strip show without the strip. Dancers, with crazy names like Vanilla Banana and Tootsie Roll, are already *déshabillée*, their charms enhanced with artistic lighting and risqué costumes. Excellent entertainment by magicians, good dancing. Crowded, uncomfortable and very expensive.

Don Camilo ✿
10 Rue des Sts-Pères, 7ᵉ
*☎ 260–82–84. Map **8**I7. Metro St-Germain-des-Prés* AE Φ
Variety show with elegance, and excellent dining available for a cabaret.

Au Lapin Agile ✿
22 Rue des Saules, 18ᵉ
*☎ 606–85–87. Map **4**C8. Metro Lamarck-Caulaincourt.*
Haunt of Montmartre artists such as Renoir and Picasso, now devoted to tourists, but still retaining some of the charms of Vieux Paris.

Le Milliardaire
68 Rue Pierre-Charron, 8ᵉ
*☎ 225–25–17. Map **7**F4. Metro Franklin-D-Roosevelt* AE Φ VISA
The sexiest strip, after the **Crazy Horse**.

Café-théâtres

The heyday of the *café-théâtre* is past, although it has certainly retained its refreshing informality. At some you eat, at others you can only drink.

If you are lucky, the show may turn out to be almost as good as the food.

Blancs-Manteaux
*15 Rue des Blancs-Manteaux, 4ᵉ ☎ 887–15–84. Map **10**H10.*
Metro Rambuteau.

Café d'Edgar
*58 Bd. Edgar-Quinet, 14ᵉ ☎ 320–85–11. Map **14**L7. Metro Edgar-Quinet.*

Café de la Gare
*41 Rue du Temple, 3ᵉ ☎ 278–52–51. Map **10**H10. Metro Hôtel-de-Ville.*

Les 400 Coups
74 Rue du Cardinal-Lemoine, 5e ☎ 633-01-21. Map ***16****K10. Metro Cardinal-Lemoine.*

Petit Casino
17 Rue Chapon, 3e ☎ 278-36-50. Map ***10****H10. Metro Rambuteau.*

Casinos

Except for a few exclusive and very private gaming clubs, it is not possible to gamble in Paris. The nearest good casino is at Enghein, 16km (10 miles) NW of the city.

Cinemas

Foreign films are either dubbed into French (VF) or presented in the original version, with sub-titles (VO). The **Gaumont**, **Pathé** and **Paramount** chains along the Champs-Élysées are best for new films, while the independents of the Left Bank, headed by the **Olympic** and **Action** organizations, present a motley and dazzling selection of revivals from every continent.

Action République
18 Rue du Faubourg-du-Temple, 11e ☎ 805-51-33. Map ***11****G11. Metro République.*
Unremittingly experimental.

La Boîte à Films
42 Av. de la Grande-Armée, 17e ☎ 622-44-21. Map ***6****E2. Metro Argentine.*
Two screens only, but more than a dozen modern classics every week.

Cinemathèque Française
Palais de Chaillot, Av. Albert-de-Mun, 16e ☎ 704-24-24. Map ***12****H2. Metro Trocadéro. Closed Mon.*
Centre Georges Pompidou (5th floor). Rue Beaubourg, 4e ☎ 278-35-57. Metro Rambuteau. Closed Tues.
France's two national film theatres, sometimes obscure, always fascinating.

Le Déjazet
41 Bd. du Temple, 3e ☎ 887-97-34. Map ***11****G11. Metro Pernety.*
The city's only all-night cinema.

Gaumont Les Halles
1-3 Rue Pierre-Lescot, Forum des Halles (Niveau 3), 1er ☎ 297-49-70. Map ***10****H9. Metro Châtelet-Les-Halles.*
Six screens in the new Forum, most modern and convenient of the commercial movie theaters.

Le Grand Rex
1 Bd. Poissonière, 2e ☎ 236-83-93. Map ***4****F9. Metro Bonne-Nouvelle.*
Last of the dinosaurs, this seats 2,800 at a single screening.

Les 14-Juillet Bastille
4 Bd. Beaumarchais, 11e ☎ 357-90-81. Map ***11****I12. Metro Bastille.*
Three screens, representing the conscience of French independent cinema.

Luxembourg
67 Rue Monsieur-Le-Prince, 6e ☎ 633-97-77. Map ***15****J8. Metro Odéon.*
Three screens, each with a regular midnight showing – a boon for insomniacs, shift-workers or those who dislike rush-hour travel.

Nickel Écoles
23 Rue des Écoles, 5e ☎ 325-72-07. Map ***15****J9. Metro Maubert-Mutualité, Cardinal-Lemoine.*
A program entirely devoted to the Marx brothers – definitely for purists.

Olympic
10 Rue Boyer-Barret, 14e ☎ 327-52-37. Metro Pernety.
Olympic Entrepot
7-9 Rue Francis-de-Pressense, 14e ☎ 542-67-42. Map ***14****M1. Metro Pernety.*
These two cinemas, with five screens altogether, plus a bar and a reasonable bookshop, make up the center of the alternative cinema in Paris. Definitely worth a visit.

La Pagode
57 bis Rue de Babylone, 7^e ☎ 705-12-15. Map ***13****J5. Metro St-François-Xavier.*
In an impressive Chinese pavilion, this is unquestionably the most beautiful cinema in the city of Paris.

Concerts

The range of music is almost matched by the spread of its habitat. Conventional *salles* vie with theaters, museums, gardens, grand houses and, best of all, the old churches of Paris, including **La Madeleine**, **St-Germain-des-Prés**, **St-Julien-le-Pauvre**, and **St-Roch**. Favorites are the summer Sun evening recitals at **Notre-Dame**. As for pop concerts, the really big ones are held at **Olympia**, both for French and for foreign performers, and there are also other smaller venues. For listings of programs see *l'Officiel des Spectacles* or *Pariscope*.

Conciergerie Museum
2 Bd. du Palais, 1er ☎ 283-85-50. Map **10***I9.*

IRCAM (Experimental Institute)
31 Rue St-Merri, 4e ☎ 277-12-33. Map **10***H10. Metro Rambuteau.*

Maison de la Radio-France
116 Av. du Président-Kennedy, 16e ☎ 524-24-24. Metro Ranelagh.

Salle Cortot
78 Rue Cardinet, 17e ☎ 763-80-16 Metro Ternes.

Salle Gaveau
45 Rue la Boétie, 8e ☎ 563-20-30. Map **2***F5. Metro Miromesnil.*

Théâtre des Champs-Élysées
15 Av. Montaigne, 8e ☎ 723-47-77. Map **7***G4. Metro Alma-Marceau.*

Rock venues

Élysées Montmartre
72 Bd. de Rochechouart, 9e ☎ 252-25-15.

Le Gibus See under *Discos*.

Olympia
28 Bd. des Capucines, 2e ☎ 742-52-86.

Le Palace See under *Discos*.

Dancing

The last tango in Paris still lives on. Dancing with strangers is viewed as a simple, entertaining diversion, just like taking tea in a café.

Adison Square Gardel
23 Rue du Cdt-Mouchotte, 14e ☎ 321-54-58. Map **14***L6. Metro Gaité* AE VISA
Tea dancing, a throwback to the 1930s in this Franco-American atmosphere, and tangos at night. There's more modern music as well.

Le Balajo
9 Rue de Lappe, 11e ☎ 700-07-87. Map **11***I12. Metro Bastille.*
Street cleaners, *concièrges*, and a host of beautiful people slumming.

La Coupole
102 Bd. Montparnasse, 14e ☎ 320-14-20. Map **14***K7. Metro Montparnasse-Bienvenue.*
Dancing down in the basement to old-fashioned tangos and waltzes. A motley crowd from politicians to showbiz personalities to students.

Mimi Pinson
79 Champs-Élysées, 8e ☎ 723-68-75. Map **6***F3. Metro George-V.*
Dancing four times weekly in the chic-est location.

Discos

The very word *discothèque* is, of course, French. Paris' discos tend to be wonderfully flashy affairs, with glittery decor and glittery people, throbbing lights, pulsating music, and a generally frenetic atmosphere. Some are more sedate, but only slightly so.

Les Bains Douches
*7 Rue du Bourg-l'Abbé, 3e*
*☎887–34–40. Map **10**G10. Metro Étienne-Marcel.*
Amusing setting in a former public bath house. All types: punks, mods, rockers, cowboys, lots of young people.

Le Boeuf sur le Toit
*34 Rue du Colisée, 8e*
*☎359–83–80. Map **7**F4. Metro Franklin-D-Roosevelt.*
Memories of Cocteau and his crowd, now patronized by more conservative types.

Bus Palladium
*6 Rue Fontaine, 9e*
*☎874–54–99. Map **4**D8. Metro Blanche.*
Hot, crowded, loud, friendly. For dancing till you drop.

Le Gibus
*18 Faubourg du Temple, 10e*
*☎700–78–80. Map **11**G11. Metro République.*
The wildest of the young crowd, all costumed in the finery of yesterday and tomorrow. The closest to a New York or London disco; today's rock music.

Katmandou
*21 Rue du Vieux-Colombier, 6e*
*☎548–12–96. Map **8**J7. Metro St-Sulpice.*
Not quite a disco, not quite a bar, but dancing. Gay women.

La Main Jaune
*Porte de Champerret, 17^e^*
☎763–26–47. Metro Porte-de-Champerret.
Roller disco on the edge of the freeway.

Martine's
Au Pavilion-Royal, Bois de Boulogne, 16^e^ ☎500–23–40. (See Bois de Boulogne for map location.) Metro Pompe, Georges-Mandel.
Sedate, older crowd, but can still be fun.

Le Palace
*8 Rue du Faubourg-Montmartre, 9^e^ ☎246–10–87. Map **9**F9. Metro Rue Montmartre* AE Φ VISA
Still going strong, Paris' best and most popular disco where absolutely anyone and everyone goes. Chic crowd – Paloma Picasso, Andy Warhol, fashion designers – mingles with hairdressers, perhaps in drag, and, in fact, Le Tout Paris. Gay nights, black nights and live concerts.

Le Sept
*7 Rue Ste-Anne, 1er*
*☎296–47–05. Map **9**G8. Metro Palais-Royale* AE Φ VISA
Chic, gay men. Good restaurant on main floor, postage-stamp-size dance floor – always extremely crowded. Women not welcome for dancing.

Jazz clubs

Once the refuge of American jazz musicians between the wars, and after World War II, Paris still retains its love for jazz, although sometimes with a slightly tired air. Nostalgic.

Birdland
*20 Rue Princesse, 6e*
*☎326–97–59. Map **15**J8. Metro St-Germain-des-Prés.*
Clubby atmosphere and fabulous collection of records.

Caveau de la Huchette
*5 Rue de la Huchette, 5e*
*☎326–65–05. Map **15**J9. Metro St-Michel* Φ
In the heart of the student-jammed Latin Quarter, very popular, excellent live music, dancing.

Dreher
*Pl. du Châtelet, 1er*
*☎233–92–80. Map **10**I9. Metro Châtelet.*
Live music with different styles – cool, salsa, reggae.

Meridien-Jazz
*Hotel Meridien, 81 Bd. Gouvion-St-Cyr, 17e*
*☎758–12–30. Map **6**E1. Metro Porte-Maillot* AE Φ ◉ VISA
Top jazz musicians and laid-back atmosphere.

Le Petit Journal
71 Bd. St-Michel, 5e
*☎ 326-28-59. Map **10**I9. Metro St-Michel.*
New Orleans jazz.

Petit Opportun
☎ 15 Rue des Lanvandières-Ste-Opportune, 1er
*☎ 236-01-36. Map **9**H9. Metro Châtelet.*
Sympathetic bar on main floor, good jazz in basement.

Le Riverbop
67 Rue St-André-des-Arts, 6e
*☎ 325-93-71. Map **10**I9. Metro St-Michel.*
Jam sessions, hang-out for musicians.

Le Slow Club
130 Rue de Rivoli, 1er
*☎ 233-84-30. Map **9**H9. Metro Louvre.*
Old cellar with nostalgic music, dancing.

Nightclubs

In Paris, as elsewhere, club normally means 'private', although there are varying degrees of privacy, particularly for visitors. If you are young, or pretty, or well-dressed (ideally all three), however, the chances are you won't be turned away. Otherwise, hotel *concièrges* are often helpful. Private clubs are stuffy about male dress, and ties are expected. Women, however, can wear what they like.

Castel ✿
15 Rue Princesse, 6e
*☎ 326-90-22. Map **15**J8. Metro St-Germain-des-Prés* AE
For many years this has been, and still is, Paris' very best, very private club. Supervised by Jean Castel, King of the Paris Night. The prettiest girls in town, and good food. Excellent bar and 'canteen' on the main floor, more elegant dining upstairs. A disco down in the basement and a video room with airplane seats on an upper floor, plus a music room. A real experience – if you're lucky enough to get through the door in the first place.

Élysées Matignon
2 Av. Matignon, 8e
*☎ 225-73-13. Map **7**F5. Metro St-Philippe-du-Roule* AE VISA
Excellent disco, bar, restaurant, with a decorative assortment of showbiz and society types. Impossible parking.

Le Privilège
3 Cité-Bergère, 9e
*☎ 523-44-62. Map **9**F9. Metro Rue Montmartre.*
Private club in the basement of **Le Palace** (see *Discos*). The trendiest hang-out of gays and models.

Régine's
49 Rue Ponthieu, 8e
*☎ 359-21-60. Map **7**F5. Metro Franklin-D-Roosevelt* AE
A slightly *démodé* but still glamorous night spot. Good food, international jet set.

Le Soixante-Dix-Huit
78 Champs-Élysées, 8e
*☎ 359-09-99. Map **6**F3. Metro George-V* AE
Going slightly downhill after its starry beginnings, but the surroundings are still fabulous. Underground pool, flying trapeze artists, elaborate light shows and a screen flashing the latest stock exchange and weather reports.

Opera

The most opulent of the arts has a fitting setting in the magnificent *Opéra*. The huge stage can play to over 2,000 spectators under the Chagall ceiling. Few other theaters in Paris have the facilities to deal with the scope of an opera production. Bookings must usually be made at least two weeks in advance.

Opéra
*Pl. de l'Opéra, 9e ☎ 742-57-50. Map **8**F7. Metro Opéra.*

Salle Favart (Opéra-Comique)
*5 Rue Favart, 2e ☎ 296-12-20. Map **9**F8. Metro Richelieu-Drouot.*

Théâtre Musical de Paris
*Pl. du Châtelet, 1er ☎ 233-44-44. Map **10**I9. Metro Châtelet.*

Revues

(See *Cabarets.*) Combining tack with taste, Parisian revues blend nudity with entertainment and unabashed glamour. The formula differs, but establishments usually require customers to spend generously on drinks or dinner. The clientele tends to be made up of expense-account executives entertained by Parisian businessmen, or, perhaps, tourists gawking at the feathers, the sequins and skin.

Alcazar de Paris
62 Rue Mazarine, 6^e
*☎ 329-02-20. Map **9**I8. Metro Odéon* AE Φ VISA
Slightly raunchy review, often with transvestites, often satirical. It does help to be able to understand French.

Crazy Horse Saloon See *Cabarets.*

Folies Bergère ✿
32 Rue Richer, 9^e
*☎ 246-77-11. Map **4**E9. Metro Le Peletier.*
Strictly a theater, with no dinner or drinks required. Payment is simply made by buying a ticket for a seat. Glorious history of Maurice Chevalier, Mistinguett and the stars of Paris, now, unfortunately, rather sad.

Lido
116 Champs-Élysées, 8^e
*☎ 563-11-61. Map **6**F3. Metro George-V* AE Φ VISA
Paris' most lavish revue, with good dancers, acrobats, and magician. Very expensive; mediocre food.

Moulin Rouge
*Pl. Blanche, 9e ☎ 606-00-19. Map **4**D7. Metro Blanche* AE Φ
Immortalized by Toulouse-Lautrec. The same management as the **Lido** (above) but cheaper.

Paradis Latin
*28 Rue du Cardinal-Lemoine, 5e ☎ 325-28-28. Map **16**K10. Metro Cardinal-Lemoine* AE Φ
Wonderful architecture in an old Eiffel warehouse, with a spectacle devised by Jean-Marie Rivière, old-time master of ceremonies.

Theaters

Over a hundred theaters offer more variety than quality – Paris has always preferred the revue, but theater-lovers keep trying.

Antoine
14 Bd. de Strasbourg, 10^e
*☎ 208-77-71. Map **5**F10. Metro Strasbourg-St-Denis.*
Upper crust 'Boulevard' theater.

Les Bouffes du Nord
*209 Rue du Faubourg St-Denis, 10^e ☎ 607-73-73. Map **5**D11. Metro La Chapelle.*
Home of Peter Brook's experimental company.

La Cartoucherie
Route de la Pyramide, Bois de Vincennes, 12^e
☎ 328-97-04/374-99-61/ 328-36-36. (See Vincennes for map location.) Metro Château-de-Vincennes, then bus no. 306.
Three theaters grouped in the pleasant Bois de Vincennes.

La Comédie Française
2 Rue de Richelieu, 1er
*☎ 296-10-20. Map **9**H8. Metro Palais-Royal.*
Respectable seat of the French classics; Molière, Racine and other well-established playwrights are performed.

Lucernaire Forum
*53 Rue Notre-Dame-des-Champs, 6e ☎ 544-57-34. Map **14**K7. Metro Vavin.*
Up to six small-scale plays in a day.

Odéon
Pl. de l'Odéon, 6^e
*☎ 325-70-32. Map **15**J8. Metro Odéon.*
Another national theater, bolder than its rival, the *Comédie Française*.

Théâtre National de Chaillot
Pl. du Trocadéro, 16^e
*☎ 505-14-50. Map **12**H2. Metro Trocadéro.*
Famous in the 1950s, and today for its technical facilities.

Théâtre Présent
211 Av. Jean-Jaurès, 19^e
☎ 203-02-55. Metro Porte-de-Pantin.
Seldom fails to surprise.

Ballet
1 Éspace Marais
2 Opéra
3 Théâtre de la Ville

Bars
4 Bedford Arms
5 Centreville
6 Closerie des Lilas
7 La Coupole
8 Fouquet's
9 Harry's Bar
10 Kenz
11 Rosebud
12 Le Village

Cabarets
13 Caveau des Oubliettes
14 Chez Félix
15 Club des Poètes
16 Crazy Horse Saloon
17 Don Camilo
18 Au Lapin Agile
19 Le Milliardaire

Café-théâtres
20 Blancs-Manteaux
21 Café d'Edgar
22 Café de la Gare
23 Les 400 Coups
24 Petit Casino

Cinemas
25 Action République
26 Cinemathèque Française
27 Le Déjazet
28 Gaumont Les Halles
29 Le Grand Rex

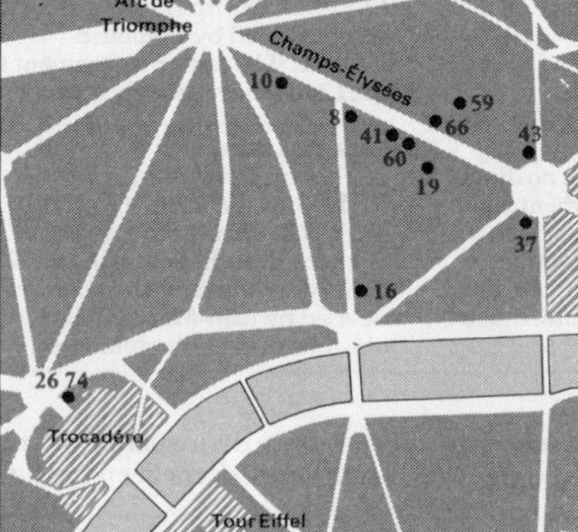

30 Les 14-Juillet Bastille
31 Luxembourg
32 Nickel Écoles
33 La Pagode

Concerts
34 Conciergerie Museum
35 IRCAM (Experimental Institute)
36 Salle Gaveau
37 Théâtre des Champs Élysées

Rock Venues
38 Élysées Montmartre
39 Olympia

Dancing
40 La Coupole
41 Mimi Pinson

Discos
42 Les Bains Douches
43 Le Boeuf sur le Toit
44 Bus Palladium
45 Le Gibus
46 Katmandou
47 Le Palace
48 Le Sept

Jazz
49 Birdland
50 Caveau de la Huchette
51 Dreher
52 Le Petit Journal
53 Petit Opportun
54 Le Riverbop
55 Le Slow Club

Nightclubs
56 Castel
57 Élysées Matignon
58 Le Privilège
59 Régine's
60 Le Soixante-Dix-Huit

Opera
61 Opéra
62 Salle Favart (Opéra-Comique)
63 Théâtre Musical de Paris

Revues
64 Alcazar de Paris
65 Folies Bergère
66 Lido
67 Moulin Rouge
68 Paradis Latin

Theaters
69 Antoine
70 Les Bouffes du Nord
71 La Comédie Française
72 Lucernaire Forum
73 Odéon
74 Théâtre National de Chaillot

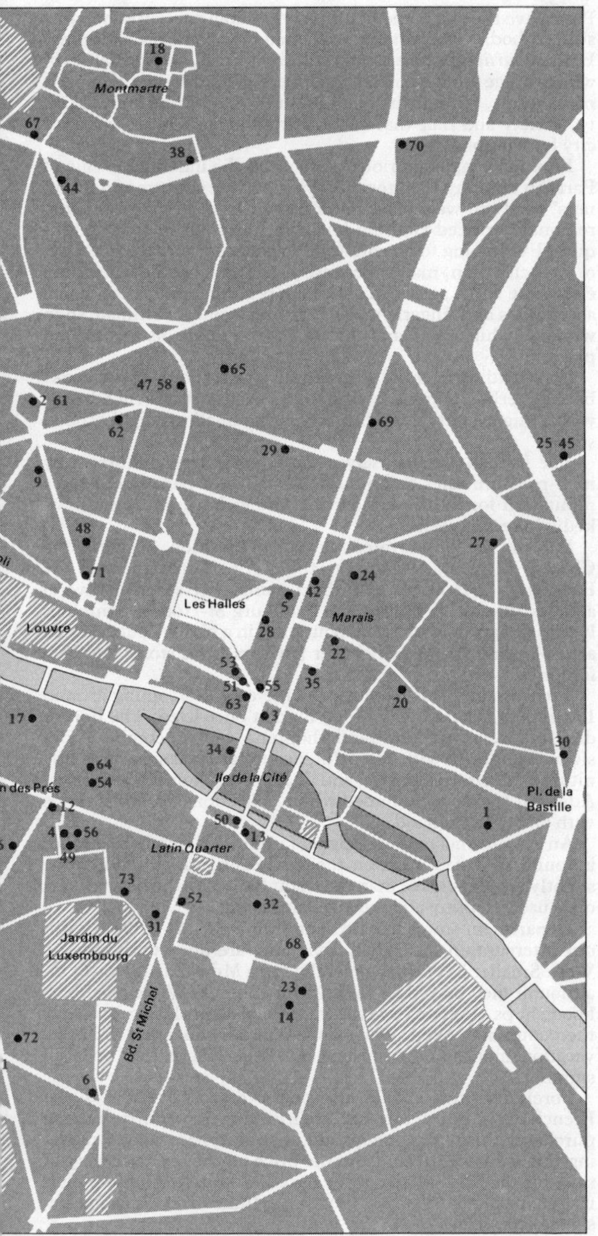

Montmartre
Les Halles
Louvre
Marais
Ile de la Cité
Pl. de la Bastille
Latin Quarter
Jardin du Luxembourg
Bd. St Michel

Shopping

Paris gave the world the boutique, the small specialty shop that still embodies the intimate character of Parisian shopping. Entire *quartiers* are blanketed with boutiques, the specialties of which range from antiques to zippers. There are good department stores, but it is the boutiques that exhibit the individuality, variety and flair that makes Paris Europe's most seductive city for shopping.

Fine tailoring, luxurious fabrics and the indefinable chic of Parisian clothing is epitomized by the haute couture and designers' ready-to-wear. But Paris fashion is also translated into reasonably priced clothing found in hundreds of small boutiques. Everything to do with fashion is a good buy, provided it is of French origin, mainly because you cannot get the same thing elsewhere at the same price. French perfume, cosmetics, home accessories and lingerie make Paris the woman's ultimate shop window, while men's and children's wear take a distinct second place.

Food and everything related to it – kitchen gadgets, cookbooks, herbs, linens – is especially close to the French heart, with a huge variety available in even the smallest neighborhood shops.

The French are themselves careful shoppers, unhurried by high-pressure sales techniques. While sales personnel have a reputation for indifferent service, things have improved markedly in recent years.

Much of the 8ᵉ is devoted to expensive fashion, primarily the Champs-Élysées, Av. Victor-Hugo, Av. Montaigne and the Faubourg St-Honoré. Off the Champs-Élysées run several arcades filled with shops. The Faubourg St-Honoré combines luxury shopping with small boutiques in a highly concentrated area. Around the Opéra cluster jewelers, shoe stores and perfumeries.

Trendier and less expensive is the area blossoming around Les Halles, where the old food market once lived. The Forum des Halles, an underground shopping center, combines designer boutiques with colourful, avant-garde fashion, plus furniture, *batterie de cuisine* and interesting home accessories. Adjacent streets are jammed with a collection of original shops with offbeat merchandise.

An eclectic mélange of designer fashion and trendy boutiques is found in St-Germain on the Left Bank, which tends to be slightly less expensive than the Right Bank. All the flea markets offer used clothing and army surplus goods.

Department stores remain open from 9:30am–6:30pm without interruption Mon–Sat, and some are open until 8pm on Wed. Smaller boutiques generally open Mon–Sat 10am–6pm, although they may close for an hour at lunch. While neighborhood shops often observe the traditional Mon closing, stores in the center stay open. And, while Aug was once the universal vacation month, now most of the larger shops stay open all summer.

Foreign visitors should ask for the *détaxe*, a refund of the French excise tax, returnable upon leaving the country with the purchases. Also, many shops advertise 'duty-free' goods, meaning this tax is deducted from the price on the spot. Be wary of this, for the basic price may be raised. Comparison shopping is useful, particularly when buying perfumes and choosing designer accessories.

Cuisine

Cookware

Paris is a cook's heaven. No other city can compare with the array of food-related objects, often cheaper and sometimes simply unobtainable elsewhere. Department stores all have large cookware departments, but it is more fun to go directly to the major specialists. Be prepared to pay cash, and ask for shipping and *détaxe* information.

Dehillerin ✿
*18 Rue Coquillière, 1er. Map **9**G9. Metro Étienne-Marcel.*
Perhaps the best restaurant supply house in the world, this store also sells happily on a smaller scale. Outstanding buys in copper, carbon steel knives, casseroles of all description. Free catalogue (also in English) and amiable service from Gaston. Excellent shipping service.

MORA
*13 Rue Montmartre, 1er. Map **9**G9. Metro Étienne-Marcel.*
Smaller selection is offered than in the above supply house, but still a store for true professionals. You may find the cool, even off-hand service difficult to take.

A. Simon
*36 Rue Étienne-Marcel, 2e, and 48 Rue Montmartre, 1er. Map **9**G9. Metro Étienne-Marcel.*
Divided into two stores, one with metalware, electrical appliances and knives; the other devoted to pottery, glassware and a reasonable selection of porcelain. Good, colorful displays and helpful personnel make shopping here a pleasure.

Food and drink

Every neighborhood has its *charcuteries*, selling pork products, prepared foods and a bit of everything, and its *fromageries*, *caves* and *pâtisseries*. The areas around the Pl. de la Madeleine and Les Halles are particularly exciting.

Androuet
*41 Rue d'Amsterdam, 8e. Map **3**E7. Metro St-Lazare.*
Owned by Pierre Androuet, this store is a temple to cheese. Special boxes for traveling.

Battendier
*8 Rue Coquillière, 1er. Map **9**G9. Metro Étienne-Marcel* AE VISA
A chic *charcuterie* known for its sausages, ham and pâtés.

Bertillon
*31 Rue St Louis-en-l'Ile, 4e. Map **10**J10. Metro Pont-Marie.*
Superb ice cream and sorbets, made from the freshest fruits that change with the seasons.

Caves de la Madeleine
*25 Rue Royale, 8e. Map **8**G6. Metro Madeleine* VISA
Nestled in a delightful mews and run by Englishman Steven Spurrier. A wide selection of high-quality wines and spirits. Gift wrapping and a delivery service.

Comptoir Gourmand
*32 Pl. de la Madeleine, 8e. Map **8**F6. Metro Madeleine* AE Φ VISA
Products from Michel Guérard, one of France's most innovative three-star chefs, and his native southwest.

Fauchon
*26 Pl. de la Madeleine, 8e. Map **8**F6. Metro Madeleine* AE Φ MC VISA
One of the world's most celebrated food stores, with two large boutiques, Fauchon carries over 20,000 products. Wonderful gift service; will ship anywhere.

La Ferme St-Hubert
*21 Rue Vignon, 8e. Map **8**F7. Metro Madeleine.*
Superb cheeses; helpful personnel.

Hédiard
*21 Pl. de la Madeleine, 8e. Map **8**F6. Metro Madeleine* AE Φ VISA
A smaller Fauchon, with exotic products and spices, rare fruits and an outstanding wine selection. Five Paris branches.

Labeyrie
*6 Rue Montmartre, 2e. Map **9**G9. Metro Étienne-Marcel.*
Foie gras, truffles, confits of duck and goose, and all the wonderful foods of the Landes region.

Legrand ✿
1 Rue de la Banque, 2ᵉ. Map ***9****G8. Metro Bourse.*
Reasonably priced wines and alcohol, and interesting culinary products.

Lenôtre
44 Rue d'Auteuil, 16ᵉ. Metro Michelange-Auteuil.
Now a famous chef, Lenôtre was first a caterer and then became a really outstanding *pâtissier*. Excellent chocolates, ice cream and prepared food.

À l'Olivier ✿
23 Rue de Rivoli, 1ᵉʳ. Map ***10****I10. Metro Hôtel-de-Ville.*
Oil of every imaginable variety, including sheeps' feet oil (for mechanics), but most of all, olive oil.

Piètrement
8 Rue Montmartre, 1ᵉʳ. Map ***9****G9. Metro Étienne-Marcel.*
Foie gras, truffles, dried mushrooms. Charming service.

Poilâne
8 Rue du Cherche-Midi, 6ᵉ. Map ***14****J7. Metro St-Sulpice.* ***49*** *Bd. de Grenelle, 16ᵉ. Map* ***12****I2. Metro Bir-Hakeim. Forum des Halles, 1ᵉʳ. Map* ***10****H9. Metro Châtelet-Les-Halles.*
Baked in wood-fueled ovens, containing no preservatives, Lionel Poilane's crusty loaves are the best in Paris.

Soleil de Provence
6 Rue du Cherche-Midi, 6ᵉ. Map ***14****J7. Metro St-Sulpice.*
Fruity olive oil, honeys and olive oil soap.

Department stores

Bazar de l'Hôtel de Ville ✿
55 Rue de la Verrerie, 4ᵉ. Map ***10****I10. Metro Hôtel-de-Ville* VISA
Excellent sporting goods, garden tools, books, records, and a dazzling array of hardware in the basement.

Bon Marché
38 Rue de Sèvres, 7ᵉ. Map ***14****J6. Metro Sèvres-Babylone* AE Φ VISA
A true department store comprising fresh foods along with clothing, home furnishings and a wide selection of linens.

FNAC ✿
Forum des Halles, 1ᵉʳ. Map ***10****H9. Metro Châtelet-Les-Halles.* ***136*** *Rue de Rennes, 14ᵉ. Map* ***14****K6. Metro Montparnasse-Bienvenue.* ***26*** *Av. Wagram, 8ᵉ. Map* ***6****E3. Metro Charles-de-Gaulle-Étoile.*
Discount records, books, small appliances, sporting goods, photo equipment. The Forum store specializes in records, audio-visual supplies, photo goods and sporting goods; Montparnasse concentrates on video and books; and Av. Wagram stocks the largest selection of audio-visual goods.

Galeries Lafayette
40 Bd. Haussmann, 9ᵉ. Map ***8****F7. Metro Chaussée-d'Antin, Auber. Maine-Montparnasse Centre, 14ᵉ. Map* ***14****K6. Metro Montparnasse-Bienvenue* AE Φ VISA
A serious attempt to update its fashion image has turned both branches of this store into trendy fashion spots, with vast home furnishings departments and a wide selection of porcelain, glassware and cookware. A variety of good, slick ideas, and plenty of color.

Printemps
64 Bd. Haussmann, 9ᵉ. Map ***8****F7. Metro Havre-Caumartin, Auber* AE CB Φ MC VISA
Elegant, with deluxe ready-to-wear on the 'Rue de La Mode', and a magnificent stained glass cupola that is a historical monument. Wide range of lingerie, gourmet boutiques, and a top-floor restaurant renowned for its Art Nouveau decor.

Samaritaine ✿
Pont Neuf, 1ᵉʳ. Map ***9****H9. Metro Pont-Neuf.*
An old-fashioned store noted for its uniforms (chef's clothes and bartenders' outfits), sporting goods, and household items. The 10th story of Magasin 2 offers an unparaleled view over the city.

Aux Trois Quartiers
17 Bd. de la Madeleine, 8ᵉ. Map ***8****F7. Metro Madeleine* AE CB Φ MC VISA
A quiet store with polite sales personnel and attentive service. A wide selection of gifts, pleasant accessories and linens. Rarely crowded.

Drugstores

These have nothing to do with American-style drugstores, although they all have pharmacies. Parisian drugstores are mini-shopping centers, meeting places and classy emergency shops that often include cinemas and restaurants among their distractions. Open daily from 9am to after midnight, they have counters devoted to books, perfume, food, gifts, toys and tobacco. Excellent selection of newspapers and periodicals in foreign languages.

149 Bd. St-Germain 6e. *Map* ***8****I7*. Metro St-Germain-des-Prés AE Φ MC VISA

133 Av. des Champs-Élysées 8e. *Map* ***6****F3*. Metro George-V AE Φ MC VISA

1 Av. Matignon 8e. *Map* ***7****F5*. Metro Franklin-D-Roosevelt AE CB Φ MC VISA

6 Bd. des Capucines 9e. *Map* ***8****F8*. Metro Opéra AE Φ VISA

Fashion

Bargains

Couturiers and ready-to-wear designers often sell last season's styles, with or without the labels (*dégriffé*), at half-price. The Rue St-Placide, 6e (*Metro Sèvres-Babylone*) is lined with discount stores for men, women and children.

Bab's ✿
34 Pl. du Marché-St-Honoré, 1er. Map ***8****G7. Metro Tuileries. 29 Av. Marceau, 16e. Map* ***6****G3. Metro Alma-Marceau* AE VISA
Nina Ricci, Guy Laroche and others. Gorgeous silk blouses.

Bidermann ✿
114 Rue de Turenne, 3e. Map ***11****H11. Metro Filles-du-Calvaire.*
Suits for men by St Laurent and others.

Gigi's Soldes ✿
30 Pl. du Marché-St-Honoré, 1er. Map ***8****G7. Metro Tuileries* AE Φ VISA
French and Italian shoes, superb boots for men and women.

Mendès ✿
65 Rue Montmartre, 2e. Map ***9****G9. Metro Sentier.*
Last season's St Laurent, Chanel and Valentino outfits. Worth a quick visit.

Minika ✿
38 Pl. du Marché-St-Honoré, 1er. Map ***8****G7. Metro Tuileries* VISA
Children's wear, with a beauty salon for them too. For indulgent parents.

La Soldetière ✿
76 Rue de la Pompe, 16e. Metro Pompe.
A good range of children's clothing from top houses. Reasonable prices.

Children's clothing

Exquisite layettes and hand-embroidered gowns can still be found in Paris but children's fashions are extremely expensive. Many designers (Dior, Hechter and others) make a children's line. The best selection is in department stores.

Men's clothing

French styling combines English conservatism with Italian flair. Many couturiers design men's lines (see women's *Couturier boutiques*). Men's clothing is not a good buy in France, with a few exceptions.

Arnys
14 Rue de Sèvres, 7e. Map ***14****J6. Metro Sèvres-Babylone* AE Φ MC VISA

Michel Axel
121 Bd. St-Germain, 6e. Map ***8****I7. Metro St-Germain-des-Prés* AE Φ MC VISA

Charvet
*8 Pl. Vendôme, 1er. Map **8**G7. Metro Tuileries* Φ VISA

Daniel Hechter
*12 Faubourg St-Honoré, 1er. Map **8**G6. Metro Concorde.* AE Φ ●● VISA

Island
*3 Rue Montmartre, 1er. Map **10**G9. Metro Étienne-Marcel. 5 Pl. des Victoires, 4e. Map **9**G8. Metro Bourse* AE

Jarvis
*48 Galerie Vivienne, 2e. Map **9**F8. Metro Bourse.*

Jeff Sayre
*4 Pl. André-Malraux, 1er. Map **9**G8. Metro Palais-Royal* AE Φ VISA
*9 Rue de la Cossonerie, 1er. Map **10**H9. Metro Les Halles.*

Unisex fashion

Altona
*6 Rue de l'Odéon, 6e. Map **15**J8. Metro Odéon. 19 Rue du Jour, 1er. Map **10**G9. Metro Les Halles* VISA
Utilitarian chic cavalry jackets, oversized trousers, canvas goods, sweaters.

Jess ❀
*Corner of Bd. St-Germain and Rue de l'Ancienne-Comédie, 6e. Map **15**J8. Metro Odéon* AE Φ VISA
Trousers, sweaters, jackets, leather overalls. Selection of stylish workwear.

Women's clothing

Haute couture

Opulent, made-to-measure clothing is the specialty that made the Paris fashion industry the best and most famous in the world. Each couturier has a distinct style which can be seen during the showings, normally in Jan (for summer) and July (for winter clothing) when the new collections are modeled for prospective clients. Tickets for these fashion showings can be obtained through hotel *concierges*, or directly from the couture houses.

Pierre Balmain
*44 Rue François-1er, 8e ☎ 720-35-34. Map **7**F4. Metro George-V* AE Φ

Pierre Cardin
*27 Av. de Marigny, 8e ☎ 266-92-25. Map **7**F5. Metro Champs-Élysées-Clémenceau* AE Φ

Chanel
*31 Rue Cambon, 1er ☎ 261-54-55. Map **8**G7. Metro Madeleine* AE

Christian Dior
*30 Av. Montaigne, 8e ☎ 723-54-44. Map **7**G4. Metro Alma-Marceau* AE Φ

Louis Féraud
*88 Faubourg St-Honoré, 1er ☎ 260-08-08. Map **8**F6. Metro Madeleine* AE Φ ●● VISA

Ted Lapidus
*37 Av. Pierre-1er-de-Serbie, 8e ☎ 720-69-33. Map **6**G3. Metro Alma-Marceau* AE Φ ●●

Guy Laroche
*29 Av. Montaigne, 8e ☎ 723-78-72. Map **7**G4. Metro Alma-Marceau* AE Φ VISA

Hanae Mori
17 Av. Montaigne, 8e ☎ 723–52–03. Map 7G4. Metro Alma-Marceau AE

Nina Ricci
38 Av. Montaigne, 8e ☎ 723–78–88. Map 7G4. Metro Franklin-D-Roosevelt AE Φ VISA

Yves St-Laurent
5 Av. Marceau, 8e ☎ 723–72–71. Map 6G3. Metro Alma-Marceau.

Jean-Louis Scherrer
51 Av. Montaigne, 8e ☎ 359–55–39. Map 7G4. Metro Alma-Marceau.

Torrente
9 Faubourg St-Honoré, 1er ☎ 266–14–14. Map 8G6. Metro Concorde AE Φ MC

Emmanuel Ungaro
2 Av. Montaigne, 8e ☎ 723–61–94. Map 7G4. Metro Alma-Marceau AE Φ VISA

Couturier boutiques

Designers clothing, ready-to-wear and at much lower prices than the haute couture, is still expensive but stunning, with high-quality styling, fabrics and workmanship.

Pierre Balmain
237 Rue St-Honoré, 1er. Map 8G7. Metro Tuileries. 44 Rue Francois-1er, 8e. Map 7G4. Metro Franklin-D-Roosevelt AE Φ
Slightly boring collection, but simple and safe.

Pierre Cardin
27 Av. de Marigny, 8e. Map 7F5. Metro Champs-Élysées-Clémenceau AE Φ
Eccentric women's fashions; men's clothing as well.

Chanel
31 Rue Cambon, 1er. Map 8G7. Metro Concorde AE
Little suits, quilted handbags, jewelry; a direct reflection of the couture.

Christian Dior
26–32 Av. Montaigne, 8e. Map 7G4. Metro Alma-Marceau AE Φ VISA
Discreet daytime dresses, glamorous evening wear; sportswear in the boutique Tricots.

Louis Féraud
47 Rue Bonaparte, 6e. Map 14J7. Metro St-Sulpice. 88 Faubourg St-Honoré, 1er. Map 8F5. Metro Champs-Élysées-Clémenceau AE VISA
A favorite of showbiz clients, noted for long gowns.

Givenchy
3 Av. George-V, 8e. Map 7G4. Metro Alma-Marceau. 66 Av. Victor-Hugo, 8e. Map 6F2. Metro Victor-Hugo AE Φ
Once an elegant, creative designer but without a good collection for several seasons. Wide selection of classics.

Lanvin
22 Faubourg St-Honoré, 1er. Map 8G6. Metro Concorde AE Φ VISA
A far cry from the famous couture house of the 1920s.

Ted Lapidus
37 Av. Pierre-1er-de-Serbie, 8e. Map 6G3. Metro George-V AE CB Φ MC VISA
Good casualwear, especially coats, and lovely fabrics. Five other branches.

Guy Laroche ✤
27 Av. Montaigne, 8e. Map 7G4. Metro Alma-Marceau Φ VISA
The least expensive designer ready-to-wear; nothing too way out but everything very wearable if you like a 'good', timeless look. Four other boutiques.

Hanae Mori
17 Av. Montaigne, 8e. Map 7G4. Metro Franklin-D-Roosevelt AE
Sumptuous silks, Japanese-inspired design. Free alteration service.

Nina Ricci
*38 Av. Montaigne, 8ᵉ. Map **7**G4. Metro Franklin-D-Roosevelt* AE Φ VISA
Safe fashions in beautiful fabrics. Sale models in basement.

St-Laurent Rive Gauche
*12 Rond-Point, 8ᵉ. Map **7**F5. Metro Franklin-D-Roosevelt* AE Φ VISA
Elegant, classic, with dash and versatility. Collectible fashions that can be built on each season. Four other branches.

Torrente
*9 Faubourg St-Honoré, 1ᵉʳ. Map **8**G6. Metro Concorde* AE Φ VISA
Classic but relatively unimaginative. Not too expensive, but not too chic.

Ungaro
*2 Av. Montaigne, 8ᵉ. Map **7**G4. Metro Alma-Marceau. 25 Faubourg St-Honoré, 1ᵉʳ. Map **8**G6. Metro Concorde* AE Φ VISA
Sumptuous fabrics and exotic combinations of patterns. Very expensive.

Boutiques

Agnes B
*3 Rue du Jour, 1ᵉʳ. Map **9**G9. Metro Les Halles* AE Φ
Smart quilted coats, sportswear in wild colors.

Anastasia
*18 Rue de l'Ancienne-Comédie, 6ᵉ. Map **9**I8. Metro Odéon* AE
Capes, romantic country clothes with a Russian flair.

Michel Axel
*121 Bd. St-Germain, 6ᵉ. Map **8**I7. Metro St-Germain-des-Prés* AE Φ ⊕ VISA
Stylish suits, coats, sportswear; elegant evening dresses.

Dorothée Bis
*17 Rue de Sèvres, 6ᵉ. Map **14**J7. Metro Sèvres-Babylone. 10 Rue Tronchet, 9ᵉ. Map **8**F7. Metro Madeleine. Forum des Halles, 1ᵉʳ. Map **10**H9. Metro Châtelet-Les-Halles* AE VISA
Young, inventive clothes in bright colours and avant-garde styles. Dorotennis sportswear.

Boa
*113 Rue St-Denis, 1ᵉʳ. Map **9**H9. Metro Châtelet-Les-Halles* AE Φ VISA
Eccentric, original fashion.

Cacharel
*165 Rue de Rennes, 6ᵉ. Map **14**J7. Metro St-Sulpice. 34 Rue Tronchet, 9ᵉ. Map **8**F7. Metro Madeleine. 7 Rue de Passy, 16ᵉ. Map **6**I2. Metro Passy* AE Φ ⊕ VISA
Young, classical clothes, never quite in or out of style.

Carla Viva
*12 Rue du Cygne, 1ᵉʳ. Map **9**H9. Metro Les Halles* AE Φ VISA
Trousers with matching shawls; ponchos in lovely fabrics.

Castelbajac
*31 Pl. du Marché-St-Honoré, 1ᵉʳ. Map **8**G7. Metro Tuileries* AE Φ VISA
Modern sportswear in beautiful natural fabrics.

Chloé
*2 bis and 3 Rue de Gribeauval, 6ᵉ. Map **8**I7. Metro Rue-du-Bac. 60 Rue Faubourg St-Honoré, 1ᵉʳ. Map **8**G6. Metro Concorde* AE Φ ⊕ VISA
Trend-setting and elegant clothes designed by Karl Lagerfeld.

Coulountjios ✿
*3 Rue du Cygne, 1ᵉʳ. Map **9**H9. Metro Les Halles.*
Exciting furs with hand-painted linings.

Emesse ✿
*11 Rue de Turbigo, 1ᵉʳ. Map **10**G9. Metro Les Halles* AE
Superbly tailored trouser suits, skirts in pure wool.

France Faver
*79 Rue des Sts-Pères, 6ᵉ. Map **8**I7. Metro Sèvres-Babylone* AE ⊕ VISA
Semi-made-to-measure clothing, elegant and refined. Lovely hats.

Daniel Hechter
*12 Faubourg St-Honoré, 1ᵉʳ. Map **8**G6* AE Φ ⊕ VISA
Young, classic sportswear, well-cut and conservative. Four other branches.

Kenzo ✿
*3 Pl. des Victoires, 1ᵉʳ. Map **9**G8. Metro Bourse* AE VISA
One of Paris's most innovative designers, Kenzo introduces off-beat styles often later adopted by the stuffier couturiers. Fabric and workmanship not always of high quality.

MicMac ✿
13 Rue Tournon, 6e. Map ***9****J8. Metro Mabillon. 46 Av. Victor-Hugo, 16e. Map* ***6****F2. Metro Victor-Hugo. Forum des Halles, 1er. Map* ***10****H9. Metro Châtelet-Les-Halles* AE VISA
Dashing sportswear, chic summer clothing.

Thierry Mugler
10 Pl. des Victoires, 1er. Map ***9****G8. Metro Bourse* AE Φ VISA
Tough chic.

Georges Rech ✿
54 Rue Bonaparte, 6e. Map ***14****J7. Metro St-Germain-des-Prés. 23 Av. Victor-Hugo, 16e. Map* ***6****F2. Metro Charles-de-Gaulle-Étoile* AE Φ VISA
Smart, wearable clothes co-ordinated in chic ensembles.

Sonia Rykiel
4 and 6 Rue de Grenelle, 6e. Map ***8****I7. Metro St-Sulpice. 70 Faubourg St-Honoré, 1er. Map* ***8****G6. Metro Concorde* AE
Sleek, unlined knits and accessories, plus feathered and sequined evening wear. Original and amusing.

Sara Shelburne
10 Rue du Cygne, 1e. Map ***9****H9. Metro Les Halles.*
Hand-made fabrics for lavish evening dresses at reasonable prices. Whimsical jewelery, some made-to-measure.

Stréa
64 Rue de Rennes, 6e. Map ***14****J7. Metro Sèvres-Babylone* AE Φ
Top designers, unusual accessories.

Ventilo
59 Rue Bonaparte, 6e. Map ***14****J7. Metro St-Germain-des-Prés* AE Φ VISA
Handsome dresses and separates in unusual fabrics.

Victoire
12 Pl. des Victoires, 1er. Map ***9****G8. Metro Bourse* AE Φ VISA
Top designers, very chic with relaxed sales personnel. Co-ordinated accessories.

Shoes

Most shoe stores carry goods for men and women, and many stock handbags and luggage. While the well-known labels are expensive, Paris is still a wonderful place for shoes.

Bally
11 Bd. de la Madeleine, 1er. Map ***8****F7. Metro Madeleine. 35 Bd. des Capucines, 9e. Map* ***8****F7. Metro Opéra* AE Φ MC VISA *Twenty other branches.*

Bazile
55 Rue Bonaparte, 6e. Map ***14****J7. Metro St-Germain-des-Prés. 5 Rue Tronchet, 9e. Map* ***8****F7. Metro Madeleine. 125 Rue de la Pompe, 16e. Metro Pompe* AE Φ MC VISA

Carel
41 Bd. des Capucines, 9e. Map ***8****F7. Metro Madeleine* AE Φ MC VISA
Six other branches.

Céline
58 Rue de Rennes, 6e. Map ***14****J7. Metro St-Germain-des-Prés. 24 Rue François-1er, 8e. Map* ***7****G4. Metro Franklin-D-Roosevelt. 3 Av. Victor-Hugo, 16e. Map* ***6****F2. Metro Charles-de-Gaulle-Étoile* AE Φ VISA

Robert Clergerie
5 Rue du Cherche-Midi, 6e. Map ***14****J7. Metro Sèvres-Babylone* AE VISA

Freelance
22 Rue Mondétour, 1er. Map ***9****H9. Metro Étienne-Marcel, Les Halles* AE VISA

Maud Frizon
7 Rue de Grenelle, 6e. Map ***14****J7. Metro Sèvres-Babylone. 83 Rue des Sts-Pères, 6e. Map* ***8****I7. Metro St-Germain-des-Prés* AE Φ VISA

Charles Jourdan
*12 Faubourg St-Honoré, 1er. Map **8**G6. Metro Concorde. 5 Bd. de la Madeleine, 1er. Map **8**F7. Metro Madeleine. 60 Rue de Rennes, 6e. Map **14**J7. Metro St-Germain-des-Prés. 86 Av. Champs-Élysées, 8e. Map **7**F4. Metro Franklin-D-Roosevelt. Forum des Halles, 1er. Map **8**I7. Metro Les Halles* AE CB Φ MC VISA

Stephane Kélian
*62 Rue des Sts-Pères, 6e. Metro St-Germain-des-Prés. Forum des Halles, 1er. Map **8**I7. Metro Châtelet-Les-Halles* VISA

Andrea Pfister
*4 Rue Cambon, 1er. Map **8**G7. Metro Concorde. 56 Rue du Four, 6e. Map **15**J8. Metro Mabillon* AE CB Φ MC VISA

Sacha
*15 Rue de Turbigo, 2e. Map **10**G9. Metro Étienne-Marcel. 24 Rue de Buci, 6e. Map **9**I8. Metro St-Germain-des-Prés. 43 Bd. Haussmann, 9e. Map **8**F7. Metro Havre-Caumartin* AE Φ VISA

St-Laurent See *Couturier boutiques.*

Household accessories, china, glass, silver

Au Bain Marie
*2 and 4 Rue du Mail, 2e. Map **9**G9. Metro Bourse* AE
Charming, old-fashioned objects and linens.

Baccarat
*30 bis Rue du Paradis, 10e. Map **5**E10. Metro Château-d'Eau* AE VISA
World-renowned crystal, beautiful gifts.

Christofle
*12 Rue Royale, 8e. Map **8**G6. Metro Madeleine* AE Φ MC VISA
Magnificent silver flatware in modern and retro patterns.

Lalique
*11 Rue Royale, 8e. Map **8**G6. Metro Madeleine* VISA
Collection of crystal, particularly frosted Art Nouveau and Deco patterns.

Limoges-Unic ✿
*12 and 58 Rue du Paradis, 10e. Map **5**E10. Metro Château-d'Eau* AE Φ VISA
Outlet for France's famed porcelain.

Puiforcat
*129 Bd. Haussmann, 9e. Map **8**F6. Metro St-Augustin* Φ VISA
Well-designed silver, good selection of gifts.

Jewelry

As in fashion, Paris has the haute couture of jewelry (*haute joaillerie*) and the ready-to-wear: Both are extremely stylish, a wide and interesting range is offered and, compared with the rest of the world, items are competitively priced.

The 'hautes' are, broadly speaking, grouped together, all clustered around the Pl. Vendôme.

Boucheron
*26 Pl. Vendôme, 1er. Map **8**G7. Metro Opéra, Concorde* AE Φ VISA

Cartier
*13 Rue de la Paix, 1er. Map **8**F7. Metro Opéra* AE Φ VISA

Ilias Lalaounis
*364 Rue St-Honoré, 1er. Map **8**G7. Metro Opéra, Madeleine* AE Φ

Van Cleef et Arpels
*22 Pl. Vendôme, 1er. Map **8**G7. Metro Opéra-Pyramides* AE Φ

Zolotas
*370 Rue St-Honoré, 1er. Map **8**G7. Metro Madeleine, Concorde* AE Φ

Jewelry boutiques

Comptoir du Kit
42 Galerie Vivienne, 4e. Map ***9****F8. Metro Bourse* VISA

Estelle
111 Rue St-Denis, 2e. Map ***9****H9. Metro Les Halles. Forum des Halles, 1er. Map* ***10****H9. Metro Châtelet-Les-Halles* AE VISA

Fabrice
26, 33 and 54 Rue Bonaparte, 6e. Map ***9****I8. Metro St-Germain-des-Prés* AE Φ VISA

IBU Gallery
8 Rue du Cherche-Midi, 6e. Map ***8****J7. Metro Sèvres-Babylone.*

Leather goods

La Bagagerie ♣
41 Rue du Four, 6e. Map ***15****J8. Metro St-Germain-des-Prés.* ***13 Rue*** *Tronchet, 8e. Map* ***8****F7. Metro Madeleine.* ***74 Rue de Passy, 16e****. Metro Muette* AE Φ VISA

Hermès
24 Faubourg St-Honoré, 1er. Map ***8****F6. Metro Madeleine* AE Φ VISA

Lancel
43 Rue de Rennes, 6e. Map ***14****J7. Metro St-Germain-des-Prés. 4 Rond Point des Champs-Élysées, 8e. Map* ***14****J7. Metro Franklin-D-Roosevelt* AE Φ VISA

Louis Vuitton
78 bis Av. Marceau, 8e. Map ***6****F3. Metro Charles-de-Gaulle-Étoile.*

Lingerie

Beautiful French underwear is considered nearly as important as outerwear, and men's underwear is sexy as well. Lingerie shops often sell swimsuits.

Berlé
14 Rue Clément Marot, 8e. Map ***7****G4. Metro Franklin-D-Roosevelt.*

Cadolle
14 Rue Cambon, 1er. Map ***8****G7. Metro Concorde.*

Erès
2 Rue Tronchet, 8e. Map ***8****F7. Metro Madeleine* AE Φ VISA

Sabbia Rosa
71 Rue des Sts-Pères, 7e. Map ***8****I7. Metro Sèvres-Babylone* AE Φ VISA

Markets

Flea markets

Each weekend Paris blossoms with flea markets on the periphery selling mainly antiques of varying quality, old clothes, books, and just plain junk. Open Sat, Sun and sometimes Mon, they invite bargaining. Most vendors will not accept credit cards, but many will ship. The most famous flea market is the *Marché aux Puces* at Porte de Clignancourt.

Marché d'Aligre Pl. d'Aligre, 12e. Metro Ledru-Rollin
Puces de Didot Av. Georges Lafenêstre. Metro Porte-de-Vanves

Puces de Kremlin-Bicêtre La Route de Paris. Metro Porte-d'Italie
Puces de Montreuil Porte de Montreuil. Metro Porte-de-Montreuil

Food markets

Every neighborhood has its street market selling mainly food. Straw baskets and kitchen gadgets can also be good buys. In addition there are several streets known for outdoor food shops, primarily the Rue Mouffetard (Metro Censier-Daubenton) and the Rue Cler (Metro École-Militaire). These are some of the better, more central markets.

Av. Président-Wilson 16e. *Map* ***6**G3.* Metro Alma-Marceau
Av. de Saxe 7e. *Map* ***13**J4.* Metro École-Militaire
Bd. de Grenelle 15e. *Map* ***12**J3.* Metro La Motte Picquet-Grenelle
Cité Berryer 26 Rue Royale, 8e. *Map* ***8**G6.* Metro Madeleine

Miscellaneous markets

Animals
Quais de Louvre and Mégisserie 1er. *Map* ***9**H8&19.* Metro Palais-Royal, Pont-Neuf
Birds
Pl. Louis-Lépine 4e. *Map* ***9**I9.* Metro Cité. Sun
Books (bouquinists)
Quais des Grands-Augustins, Conti and Malaquais 6e. *Map* ***9**I8.* Metro St-Michel
Quais de Louvre and Mégisserie 1er. *Map* ***9**H8&I9.* Metro Palais-Royal, Pont-Neuf
Quai Voltaire 6e. *Map* ***8**H7.* Metro Rue-du-Bac
Flowers
Pl. Louis-Lépine Quai de la Corse, 4e. *Map* ***9**I9.* Metro Cité
Pl. de la Madeleine 1er. *Map* ***8**F6.* Metro Madeleine
Pl. de la République 3e. *Map* ***11**G11.* Metro République
Pl. des Ternes 8e. *Map* ***6**E3.* Metro Ternes
Stamps
Av. Gabriel 1er, *Map* ***7**F5.* Metro Franklin-D-Roosevelt
Textiles
Marché St-Pierre Pl. St-Pierre. *Map* ***4**D9.* Metro Anvers

Perfume and cosmetics

Many shops offer 'duty-free' perfumes, meaning that the price is lowered by the excise tax, and many just offer discounts. Comparison shopping is useful, since the best prices are at the duty-free airport shop, although the selection there is certainly more limited.

Dozens of shops surround the Opéra, all selling the major brands of cosmetics and perfumes. These are the slightly more unusual ones.

American Perfumery ✿
31 Rue de la Sourdière, 1er. Map ***8**G7. Metro Tuileries.*
Major brands at discounts.

L'Artisan Parfumeur
84 bis Rue de Grenelle, 6e. Map ***8**I6. Metro Rue-du-Bac* AE
Charming, unusual scents such as grapefruit and cinnamon, lovely potpourris and gifts for men and women.

Dans un Jardin
80 Rue du Bac, 6e. Map ***8**I6. Metro Rue-du-Bac* VISA
Custom-made perfumes and unusual gifts.

Guerlain
68 Champs–Élysées, 8e. Map ***6****F3. Metro George-V. 2 Pl. Vendôme, 1er. Map* ***8****G7. Metro Tuileries. 29 Rue de Sèvres, 6e. Map* ***14****J7. Metro Sèvres-Babylone.*

Roger et Gallet
62 Faubourg St-Honoré, 1er. Map ***8****F6. Metro Madeleine* AE Φ VISA
Lovely soaps, eau de toilette, bath accessories for men and women.

Sur la Place
12 Pl. St-Sulpice, 6e. Map ***14****J7. Metro St-Sulpice.*
Old-fashioned bath jellies, algae from Britanny, natural beauty products.

Michel Swiss ✿
16 Rue de la Paix, 1er. Map ***8****F7. Metro Opéra* AE Φ VISA

Textiles

The backbone of the fashion industry, French textiles are sumptuous, beautifully designed and often reasonably priced.

Alexandra
95 Faubourg St-Honoré, 1er. Map ***8****G6. Metro Concorde.*

Bouchara ✿
54 Bd. Haussmann, 9e. Map ***8****F7. Metro Havre-Caumartin* VISA
Five other branches.

Max
70 Champs-Élysées, 8e. Map ***7****F4. Metro George-V* AE VISA

Rodin
36 Champs-Élysées, 8e. Map ***7****F4. Metro Franklin-D-Roosevelt* VISA

Toys

For toy shops see *Paris for children*.

Clothing sizes

When shops give clothing sizes in centimetres, use the following conversion scale to determine the correct size

12 *in*	16	20	24	28	32	36	40	44	48
30 *cm*	40	50	60	70	80	90	100	110	120

When standardized codes are used, although these may be found to vary considerably, the following provides a useful guide.

Women's clothing sizes

UK/US sizes	8/6	10/8	12/10	14/12	16/14	18/16
French sizes	38/34N	40/36N	42/38N	44/40N	46/42N	48/44N
Bust in/cm	31/80	32/81	34/86	36/91	38/97	40/102

Men's clothing sizes

European code (suits)	44	46	48	50	52	54	56
Chest in/cm	34/86	36/91	38/97	40/102	42/107	44/112	46/117
Collar in/cm	13½/34	14/36	14½/37	15/38	15½/39	16/41	16½/42
Waist in/cm	28/71	30/76	32/81	34/86	36/91	38/97	40/102
Inside leg in/cm	28/71	29/74	30/76	31/79	32/81	33/84	34/86

Men's and women's shoe sizes

UK/US sizes	3/4½	4/5½	5/6½	6/7½	7/8½	8/9½	9/10½	10/11½	11/12½
European	36	37	38	39	40	41	42	43	44

Biographies

A list of the famous whose names are linked with Paris would be endless. The following personal selection pays particular attention to those mentioned in this book.

Balzac, Honoré de *(1799–1850)*
Author of the great series of novels and stories called *La Comédie Humaine*. Many of these portray intimately the life of Paris, its inhabitants and their social mores.

Barrault, Jean-Louis *(born 1910)*
Author, outstanding artist of mime and director, who became internationally famous after his performance in Marcel Carne's celebrated film *Les Enfants du Paradis* (1944).

Chevalier, Maurice *(1888–1972)*
Actor, dancer and singer, who often appeared in English-speaking films as the embodiment of urbane Parisian charm.

Clémenceau, Georges *(1841–1929)*
Politician and journalist. Known as 'the tiger' because of his tough belligerence. Clémenceau was Premier in 1906–09 and 1917–20.

Cocteau, Jean *(1889–1963)*
A flamboyant genius who achieved fame as an artist, novelist (*Les Enfants Terribles*), screenwriter and film director (*La Belle et la Bête*), and playwright (*Orphée*).

Colbert, Jean-Baptiste *(1619–83)*
Most effective of Louis XIV's ministers. His wise financial policies greatly enriched the state.

Colette *(1873–1954)*
Author of vividly sensual and perceptive novels, such as *Chéri* and *La Chatte*. She lived for a time in the Palais-Royal.

De Gaulle, Charles *(1890–1970)*
Soldier and statesman. After leading the Free French during the war, he headed a provisional government from 1944–46. In 1958 he came out of retirement to lead France again and draw up a new constitution, resigning in 1969.

Dreyfus, Alfred *(1859–1935)*
Jewish army officer imprisoned in 1894 on a false charge of treason. The subsequent attempts by Zola and others to exonerate him split France into bitterly opposed factions and opened up an ugly blister of anti-Semitism.

Gambetta, Léon Michel *(1838–82)*
French leader during the Franco-Prussian War of 1870–71. He is famous for his daring escape from Paris by balloon when the city was under siege.

Geneviève, Saint *(c.422–512)*
Patron saint of Paris. She calmed the Parisians by correctly predicting that Attila the Hun would not attack the city in AD 451. Ten years later, she smuggled in food when Paris was besieged by the Franks.

Giscard d'Estaing, Valéry *(born 1926)*
Finance minister under de Gaulle. Leader of Independent Republican Party from 1967. President of France 1974–81.

Haussmann, Georges Eugène *(1809–91)*
As Prefect of the Seine under Napoleon III, he reshaped large areas of Paris, creating boulevards, squares, parks and bridges. His grand, triumphal style is now an integral part of the city's personality.

Hugo, Victor *(1802–85)*
A towering figure in French literature and the leader of the Romantic movement in France. Author of *Notre-Dame de Paris*

(*The Hunchback of Notre Dame*) and *Les Misérables*, he was also a member of parliament. As writer and politician he was a fierce champion of liberty and justice.

Lafayette, Marquis de (*1757–1834*)
A dashing and glamorous figure who fought against Britain in the American War of Independence, commanded the Paris National Guard after the fall of the Bastille, and was the main author of the Declaration of Rights.

Malraux, André (*1901–76*)
Novelist, art historian, revolutionary fighter, resistance hero and de Gaulle's Minister of Culture from 1958–69.

Mansart, François (*1598–1668*)
Architect who created the Classical style in French architecture, for example the Hôtel Carnavalet, and gave his name to the high-pitched Mansard roof.

Mansart, Jules Hardouin- (*1645–1708*)
Great nephew of François and chief architect to Louis XIV. His designs include the Grand Trianon and the Dôme church.

Mazarin, Jules (*1602–61*)
Cardinal and statesman. Chief Minister of France during the regency of Anne of Austria, mother of Louis XIV.

Mitterand, François (*born 1916*)
Leader of the Socialist Party and President of the Republic since 1981. His election was hailed with wild celebration in the streets of Paris by young supporters of the Left.

Piaf, Edith (*1915–63*)
Singer, actress and cabaret performer, whose small size and lively personality won her the nickname '*La Môme*' (the sparrow), and whose inspired rendering of such songs as *La Vie en Rose*, *Milord* and *Je ne regrette rien* seemed to epitomize the spirit of Paris.

Pompadour, Marquise de (*1721–64*)
Mistress of Louis XV and a ruthless political intriguer. For 20yr she unofficially controlled the French government. A lavish patron of the arts, she also helped to lead France into financial, political and military disaster.

Pompidou, Georges (*1911–74*)
De Gaulle's successor as president, he remained in office until his death. Many of the new building developments in Paris have resulted from his campaign to 'modernize' the city.

Proust, Marcel (*1871–1922*)
One of the most influential novelists of all time. His fame rests on a seven-part work, *À la Recherche du Temps Perdu* (*Remembrance of Things Past*), a minutely detailed and searching autobiographical work. Proust was born in Paris and lived there for most of his life.

Richelieu, Armand Jean du Plessis (*1585–1642*)
Cardinal and effective ruler of France under Louis XIII, he greatly increased the power of France and the crown. He was an energetic patron of literature and founded the Académie Française.

Robespierre, Maximilien (*1758–94*)
Revolutionary leader and architect of the Reign of Terror, he was executed in his turn on the guillotine.

Sartre, Jean-Paul (*1886–1980*)
Novelist, playwright, existentialist philosopher, left-wing polemicist and doyen of the Left Bank intelligentsia. He expounded his ideas in philosophical works such as *L'Être et le Néant* (*Being and Nothingness*) and in novels such as *Les Chemins de la Liberté* (*Roads to Freedom*).

Paris for children

Paris is a city of adult pleasures where the world of childhood innocence is a restricted domain – and perhaps all the more cherished on that account. The needs of children are catered to in many imaginative ways, and Paris can be a rich and exciting place for the young. But it can also be frustrating and claustrophobic, especially for active and restless youngsters. The perfect illustration is the Parisian park. Although the city has a large amount of green space per inhabitant, much of it is in the form of small, well-tailored public gardens bristling with signs telling visitors to keep off the grass. The inevitable children's play area, with its sandbox and sometimes slide and swings, is a welcome feature but no substitute for the open space where children can kick a ball or roll in the grass. On the positive side, the larger parks offer more exciting distractions such as donkey rides and miniature farms, and there are many fun places for children: zoos, museums, theaters, circuses.

Having children with you in Paris means careful planning if they are to get the best out of their stay. A good way to keep abreast of children's events is to read the section 'Pour les jeunes' in the weekly event guide called *l'Officiel des Spectacles*.

Parks and zoos

Top of the list is the **Jardin d'Acclimatation** (☎ ✈) which is a veritable children's paradise on the edge of the *Bois de Boulogne* offering enough distractions to please the most demanding youngster, including a puppet show, distorting mirrors, an archery range, miniature golf (minigolf), driving in mini-cars organized by the police, a dolphinarium and a small zoo. Kids will enjoy riding there on a miniature train from Porte Maillot. The rest of the Bois is not ideal for children, for the most part, but there is a boating lake.

The Bois de *Vincennes* also has boating lakes and the best zoo in the city. Another but less exciting zoo is to be found in the *Jardin des Plantes.* Other parks to take children to are: the *Buttes Chaumont*, with dramatic scenery, grass to walk on, roller-skating, boating and donkey rides; the *Champs-de-Mars*, with a playground for skate-boards and roller-skating, donkey-rides, and puppet shows; the *Luxembourg* gardens, which is excellent, with donkey rides, a pond for toy boats and a large marionette theater; the *Palais de Chaillot* gardens, E side, for an underground aquarium and small playground; **Ranelagh Gardens** (*Av. Raphael, 16ᵉ*) for a playground, cycling and roller-skating track, donkey rides, merry-go-round, puppet shows; and the *Tuileries* gardens, which has small play areas, donkey rides, puppet shows and two ponds for toy boats.

Museums and workshops

The main museums that give special emphasis to children and with supervised activities are the *en Herbe* museum in the Jardin d'Acclimatation, the **Musée des Enfants** (part of the *Art Moderne de la Ville de Paris* museum), the *Arts Décoratifs* museum and the *Pompidou Centre*. But for sheer old-fashioned fun there is no museum that can beat the *Grévin* with its waxworks and conjuring show. Other museums that children enjoy visiting are: the *Arts et Traditions Populaires* museum with everyday objects from past life in France, including toys; the *Palais de la Découverte*, a science museum with a planetarium; the **Army Museum** at *Les Invalides*; the

Marine museum; and the technical museum in the *Conservatoire des Arts et Métiers*, with its push-button working models of machines.

There are a number of workshops offering a range of crafts and activities for children. Here are some of them.

L'Abécédaire 68 Rue Crozatier, 12e ☎343–25–36
L'Atelier 130 Rue de Vaugirard, 6e ☎548–39–95
Atelier d'Art Enfantin 11 Rue de Clichy, 9e ☎874–68–48
Atelier Chouette 8 Passage des Entrepreneurs, 15e ☎250–97–60
Centre Franco-Americain 261 Bd. Raspail, 14e ☎033–99–92
Maison des Jeunes et de la Culture 53 Rue de Courcelles, 8e ☎267–21–70. (Branches also in 11e, 13e, 16e and 17e)

Theaters, movies, circuses and other events

Apart from the puppet shows in the parks (see opposite), there are many theaters that stage special performances for children. A list of these, along with other children's events such as children's movies and circuses, can be found in the 'Pour les jeunes' section of *l'Officiel des Spectacles*. For a list of café-theaters which often have matinées for children, see *Nightlife*.

Other ideas

Most children enjoy climbing up to the high vantage points of Paris (*Tour Eiffel*, *Tour Montparnasse*, *Arc de Triomphe*, *Notre-Dame*, *Sacré-Coeur*) or, by contrast, plunging underground into the Sewers – *Égouts* and *Catacombs*, but the latter is not for the squeamish.

The Sun bird market on the *Ile de la Cité* is always crowded, and river and canal trips are also popular with the young. And if you go up to *Montmartre* you can take them on the funicular railway. There are also annual events that always prove to be great attractions for kids, such as the Fête du Pont-Neuf, the Marais Festival and the Feux de St-Jean (see *Calendar of events* in *Planning* for full list).

Toy shops

French toys can be sophisticated, well-designed and expensive. Many are quite beautiful, particularly marionettes, model cars and boats, and dolls.

Ali Baba 29 Av. de Tourville, 7e. Metro École-Militaire AE Ⓓ VISA
L'Automobiliste 42 Rue du Bac, 6e. Metro Bac
Le Canard à Roullettes 60 Rue Mazarine, 6e. Metro St-Germain-des-Prés
Farandole 48 Av. Victor-Hugo, 8e. Metro Victor-Hugo
Le Nain Bleu 406 Rue St-Honoré, 1er. Metro Concorde AE VISA

For information on children's clothes see *Shopping*.

Baby sitters

The following operate baby-sitting services.

Baby Fare 15 Rue Saussier-Leroy, 17e
Catholic Institute 21 Rue d'Assas, 6e ☎548–31–70
General Association of Paris Medical Students 105 Bd. de l'Hôpital, 13e ☎586–19–42. (Daily 14.00–19.00)
Kid Service 17 Rue Molière, 1er ☎296–04–16
Nurse Service 33 Rue Fortuny, 17e ☎622–26–22
La Panthère Rose 1 Rue Cherubini, 1er ☎296–64–05

For information about sports, including roller-skating and skate-boarding, see *Sports and activities*.

Sports and activities

In a city as devoted to urban pleasures as Paris it is perhaps surprising to find that there is a rich choice of sports both for those who want to take part and for those who prefer to watch. Within the city boundaries, where space is at a premium, it is easier to pursue indoor than outdoor sports, but on the periphery a full range of open-air sports is available. Pursuing a sport in Paris can be an expensive business, but is not necessarily so. Many facilities, often in the form of multi-purpose leisure complexes, are provided by the City of Paris, and these can be used by the public at relatively low cost. For details contact **Bureau des Sports** (*Mairie de Paris, 75004 Paris ☎ 277-15-50 ext 30-57*). For a list that includes private multi-purpose clubs get in touch with the organization **CIKJ** (*101 Quai Branly, 75015 Paris ☎ 566-40-20*). A very useful reference book for the active sportsman or sportswoman is *Tous les Sports à Paris* by Marie-Aline Janneau (*published by Diane de Selliers, 20 Rue Raffet, 75016 Paris*). Some sporting facilities are also listed in the weekly magazines *L'Officiel des Spectacles* and *Pariscope*. For the spectator, the best way to keep abreast of events is to read the daily sports newspaper *L'Équipe*.

Conveniently, the 16ᵉ contains the major tennis and soccer stadiums **Roland Garros** and **Parc des Princes**, as well as **Longchamp** and **Auteuil** racecourses in the Bois de Boulogne.

As a starting point, the following is an A–Z guide to the main sports, games and other leisure activities in and around Paris for both participant and spectator.

Athletics

There are numerous centers in Paris where you can practice athletics. Contact the **Fédération Française d'Athlétisme** (*10 Rue de Faubourg-Poissonière, 75010 Paris ☎ 770-90-61*), or the **Bureau des Sports** (*Mairie de Paris, 17 Bd. Morland, 75004 Paris ☎ 277-15-50 ext 30-57*).

Auto racing

One of the world's great auto-racing circuits is at **Le Mans**, about 184km (115 miles) SW of Paris, where the 24hr road race takes place every year in mid-June. For information contact the **Fédération Française de Sport Automobile** (*136 Rue de Longchamp, 75016 Paris ☎ 727-97-39*).

Bicycling

Cycle racing is another French mania culminating in the annual Tour de France which finishes in Paris in July. A good idea is to make use of the *Train plus vélo* scheme offered by the French National Railways (SNCF) which gives you a day's excursion with bicycle rental thrown in. For details contact **Bicky Club** (*7 Rue Ambroise-Thomas, 75009 Paris ☎ 523-36-62*).

For general inquiries get in touch with the **Fédération Française du Cyclisme** (*43 Rue de Dunkerque, 75010 Paris ☎ 285-41-20*).

Boating

Bois de Boulogne Metro Porte-Dauphine.
Bois de Vincennes Metro Château-de-Vincennes.
Parc de Buttes-Chaumont Metro Buttes-Chaumont.

Boules

This game, and its close relative, *pétanque*, are national obsessions in France. Walk into almost any park in Paris on a

Sat or Sun afternoon, and you will find a series of amateur matches in progress on any convenient patch of earth or gravel. To find out more contact:

Bureau des Sports of the Mairie de Paris For address see *Athletics*. For a list of *boulodromes*:

Comité Regional Bouliste 66 Bd. du Montparnasse, 75014 Paris ☎538–68–11

Fédération Française de Pétanque et de Jeu Provençal 9 Rue Duperré, 75009 Paris ☎874–61–63

Bowling

The largest alley is the **Bowling de Paris** (*Jardin d'Acclimatation, Bois de Boulogne ☎ 747–77–55*). Other 'bowlings' are advertised in *L'Officiel des Spectacles* and *Pariscope*.

Boxing

Both the English and French varieties are practiced here. For the former contact the **Fédération Française de Boxe** (*62 Rue Mollet, 75017 Paris ☎ 627–52–32*), and for the latter the **Fédération Française de Boxe Française-Savate et Disciplines Assimilées** (*25 Bd. des Italiens, 75002 Paris ☎ 742–82–27*).

Bridge

There are several good bridge clubs in Paris where you can also play backgammon and gin rummy:

Bridge Club de Paris 68 Bd. de Courcelles, 17e ☎ 763–68–31
Club Pierre Albarran 141 Av. Malakoff, 16e ☎ 500–23–25
Omar Sharif Bridge Club 7 Rue Dufrenoy, 16e ☎504–69–79. Owned by the actor and world-class player

For further information contact the **Fédération Française de Bridge** (*Comité Parisien, 105 Av. Raymond-Poincaré, 75016 Paris*).

Chess

Chess is played in many Paris cafés as well as in special clubs. The **Ligue d'Ile de France d'Échecs** (*2 Rue de Pigalle, 75009 Paris ☎ 874–02–14*) can provide information.

Dance

Whether your bent is towards classical ballet, flamenco, rock or folk, there is sure to be a dance centre in Paris to suit you. Ask at the **Fédération Française de la Danse** (*12 Rue St-Germain-l'Auxerrois, 75001 Paris ☎ 236–19–61*).

Fishing

Fédération APP de la Seine (*3 Bd. Morland, 75004 Paris ☎ 376–21–82*) for information.

Football (soccer)

The main Paris stadium is the **Parc des Princes** (*Porte de St-Cloud, 16e*) near the S end of the Bois de Boulogne, where such events as the French Cup Final (May or June) are held. For more details contact the **Fédération Française de Football** (*60 bis Av. d'Iéna, 75016 Paris ☎ 720–65–40*) or the **Ligue de l'Ile de France** (*5 Pl. de Valois, 75001 Paris ☎ 261–56–47*).

Gardens

There are floral gardens in the **Bois de Vincennes** and the **Bois de Boulogne**, and the **Parc de Bagatelle** also forms part of the latter. Also worth a visit are the **Jardin des Plantes** and the **Jardin Fleuriste** (*Porte d'Auteuil*) where all the capital's flowers are grown. Many châteaux in the Ile de France have beautiful gardens. Among the more unusual gardens are the **Albert Kahn Gardens** (*Boulogne-Billancourt*) and in a town just outside Paris, **L'Häy-les-Roses**, which has a rose museum.

Golf

Most of the best golf courses belong to clubs, which will admit players on payment of a green fee. Details from the **Fédération Française de Golf** (*69 Av. Victor-Hugo, 75016 Paris ☎ 500–62–20*).

Gymnastics

Plenty of gymnasiums in Paris. Contact the city's **Bureau des Sports** (for address see *Athletics*) or the **Fédération Française d'Éducation Physique et de Gymnastique Volontaire** (*2 Rue de Valois, 75001 Paris ☎ 261–38–44*).

Health clubs

Although there are many health clubs in Paris, most are open to members only. However, **La Sauna du Louvre** (*274 Rue St-Honoré, 1er ☎ 260–61–26*) is open to visitors. Many hotels have saunas and other health facilities for residents.

Horse racing

The principal racecourses are **Longchamp** (*Bois de Boulogne*) and **St-Cloud** (*12km (8 miles) W of Paris*) for flat-racing, and **Auteuil** (*Bois de Boulogne, metro Porte d'Auteuil*) for steeple-chasing. Other courses in or near Paris are found at Chantilly, Enghien, Evry, Maisons-Laffitte and Vincennes.

Longchamp is a superb racecourse, and has a restaurant overlooking the track. The biggest racing event, the Prix de l'Arc de Triomphe, is held there on the first Sun in Oct.

Ice-skating

There are several ice-rinks in Paris where skates can also be rented. One is the **Gaîté Montparnasse** (*27 Rue du Cdt-Mouchotte, 75014 Paris ☎ 260–15–90*). For further information try the **Fédération Française des Sports de Glace** (*42 Rue du Louvre, 75001 Paris ☎ 261–51–38*).

Language courses

For general information about courses write to **Office National des Universités et Écoles Française** (*96 Bd. Raspail, 75006 Paris ☎ 222–50–20*). The following associations organize courses for all ages and all levels.

Alliance Française 101 Bd. Raspail, 75006 Paris ☎ 544–38–28

Eurocentre de Paris 13 Passage Dauphine, 75006 Paris ☎ 325–81–40

UER Etudes Françaises pour l'Étranger Sorbonne, 46 Rue Saint-Jacques, 75230 Paris ☎ 329–12–13

Riding

There are many riding stables in the Paris region. Contact the **Ligue Équestre de Paris** (*51 Rue Dumont d'Urville, 75016 Paris ☎ 500–48–74*) – afternoons only – for details of horse shows and events.

Roller-skating

It's as fun to watch the skills of others as it is to participate at a number of outdoor roller-skating and skate-boarding *pistes* such as the big concourse at the **Palais de Chaillot**. Or try a roller-skating discotheque like **La Main Jaune** (*Pl. de la Porte Champeret, 17e ☎ 763–26–47*) where you can hire skates for the evening – open to children during the day.

Rugby

For rugby union contact the **Fédération Française de Rugby** (*7 Cité d'Antin, 75009 Paris ☎ 874–84–75*), and for rugby league (*jeu à treize*) the **Fédération Française de Jeu à XIII** (*29 Rue Coquillière, 75001 Paris ☎ 236–49–45*). Important rugby (as well as soccer) matches are held at the **Parc des Princes** (*metro Porte-de-St-Cloud*).

Skate-boarding

As with roller-skating you can skate-board on the concourse of the Palais de Chaillot as well as other unofficial *pistes*, or you can choose a special skate-board park. For a list ask the **Fédération Nationale de Surf et Skate** (*45 Av. du Penon, 40510 Seignosse ☎ (58) 43–31–22*).

Squash

Though squash is an increasingly popular sport in France, there are still relatively few courts in the center of Paris, and they usually require membership. There are excellent courts at **Tour Montparnasse** (*37 Av. du Maine, 14ᵉ* ☎ 538–66–20) and at **Le Squash Front de Seine** (*21 Rue Gaston-de-Cavaillet, 15ᵉ ☎ 575–35–37*). For more information contact the **Fédération Française de Squash** (*70 Av. Clébert, 75016 Paris ☎ 553–26–43*).

Swimming

A list of municipal pools can be obtained from the city's **Bureau des Sports** (for address see *Athletics*). Information is also available from the **Fédération Française de Natation – Comité de l'Ile de France** (*148 Av. Gambetta, 75020 Paris ☎ 364–17–02*). Meanwhile here is a selection.

Deligny Quai Anatole-France, 7ᵉ ☎ 551–72–15, a very popular place which also has other sports facilities and a bar-restaurant
Étoile 32 Rue de Tilsitt, 17ᵉ ☎ 380–50–99
Molitor (municipal) 2 Av. de la Porte-Molitor ☎ 651–10–61
Oberkampf 160 Rue Oberkampf, 11ᵉ ☎ 357–56–19
Piscine Municipal de Neuilly 50 Rue Pauline-Borghese, Neuilly ☎ 722–69–74

Tennis

Both municipal courts (for example in the Luxembourg gardens) and many private ones are available. Information from the **Ligue de Paris de Tennis** (*74 Rue de Rome, 75008 Paris ☎ 522–22–08*). Tennis clubs open to visitors include the following.

Paddair 48 Pl. des Saisons, La Défense ☎ 774–63–39
Stade Française Porte de St-Cloud ☎ 602–03–09
Tennis Club de St-James 23 Bd. Général-Koenig, Neuilly ☎ 624–11–15

The big tennis event in France is the International Championship which takes place at the end of May and beginning of June, at the **Stade Roland-Garros** (*Av. Gordon-Bennett, 16ᵉ*).

Walking and rambling

Fédération Française de Randonnée Pédestre (*92 Rue de Clignancourt, 75007 ☎ 548–04–64*) for information.

Zoos

Bois de Vincennes Metro Château-de-Vincennes
Jardin d'Acclimatation, Bois de Boulogne Metro Porte-Maillot
Jardin des Plantes Metro Jussieu

Excursions

Paris has always been the center of power, politics and the arts in France, and over the centuries great châteaux have grown up within easy striking distance of the city. Several important cathedral towns are also close at hand, as well as pretty villages and many magnificent forests, a famous feature of the Ile de France. All these sights make easy one-day excursions from Paris for the modern visitor. Here we describe in full five of the best-known sights near Paris: Chartres, Fontainebleau, Reims, Rouen and Versailles. However, there are others to choose from:

Barbizon 58km (35 miles) SE of Paris. By train, from Gare du Lyon; by car, on A6 or N7. Small village close to Fontainebleau famed for its artistic associations in the 19thC when several Romantic painters settled there. They included Rousseau and Millet whose studios are open to the public. The inn where they gathered, Pierre Ganne's, also stands.

Beauvais 76km (45 miles) N of Paris. By train, from Gare du Nord; by car, on N1. Though the center of Beauvais was destroyed in a 1940 air raid, the marvelous Gothic cathedral miraculously survived.

Chantilly 50km (30 miles) N of Paris. By train, from Gare du Nord; by car, on N16. Famed for its cream, its hand-worked lace, and its racecourse, but most of all for its supremely elegant château.

Compiègne 82km (50 miles) NE of Paris. By train, from Gare du Nord; by car, on A1. The impressive palace here was a favorite royal hunting residence, and is surrounded by the majestic Compiègne Forest, where in 1918 and 1940 two very different armistices were signed.

Malmaison 15km (10 miles) W of Paris. By metro/RER to Rueil-Malmaison; by car, N13 via La Défense. The château of Napoleon and Josephine, now a fascinating museum.

St-Germain-en-Laye 21km (12 miles) W of Paris. By metro/RER to St-Germain-en-Laye; by car, on N13. Smart suburb of Paris; old streets, château, museum of French national antiquities.

Senlis 51km (30 miles) NE of Paris. By train, from Gare du Nord; by car, on A1. Old town with narrow streets, a ruined royal castle and a lovely 12thC cathedral.

Vaux-le-Vicomte 60km (35 miles) SE of Paris. By train, from Gare du Lyon; by car, on N5. Fabulous château and spacious grounds designed by Le Vau, Le Brun and Le Nôtre, still privately owned.

Chartres

88km (55 miles) SW of Paris. Population: 41,250. Getting there: By train, from Gare Montparnasse; by car, N10 or A11; by bus, tours from Cityrama (4 Pl. des Pyramides, 1er ☎ 260-30-14) and Paris-Vision (214 Rue de Rivoli, 1er ☎ 260-30-01) i 7 Cloître Notre-Dame ☎ (37) 21-54-03.

Chartres Cathedral

✗ (✗ in crypt). Cathedral open daily 7am–7pm; towers 9:30 or 10am–noon, 2–5 or 6pm; treasury 10am–noon, 2–5 or 6pm.

No one who has seen the cathedral of Notre-Dame at Chartres will ever forget the experience, for it is a building of potent beauty, a representation of the New Jerusalem on earth, as well as a shrine to the Virgin Mary. The building as it now stands was erected on the site of an earlier church which burned down in 1194, leaving only the crypt with its precious relic, the **Sancta Camisia** (now in the treasury), said to be the garment which the Virgin was wearing when she gave birth to Jesus. The fire and the survival of the relic were taken to be a sign from the Virgin that she wanted a more impressive shrine. Accordingly, enormous donations poured in from all over Christendom, and a huge army of craftsmen set to work, completing the basic structure of the cathedral in the extraordinarily short span of about 25yr. This rapidity explains the unique unity of the building as an architectural and esthetic whole.

The cathedral overflows with visual riches, but one of its most famous features is its abundant **stained glass** ★ which includes three staggering rose windows. The imagery of the stained glass, its graceful tracery depicting legends of saints, could by itself occupy many hours of study. Another attraction is the curious **maze** set into the floor of the nave near the W door, to which many people attribute an esoteric significance. The rich sculpture around the **portals** should also not be missed, nor the intricately worked **screen** ☆ separating the choir from the ambulatory. If you have time, climb up to the roof, via a stairway on the N side for a dizzying view to the N and W through the flying buttresses.

It is worthwhile taking one of the excellent English lecture tours of the cathedral conducted by the resident English guide, Malcolm Miller. Mr Miller has a rare gift for communicating his deep knowledge of the cathedral in a spicy and stimulating way. He conducts tours at Chartres all year except Feb and Mar and is the author of a short book on the cathedral which is on sale there.

Other buildings worth visiting include the churches of **St-Pierre, St-André**, **St-Martin-au-Val** and **St-Aignan** and the Bishops' Palace, now the **Musée des Beaux-Arts** (📷 *open 10am–noon, 2–6pm; closed Mon*), containing many fine works of art from medieval ivories to 18thC paintings.

The town

As for the town itself, the newer part to the S and W is not particularly remarkable, but the old district along the banks of the River Eure is beautiful and unspoiled. Here you can wander past old stone bridges, half-timbered houses and gardens reflected in the water, with the cathedral visible at every turn above the jumble of rooftops.

Hotels

Le Grand Monarque (*22 Pl. des Épars, 28000 Chartres ☎(37) 21–00–72 ▮▮▮▯ to ▮▮▮▮▮*), grand and sedate; also **Ouest** (*3 Pl. P-Semard, 28000 Chartres ☎(37) 21–43–27 ▮▮▯ to ▮▮▮▮▮*).

Restaurants

Le Buisson Ardent (*10 Rue au Lait ☎(37) 34–04–66 ▮▮▯ to ▮▮▮▮▮*), delicious and interesting food in an old Chartres house; **Le Grand Monarque** (*22 Pl. des Épars ☎(37) 21–00–72 ▮▮▮▮▮*), the hotel restaurant serves exceptionally good *nouvelle cuisine*, book in advance.

Cafés

Escalier de la Reine (*Rue du Bourg*), delicious pâtisserie; also **Salon de Thé Bergamots** (*opposite N door of cathedral*).

Fontainebleau ★

65km (40 miles) SE of Paris. Population: 19,600. Getting there: By train, from Gare de Lyon to Fontainebleau station then bus to the palace; by car, on the A6 or the N7; by bus, tours with Cityrama (4 Pl. des Pyramides, 1er ☎ (260–30–14) or Paris-Vision (214 Rue de Rivoli, 1er ☎ 260–30–01) i 38 Rue Grande ☎ (6) 422–25–68.

The palace

☎ (6) 422–34–39 Open daily Aug–Sept 10am–noon, 2pm–6pm; Oct–Mar 10am–noon, 2pm–5pm. Closed Tues.

As a former royal residence, the palace of Fontainebleau is just as interesting as Versailles and possesses a much more subtle beauty; even the name has a magical quality, deriving from a fountain in the grounds of the palace, *fontaine belle eau*, (fountain of beautiful water). The town too has its charm, a place of well-heeled grace and elegance with leafy avenues and large, quietly prosperous houses. All around it lies the lovely Fontainebleau forest.

If you have time to spare before visiting the palace, take a walk (allow 45–50min) through the thickly wooded park and approach the palace through the **formal garden** ☆ with its carp pond, its great parterres designed by Le Nôtre in 1664 and its curious statues, which include a pair of sphinxes. The fountain after which the palace was named lies to the SW of the pond.

A royal residence from the 12thC, Fontainebleau saw the birth of two French Kings, Philippe le Bel (who also died there) and Louis XIII. But the palace is linked particularly with the colorful François I (1494–1547), rake, military adventurer, friend of Leonardo da Vinci and one of the greatest royal patrons of the arts in French history. In 1528 he knocked down most of the existing medieval edifice and began to build a new château according to the Renaissance principles which had influenced him while he was campaigning in Italy. All over the building, carved in stonework and paneling, you will see the fire-breathing salamander that was his emblem. Henry II, Catherine de Medici and Henry IV added to the palace.

Most of the French sovereigns lived for a time at Fontainebleau, and the palace has witnessed a rich pageant of history: Louis XIV's decision to revoke the Edict of Nantes was made there; Pope Pius VII lived a virtual prisoner in the palace between June 1812 and Jan 1814; Napoleon I made Fontainebleau his favorite residence after the Tuileries, and it was here that he came when he abdicated in 1814 before departing for Elba.

Fontainebleau has been described as a "rendezvous of châteaux" for it is really a sprawling conglomeration of buildings of different periods, built around five courtyards. Before entering, take a walk around the palace. On the N side is the charming **Garden of Diana** ☆ with its fountain decorated with a statue of the goddess. Traveling counter-clockwise, pass into the White Horse Courtyard, or **Courtyard of Farewells** ☆ which was the scene of Napoleon's farewell to his guard. Note the graceful double horseshoe staircase with its hermetic caduceuses carved in the stonework of the balustrade.

To the right of the stairway is an arch leading into the **Fountain Courtyard** looking onto the Carp Pond. Notice on the right the two stone statues of fierce-looking Fô dogs guarding the entrance to the Empress Eugénie's Chinese salons.

Through another archway to the W is the **gilded door** ☆ which is one of the most famous features of the palace. This huge gateway, with its three superimposed loggias, was the first structure to be completed when rebuilding began in 1528.

From here the way leads NE along the facade of the ballroom. Turn left to stand between the **Oval Courtyard** to the SW, with its domed gateway, and the **Courtyard of the Kitchens** to the NE. The gateway to the latter is decorated by two huge **Hermes heads** in stone. The public entrance to the apartments is in the White Horse Courtyard.

Arguably the most remarkable room in the palace is the **François I Gallery** ★ which was decorated in the years 1534–37 by a team of Italian artists and craftsmen. The walls are adorned with 14 frescoes surrounded by rich decorative stucco work and illustrating events or allegorical subjects connected with the reign of François I. One shows an elephant decorated with fleur-de-lys as an allegory of the king's wisdom; another, symbolizing the unity of the state, depicts François I presenting a pomegranate, symbol of concord, to representatives of different classes. Another splendid Renaissance-style room is the vast **ballroom** ☆ which was designed by Philibert Delorme under Henry II. It has deep, arched bays, frescoes of mythological scenes and a coffered ceiling, the design of which is reflected in the woodwork of the floor (dating from 1835).

The rooms known as the **apartments of the King and Queen** are a rich, if often rather indigestible, confection of different periods, much of the decoration being in the overblown 19thC style of King Louis-Philippe,

Equally ornate is the series of **Napoleonic rooms**, including the Emperor's Throne Room, bedroom and council chamber. Notice that the Napoleonic bee emblem of industry and discipline figures prominently in the decoration.

Those interested in Napoleon and in militaria should visit the **Musée Napoléonien d'Art et d'Histoire Militaire** (*88 Rue St-Honoré; open Tues–Sat 14.00–17.30*) which has a splendid collection of military paraphernalia.

The forest

Ideally your visit to Fontainebleau should be a two-day affair, one to visit the palace and town, another to explore the forest. This great expanse of woodland is a remarkable natural phenomenon. Over the millennia a strange alchemy of glacial action and erosion has produced a surrealistic terrain of hills, ravines and extraordinary rock formations. Giant boulders with organic-looking contours lie everywhere, some resembling stranded whales, others sculptures by Henry Moore. No wonder the forest has been used as a setting for more than 100 films in which it has served to represent, among other things, the terrain of the Holy Land, the Wild West and the Switzerland of William Tell.

Hotels

Aigle Noir 🏛 (*27 Pl. Napoléon-Bonaparte, 77300 Fontainebleau ☎ (6) 422–32–65* ▮▮▮▮); **Napoléon** (*9 Rue Grande, 77300 Fontainebleau ☎ (6) 422–20–39* ▮▮▮□).

Restaurants

Aigle Noir (see *Hotels* above); **François 1**^er^ (*3 Rue Royale ☎ (6) 422–24–68* ▮▮□ *to* ▮▮▮□).

Reims

143km (89 miles) NE of Paris. Population: 183,600. Getting there: By train, from Gare de l'Est; by car, on the A4; by bus, tours with Cityrama (4 Pl. des Pyramides, 1er ☎ 260-30-14) and Paris-Vision (214 Rue de Rivoli, 1er ☎ 260-30-01) i 3 Bd. Paix ☎ (26) 47-04-60.

Reims is famous for two main reasons: its Gothic cathedral and the fact that it is the capital of the Champagne Country and the place where many of the big producers have their cellars. On a day excursion from Paris, try to get there early because the town has much to offer, but if possible avoid going on a Mon or Tues, when the most interesting museums are closed.

Despite the heavy damage Reims suffered in World War I, it has remained a gracious place with quietly elegant streets, solid houses, wide boulevards, fashionable shops and a lively air. Particularly fine is the **Place Royale** ☆ which was built with Classical simplicity as one unit in the 18thC.

Reims was an important city in Roman times, and some fine monuments of that era remain; the most striking is the **Mars Gate** near the station. This three-arched edifice is thought to have been the largest of its kind in the Roman Empire. The mythological themes carved on it include the story of Romulus and Remus, and local etymology has it that the latter was the founder of the city – hence the name. The Roman forum also survives, in the center of the **Place du Forum**, and includes among other things an imposing vaulted colonnade which has been beautifully restored.

Notre-Dame Cathedral ★ (*open 8am–7pm*), begun in 1211, is one of the chain of great Gothic churches which includes Chartres, Amiens and Notre-Dame de Paris. Its special importance lies in the fact that all but three kings of France were crowned there. It was one of Joan of Arc's triumphs to take the Dauphin to Reims, escorting him with an army of 12,000 men through English-held territory, so that he could be crowned as Charles VII there in 1429.

The cathedral is not as overwhelming as that of Chartres, but it has a graceful splendor. The W facade, with its three great portals and its mass of sculpture, has been badly eroded over the centuries, but some fine statues still survive, notably the angel to the right of the center door, whose face bears a curiously mischievous smile.

Inside, the cathedral has the typical majesty and grace of its era, with the characteristic soaring ribbed ceiling. The large rose window at the W end retains its original 13thC stained glass; most of the original glass was destroyed in World War I, but some of the modern glass is of a very high standard, most notably the three windows by Chagall at the E end, and the intriguing windows in the S transept depicting aspects of the Champagne industry.

The **Palais de Tau** (▣ *open daily 10am–noon, 2pm–6pm; closed Tues*), adjacent to the cathedral to the S, is a museum containing the cathedral treasury. It was once a royal residence, and dates from the 12thC. It was damaged in World War I and has been extensively restored. Other churches include the 11thC **Basilica of St-Remi** ☆ who was the patron saint of the town, and the small 20thC **Chapelle Foujita**, in Rue de Champ-de-Mars, which was designed and decorated by the Japanese artist Léonard Foujita who lived in France.

A delightful museum is the **Hôtel Le Vergeur** ☆ *(36 Pl. du Forum ☎ (26) 47-20-75 ▣; open Tues–Sun 2pm–6pm)* in a lovely rambling house, parts of which date from the 13thC. The museum was formerly the residence of the art collector and traveler Hugues Krafft, and the contents range from antique furniture and works of art to a priceless collection of original Dürer engravings of the *Apocalypse* and the *Passion of Christ*. The museum also illustrates the history of Reims through the ages, and the garden at the back contains a fascinating collection of old facades and doorways from the town.

Other interesting museums are the **Museé St-Denis** (*8 Rue Chanzy open daily 10am–noon, 2pm–6pm; closed Tues*), and the **Ancien Collège des Jesuites** (*1 Pl. Museux open Mon, Tues, Thurs, Fri 10am–noon, 2pm–6pm*). The Museé St-Denis is a fine arts museum with an excellent collection of sculpture, furniture, objets d'art and French paintings from the 17thC to modern times, which includes works by most of the great French painters. The Ancien Collège des Jesuites is a 17thC building with some magnificent rooms, a fine art and furniture collection and a planetarium (*Wed, Sat, Sun 2:15pm, 3:30pm, 4:45pm*).

If you are interested in champagne, a prime focus of a visit to Reims must be the cellars of one or more of the producers dotted around the suburbs of the town. At the premises of Piper-Heidsieck, for example, you descend 18m (54ft) below ground and then proceed in wagons pulled by an electric car through catacombs flanked by stacks of bottles. En route an audio-visual program is run on champagne production.

The easiest way to visit the cellars and vineyards of Reims and also of Épernay, 24km (15 miles) to the S, is to take a day trip by coach from Paris. These are arranged by Cityrama, Paris-Vision and other tour operators. If you have your own car, the brochure *The Champagne Road*, from the Tourist Office in Reims, gives details to enable you to choose your route.

The following champagne cellars in Reims and Épernay welcome visitors. Asterisks indicate appointments required.

REIMS **Abel Lepitre*** (*2 Av. du Gl-Giraud*); **Besserat de Bellefon*** (*Allée du Vignoble*); **Charles Heidsieck*** (*46 Rue de la Justice*); **Veuve Clicquot-Ponsardin** (*1 Pl. des Droits-de-l'Homme*); **George Goulet*** (*4 Av. du Gl-Giraud*); **Heidsieck & Co Monopole** (*83 Rue Coquebert*); **Henriot & Co*** (*3 Pl. des Droits-de-l'Homme*); **Krug*** (*5 Rue Coquebert*); **Lanson Père & Fils*** (*12 Bd. Lundy*); **Louis Roederer*** (*21 Bd. Lundy*); **G.H. Mumm & Co** (*34 Rue du Champ-de-Mars*); **Piper-Heidsieck** (*51 Bd. Henri-Vasnier*); **Pommery & Greno** (*5 Pl. Gl-Gouraud*); **Ruinart Père & Fils*** (*5 Rue des Crayères*); **Taittinger** (*9 Pl. St-Nicaise*).

ÉPERNAY **De Castellane*** (*57 Rue du Verdun*); **G.H. Martel & Co*** (*46 Av. Champagne*); **Mercier** (*75 Av. Champagne*); **Moët & Chandon** (*20 Av. Champagne*); **Perriet-Jouët** (*26 Av. Champagne*); **Pol Roger*** (*1 Rue Henri-Lelarge*).

Hotels

Frantel (*31 Bd. P-Doumer, 51100 Reims ☎ (26) 88–53–54*), a stylish modern hotel with above average service; **La Paix** (*9 Rue Buirette, 51100 Reims ☎ (26) 40–04–08 to*), quiet, comfortable and modern, good restaurant.

Restaurants

Le Boulingrin (*48 Rue de Mars ☎ (26) 47–39–01*), an old bistro with a more modern extension, reasonably priced set menu; **Boyer** (*184 Av. Épernay ☎ (26) 06–08–60*), one of the best restaurants in France, offering superb *nouvelle cuisine;* **Le Vigneron** (*13 Rue de l'Université ☎ (26) 88–00–31 to*), *cuisine Champenoise.*

Rouen

140km (87 miles) NW of Paris. Population: 118,350. Getting there: By train, from Gare St-Lazare; by car, on the A13, N14 or N15 ℹ 25 Pl. Cathédrale ☎ (35) 71–41–77.

For many centuries the capital of the powerful duchy of Normandy and the last bridging point of the Seine, Rouen has always been an important prize and has suffered regular sieges and ransacking, culminating in severe damage from heavy bombing by both sides in the Second World War. Despite this, it has retained an intimate domestic atmosphere, some superb church and secular architecture, fine museums, and a bustling social and shopping center. It is an ideal city for walking. The following route takes in most of the main sights, some of which are described more fully opposite.

The best place to begin is Pl. de la Cathédrale, a short walk from the railway station or parking lots. After visiting the **cathedral**, leave by the W door, and follow Rue St-Romain, along the N side. The overhanging buildings date from before 1525 when local law forbade the style to prevent streets from becoming too dark. On the right, notice the **Vieille Maison** of 1466 and the restored **Archbishop's Palace**. Note the plaque recording that Joan of Arc was condemned here in 1431 and then officially rehabilitated 25yr later.

Across the Rue de la République is the extravagantly ornate church of **St-Maclou** 🏛 † which shows the limit reached by the Flamboyant style. Pass along Rue Martainville and Rue Damiette, to see the sculpted facade of the superb **Hôtel d'Etancourt** in the Pl. du Lieutenant-Aubert, and the enormous abbey of **St-Ouen**. Note particularly the stained glass and the exhilarating **Portail des Marmousets**. Leave the abbey gardens by the restored 18thC **Hôtel de Ville** and across Pl. du Général-de-Gaulle to reach the shaded **Pl. du Rougemare**, where the cafés make an ideal place to pause.

Rue du Cordier leads from the square to Rue du Donjon, where the **Joan of Arc Tower** (🎫 *open 10am–noon, 2pm–5pm; closed Thurs and hols*) is found. This donjon with its pepperpot roof is all that remains of a castle built in 1204. Visitors can see the somber, bare room where Joan of Arc was brought before her accusers.

After leaving the tower, turn back along Rue du Donjon then turn right into Rue Jacques Villon at the end of which, on the left, is the old church of St-Laurent, which houses the **Secq des Tournelles Museum**. The **Beaux-Arts Museum** is on the opposite side of the street. After this museum the walk takes you right to Rue Thiers, then left to Rue Jeanne d'Arc until you reach the Rue du Gros Horloge, which leads, on the right, to the **Place du Vieux Marché**. This square, where Joan of Arc was burnt at the stake, combines tall timbered houses with some wonderfully successful modern architecture – a mixture also illustrated by the 16thC stained glass in the light and airy modern church.

Returning from the square to the Rue du Gros Horloge, walk along as far as the **Gros Horloge** itself and the **Belfry Museum**. Then continue along the street as far as the Rue du Bec which leads to the delightful **Palais de Justice**. However, only the central block remains from the 16thC when it was built for Normandy's parliament. From here, by turning right along Rue aux Juifs and then right again into Rue des Carmes, it is easy to get your bearings to return to the Pl. de la Cathédrale where the walk began.

Rouen Cathedral (Notre-Dame) ★
Crypt and Lady Chapel Tours 10am, 11am, 2:15pm, 3pm, 4pm, 5pm during June–Sept and Easter, except Sun morning and other hols; rest of year Sat 2:15pm, 3pm, 4pm, Sun 3pm, 4pm.
Rouen's cathedral soars above the city in extravagant confidence. The main W facade climbs from the solid base of the St-Romain Tower on the N side and the two outer portals, sole remnants of the cathedral that burned down in 1201, to a dramatic skyline, the late 15thC work of Guillaume Pontis. It reaches its climax in the **Tour de Beurre** (Butter Tower) on the S side, which was paid for by indulgences granted to allow citizens to eat butter during Lent; the ornate decoration, always in proportion, typifies the Flamboyant style. The cathedral's interior is more austere but just as harmonious, highlights being the **11thC crypt** and the **Lady Chapel**, with its 14thC windows and Renaissance tombs of the two cardinals of Amboise.
Secq des Tournelles Museum ☆
Rue Jacques Villon, in the old church of St-Laurent Open 10am–noon, 2pm–6pm. Closed Tues, Weds morning and hols. (Ticket also gives entry to Beaux-Arts and Gros Horloge Belfry).
This unusual museum houses a collection of all sorts of ironwork, displayed perfectly in the church. The arches are hung with *auberge* and tradesmen's signs, and the alcoves and galleries are full of tools, jewelery and locks.
Beaux-Arts Museum
Rue Jacques Villon (For times and tickets, see Secq des Tournelles Museum.)
A considerably richer collection than the average provincial art gallery; the most interesting rooms are reached by turning left from the entrance hall. The outstanding exhibit, kept alone in an alcove, is Gerard David's *Virgin and Saints*, a work of great calmness and sensitivity. Other notable paintings include collections of Delacroix, Géricault, Jouvenet, Monet and Sisley, and single works by Ingres, Velazquez and Clouet.
Gros Horloge and Belfry Museum
(For times and tickets, see Secq des Tournelles Museum.)
The enormous and colorful Renaissance clock straddles the street named after it, adorning a gatehouse completed in 1527, inside which is the Belfry Museum where you can examine the workings of the clock, made in the late 14thC, as well as two 13thC bells. The highlight is the view of the city and Seine valley after the long climb up a spiral staircase.

Hotels

Cathédrale (*12 Rue St-Romain, 76000 Rouen ☎ 71–57–95*) is a traditional hotel; **Frantel** (*Rue Croix de Fer, 76000 Rouen ☎ (35) 98–06–98 180949*), a modern hotel offering every facility – it also has a good restaurant.

Restaurants

Two of the best, both in the Pl. du Vieux-Marché: **La Couronne** (*closed Sun, Mon*), reputedly the oldest *auberge* in France; **L'Auberge de l'Écu de France** (*closed Sun, Mon, Oct–Mar*). Both specialize in classic French cuisine. **L'Écu de France** also offers a six-course gourmet *menu dégustation* at a bargain price. **La Marée** (*closed Sun, Mon, late Jul, early Feb*) offers local seafood specialties.

Versailles ★

24km (15 miles) sw of Paris. Population: 97,150. Getting there: By train, from Gare des Invalides, Gare Montparnasse; by car, on the N10; by bus, tours with Cityrama (4 Pl. des Pyramides, 1er ☎ 260–30–14) and Paris-Vision (214 Rue de Rivoli, 1er ☎ 260–30–01) i 7 Rue Reservoirs ☎ (6) 950–36–22. Map 24.

The palace

in English and French in some parts of building For full details and opening times, write to Services des Visites, Château de Versailles, 78000 Versailles. For times of guided visits ☎ (6) 950–38–32. State apartments open daily 10am–5pm; Grand Trianon 10am–6pm; Petit Trianon 2pm–6pm; gardens open dawn to dusk.

The palace of Versailles is perhaps the greatest monument to absolute monarchy ever built. It is overwhelming, fascinating, unforgettable, but to many people not exactly beautiful. Louis XIV, the Sun King who built it, was extremely vain and his palace is an expression of egomania in stone, plaster and gold leaf.

The site was first occupied by a hunting lodge and then by a small brick-and-stone château built by Louis XIII which his son and successor Louis XIV enlarged into the present building, the work continuing from 1661 for about half a century. The architects were first Le Vau, then Jules Hardouin-Mansart. The decoration was supervised by Le Brun and the gardens were planned by Le Nôtre, creator of the *Tuileries* gardens. At the height of the building work 36,000 men and 6,000 horses were employed on the site.

In 1682 Louis decided to make Versailles the court residence and seat of government, and it retained this function until the Revolution. Thus Versailles was the capital of France for over a century. It was the scene of a glittering court which in its heyday included a thousand nobles who lived in the palace itself, along with a vast retinue of servants.

Approaching the palace from the station and the Av. de Paris, the grand stables are to the right and left of the vast **Place d'Armes** in front of the palace. Passing through the great wrought-iron gates, the visitor enters the enormous courtyard with its equestrian statue of *Louis XIV*, erected by King Louis-Philippe, in the middle. Enter by the doorway on the right of the courtyard, and follow the stairway to the upper chapel vestibule, from where the **chapel**☆ can be seen. Dedicated to St Louis (King Louis XI of France), it is a frothy confection in white and gold with a sumptuously painted ceiling.

From here you pass into the series of **State apartments**☆ leading into the astonishing **Hall of Mirrors**★ where the 17 windows that overlook the gardens are matched on the opposite wall by a row of arches filled with reflecting glass.

Beside the Hall of Mirrors are the sumptuous **King's apartments**☆ with the bed where each morning and night the monarch's *levée* and *couchée* took place in front of the assembled courtiers. Louis XIV died of gangrene on this bed on Sept 1, 1715.

At the opposite end of the Hall of Mirrors are the **Queen's apartments**☆ followed by the **Coronation Room** and then the s wing, the first floor of which is taken up almost entirely by the **Hall of Battles**, built by Louis-Philippe, containing 33 paintings of war scenes. Also on the first floor are several rooms, including the **private apartments of the King and Queen**☆

The **Royal Opera**☆ which occupies the end of the N wing, can also be visited only on a guided tour. Its interior is entirely of wood, ornately carved and painted in gold, blue and pink.

The gardens

To understand Versailles fully it is necessary to appreciate that the whole complex, palace and gardens, is a kind of symbolic Utopia in which one theme is constantly emphasized: that of a solar deity around which everything revolves, just as the state revolves around the king. This comes across particularly clearly in the **gardens**★ which were laid out by Le Nôtre in a series of highly formal terraces adorned with parterres, statues, vases and fountains. Here nature is subdued and constrained as a demonstration of the power of the Sun King who, in the gardens, is represented as Apollo.

Bear this in mind as you approach the main focus of the garden, the fountain of Apollo, through a long avenue, flanked by statues and with a carpet of lawn stretching down the middle. The figure of Apollo in his chariot emerges out of the water, just as in legend the sun rose out of the sea at daybreak. If you want to witness the amazing spectacle of the illuminated **fountains**★ in operation, telephone for details of times and tickets (☎*(6) 950–36–22*).

Beyond the fountain of Apollo stretches the **Grand Canal**, on which there once sailed a flotilla of small-scale ships and gondolas. Today you can rent a boat to row on the canal in more modest style. The waterway forms a cross, the northern arm of which leads to where the **Grand Trianon**☆ and **Petit Trianon**☆ are situated. Both of these are worth a visit, the former with its pink marble colonnade and lavish interior, the latter more elegant and restrained with its exquisite theater in which Marie-Antoinette used to act. Close by is the **hamlet**, a collection of mock-rustic buildings where the same queen used to play at leading the simple life.

The town

The name of Versailles is so closely linked with the palace that the town itself tends to be neglected by tourists. It is worth knowing, however, that Versailles is one of the earliest examples of what we now call town planning. It was built by royal command in the 17thC after its layout had been carefully designed. Its regular, grid-like pattern of streets and squares (exemplified in the elegant Pl. Hoche) inspired the designers of such cities as St Petersburg, Washington and Karlsruhe. Today it preserves a wealth of domestic architecture from the time of Louis XV and XVI. Two churches worth visiting are **Notre-Dame**, built by J.H. Mansart in the 1680s, and **St-Louis**, built by Mansart de Sagonne in the mid-18thC.

Hotel

St-Louis (*28 Rue St-Louis, 78000 Versailles* ☎*(6) 950–23–55* ▮▮▮□).

Restaurants

Boule d'Or (*25 Rue Maréchal Foch* ☎*(3) 950–22–97* ▮▮▮□ *to* ▮▮▮▮▮); **La Flotille**, a delightful café near the E end of the canal in the palace gardens; **Trois Marches** (*3 Rue Colbert* ☎*(3) 950–13–21* ▮▮▮▮▮).

A guide to French

This glossary covers the basic language needs of the traveler: for pronunciation, essential vocabulary and simple conversation, finding accommodations, visiting the bank, shopping, using public transport or a car, and for eating out.

Pronunciation

It is impossible to give a summary of the subtlety and richness of the French language, but there are some general tips about pronunciation that should be remembered.

French tends to be pronounced in individual syllables rather than in rhythmic feet, so that the word *institution* has four stresses in French and only two in English. In French the voice usually rises at the ends of words and sentences whereas it drops in English. French vowels and consonants are shorter, softer and more rounded than their English counterparts.

The French language is full of characteristic sounds – the r, the u, the frequent eau sound and the nasal sounds (e.g. an, en, ien, in, ain, on, un). The best way to acquire these is to speak English whilst mimicking a strong French accent. The great poet Verlaine used this method with his English pupils.

Vowels

a		short, as in hat; e.g. haricot
	before i	long, as in hay; e.g. aimer
	before m,n	as the o in hot; e.g. dance
e	at beginning of word	as the e in let; e.g. exemple
	at end of syllable	as the ir in irk; e.g. repas
	before m,n	as the a in arm; e.g. emploi
	before r or z at end of word	as the a in lady; e.g. chercher, venez
é		as the a in baby; e.g. bébé
è		as the ai in air; e.g. frère
i		as the ee in seek; e.g. rire
	before m,n	as the a in pan; e.g. vin
o		short, as in song; e.g. tomate
	before i	as the wh in white; e.g. soif
	before n	as the or in torn; e.g. Londres
u		as the u in tune; e.g. jupe

Consonants

c	before a,o,u	hard, as in cat; e.g. canard
	before e,i,y	as the s in sight; e.g. cèpe
	before h	as the sh in shock; e.g. chic
ç		as the c in facet; e.g. façon
g	before a,o,u	as in gun; e.g. gaz
	before e,i,y	as the dg in ledge; e.g. Gigi
	before n	as the n in onion; e.g. Cognac
h		never sounded
j		as the s in leisure; e.g. jupe
m,n	at end of word	not sounded, except with slight nasal twang; e.g. nom —
r		rolled in back of throat
s	at end of word	usually silent; e.g. Paris
t	at end of word	usually silent; e.g. tôt
x	at end of word	usually silent, e.g. prix

Letter Groups

(e) au (x)	as in oh; e.g. gâteaux
ail (le)	as in eye; e.g. volaille
(a) (e) in	as in pan, plus nasal twang; e.g. pain
(a) (e) ine	as en in men; e.g. Madeleine
il (le) at end of word	usually ee as in see; e.g. rouille (except ville, pronounced "veel")
ine	as in green; e.g. poitrine

Reference words

Monday lundi
Tuesday mardi
Wednesday mercredi
Thursday jeudi
Friday vendredi
Saturday samedi
Sunday dimanche

January janvier
February février
March mars
April avril
May mai
June juin
July juillet
August août
September septembre
October octobre
November novembre
December décembre

1	un	11	onze	21	vingt-et-un
2	deux	12	douze	22	vingt-deux
3	trois	13	treize	30	trente
4	quatre	14	quatorze	40	quarante
5	cinq	15	quinze	50	cinquante
6	six	16	seize	60	soixante
7	sept	17	dix-sept	70	soixante-dix
8	huit	18	dix-huit	80	quatre-vingts
9	neuf	19	dix-neuf	90	quatre-vingt-dix
10	dix	20	vingt	100	cent

First premier, -ière
Second second, -e
Third troisième
Fourth quatrième
. . . . o'clock . . . heures
Quarter-past . . . . et quart
Half-past . . . . et demie
Quarter to . . . . moins le/un quart
Quarter to six six heures moins le quart

Mr monsieur/M.
Mrs madame/Mme
Miss mademoiselle/Mlle
Ladies dames
Men/gentlemen hommes/messieurs

Basic communication

Yes oui (si, for emphatic contradiction)
No non
Please s'il vous plaît
Thank you merci
I'm very sorry je suis désolé/pardon, excusez-moi
Excuse me pardon/excusez-moi
Not at all/you're welcome de rien
Hello bonjour, salut (familiar), allo (on telephone)
Good morning bonjour
Good afternoon bonjour
Good night bonsoir/bonne nuit
Goodbye au revoir, adieu (final or familiar)
Morning matin (m)
Afternoon après-midi (m/f)
Evening soir (m)
Night nuit (f)
Yesterday hier
Today aujourd'hui
Tomorrow demain
Next week la semaine prochaine
Last week la semaine dernière
. . . . days ago il y a . . . . jours
Month mois (m)
Year an (m)/année (f)
Here ici
There là
Over there là-bas
Big grand, -e
Small petit, -e
Hot chaud, -e
Cold froid, -e
Good bon, bonne
Bad mauvais, -e
Well bien
Badly mal
With avec
And et
But mais
Very très
All tout, -e
Open ouvert, -e
Closed fermé, -e
Left gauche
Right droite
Straight on tout droit
Near près/proche
Far loin
Up en haut
Down en bas
Early tôt
Late tard
Quickly vite
Pleased to meet you. Enchanté
How are you? Comment ça va? (Formal: comment allez vous?
Very well, thank you. Très bien, merci.
Do you speak English? Parlez-vous anglais?
I don't understand. Je ne comprends pas.
I don't know. Je ne sais pas.
Please explain. Pourriez-vous m'expliquer?
Please speak more slowly. Parlez plus lentement, s'il vous plaît.

My name is . . . . Je m'appelle . . . .
I am American/English. Je suis americain, -e/anglais, -e.
Where is/are? Où est/sont . . . ?
Is there a . . . . ? Y a-t-il un, une . . . . ?
What? Comment?
How much? Combien?
That's too much. C'est trop.
Expensive cher (chère)
Cheap pas cher/bon marché
I would like . . . . je voudrais . . . .
Do you have . . . . ? Avez-vous . . . . ?
Just a minute. Attendez une minute. (**On telephone:** *ne quittez pas!*)
That's fine/OK. Ça va/OK/ça y est/d'accord.
What time is it? Quelle heure est-il?
I don't feel well. Je ne me sens pas bien/j'ai mal.

Accommodations

Making a reservation by letter

Dear Sir, Madam,
Monsieur, Madame,
I would like to reserve one double room (with bathroom), one twin-bedded room
Je voudrais réserver une chambre pour deux personnes (avec salle de bain), une chambre avec deux lits
and one single room (with shower) for 7 nights from
et une chambre pour une personne (avec douche) pour 7 nuits à partir
12th August. We would like bed and breakfast/half board/full board,
du 12 août. Nous désirons le petit déjeuner/la demi-pension/pension,
and would prefer rooms with a sea view.
et préférerions des chambres qui donnent sur la mer.
Please send me details of your terms with the confirmation.
Je vous serais obligé de m'envoyer vos conditions et tarifs avec la confirmation.
Yours sincerely,
Veuillez agréer, Monsieur, l'expression de mes sentiments distingués.

Arriving at the hotel

I have a reservation. My name is . . . .
J'ai une réservation. Je m'appelle . . . .
A quiet room with bath/shower/toilet/wash basin
Une chambre tranquille avec bain/douche/toilettes/lavabo
. . . . overlooking the sea/park/street/back.
. . . . qui donne sur la mer/le parc/la rue/la cour.
Does the price include breakfast/service/tax?
Ce prix comprend-il le petit déjeuner/la service/les taxes?
This room is too large/small/cold/hot/noisy.
Cette chambre est trop grande/petite/froide/chaude/bruyante.
That's too expensive. Have you anything cheaper?
C'est trop cher. Avez-vous quelque chose de moins cher?
Where can I park my car? Où puis-je garer ma voiture?
Is it safe to leave the car on the street? Est-ce qu'on peut laisser la voiture dans la rue?

Floor/story étage (m)
Dining room/restaurant salle à manger (f)/restaurant (m)
Lounge salon (m)
Porter portier/concierge (m) porteur (station)
Manager directeur (m)
Have you got a room? Avez-vous une chambre?
What time is breakfast/dinner? À quelle heure est le petit déjeuner/dîner?
Can I drink the tap water? L'eau du robinet est–elle potable?
Is there a laundry service? Y a-t-il un service de blanchisserie?
What time does the hotel close? À quelle heure ferme l'hôtel?
Will I need a key? Aurai-je besoin d'une clé?
Is there a night porter? Y a-t-il un portier de nuit?
I'll be leaving tomorrow morning. Je partirai demain matin.
Please give me a call at . . . . Voulez-vous m'appeler à . . . .
Come in! Entrez!

Shopping

Where is the nearest/a good . . . .? Où est le . . . . le plus proche?/Où y a-t-il un bon . . . .?
Can you help me/show me . . . .? Pouvez-vous m'aider/voulez-vous me montrer . . . .?
I'm just looking. Je regarde.
Do you accept credit cards/travelers checks? Est-ce que vous prenez des cartes de credit/chèques de voyage?
Can you deliver to . . . .? Pouvez-vous me le livrer à . . . .?
I'll take it. Je le prends.
I'll leave it. Je ne le prends pas.
Can I have it tax-free for export? Puis-je l'avoir hors tax pour exportation?
This is faulty. Can I have a replacement/refund? Celui-ci ne va pas. Voulez-vous me l'échanger?
I don't want to spend more than . . . . Je ne veux pas mettre plus de . . . .
I'll give . . . . for it. Je vous donne . . . .
Can I have a stamp for . . . .? Donnez-moi un timbre pour . . . . s'il vous plaît.

Shops

Antique shop antiquaire (m/f)
Art gallery galérie d'art (f)
Bakery boulangerie (f)
Bank banque (f)
Beauty salon salon de beauté (m)
Bookshop librairie (f)
Butcher boucherie (f)
Horse butcher boucherie chevaline (f)
Pork butcher charcuterie (f)
Tripe butcher triperie (f)
Cake shop pâtisserie (f)
Chemist/pharmacy /drugstore pharmacie (f) (m)
Clothes shop magasin de vêtements/de mode (m)
Dairy crèmerie (f)
Delicatessen épicerie fine (f)/ charcuterie (f)
Department store grande surface (f)/grand magasin (m)
Fish store marchand de poisson/poissonier (m)
Florist fleuriste (m/f)
Greengrocer marchand de légumes/primeurs (m)
Grocer épicier (m)
Haberdashery mercier (m)
Hairdresser coiffeur (m)
Hardware store droguerie (f)
Jeweller bijouterie/joaillerie (f)
Market marché (m)
Newsstand marchand de journaux (m)
Optician opticien (m/f)
Perfumery parfumerie (f)
Photographic shop magasin de photographie (m)
Post office bureau de poste (m)
Shoe shop magasin de chaussures (m)
Souvenir shop magasin de cadeaux/souvenirs (m)
Stationer papeterie (f)
Supermarket supermarché (m)
Tailor tailleur (m)
Tobacconist bureau de tabac (m)
Tourist office syndicat d'initiative (m)
Toy shop magasin de jouets (m)
Travel agent agence de voyage (f)

At the bank

I would like to change some dollars/pounds/travelers checks.
Je voudrais changer des dollars/livres/chèques de voyage.
What is the exchange rate?
Quel est le taux?/le cours du change?
Can you cash a personal check?
Pouvez-vous encaisser un chèque personnel?
Can I obtain cash with this credit card?
Puis-je obtenir de l'argent avec cette carte de crédit?
Do you need to see my passport?
Voulez-vous voir mon passeport?

Some useful goods

Antiseptic cream crème antiseptique (f)
Aspirin aspirine (f)
Bandages pansements (m) bandes (f)
Cotton coton hydrophile (m)
Diarrhea/upset stomach pills comprimés (m) pour la diarrhée/l'estomac dérangé
Indigestion tablets comprimés pour l'indigestion
Insect repellant anti-insecte (m)
Laxative laxatif (m)
Sanitary napkins serviettes hygiéniques (f)

Shampoo shampooing (m)
Shaving cream crème à raser (f)
Soap savon (m)
Sticking plaster sparadrap (m)
String ficelle (f)
Sunburn cream crème écran solaire (f)
Sunglasses lunettes de soleil (f)
Suntan cream/oil crème solaire (f)/huile bronzante (f)
Tampons tampons (m)
Tissues mouchoirs en papier (m)
Toothbrush brosse à dents (f)
Toothpaste (pâte) dentifrice (f)
Travel sickness pills comprimés pour les maladies de transport

---

Bra soutien-gorge (m)
Coat manteau (m)
Dress robe (f)
Jacket veste/jaquette (f)
Pants slip (m)
Pullover pull (m)
Shirt chemise (f)
Shoes souliers (m)/ chaussures (f)
Skirt jupe (f)
Socks chaussettes (f)
Stockings/tights bas/collants (m)
Swimsuit maillot de bain (m)
Trousers pantalon (m)

Film film (m)/pellicule (f)
Letter lettre (f)
Money order mandat (m)
Postcard carte postale (f)
Stamp timbre(m)
Telegram télégramme (m)

Driving

Service station station de service (f)
Fill it up. Plein, s'il vous plaît.
Give me . . . . francs worth. Donnez m'en pour . . . francs.
I would like . . . . liters of gasoline. Je voudrais . . . . litres d'essence.
Can you check the . . . .? Voulez-vous vérifier . . . .?
There is something wrong with the . . . . Il y a quelque chose qui ne va pas dans le . . . .
Battery batterie (f)
Brakes freins (m)
Exhaust échappement (m)
Lights phares (m)
Oil huile (f)
Tires pneus (m)
Water eau (f)
Windscreen pare-brise (m)
My car won't start. Ma voiture ne veut pas démarrer.
I have broken down/had a flat tire. Je suis tombé en panne/J'ai eu une crevaison.
The engine is overheating. Le moteur chauffe.
How long will it take to repair? Il faudra combien de temps pour la réparer?

Car rental

Is full/comprehensive insurance included? Est-ce que l'assurance tous–risques est comprise?
Is it insured for another driver? Est-elle assurée pour un autre conducteur?
Unlimited mileage kilométrage illimité
Deposit caution (f)
By what time must I return it? À quelle heure devrais-je la ramener?
Can I return it to another depot? Puis-je la ramener à une autre agence?
Is the gas tank full? Est-ce que le réservoir est plein?

Road signs

Aire (de repos) **highway rest stop**
Autres directions **other directions**
Centre ville **town center**
Chaussée deformée **irregular surface**
Déviation **diversion**
Passage à niveau **level crossing**
Passage protégé **priority for vehicles on main road**
Péage **toll point**
Priorité à droite **priority for vehicles coming from the right**
Ralentir **slow down**
Rappel **remember that a previous sign still applies**
Route barrée **road blocked**
Sortie de secours **emergency exit**
Stationnement interdit **no parking**
Stationnement toléré **literally, parking tolerated**
Toutes directions **all directions**
Verglas **(black) ice on road**

Other methods of transport

Aircraft avion (m)
Airport aéroport (m)
Bus autobus (m)
Bus stop arrêt d'autobus (m)
Coach car (m)
Ferry/boat Ferry/bâteau/bac (m)
Ferry port port du ferry/bâteau/bac (m)

Hovercraft hovercraft/aéroglisseur (m)
Station gare (f)
Train train (m)
Ticket billet (m)
Ticket office guichet (m)
Single billet simple
Round trip billet aller-retour
Half fare demi-tarif
First/second class première/seconde classe
Sleeper/couchette wagon-lit (m)

When is the next . . . . for . . . .? À quelle heure est le prochain . . . . pour . . . .?
What time does it arrive? À quelle heure arrive-t-il?
What time does the last . . . . for . . . . leave? À quelle heure part le dernier . . . . pour . . . .?
Which platform/quay/gate? Quel quai/port?
Is this the . . . . . for . . . .? Est-ce que c'est bien le . . . . pour . . . .?
Is it direct? Where does it stop? C'est direct? Où est-ce qu'il s'arrête?
Do I need to change anywhere? Est-ce que je dois changer?
Please tell me where to get off? Pourrez-vous me dire ou je devrai descendre?
Take me to . . . . . Conduisez-moi à . . . . .
Is there a buffet car? Y a-t-il un wagon-restaurant?

Food and drink

Have you a table for . . . .? Avez-vous une table pour . . . .?
I want to reserve a table. Je veux réserver une table.
A quiet table. Une table bien tranquille.
A table near the window. Une table près de la fenêtre.
Could we have another table? Est-ce que nous pourrions avoir une autre table?
Set menu Menu prix-fixe
I did not order this Je n'ai pas commandé cela
Bring me another . . . . Apportez-moi encore un . . . .
The bill please L'addition s'il vous plaît
Is service included? Le service, est-il compris?

Breakfast petit déjeuner (m)
Lunch déjeuner (m)
Dinner dîner (m)
Hot chaud
Cold froid
Glass verre (m)
Bottle bouteille (f)
Half-bottle demi-bouteille
Beer/lager bière (f)/lager (m)
Draft beer bière pression
Orangeade/lemonade sirop d'orange/de citron (m)
Mineral water eau minérale (f)
Carbonated gazeuse
Still non-gazeuse
Fruit juice jus de fruit (m)
Red wine vin rouge (m)
White wine vin blanc
Rosé wine vin rosé
Vintage année (f)
Dry sec
Sweet doux (of wine)
Salt sel (m)
Pepper poivre (m)
Mustard moutarde (f)
Oil huile (m)
Vinegar vinaigre (m)
Bread pain (m)
Butter beurre (m)
Cheese fromage (m)
Milk lait (m)
Coffee café (m)
Tea thé (m)
Chocolate chocolat (m)
Sugar sucre (m)
Steak biftek (m)
well done bien cuit
medium à point
rare saignant
very rare bleu

Menu decoder

Agneau **lamb**
Agneau de pré salé **young lamb grazed in fields bordering the sea**
Aiglefin **haddock**
Aigre–doux **sweet and sour**
Aiguillettes **thin slices**
Ail **garlic**
Ailerons **chicken wings**
Aïoli **garlic mayonnaise**
Allumettes **puff pastry strips garnished or filled**
Alouette **lark**
Ananas **pineapple**
Anchoïade **anchovy paste, usually served on crispy bread**
Anchois **anchovies**
Andouillette **chitterling sausage**
Anguille **eel**
Arachides **peanuts**
Artichaut **artichoke**
Asperges **asparagus**
Assiette assortie **mixture of cold hors d'oeuvre**
Baguette **long bread loaf**
Banane **banana**
Barbue **brill**
Barquette **pastry boat**
Basilic **basil**
Baudroie **monkfish**
Belons **flat shelled oysters**

Betterave beetroot
Beurre butter
Biftek beefsteak
Bignorneaux winkles
Bisque shellfish soup
Blanchailles whitebait
Blanquette 'white' stew thickened with egg yolk
Bombe elaborate ice cream
Bouchée tiny vol-au-vent
Boudin (noir ou blanc) (black or white) sausage pudding
Bouillabaisse Mediterranean fish soup which must include fresh fish and saffron
Bouillon broth
Bourride Provençal soup of mixed fish with *aïoli*
Brandade de morue purée of salt cod, milk and garlic (Provençal dish)
Brioche soft bread made from a rich yeast dough
(à la) Broche spit roasted
Brochet pike
Brochette (de) meat or fish on a skewer
Cabillaud cod
Calmar squid
Canard duck
Carré (d'agneau) loin (of lamb)
Cassis black currants
Cassoulet casserole from Languedoc with beans, *confit d'oie* and pork
Cèpes prized wild, dark brown mushrooms
Cervelles brains
Champignons mushrooms
Chanterelles, girolles apricot-colored mushroom
Chantilly whipped cream with sugar
Chicorée curly endive/chickory
Chou light puff pastry/cabbage
Choucroute pickled white cabbage/sauerkraut
Choufleur cauliflower
Citron lemon
Citron vert lime
Civet de lièvre jugged hare
Colin hake
Concombre cucumber
Confit meat covered in its own fat, cooked and preserved
Confit d'oie preserved goose
Confiture jam
Contre-filet sirloin steak
Coquillages shellfish
Coquille St Jacques scallops, usually cooked in wine
Côte, côtelette chop, cutlet
Coupe ice cream dessert
Crabe crab
Crème cream
Crêpe thin pancake
Cresson watercress
Crevettes grises shrimps
Crevettes roses prawns
Croque-monsieur toasted cheese and ham sandwich
Croustade small bread or pastry mold with a savory filling
(en) Croûte cooked in a pastry case
Cru raw
Crudités selection of raw sliced vegetables
Cuisses (de grenouilles) (frogs) legs
Cuit cooked
Culotte de boeuf rump of beef
Darne thick slice, usually of fish
Daube meat slowly braised in a rich wine stock
Daurade sea bream
Dindon turkey
Écrevisses freshwater crayfish
Émincé thinly sliced
Endive endive
Épaule (d'agneau) shoulder (of lamb)
Éperlans smelts
Épices spices
Épinards spinach
Escabèche various fish, fried, marinated and served cold
Escargots snails
Estouffade a stew marinated and fried then slowly braised
Estragon tarragon
Faisan pheasant
Farci stuffed
Faux filet sirloin steak
Fenouil fennel
Feuilleté light flaky pastry
Filet fillet
Flageolets fava beans
Flétan halibut
Foie liver
Foie gras goose liver
(au) Four cooked in the oven
Fourré stuffed
Frais, fraîche fresh
Fraises strawberries
Framboises raspberries
Frappé surrounded by crushed ice
Fricadelle kind of meat ball
Frit fried
Frites chips/french fries
Fritots fritters
Fruits de mer seafood
Fumé smoked
Galantine cooked meat, fish or vegetables served cold in a jelly
Galette flaky pastry case
Gambas large prawns
Garbure very thick soup
Garni garnished
Gâteau cake
Gibier game
Gigot (d'agneau) leg (of lamb)
Glace ice cream
Glacé iced, frozen, glazed
(au) Gratin crisp browned topping of breadcrumbs and cheese

Grenouilles frogs
Grillé grilled
Grive thrush
Hachis minced
Harengs herrings
Haricot stew with vegetables/beans
Haricot verts green beans
Homard lobster
Huile (d'olive) (olive) oil
Huîtres oysters
Jambon ham
Laitue lettuce
Langouste spiny lobster or crayfish
Langoustines Dublin bay prawns
Langue (de boeuf) (ox) tongue
Lapin rabbit
Légumes vegetables
Lièvre hare
Loup de mer sea bass
Magret (de canard) breast (of duck)
Maïs sweet corn
Maquereaux mackerel
Marcassin young wild boar
Marrons chestnuts
Matelote freshwater fish stew
Merlin whiting
Morilles edible dark brown fungi
Morue cod
Moules mussels
Moules marinière mussels cooked with white wine and shallots
Museau de porc pig's snout
Navarin stew of lamb and young root vegetables
Noix nuts, usually walnuts
Noix de veau rump of veal
Oeufs eggs
Oie goose
Oignons onions
Oseille sorrel
Oursins sea urchins
Palourdes clams
Pamplemousse grapefruit
(en) Papillote cooked in oiled or buttered paper
Pâte pastry
Paupiette thin slices of meat or fish rolled up and filled
Pêche peach
Perdreau partridge
Persil parsley
Petit salé salted pork
Petits fours tiny cakes and sweets
Petits pois peas
Pieds de porc pigs' trotters
Pignons pine nuts
Piments doux sweet peppers
Pintade guinea fowl
Pissaladière bread dough or pizza covered with tomatoes
Pissenlits dandelion leaves, used in salads
Pistou vegetable soup with a paste of garlic, basil and oil
Poché poached
Pochouse fish stew
Poire pear
Poireaux leeks
Poisson fish
Poitrine de porc belly of pork
Pomme apple
Pomme (de terre) potato
Porc pork
Poularde capon
Poulet young spring chicken
Poulpe octopus
Poussin very small baby chicken
Primeurs young vegetables or wines
(à la) Provençale with tomatoes, garlic, olive oil, etc
Quenelles light dumplings of fish or poultry
Queue de boeuf oxtail
Quiche egg- and milk-based pie
Radis radishes
Raie skate
Raifort horseradish
Ris (de veau) (calf's) sweetbreads
Riz rice
Rognons kidneys
Romarin rosemary
Rôti roast
Rouget red mullet
Rouille garlic and chilli sauce usually served with fish soups
Safran saffron
Saint Pierre John Dory
Salade Niçoise salad including tomatoes, beans, potatoes, black olives and tuna
Sanglier wild boar
Saucisses fresh wet sausage
Saucisson dry sausage (salami-type)
Sauge sage
Saumon salmon
Selle (d'agneau) saddle (of lamb)
Suprême de volaille chicken breast and wing fillet
Tapenade purée of black olives and olive oil
Tête (de veau) (calf's) head
Thon tuna fish
Thym thyme
Timbale dome-shaped mold or the pie cooked within it
Tournedos small thick round slices of beef fillet
Tourte covered tart
Tranche slice
Truffes truffles
Truite trout
Truite saumonée salmon trout
(à la) Vapeur steamed
Veau veal
Viande meat
Vinaigrette oil and vinegar dressing
Volaille poultry
Vol-au-vent puff pastry case

Index

General index 212
Gazetteer of street names 220

With the exception of a few of the most notable, such as the Deux Magots café and the Crillon hotel, individual hotels, restaurants, cafés and shops have not been indexed, because they appear in alphabetical order within their appropriate sections. The sections themselves, however, have been indexed. Similarly, although most streets are listed in the gazetteer and not in the index, a few exceptions, such as the Champs-Élysées, are indexed as well.

Page numbers in bold type indicate the main entry.

Index

Gazetteer of street names

Numbers after the street name refer to pages on which the street is mentioned in the book. Map references refer to the maps that follow this gazetteer.

It has not been possible to label every street drawn on the maps, although of course all major streets and most smaller ones have been named. However, even streets not labeled have been given map references in this gazetteer, because this serves as an approximate location which will nearly always be sufficient for you to find your way.

D

E

F

G

T

U

V

W

PARIS

1

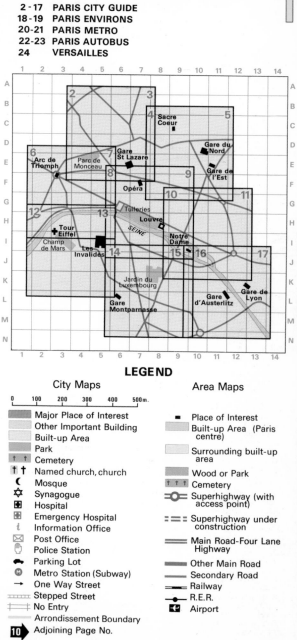

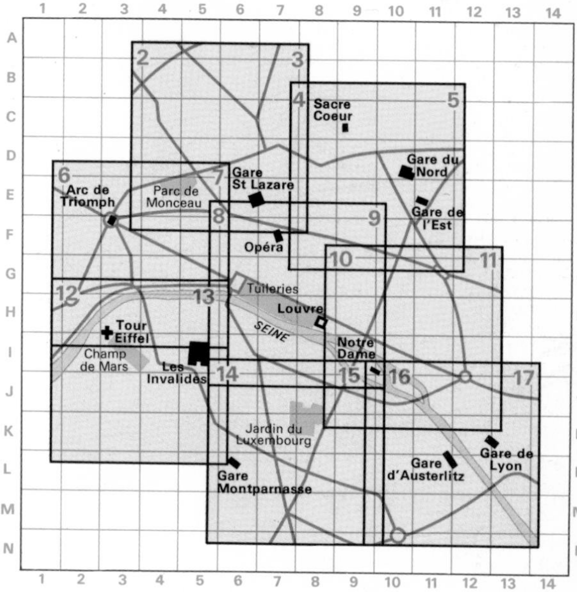

LEGEND

City Maps

0 100 200 300 400 500m.

- Major Place of Interest
- Other Important Building
- Built-up Area
- Park
- Cemetery
- Named church, church
- Mosque
- Synagogue
- Hospital
- Emergency Hospital
- Information Office
- Post Office
- Police Station
- Parking Lot
- Metro Station (Subway)
- One Way Street
- Stepped Street
- No Entry
- Arrondissement Boundary
- 10 Adjoining Page No.

Area Maps

- Place of Interest
- Built-up Area (Paris centre)
- Surrounding built-up area
- Wood or Park
- Cemetery
- Superhighway (with access point)
- Superhighway under construction
- Main Road-Four Lane Highway
- Other Main Road
- Secondary Road
- Railway
- R.E.R.
- Airport

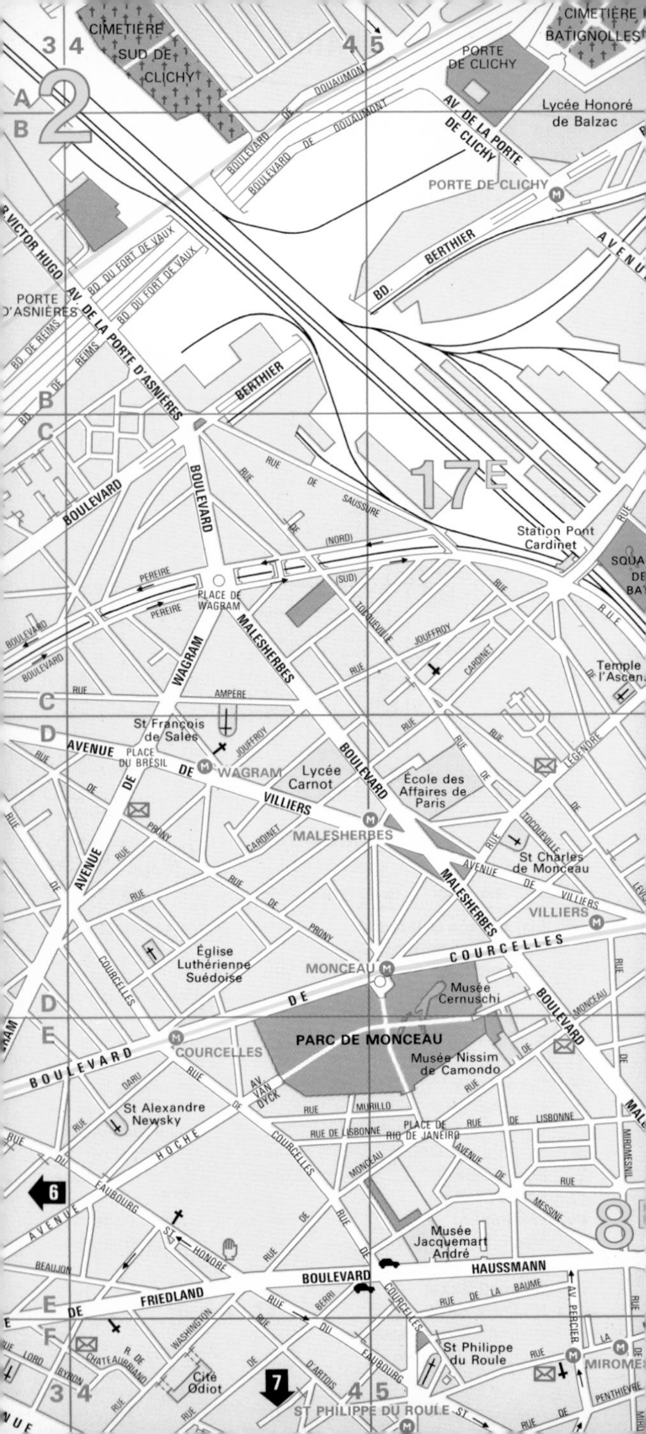

CIMETIÈRE SUD DE CLICHY
CIMETIÈRE BATIGNOLLES
PORTE DE CLICHY
Lycée Honoré de Balzac
BOULEVARD DE DOUAUMONT
AV. DE LA PORTE DE CLICHY
PORTE DE CLICHY
BD. BERTHIER
AV. VICTOR HUGO
BD. DU FORT DE VAUX
PORTE D'ASNIÈRES
AV. DE LA PORTE D'ASNIÈRES
BD. DE REIMS
BERTHIER
17E
RUE DE SAUSSURE
Station Pont Cardinet
SQUARE DES BATIGNOLLES
BOULEVARD
BOULEVARD PEREIRE
(NORD)
(SUD)
PLACE DE WAGRAM
AVENUE DE WAGRAM
BOULEVARD MALESHERBES
RUE TOCQUEVILLE
RUE JOUFFROY
RUE CARDINET
RUE AMPÈRE
Temple de l'Ascension
St François de Sales
AVENUE DE VILLIERS
PLACE DU BRÉSIL
WAGRAM
Lycée Carnot
École des Affaires de Paris
RUE LEGENDRE
RUE DE PRONY
MALESHERBES
St Charles de Monceau
VILLIERS
Église Luthérienne Suédoise
MONCEAU
BOULEVARD DE COURCELLES
Musée Cernuschi
RUE DE MONCEAU
PARC DE MONCEAU
COURCELLES
Musée Nissim de Camondo
RUE DARU
AV. VAN DYCK
St Alexandre Newsky
RUE MURILLO
RUE DE LISBONNE
PLACE DE RIO DE JANEIRO
AVENUE HOCHE
AVENUE DE MESSINE
RUE MIROMESNIL
6
RUE DU FAUBOURG ST HONORÉ
AVENUE BEAUJON
Musée Jacquemart André
BOULEVARD HAUSSMANN
8
AVENUE DE FRIEDLAND
RUE DE LA BAUME
AV. PERCIER
RUE BERRI
RUE WASHINGTON
RUE LORD BYRON
R. DE CHATEAUBRIAND
Cité Odiot
7
RUE D'ARTOIS
St Philippe du Roule
MIROMESNIL
RUE DE PENTHIÈVRE
ST PHILIPPE DU ROULE
A B C D E F
3 4 5

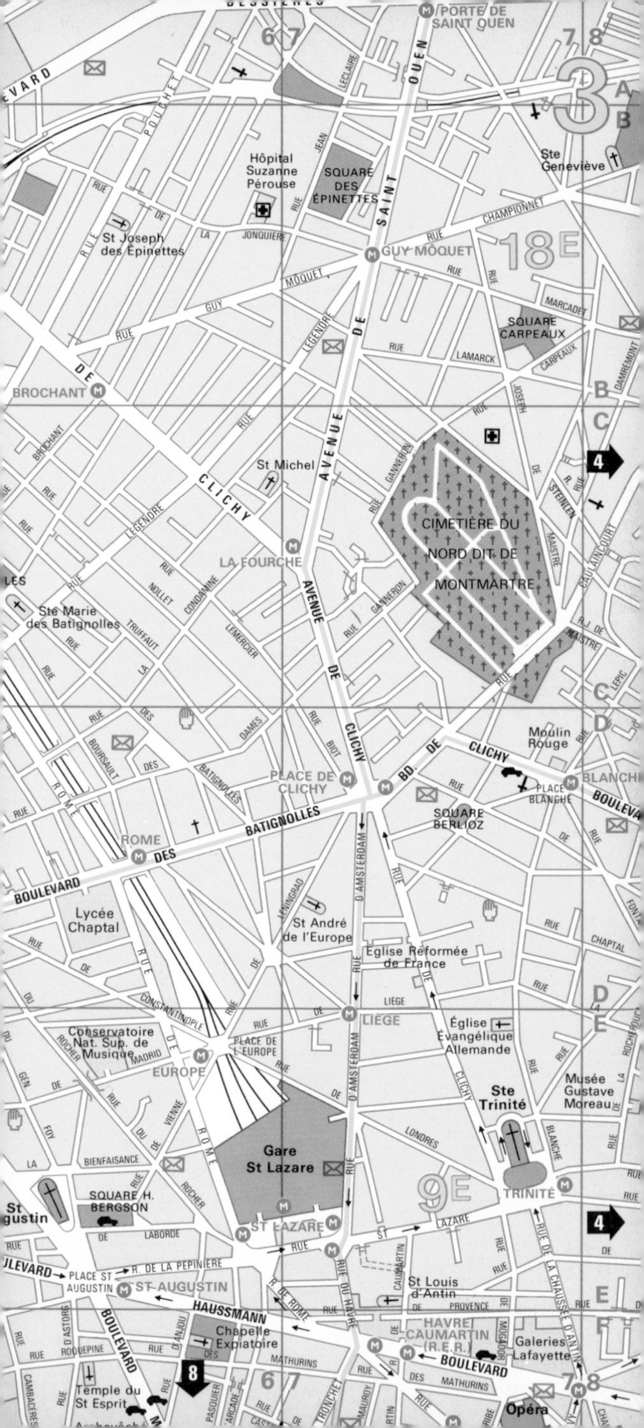

PORTE DE SAINT OUEN
3
18E
Hôpital Suzanne Pérouse
SQUARE DES ÉPINETTES
St Joseph des Épinettes
Ste Geneviève
GUY MÔQUET
SQUARE CARPEAUX
BROCHANT
St Michel
LA FOURCHE
CIMETIÈRE DU NORD DIT DE MONTMARTRE
Ste Marie des Batignolles
AVENUE DE CLICHY
AVENUE DE SAINT OUEN
BOULEVARD DES BATIGNOLLES
BD. DE CLICHY
PLACE DE CLICHY
Moulin Rouge
BLANCHE
PLACE BLANCHE
SQUARE BERLIOZ
ROME
Lycée Chaptal
St André de l'Europe
Eglise Réformée de France
LIÈGE
Église Évangélique Allemande
Conservatoire Nat. Sup. de Musique
PLACE DE L'EUROPE
EUROPE
Ste Trinité
Musée Gustave Moreau
Gare St Lazare
9E
TRINITÉ
SQUARE H. BERGSON
St Augustin
ST LAZARE
PLACE ST AUGUSTIN
ST AUGUSTIN
HAUSSMANN
St Louis d'Antin
HAVRE CAUMARTIN (R.E.R.)
Chapelle Expiatoire
Galeries Lafayette
Temple du St Esprit
Opéra
4
8

4
Temple de Montmartre
Musée d'Art Juif
LAMARCK CAULAINCOURT
CIM. ST VINCENT
Musée de Montmartre
Basilique du Sacré Cœur
St Pierre de Montmartre
PL. DU TERTRE
SQ. JEHAN RICTUS
SQUARE WILLETTE
Moulin Rouge
ABBESSES
BLANCHE
PLACE BLANCHE
St Jean de Montmartre
PL. SAINT PIERRE
PL. CHARLES DULLIN
ANVERS
BOULEVARD DE CLICHY
BOULEVARD DE ROCHECHOUART
PIGALLE
PLACE PIGALLE
Lycée J. Decour
ST GEORGES
Musée Gustave Moreau
9E
SQUARE DE MONTHOLON
TRINITÉ
N.D. de Lorette
N.D. DE LORETTE
CADET
LE PELETIER
Folies Bergère
St Eugène Ste Cécile
Galeries Lafayette
CHAUSSÉE D'ANTIN
Temple de la Rédemption
Conservatoire Nat. d'Art Dramatique
Opéra
HAUSSMANN
RICHELIEU DROUOT
Musée Grévin
BD. MONTMARTRE
RUE MONTMARTRE
BD. POISSONNIÈRE
BD. DES ITALIENS
CAPUCINES
Opéra Studio
PLACE DE L'OPÉRA
PASS. DES PANORAMAS
BONNE NOUVELLE
QUATRE SEPTEMBRE
La Bourse
BOURSE
2E
SQUARE LOUVOIS
Bibliothèque National
SENTIER

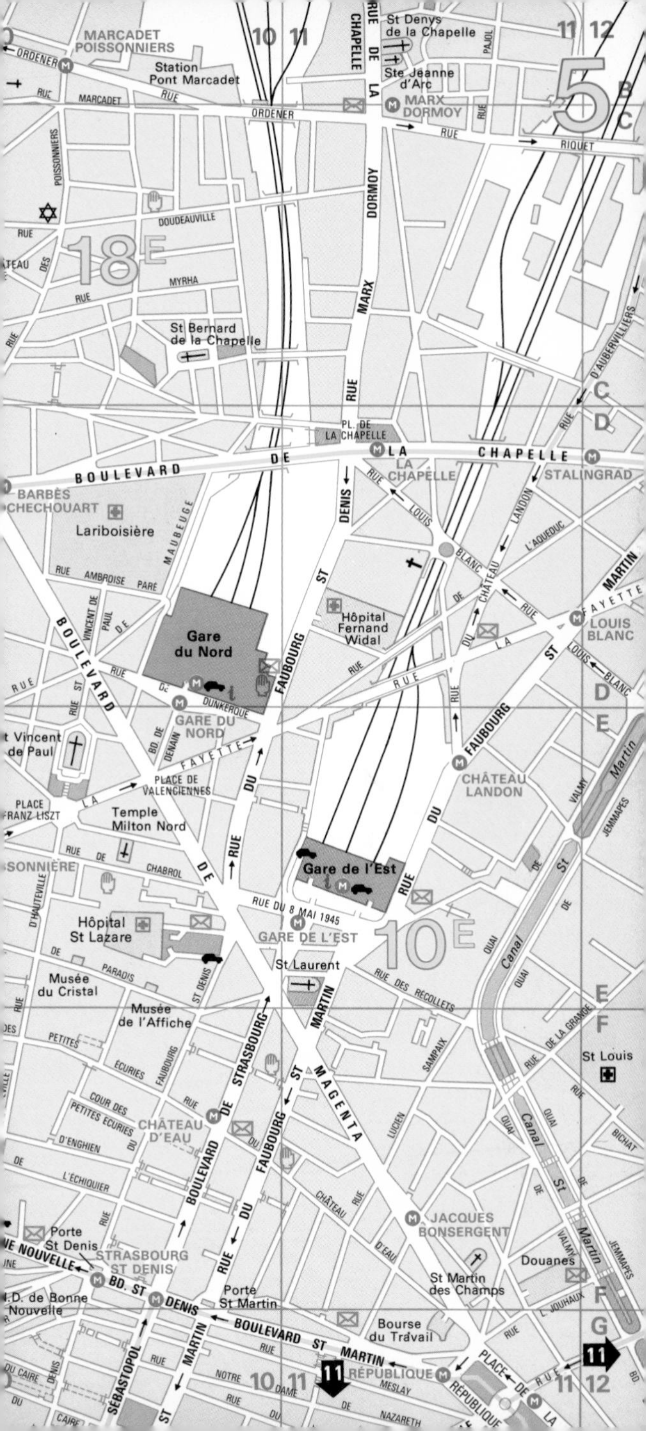

MARCADET POISSONNIERS
Station Pont Marcadet
St Denys de la Chapelle
Ste Jeanne d'Arc
MARX DORMOY
RUE DE LA CHAPELLE
RUE ORDENER
RUE MARCADET
RUE RIQUET
PAJOL
5
18E
DOUDEAUVILLE
MYRHA
RUE MARX DORMOY
St Bernard de la Chapelle
PL. DE LA CHAPELLE
BOULEVARD DE LA CHAPELLE
LA CHAPELLE
STALINGRAD
BARBÈS ROCHECHOUART
Lariboisière
RUE AMBROISE PARÉ
MAUBEUGE
RUE LOUIS BLANC
L'AQUEDUC
D'AUBERVILLIERS
Gare du Nord
GARE DU NORD
DUNKERQUE
Hôpital Fernand Widal
LOUIS BLANC
RUE LA FAYETTE
RUE DU FAUBOURG ST DENIS
RUE DU FAUBOURG ST MARTIN
RUE DU CHÂTEAU LANDON
CHÂTEAU LANDON
St Vincent de Paul
PLACE DE VALENCIENNES
PLACE FRANZ LISZT
Temple Milton Nord
BOULEVARD DE MAGENTA
RUE DE CHABROL
Gare de l'Est
RUE DU 8 MAI 1945
GARE DE L'EST
10E
Hôpital St Lazare
St Laurent
Musée du Cristal
Musée de l'Affiche
RUE DE PARADIS
RUE DES RÉCOLLETS
QUAI DE VALMY
QUAI DE JEMMAPES
Canal St Martin
St Louis
PETITES ÉCURIES
COUR DES PETITES ÉCURIES
RUE D'ENGHIEN
RUE DE L'ÉCHIQUIER
CHÂTEAU D'EAU
BOULEVARD DE STRASBOURG
RUE DU FAUBOURG ST DENIS
MAGENTA
LUCIEN SAMPAIX
RUE DE LA GRANDE
BICHAT
JACQUES BONSERGENT
Douanes
St Martin des Champs
Porte St Denis
STRASBOURG ST DENIS
BD. ST DENIS
N.D. de Bonne Nouvelle
Porte St Martin
BOULEVARD ST MARTIN
Bourse du Travail
RÉPUBLIQUE
PLACE DE LA RÉPUBLIQUE
RUE MESLAY
RUE NOTRE DAME
RUE DE NAZARETH
SÉBASTOPOL
RUE ST MARTIN
RUE DU CAIRE
L. JOUHAUX
10 11 12

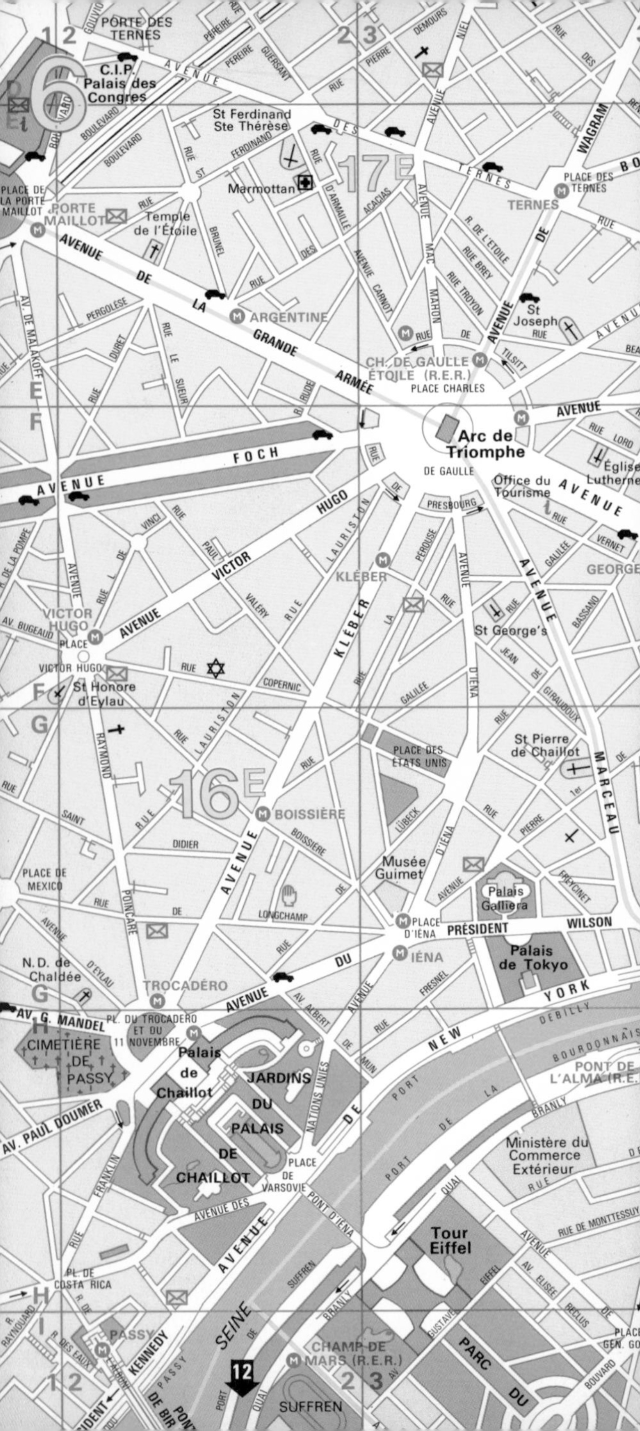

PORTE DES TERNES
C.I.P. Palais des Congres
St Ferdinand Ste Thérèse
Marmottan
Temple de l'Étoile
PLACE DE LA PORTE MAILLOT
PORTE MAILLOT
AVENUE DE LA GRANDE ARMÉE
ARGENTINE
17E
TERNES
PLACE DES TERNES
St Joseph
CH. DE GAULLE ÉTOILE (R.E.R.)
PLACE CHARLES DE GAULLE
Arc de Triomphe
Église Lutherne
Office du Tourisme
AVENUE FOCH
AVENUE VICTOR HUGO
KLÉBER
AVENUE KLÉBER
VICTOR HUGO
PLACE VICTOR HUGO
St Honore d'Eylau
St George's
PLACE DES ÉTATS UNIS
St Pierre de Chaillot
AVENUE MARCEAU
16E
BOISSIÈRE
PLACE DE MEXICO
Musée Guimet
Palais Galliera
PLACE D'IÉNA
AVENUE DU PRÉSIDENT WILSON
IÉNA
Palais de Tokyo
N.D. de Chaldée
TROCADÉRO
AV. G. MANDEL
PL. DU TROCADERO ET DU 11 NOVEMBRE
CIMETIÈRE DE PASSY
Palais de Chaillot
JARDINS DU PALAIS DE CHAILLOT
AV. PAUL DOUMER
AVENUE DE NEW YORK
PONT DE L'ALMA (R.E.)
Ministère du Commerce Extérieur
PLACE DE VARSOVIE
PONT D'IÉNA
Tour Eiffel
PL. DE COSTA RICA
PASSY
SEINE
12
CHAMP DE MARS (R.E.R.)
PARC DU
SUFFREN

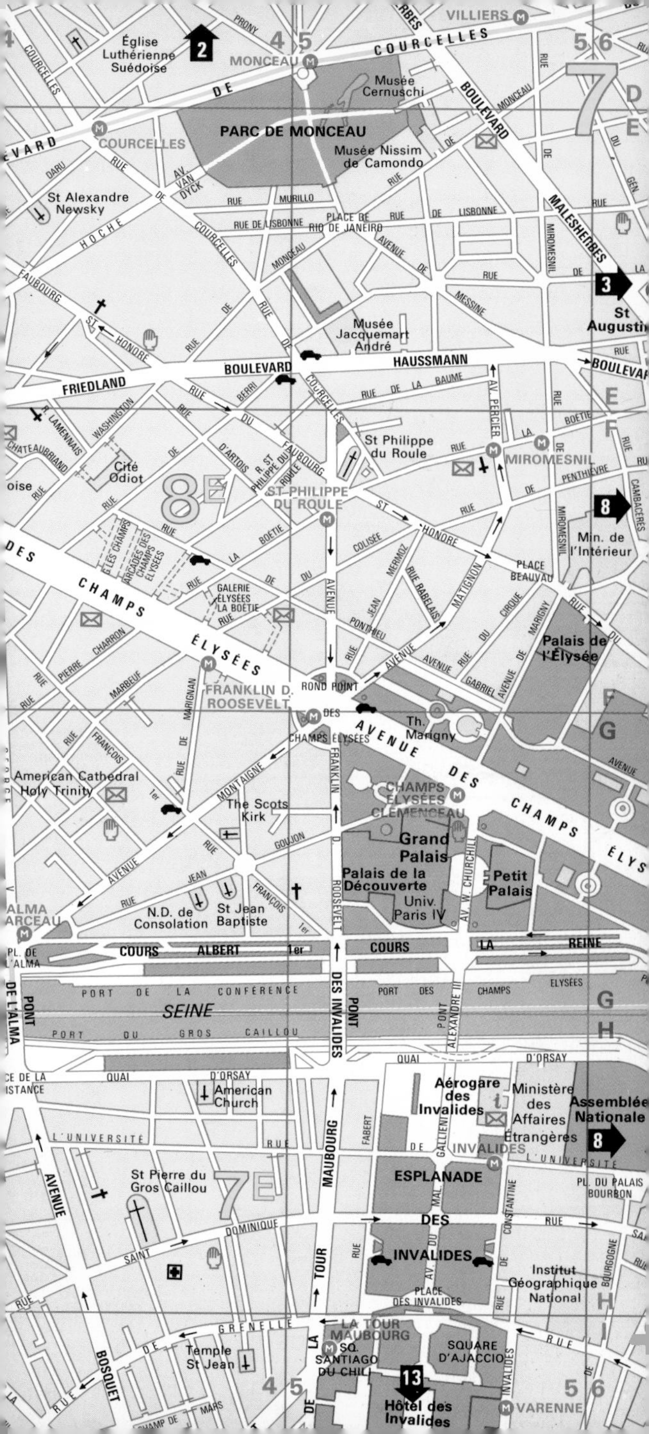

Église Luthérienne Suédoise
Monceau
Courcelles
Villiers
Musée Cernuschi
Parc de Monceau
Musée Nissim de Camondo
St Alexandre Newsky
Place de Rio de Janeiro
Boulevard Malesherbes
St Augustin
Musée Jacquemart André
Boulevard Haussmann
Friedland
St Philippe du Roule
Miromesnil
Cité Odiot
8E
Min. de l'Intérieur
Place Beauvau
Galerie Élysées La Boétie
Champs Élysées
Palais de l'Élysée
Rond Point
Franklin D. Roosevelt
Th. Marigny
Avenue des Champs Élysées
Champs Élysées Clemenceau
American Cathedral Holy Trinity
The Scots Kirk
Grand Palais
Palais de la Découverte
Univ. Paris IV
Petit Palais
N.D. de Consolation
St Jean Baptiste
Alma Marceau
Cours Albert 1er
Cours la Reine
Port de la Conférence
Seine
Port du Gros Caillou
Pont de l'Alma
Pont des Invalides
Pont Alexandre III
Quai d'Orsay
American Church
Aérogare des Invalides
Ministère des Affaires Étrangères
Assemblée Nationale
Invalides
St Pierre du Gros Caillou
7E
Esplanade des Invalides
Institut Géographique National
Place des Invalides
La Tour Maubourg
Sq. Santiago du Chili
Square d'Ajaccio
Temple St Jean
Hôtel des Invalides
Varenne

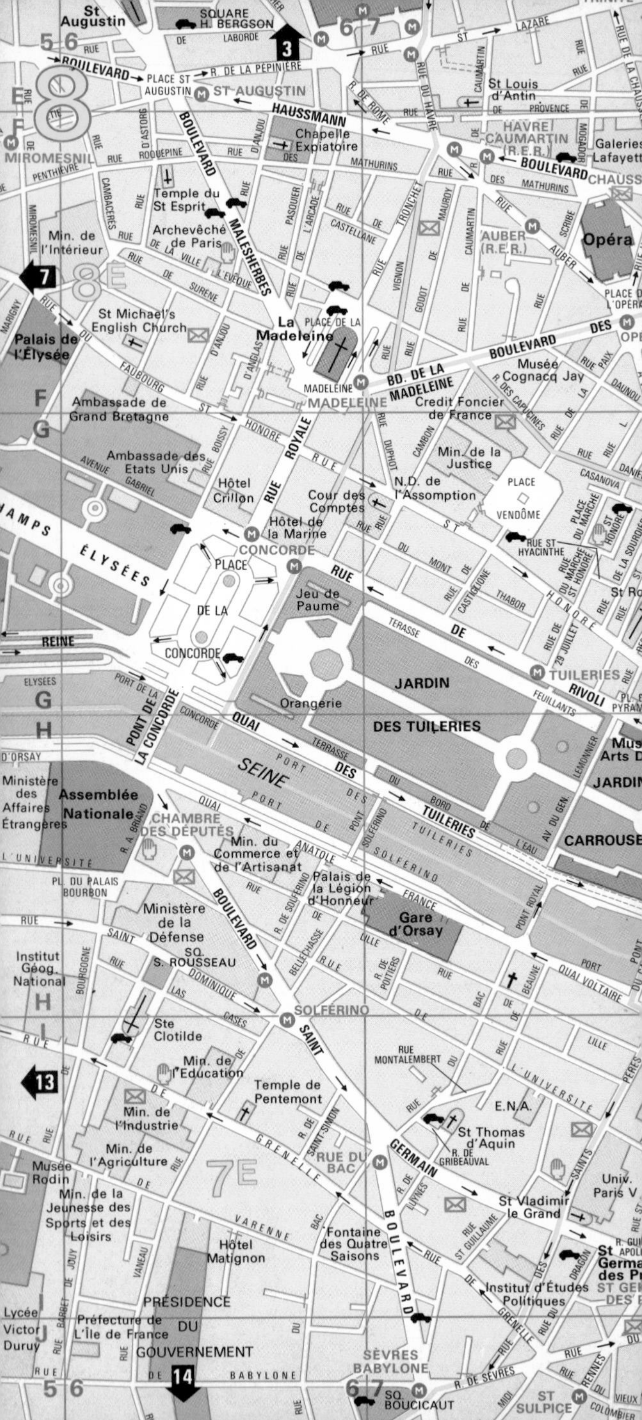

8
8E
7E
St Augustin
Square H. Bergson
Place St Augustin
St Augustin
Boulevard Haussmann
R. de la Pépinière
Rue de Laborde
Rue Lazare
Rue du Havre
R. de Rome
Rue Caumartin
St Louis d'Antin
Rue de Provence
Havre Caumartin (R.E.R.)
Chapelle Expiatoire
Rue des Mathurins
Galeries Lafayette
Boulevard Haussmann
Miromesnil
Rue de Penthièvre
Rue Roquépine
Rue d'Astorg
Rue Cambacérès
Temple du St Esprit
Boulevard Malesherbes
Archevêché de Paris
Min. de l'Intérieur
Rue de la Ville l'Évêque
Rue de Surène
Rue Pasquier
Rue de l'Arcade
Rue de Castellane
Rue Tronchet
Rue Vignon
Rue Godot de Mauroy
Rue Caumartin
Auber (R.E.R.)
Rue Auber
Rue Scribe
Opéra
Place de l'Opéra
St Michael's English Church
Palais de l'Élysée
Rue du Faubourg St Honoré
La Madeleine
Place de la Madeleine
Madeleine
Bd. de la Madeleine
Boulevard des Capucines
Musée Cognacq Jay
R. des Capucines
Rue de la Paix
Rue Daunou
Credit Foncier de France
Ambassade de Grand Bretagne
Rue d'Anjou
Rue d'Anglas
Rue Boissy
Rue Royale
Rue St Honoré
Rue Duphot
Rue Cambon
Min. de la Justice
Place Vendôme
Rue Casanova
Ambassade des Etats Unis
Avenue Gabriel
Hôtel Crillon
Cour des Comptes
N.D. de l'Assomption
Hôtel de la Marine
Concorde
Avenue des Champs Élysées
Place de la Concorde
Rue du Mont Thabor
Rue de Castiglione
Rue St Hyacinthe
Place du Marché St Honoré
Rue du Marché St Honoré
Rue de la Sourdière
St Roch
Rue de Rivoli
Rue du 29 Juillet
Jeu de Paume
Terasse des Feuillants
Tuileries
Cours la Reine
Jardin des Tuileries
Orangerie
Port de la Concorde
Pont de la Concorde
Quai des Tuileries
Terrasse du Bord de l'Eau
Seine
Port des Tuileries
Port de Solférino
Pont Solférino
Av. du Gen. Lemonnier
Mus. Arts D.
Jardin du Carrousel
Quai d'Orsay
Ministère des Affaires Étrangeres
Assemblée Nationale
Chambre des Députés
Quai Anatole France
R. A. Briand
Min. du Commerce et de l'Artisanat
Rue de l'Université
Pl. du Palais Bourbon
Palais de la Légion d'Honneur
Gare d'Orsay
Pont Royal
Quai Voltaire
Rue de Solférino
Rue de Bellechasse
Rue de Lille
R. de Poitiers
Rue du Bac
Rue de Beaune
Ministère de la Défense
Sq. S. Rousseau
Rue Saint Dominique
Boulevard Saint Germain
Institut Géog. National
Rue de Bourgogne
Rue Las Cases
Solférino
Ste Clotilde
Min. de l'Education
Rue Montalembert
Rue de l'Université
Rue des Saints Pères
Temple de Pentemont
Min. de l'Industrie
Rue de Grenelle
R. de St Simon
Rue du Bac
E.N.A.
St Thomas d'Aquin
R. de Gribeauval
Min. de l'Agriculture
R. de Luynes
St Vladimir le Grand
Univ. Paris V
Musée Rodin
Min. de la Jeunesse des Sports et des Loisirs
Rue de Varenne
Fontaine des Quatre Saisons
Rue St Guillaume
Rue du Dragon
St Germain des Prés
Hôtel Matignon
Boulevard Raspail
Institut d'Études Politiques
Rue de Grenelle
Rue de Vaneau
Rue de Babylone
Présidence du Gouvernement
Préfecture de l'Île de France
Lycée Victor Duruy
Rue Barbet de Jouy
Sèvres Babylone
R. de Sèvres
Sq. Boucicaut
Rue de Rennes
St Sulpice
Rue du Vieux Colombier
Rue du Cherche Midi
3
7
13
14
5 6
6 7
E
F
G
H
I
J

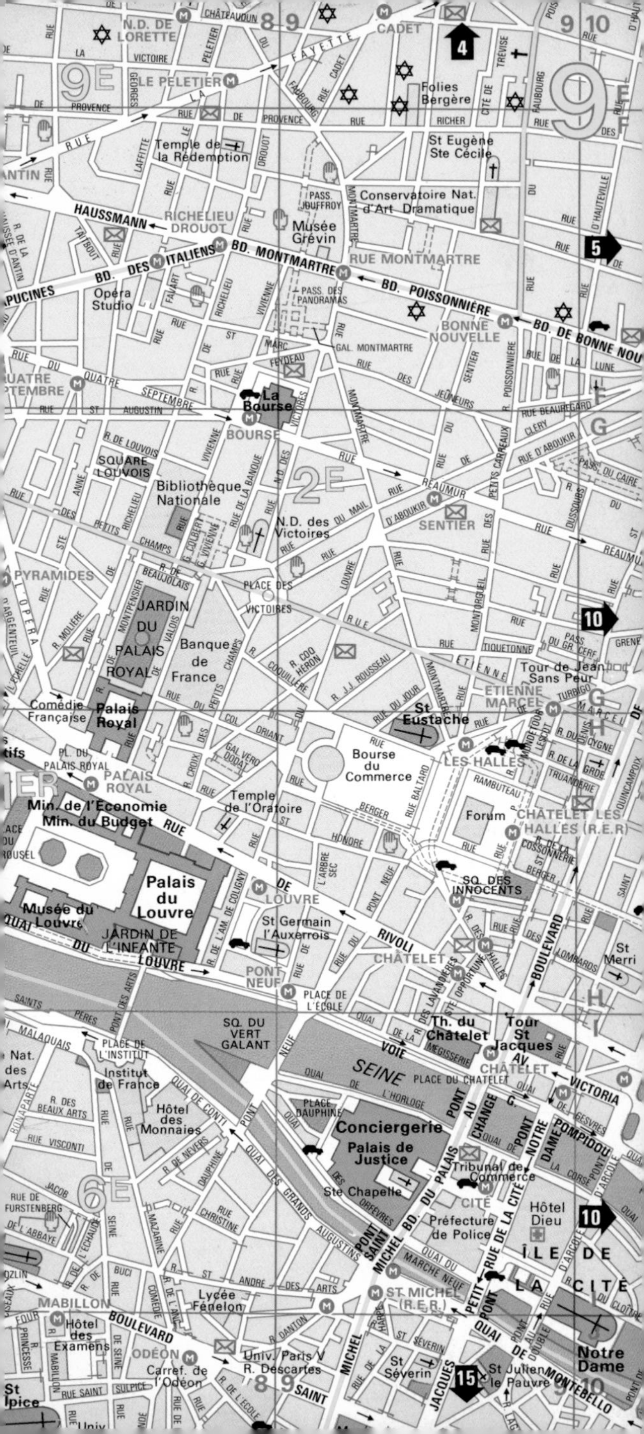

9E
2E
6E
N.D. DE LORETTE
LE PELETIER
CADET
Folies Bergère
St Eugène Ste Cécile
Temple de la Rédemption
Conservatoire Nat. d'Art Dramatique
HAUSSMANN
RICHELIEU DROUOT
Musée Grévin
BD. DES ITALIENS
BD. MONTMARTRE
RUE MONTMARTRE
BD. POISSONNIÈRE
BD. DE BONNE NOUVELLE
BONNE NOUVELLE
Opéra Studio
PASS. DES PANORAMAS
GAL. MONTMARTRE
QUATRE SEPTEMBRE
La Bourse
BOURSE
SQUARE LOUVOIS
Bibliothèque Nationale
N.D. des Victoires
SENTIER
RÉAUMUR
PYRAMIDES
PLACE DES VICTOIRES
JARDIN DU PALAIS ROYAL
Banque de France
Tour de Jean Sans Peur
ÉTIENNE MARCEL
St Eustache
Comédie Française
Palais Royal
PALAIS ROYAL
Bourse du Commerce
LES HALLES
Forum
CHÂTELET LES HALLES (R.E.R)
Min. de l'Économie
Min. du Budget
Temple de l'Oratoire
Palais du Louvre
Musée du Louvre
JARDIN DE L'INFANTE
LOUVRE
St Germain l'Auxerrois
SQ. DES INNOCENTS
RIVOLI
CHÂTELET
St Merri
PONT NEUF
PLACE DE L'ÉCOLE
SQ. DU VERT GALANT
Th. du Châtelet
Tour St Jacques
SEINE
PLACE DU CHATELET
VICTORIA
Institut de France
Hôtel des Monnaies
PLACE DAUPHINE
Conciergerie
Palais de Justice
Tribunal de Commerce
CITÉ
Ste Chapelle
Préfecture de Police
Hôtel Dieu
ÎLE DE LA CITÉ
ST MICHEL (R.E.R.)
MABILLON
Lycée Fénelon
Hôtel des Examens
ODÉON
Carref. de l'Odéon
Univ. Paris V R. Descartes
St Séverin
St Julien le Pauvre
Notre Dame
QUAI DE MONTEBELLO
4
5
10
10
15

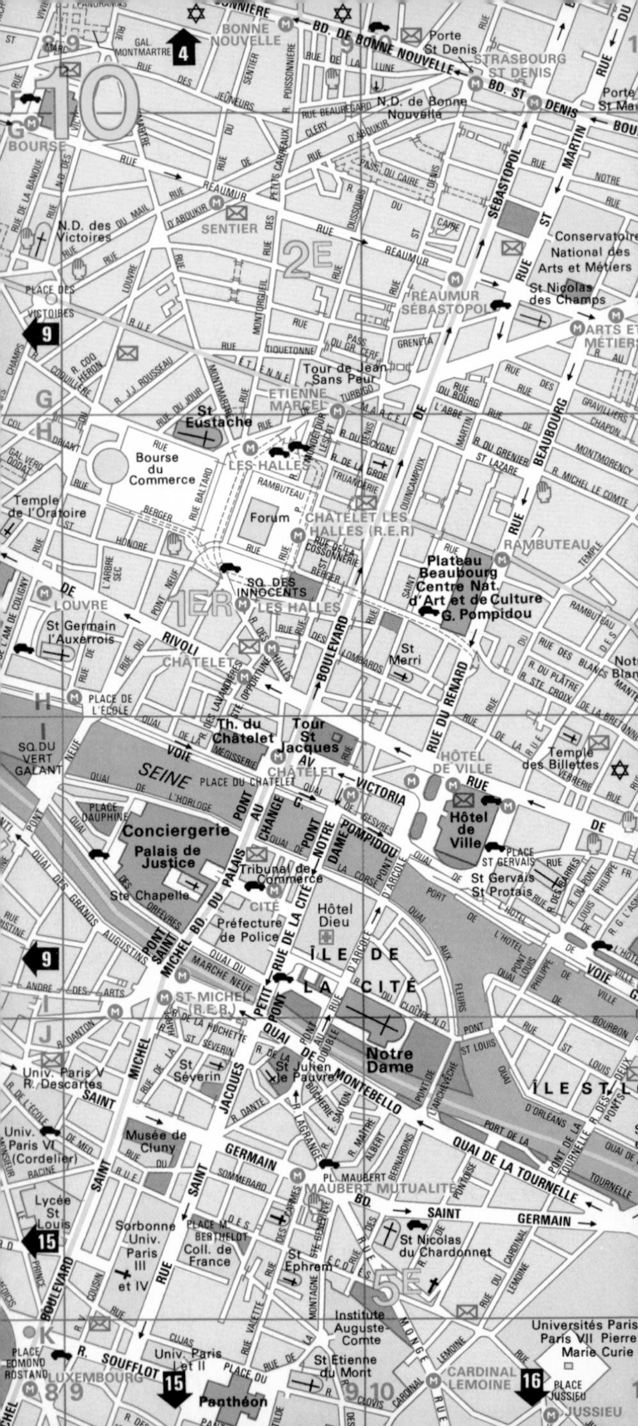

JACQUES BONSERGENT
10E
St Martin des Champs
Douanes
Bourse du Travail
GONCOURT
11E
St Joseph
RÉPUBLIQUE
PLACE DE LA RÉPUBLIQUE
TEMPLE
Ste Elisabeth
SQUARE DU TEMPLE
Carreau du Temple
AVENUE DE LA RÉPUBLIQUE
PARMENTIER
OBERKAMPF
BOULEVARD VOLTAIRE
FILLES DU CALVAIRE
3E
BD. DU TEMPLE
BD. DES FILLES DU CALVAIRE
Musée de la Chasse
ST AMBROISE
ST SÉBASTIEN FROISSART
St Croix St Jean
RICHARD LENOIR
St Denys du St Sacrement
Musée Bricard
BOULEVARD BEAUMARCHAIS
CHEMIN VERT
Musée Carnavalet
Hôtel Lamoignon
Foyer de l'Âme
BRÉGUET SABIN
Notre Dame de l'Espérance
PLACE DES VOSGES
RIVOLI
ST PAUL
St Paul St Louis
RUE ST ANTOINE
Hôtel Sens
4E
PLACE DE LA BASTILLE
Ste Marie
BASTILLE
POMPIDOU
SQ. H. GALLI
BD. HENRI IV
SULLY MORLAND
Bibl. de l'Arsenal
BD. PONT DE SULLY
BOULEVARD MORLAND
Préfecture de Paris
Gare de l'Arsenal
RUE DE LYON
Quinze Vingts
St Antoine des Quinze Vingts
12E
SEINE
PORT SAINT BERNARD
PONT MORLAND
QUAI DE LA RAPÉE

12
Palais de Tokyo
Palais de Chaillot
JARDINS DU PALAIS DE CHAILLOT
CIMETIÈRE DE PASSY
TROCADÉRO
PLACE D'IÉNA
IÉNA
AVENUE DU PRÉSIDENT WILSON
AV. PAUL DOUMER
PLACE DE VARSOVIE
PONT D'IÉNA
PONT DE L'ALMA (R.E.R.)
Ministère du Commerce Extérieur
Tour Eiffel
16E
PL. DE COSTA RICA
PASSY
SEINE
CHAMP DE MARS (R.E.R.)
SUFFREN
PARC DU CHAMP DE MARS
PONT DE BIR HAKEIM
Ministère des Transports
BIR HAKEIM
VILLAGE SUISSE
PLACE DUPLEIX
St Léon
DUPLEIX
LA MOTTE PICQUET GRENELLE
Foyer de Grenelle
Totem
Reflet
Lutécien
Nikko
Perspective
Panorama
AVENUE EMILE ZOLA
AV. ÉMILE ZOLA
CHARLES MICHELS
15E
PLACE DU COMMERCE
COMMERCE
PLACE VIOLET
St Jean Baptiste de Grenelle
Temple de Résurrection
SQUARE ST LAMBERT
FÉLIX FAURE
Boucicaut
BOUCICAUT

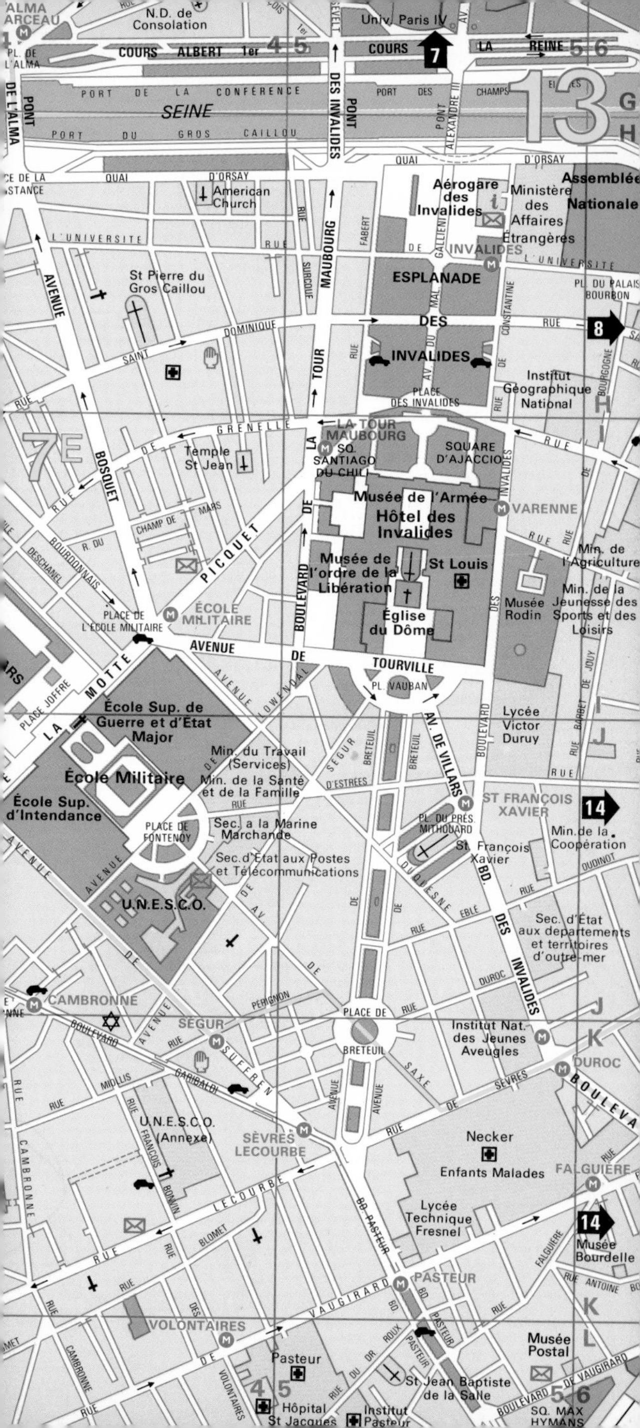

13
7E
N.D. de Consolation
Univ. Paris IV
COURS ALBERT 1er
COURS LA REINE
SEINE
PORT DE LA CONFÉRENCE
PORT DU GROS CAILLOU
PORT DES CHAMPS ÉLYSÉES
PONT DE L'ALMA
PONT DES INVALIDES
PONT ALEXANDRE III
QUAI D'ORSAY
American Church
Aérogare des Invalides
Ministère des Affaires Étrangères
Assemblée Nationale
INVALIDES
ESPLANADE DES INVALIDES
St Pierre du Gros Caillou
RUE SAINT DOMINIQUE
RUE DE L'UNIVERSITÉ
AVENUE BOSQUET
BOULEVARD DE LA TOUR MAUBOURG
PLACE DES INVALIDES
Institut Géographique National
RUE DE GRENELLE
LA TOUR MAUBOURG
SQ. SANTIAGO DU CHILI
SQUARE D'AJACCIO
Temple St Jean
Musée de l'Armée
Hôtel des Invalides
VARENNE
Musée de l'ordre de la Libération
St Louis
Min. de l'Agriculture
Min. de la Jeunesse des Sports et des Loisirs
Musée Rodin
Église du Dôme
AVENUE DE TOURVILLE
PL. VAUBAN
PLACE DE L'ÉCOLE MILITAIRE
ÉCOLE MILITAIRE
AVENUE PICQUET
AVENUE DE LA MOTTE PICQUET
PLACE JOFFRE
École Sup. de Guerre et d'État Major
École Militaire
École Sup. d'Intendance
AVENUE LOWENDAL
Min. du Travail (Services)
Min. de la Santé et de la Famille
RUE D'ESTRÉES
AV. DE VILLARS
Lycée Victor Duruy
ST FRANÇOIS XAVIER
PL. DU PRÉS. MITHOUARD
St François Xavier
Min. de la Coopération
PLACE DE FONTENOY
Sec. à la Marine Marchande
Sec. d'État aux Postes et Télécommunications
U.N.E.S.C.O.
Sec. d'État aux departements et territoires d'outre-mer
BD. DES INVALIDES
CAMBRONNE
SÉGUR
PLACE DE BRETEUIL
Institut Nat. des Jeunes Aveugles
DUROC
BOULEVARD GARIBALDI
RUE DE SÈVRES
U.N.E.S.C.O. (Annexe)
SÈVRES LECOURBE
Necker Enfants Malades
FALGUIÈRE
RUE LECOURBE
Lycée Technique Fresnel
BD. PASTEUR
PASTEUR
Musée Bourdelle
RUE DE VAUGIRARD
VOLONTAIRES
Musée Postal
Pasteur
St Jean Baptiste de la Salle
Hôpital St Jacques
Institut Pasteur
SQ. MAX HYMANS
BOULEVARD DE VAUGIRARD
14
8

Hôtel Matignon
Présidence du Gouvernement
Fontaine des Quartre Saisons
St Vladimir le Grand
Institut d'Études Politiques
Lycée Victor Duruy
Préfecture de l'Île de France
Min. de la Coopération
Laennec
Sq. Boucicaut
Sèvres Babylone
St Ignace
St Sulpice
Sec. d'État aux departements et territoires d'outre-mer
Vaneau
Rennes
Institut Catholique
Duroc
St Placide
Alliance Française
Necker
Enfants Malades
Falguière
Collège Stanislas
N.D. des Champs
École St Sulpice
Place du 18 Juin 1940
Musée Bourdelle
Montparnasse Bienvenüe
N.D. des Champs
Pl. Bienvenüe
Tour Montparnasse
Vavin
Musée Postal
Place R. Dautry
Gare Montparnasse
Sq. Max Hymans
Edgar Quinet
Raspail
Cimitière du Sud du Montparnasse
Gaîté
École Spéciale d'Architecture
Hôpital Léopold Bellan
Place de Moro Giafferi
Pernéty
Denfert Rochereau
Mouton Duvernet
Villa Adrienne
Boulevard Raspail
Boulevard du Montparnasse
Avenue du Maine
Rue de Vaugirard
Rue de Sèvres
Rue de Babylone
Rue de Varenne
Rue du Bac
Rue de Rennes
Av. du Gén. Leclerc
Rue Froidevaux
Rue Daguerre
Rue Gassendi
Rue Raymond Losserand
Rue Didot
Rue d'Alésia
7E
6E
15E
14E
8
13

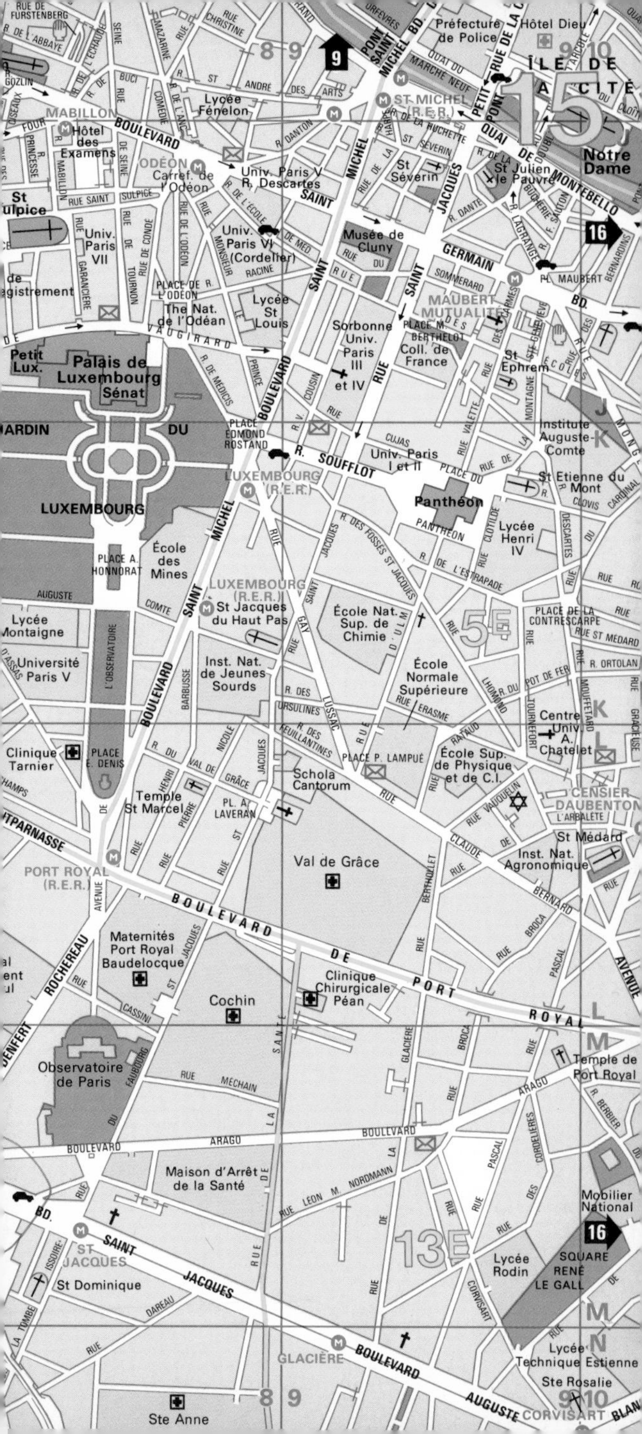

Préfecture de Police
Hôtel Dieu
ÎLE DE LA CITÉ
15
Notre Dame
9
16
MABILLON
Hôtel des Examens
ODÉON
Carref. de l'Odéon
Univ. Paris V R. Descartes
ST MICHEL (R.E.R.)
Lycée Fénelon
St Séverin
St Julien le Pauvre
St Sulpice
Univ. Paris VII
Univ. Paris VI (Cordelier)
Musée de Cluny
The Nat. de l'Odéan
Lycée St Louis
Sorbonne Univ. Paris III et IV
Coll. de France
MAUBERT MUTUALITÉ
St Ephrem
Petit Lux.
Palais de Luxembourg Sénat
JARDIN DU LUXEMBOURG
PLACE EDMOND ROSTAND
Univ. Paris I et II
Institute Auguste-Comte
LUXEMBOURG (R.E.R.)
Panthéon
St Etienne du Mont
Lycée Henri IV
PLACE A. HONNORAT
École des Mines
LUXEMBOURG (R.E.R.)
St Jacques du Haut Pas
École Nat. Sup. de Chimie
PLACE DE LA CONTRESCARPE
5E
Lycée Montaigne
Université Paris V
Inst. Nat. de Jeunes Sourds
École Normale Supérieure
Centre Univ. A. Chatelet
Clinique Tarnier
PLACE E. DENIS
Temple St Marcel
PL. A. LAVERAN
Schola Cantorum
PLACE P. LAMPUÉ
École Sup. de Physique et de C.I.
CENSIER DAUBENTON
St Médard
Inst. Nat. Agronomique
PORT ROYAL (R.E.R.)
Val de Grâce
BOULEVARD DE PORT ROYAL
Maternités Port Royal Baudelocque
Cochin
Clinique Chirurgicale Péan
Observatoire de Paris
Temple de Port Royal
BOULEVARD ARAGO
Maison d'Arrêt de la Santé
Mobilier National
ST JACQUES
BD. SAINT JACQUES
St Dominique
13E
Lycée Rodin
SQUARE RENÉ LE GALL
Lycée Technique Estienne
Ste Rosalie
GLACIÈRE
BOULEVARD AUGUSTE BLANQUI
CORVISART
Ste Anne
8 9
9 10

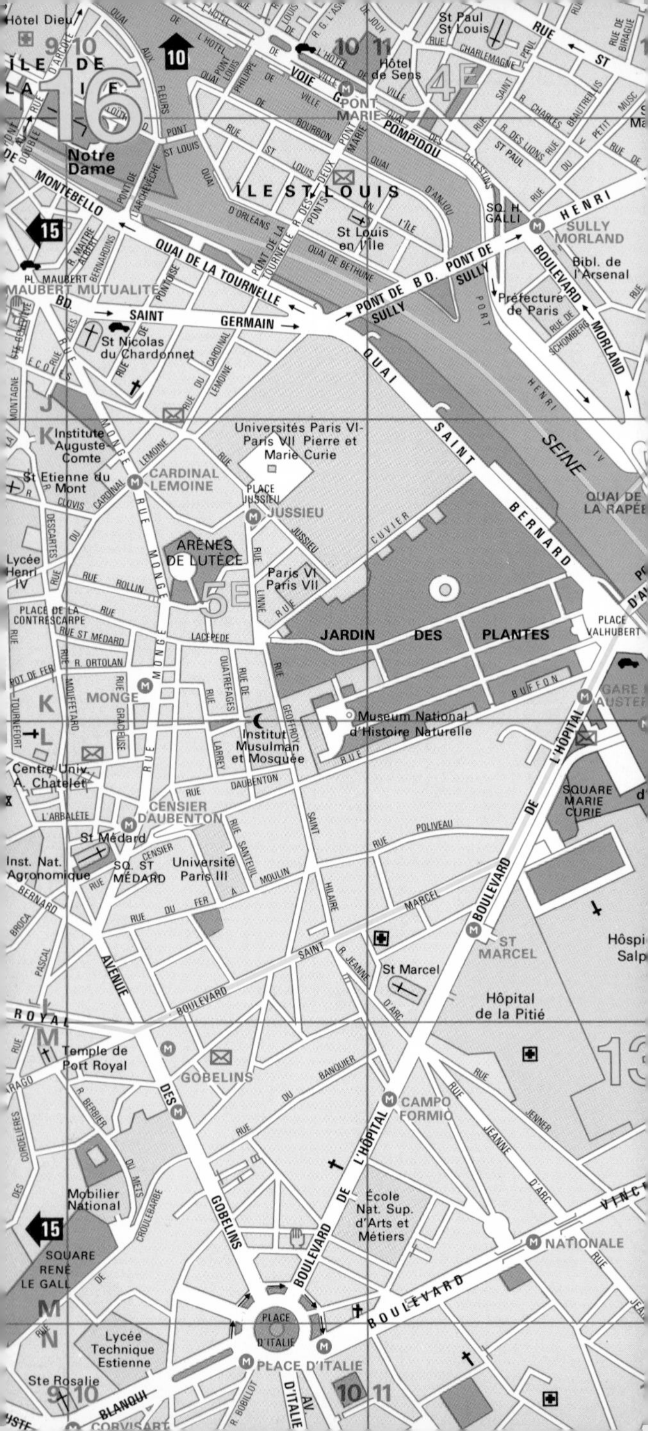

Hôtel Dieu
ÎLE DE LA CITÉ
16
Notre Dame
10
St Paul
St Louis
Hôtel de Sens
4E
PONT MARIE
VOIE G. POMPIDOU
ÎLE ST LOUIS
St Louis en l'Île
QUAI DE BETHUNE
QUAI DE LA TOURNELLE
MONTEBELLO
15
MAUBERT MUTUALITÉ
BD. SAINT GERMAIN
St Nicolas du Chardonnet
PONT DE SULLY
BD. HENRI IV
SQ. H. GALLI
SULLY MORLAND
Bibl. de l'Arsenal
Préfecture de Paris
BOULEVARD MORLAND
QUAI SAINT BERNARD
SEINE
QUAI DE LA RAPÉE
Universités Paris VI-Paris VII Pierre et Marie Curie
Institute Auguste-Comte
St Etienne du Mont
CARDINAL LEMOINE
PLACE JUSSIEU
JUSSIEU
ARÈNES DE LUTÈCE
Lycée Henri IV
Paris VI
Paris VII
5E
PLACE DE LA CONTRESCARPE
JARDIN DES PLANTES
PLACE VALHUBERT
GARE D'AUSTERLITZ
MONGE
Institut Musulman et Mosquée
Museum National d'Histoire Naturelle
Centre Univ. A. Chatelet
CENSIER DAUBENTON
SQUARE MARIE CURIE
St Médard
SQ. ST MÉDARD
Inst. Nat. Agronomique
Université Paris III
BOULEVARD DE L'HÔPITAL
ST MARCEL
St Marcel
Hôpital de la Pitié
BOULEVARD SAINT MARCEL
BOULEVARD ROYAL
Temple de Port Royal
GOBELINS
CAMPO FORMIO
AVENUE DES GOBELINS
Mobilier National
École Nat. Sup. d'Arts et Métiers
NATIONALE
SQUARE RENÉ LE GALL
PLACE D'ITALIE
Lycée Technique Estienne
Ste Rosalie
BOULEVARD BLANQUI
AV. D'ITALIE
CORVISART
13

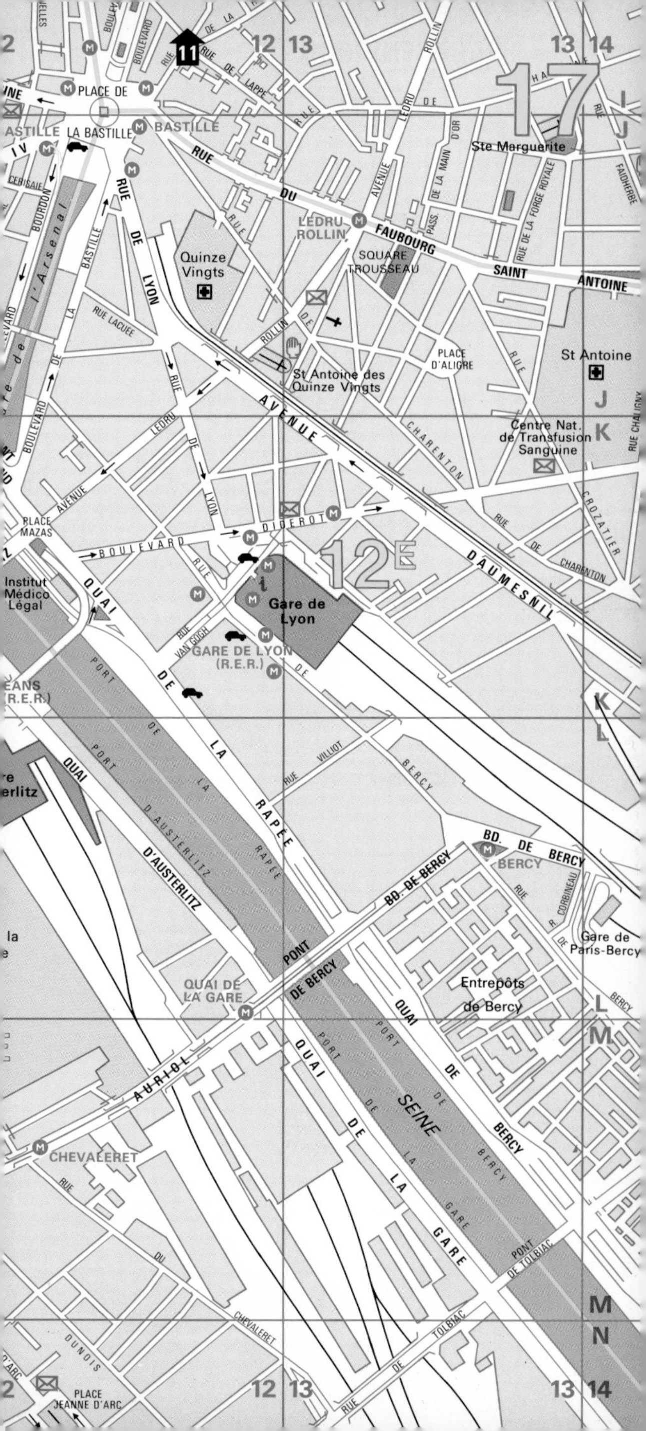

17
11
12
13
14
PLACE DE LA BASTILLE
BASTILLE
RUE DE LYON
BOULEVARD DE LA BASTILLE
BOULEVARD BOURDON
l'Arsenal
RUE CERISAIE
RUE LACUEE
RUE DE LAPPE
RUE DU FAUBOURG SAINT ANTOINE
AVENUE LEDRU ROLLIN
RUE DE LA MAIN D'OR
PASS.
RUE DE LA FORGE ROYALE
RUE FAIDHERBE
Ste Marguerite
LEDRU ROLLIN
SQUARE TROUSSEAU
Quinze Vingts
St Antoine des Quinze Vingts
PLACE D'ALIGRE
St Antoine
Centre Nat. de Transfusion Sanguine
RUE DE CHARENTON
RUE CROZATIER
RUE CHALIGNY
AVENUE DAUMESNIL
AVENUE LEDRU ROLLIN
PLACE MAZAS
BOULEVARD DIDEROT
12E
Institut Médico Légal
Gare de Lyon
GARE DE LYON (R.E.R.)
RUE VAN GOGH
QUAI DE LA RAPÉE
PORT DE LA RAPÉE
PORT D'AUSTERLITZ
QUAI D'AUSTERLITZ
RUE VILLIOT
RUE DE BERCY
BD. DE BERCY
BERCY
RUE R. CORBINEAU
Gare de Paris-Bercy
Entrepôts de Bercy
PONT DE BERCY
QUAI DE LA GARE
QUAI DE BERCY
SEINE
PORT DE BERCY
PORT DE LA GARE
QUAI DE LA GARE
PONT DE TOLBIAC
RUE DE TOLBIAC
AURIOL
CHEVALERET
RUE DU CHEVALERET
DUNOIS
PLACE JEANNE D'ARC
I
J
K
L
M
N

PARIS ENVIRONS
18
0 1 2 3 4 5 Km.
A
B
C
D
E
F
1 2
2 3
Pontoise, Rouen, Dieppe
Auvers-s-Oise
Ermont
N309
F15
N14
A15
N192
Cormeilles-en-Parisis
Forêt de St Germain
D121
Maisons-Laffitte
N308
Poissy
Argenteuil
A86
N311
Gennevil
D157
N186
Houilles
Colombes
Asniè
D311
le Vésinet
SEINE
Courbevoie
ST GERMAIN-EN-LAYE
R.E.R.
N190
Nanterre
LA DÉFENSE
N13
PORTE DE CHAMPER
Neuilly-sur-Seine
Puteaux
N187
Rueil-Malmaison
D3
PORTE MAILLOT
PORT DAUPHINE
Marly-le-Roi
Bois de Boulogne
PORTE DE LA MUETTE
N185
PORTE D'AUTEUIL
PORTE DE PASSY
Bois de la Malmaison
St Cloud
PORTE MOLITOR
Rouen
N321
N307
A13
Boulogne-Billancourt
PORTE DE ST CLOUD
PORTE DE SEVRES
N10
D182
Bois de Fausse Repose
Sèvres
VERSAILLES
Meudon
CHÂTEAU
D183
N118
D2
Clamart
D53
Bois de Meudon
N286
Rambouillet
Vélizy-Villacoublay
N306
Sce
N446
D938
D117
Bois de Verrières
N118
N444
Orleans, Chartres, Tours
Palaiseau

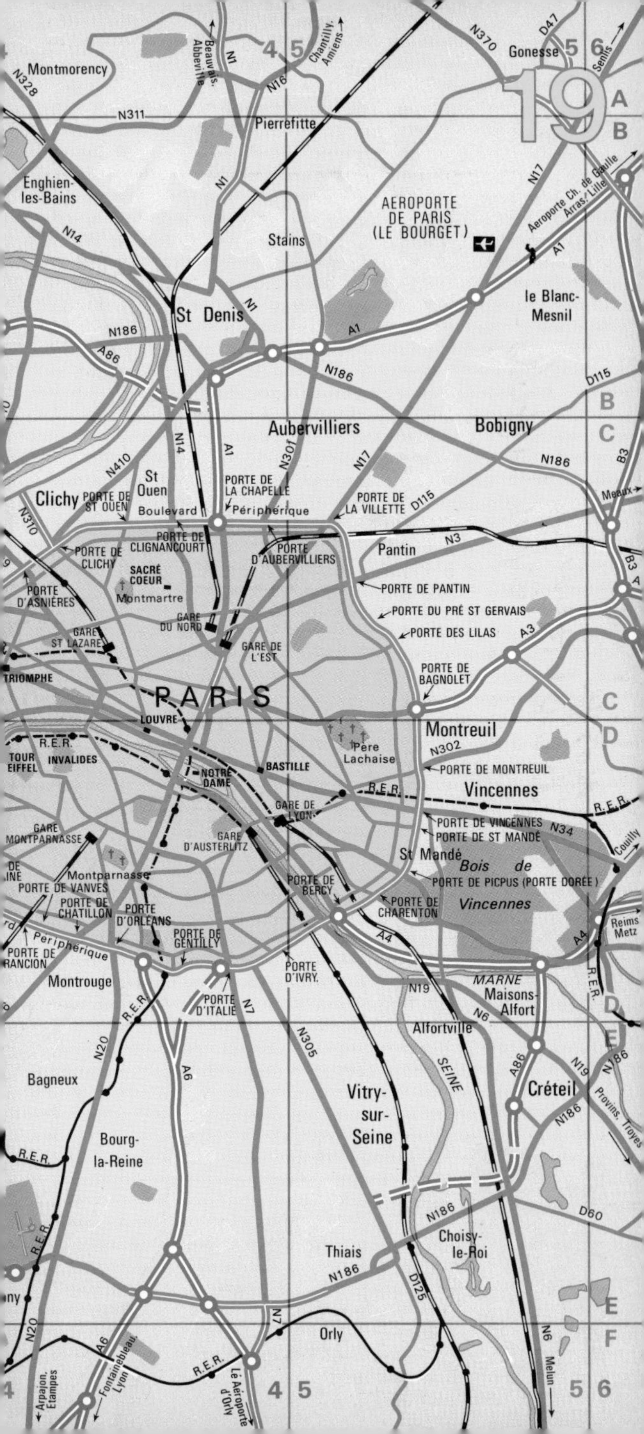
19
Montmorency
Gonesse
Pierrefitte
Enghien-les-Bains
AEROPORTE DE PARIS (LE BOURGET)
Stains
St Denis
le Blanc-Mesnil
Aubervilliers
Bobigny
Clichy
St Ouen
PORTE DE LA CHAPELLE
PORTE DE LA VILLETTE
Boulevard Périphérique
PORTE DE CLIGNANCOURT
PORTE D'AUBERVILLIERS
PORTE DE CLICHY
Pantin
SACRÉ COEUR
Montmartre
PORTE DE PANTIN
PORTE DU PRÉ ST GERVAIS
PORTE DES LILAS
GARE DU NORD
GARE DE L'EST
GARE ST LAZARE
PORTE D'ASNIÈRES
TRIOMPHE
PARIS
PORTE DE BAGNOLET
LOUVRE
Montreuil
Père Lachaise
TOUR EIFFEL
INVALIDES
NOTRE DAME
BASTILLE
PORTE DE MONTREUIL
Vincennes
GARE DE LYON
GARE MONTPARNASSE
GARE D'AUSTERLITZ
PORTE DE VINCENNES
PORTE DE ST MANDÉ
St Mandé
Bois de Vincennes
PORTE DE PICPUS (PORTE DORÉE)
Montparnasse
PORTE DE VANVES
PORTE DE CHATILLON
PORTE D'ORLEANS
PORTE DE BERCY
PORTE DE CHARENTON
PORTE DE GENTILLY
Périphérique
PORTE DE VANCION
Montrouge
PORTE D'IVRY
PORTE D'ITALIE
MARNE
Maisons-Alfort
Alfortville
SEINE
Créteil
Bagneux
Vitry-sur-Seine
Bourg-la-Reine
Choisy-le-Roi
Thiais
Orly
R.E.R.
Beauvais, Abbeville
Chantilly, Amiens
Senlis
Aeroporte Ch. de Gaulle
Arras, Lille
Meaux
Coilly
Reims Metz
Provins, Troyes
Arpajon, Étampes
Fontainebleau, Lyon
Le Aéroporte d'Orly
Melun
N1
N16
N370
D47
N328
N311
N17
N14
A1
N186
A86
D115
B3
N301
N410
N310
N3
A3
N302
N34
A4
N19
N6
N7
N20
A6
N305
D60
D125
4 5 5 6
A B C D E F

PARIS METRO

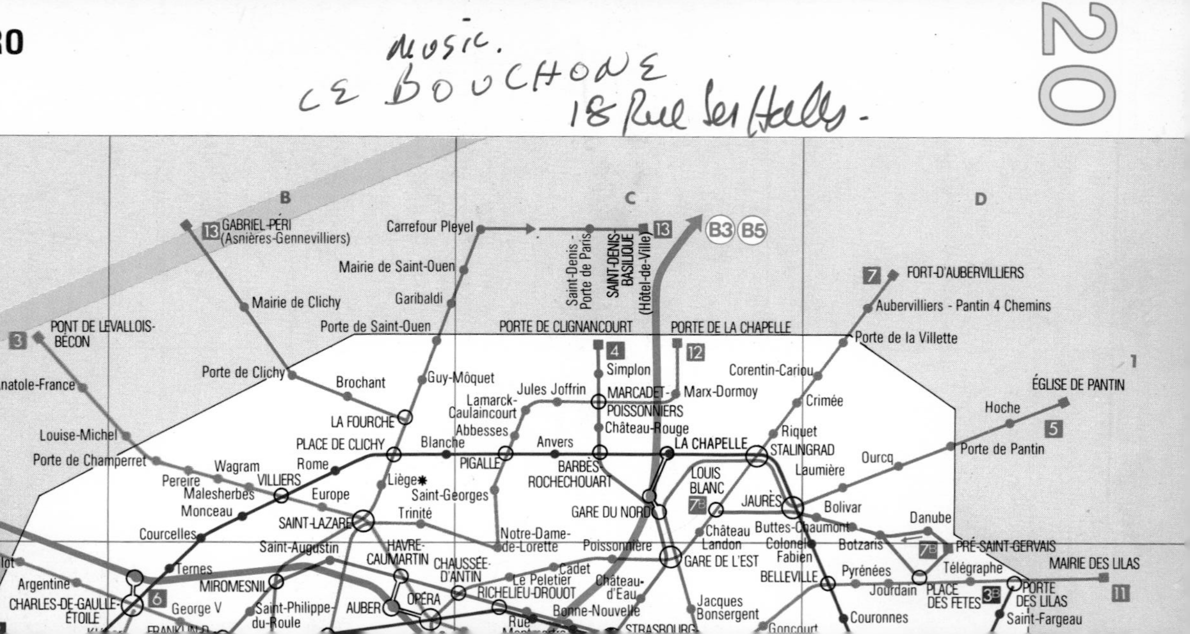

Lignes de Métro
RER LIGNE A RATP
RER LIGNE B RATP-SNCF
RER LIGNE C SNCF
Station ouverte de 5 h 30 à 20 h et fermée les Dimanches et Fêtes.
A
B
C
D
1
GABRIEL-PÉRI (Asnières-Gennevilliers)
Carrefour Pleyel
Saint-Denis - Porte de Paris
SAINT-DENIS-BASILIQUE (Hôtel-de-Ville)
B3
B5
FORT-D'AUBERVILLIERS
Aubervilliers - Pantin 4 Chemins
Porte de la Villette
Mairie de Saint-Ouen
Garibaldi
Mairie de Clichy
Porte de Saint-Ouen
PORTE DE CLIGNANCOURT
PORTE DE LA CHAPELLE
PONT DE LEVALLOIS-BÉCON
Anatole-France
Louise-Michel
Porte de Champerret
Porte de Clichy
Brochant
Guy-Môquet
LA FOURCHE
Lamarck-Caulaincourt
Jules Joffrin
Simplon
MARCADET-POISSONNIERS
Marx-Dormoy
Château-Rouge
Corentin-Cariou
Crimée
Riquet
ÉGLISE DE PANTIN
Hoche
Porte de Pantin
Ourcq
Laumière
STALINGRAD
LA CHAPELLE
Abbesses
Anvers
Blanche
PIGALLE
PLACE DE CLICHY
BARBÈS-ROCHECHOUART
Wagram
Rome
Pereire
Malesherbes
VILLIERS
Europe
Liège
Saint-Georges
GARE DU NORD
LOUIS BLANC
JAURÈS
Bolivar
Monceau
SAINT-LAZARE
Trinité
Notre-Dame-de-Lorette
Poissonnière
Château Landon
Buttes-Chaumont
Danube
PRÉ-SAINT-GERVAIS
Courcelles
Saint-Augustin
HAVRE-CAUMARTIN
CHAUSSÉE-D'ANTIN
Cadet
Le Peletier
RICHELIEU-DROUOT
Château-d'Eau
GARE DE L'EST
Colonel Fabien
Botzaris
Télégraphe
MAIRIE DES LILAS
PONT DE NEUILLY
Les Sablons
Porte Maillot
Argentine
CHARLES-DE-GAULLE-ÉTOILE
Ternes
MIROMESNIL
George V
Saint-Philippe-du-Roule
AUBER
OPÉRA
Bonne-Nouvelle
Jacques Bonsergent
BELLEVILLE
Pyrénées
Jourdain
PLACE DES FETES
PORTE DES LILAS
Saint-Fargeau
Couronnes
A1

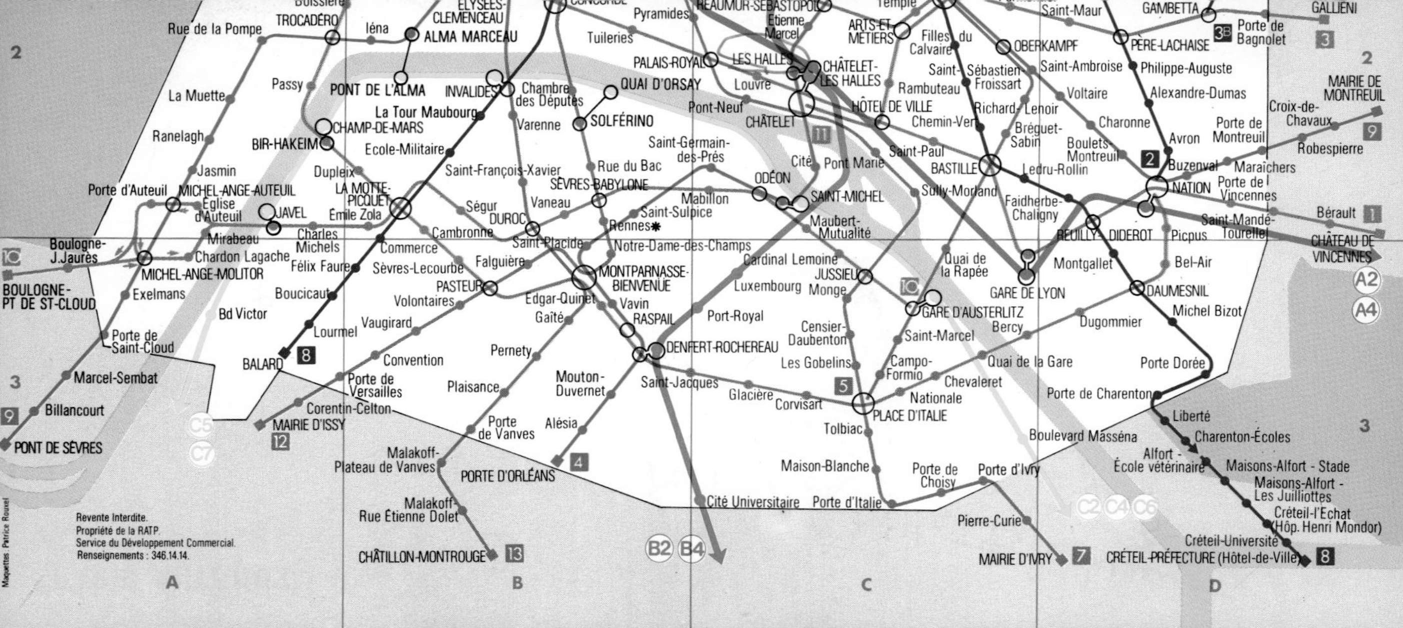

Rue de la Pompe
TROCADÉRO
Iéna
ALMA MARCEAU
ELYSÉES-CLEMENCEAU
Pyramides
RÉAUMUR-SÉBASTOPOL
Étienne Marcel
ARTS-ET-MÉTIERS
Filles du Calvaire
Saint-Maur
GAMBETTA
Porte de Bagnolet
GALLIENI
2
La Muette
Passy
PONT DE L'ALMA
INVALIDES
Chambre des Députés
Tuileries
QUAI D'ORSAY
PALAIS-ROYAL
LES HALLES
CHÂTELET-LES HALLES
Saint-Sébastien-Froissart
OBERKAMPF
Saint-Ambroise
PÈRE-LACHAISE
Philippe-Auguste
Alexandre-Dumas
MAIRIE DE MONTREUIL
Croix-de-Chavaux
Robespierre
Ranelagh
CHAMP-DE-MARS
BIR-HAKEIM
La Tour Maubourg
Ecole-Militaire
Varenne
SOLFÉRINO
Louvre
Pont-Neuf
CHÂTELET
HÔTEL DE VILLE
Rambuteau
Chemin-Vert
Richard-Lenoir
Bréguet-Sabin
Voltaire
Charonne
Boulets-Montreuil
Avron
Porte de Montreuil
Jasmin
Dupleix
Saint-François-Xavier
Rue du Bac
Saint-Germain-des-Prés
Cité
Pont Marie
Saint-Paul
BASTILLE
Ledru-Rollin
Buzenval
Maraîchers
Porte d'Auteuil
MICHEL-ANGE-AUTEUIL
Église d'Auteuil
JAVEL
LA MOTTE-PICQUET
Émile Zola
Ségur
SÈVRES-BABYLONE
Vaneau
DUROC
Mabillon
ODÉON
SAINT-MICHEL
Sully-Morland
Faidherbe-Chaligny
NATION
Porte de Vincennes
Bérault
Saint-Mandé-Tourelle
CHÂTEAU DE VINCENNES
Boulogne-J.Jaurès
Mirabeau
Charles Michels
Cambronne
Saint-Sulpice
Rennes*
Saint-Placide
Notre-Dame-des-Champs
Maubert-Mutualité
REUILLY-DIDEROT
Picpus
Chardon Lagache
MICHEL-ANGE-MOLITOR
Félix Faure
Commerce
Sèvres-Lecourbe
Falguière
MONTPARNASSE-BIENVENÜE
Cardinal Lemoine
JUSSIEU
Monge
Quai de la Rapée
GARE DE LYON
Montgallet
Bel-Air
BOULOGNE-PT DE ST-CLOUD
Exelmans
Boucicaut
PASTEUR
Volontaires
Edgar-Quinet
Vavin
Luxembourg
GARE D'AUSTERLITZ
DAUMESNIL
Michel Bizot
A2
A4
Bd Victor
Vaugirard
Gaîté
RASPAIL
Port-Royal
Censier-Daubenton
Saint-Marcel
Bercy
Dugommier
Porte de Saint-Cloud
Lourmel
BALARD
8
Convention
Pernety
DENFERT-ROCHEREAU
Les Gobelins
Campo-Formio
Quai de la Gare
Porte Dorée
3
Marcel-Sembat
Porte de Versailles
Plaisance
Mouton-Duvernet
Saint-Jacques
Glacière
Corvisart
PLACE D'ITALIE
Nationale
Chevaleret
Porte de Charenton
Billancourt
Corentin-Celton
MAIRIE D'ISSY
12
Porte de Vanves
Alésia
Tolbiac
Boulevard Masséna
Liberté
Charenton-Écoles
PONT DE SÈVRES
9
C5
C7
Malakoff-Plateau de Vanves
PORTE D'ORLÉANS
4
Maison-Blanche
Porte de Choisy
Porte d'Ivry
Alfort-École vétérinaire
Maisons-Alfort - Stade
Maisons-Alfort - Les Juilliottes
Créteil-l'Echat (Hôp. Henri Mondor)
Malakoff-Rue Étienne Dolet
Cité Universitaire
Porte d'Italie
C2
C4
C6
Pierre-Curie
Créteil-Université
CHÂTILLON-MONTROUGE
13
B2
B4
MAIRIE D'IVRY
7
CRÉTEIL-PRÉFECTURE (Hôtel-de-Ville)
Revente Interdite.
Propriété de la RATP.
Service du Développement Commercial.
Renseignements : 346.14.14.
Maquettes: Patrice Rouxel
A
B
C
D

PARIS AUTOBUS

Port D la Villette - Museum prt.

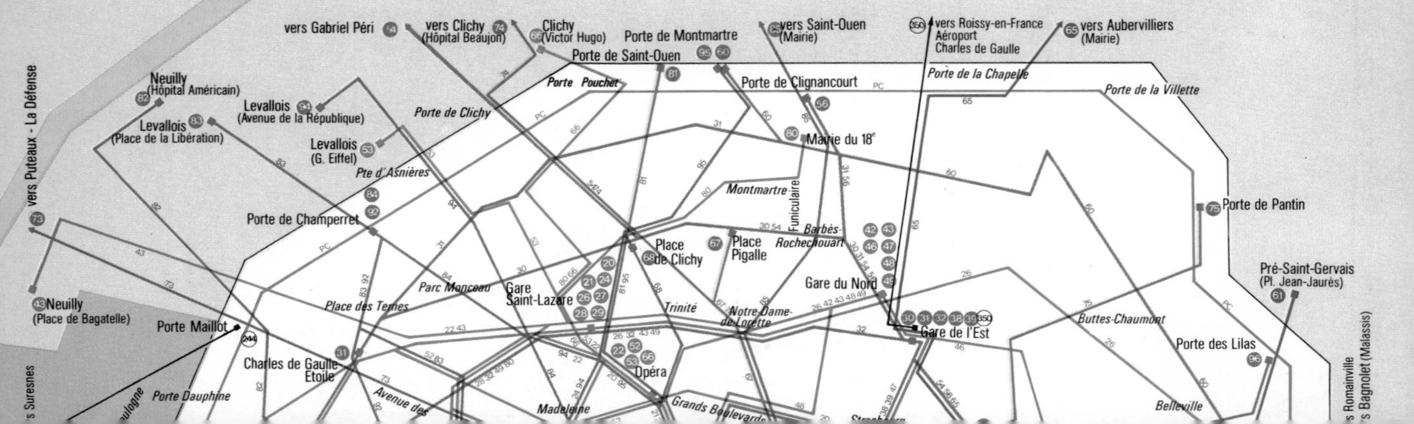

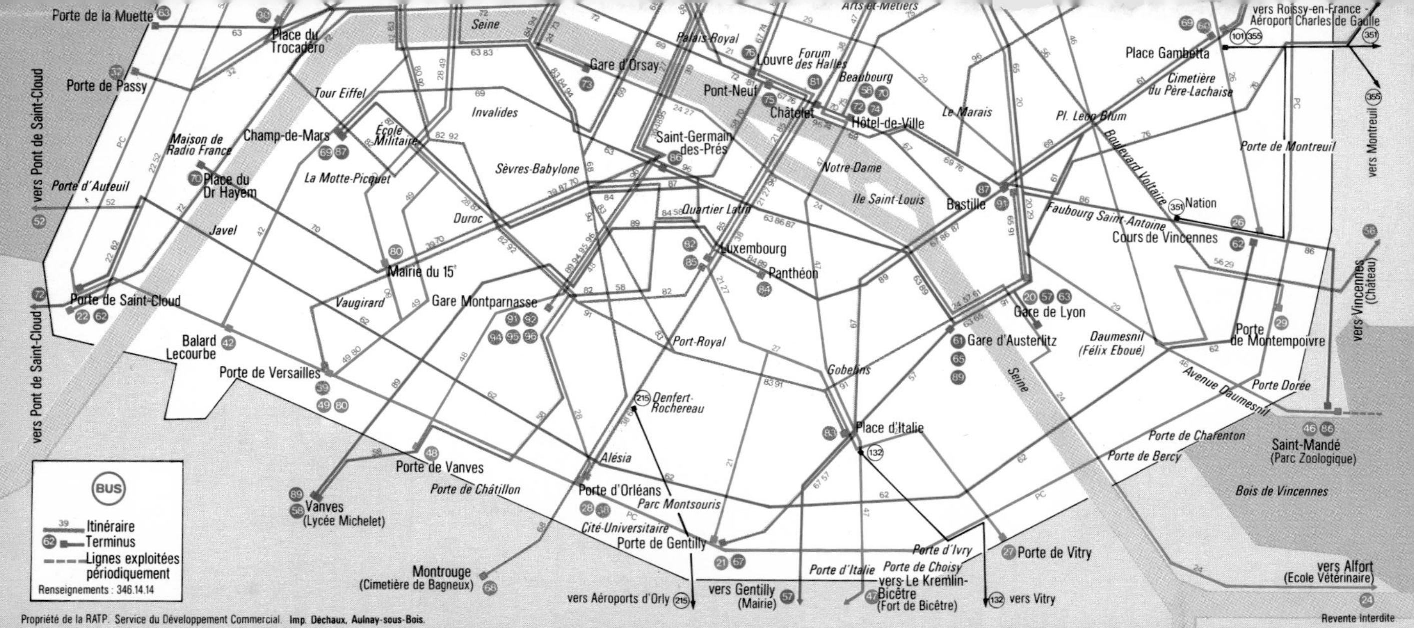
Porte de la Muette
Place du Trocadéro
Porte de Passy
Tour Eiffel
Invalides
Seine
Gare d'Orsay
Palais-Royal
Louvre
Forum des Halles
Beaubourg
Arts-et-Métiers
Pont-Neuf
Châtelet
Hôtel-de-Ville
Le Marais
Pl. Léon Blum
Boulevard Voltaire
Place Gambetta
Cimetière du Père-Lachaise
vers Roissy-en-France - Aéroport Charles de Gaulle
vers Montreuil
Porte de Montreuil
vers Pont de Saint-Cloud
Champ-de-Mars
École Militaire
Maison de Radio France
Place du Dr Hayem
Porte d'Auteuil
La Motte-Picquet
Sèvres-Babylone
Saint-Germain des-Prés
Notre-Dame
Ile Saint-Louis
Bastille
Nation
Faubourg Saint-Antoine
Cours de Vincennes
vers Vincennes (Château)
Javel
Duroc
Quartier Latin
Luxembourg
Panthéon
Mairie du 15e
Porte de Saint-Cloud
Vaugirard
Gare Montparnasse
Gare de Lyon
Gare d'Austerlitz
Daumesnil (Félix Eboué)
Porte de Montempoivre
Balard Lecourbe
Porte de Versailles
Port-Royal
Gobelins
Avenue Daumesnil
Porte Dorée
Denfert-Rochereau
Place d'Italie
Porte de Charenton
Porte de Bercy
Saint-Mandé (Parc Zoologique)
Bois de Vincennes
Alésia
Porte de Vanves
Porte de Châtillon
Porte d'Orléans
Parc Montsouris
Cité-Universitaire
Porte de Gentilly
Vanves (Lycée Michelet)
Porte d'Ivry
Porte de Vitry
Porte d'Italie
Porte de Choisy
vers Le Kremlin-Bicêtre (Fort de Bicêtre)
vers Alfort (Ecole Vétérinaire)
Montrouge (Cimetière de Bagneux)
vers Aéroports d'Orly
vers Gentilly (Mairie)
vers Vitry
BUS
Itinéraire
Terminus
Lignes exploitées périodiquement
Renseignements : 346.14.14
Propriété de la RATP. Service du Développement Commercial. Imp. Déchaux, Aulnay-sous-Bois.
Revente Interdite

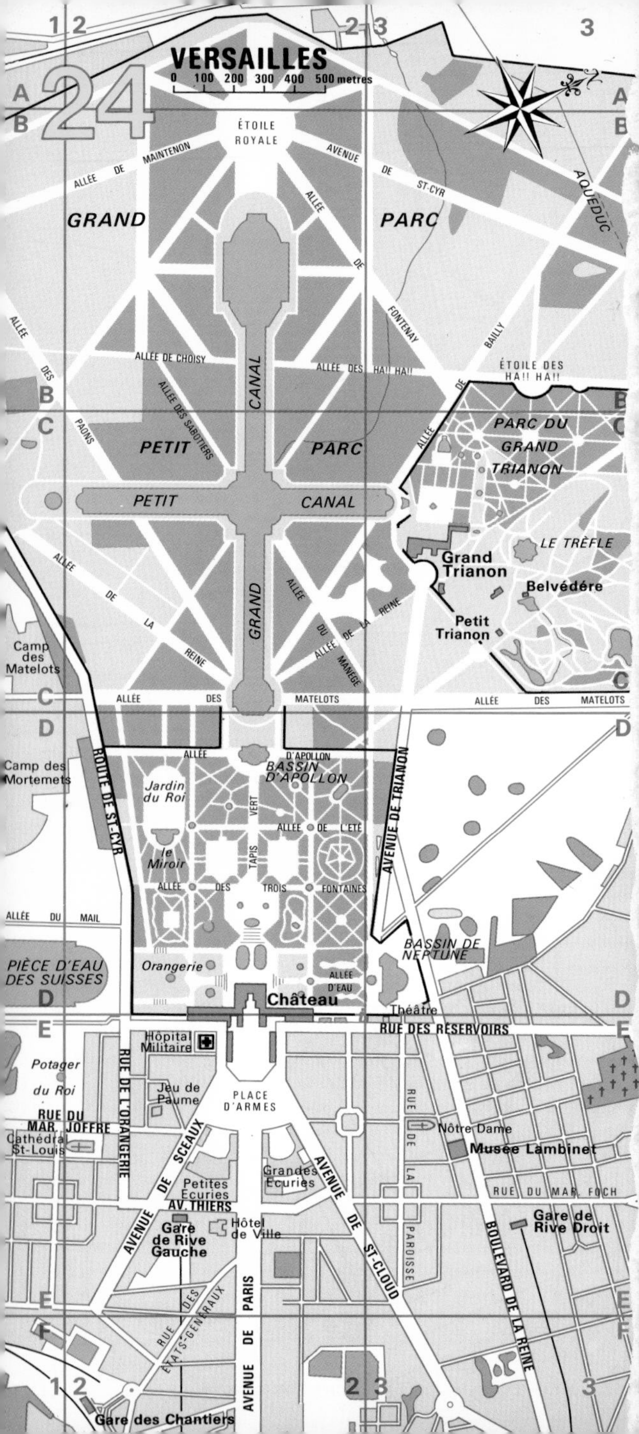
24
VERSAILLES
0 100 200 300 400 500 metres
ÉTOILE ROYALE
ALLÉE DE MAINTENON
AVENUE DE ST-CYR
AQUEDUC
GRAND PARC
ALLÉE DE FONTENAY
ALLÉE DE BAILLY
ALLÉE DES PAONS
ALLÉE DE CHOISY
ALLÉE DES HA!! HA!!
ÉTOILE DES HA!! HA!!
ALLÉE DES SABOTIERS
CANAL
PETIT PARC
PARC DU GRAND TRIANON
PETIT CANAL
LE TRÈFLE
Grand Trianon
Belvédére
Petit Trianon
ALLÉE DE LA REINE
GRAND
ALLÉE DU MANEGE
Camp des Matelots
ALLÉE DES MATELOTS
Camp des Mortemets
ROUTE DE ST-CYR
ALLÉE D'APOLLON
BASSIN D'APOLLON
Jardin du Roi
TAPIS VERT
ALLÉE DE L'ETÉ
AVENUE DE TRIANON
le Miroir
ALLÉE DES TROIS FONTAINES
ALLÉE DU MAIL
BASSIN DE NEPTUNE
PIÈCE D'EAU DES SUISSES
Orangerie
ALLÉE D'EAU
Château
Théâtre
RUE DES RÉSERVOIRS
Hôpital Militaire
Potager du Roi
RUE DE L'ORANGERIE
Jeu de Paume
PLACE D'ARMES
RUE DU MAR. JOFFRE
Cathédral St-Louis
AVENUE DE SCEAUX
Nôtre Dame
Musée Lambinet
Grandes Ecuries
Petites Ecuries
AVENUE DE ST-CLOUD
RUE DE LA PAROISSE
RUE DU MAR. FOCH
AV. THIERS
Gare de Rive Gauche
Hôtel de Ville
Gare de Rive Droit
BOULEVARD DE LA REINE
RUE DES ÉTATS-GÉNÉRAUX
AVENUE DE PARIS
Gare des Chantiers